The One Year Daily Acts of Friendship is a perfect combination of heartfelt stories, biblical truth, and practical application. Julie, Kendra, and Kristin prove (once again) to be both witty and wise by giving us a devotional that helps ᴛᴏ cultivate authentic friendships, one step at a time. I've already seen huge ɡ⸺ ᵇ my neighborhood relationships after just one week of implemen⸺ ⸺. I love it!

AMINTA GEISLER, host of the *Mint* podcast and diᵣ ⸺ Ministries

Navigating friendships as an adult can ᵇ⸺ ⸺ᴄted. It's necessary to dedicate time and effort to ɡ⸺ ⸺ost of us don't have the time and effort to put into our frᵢ⸺ ᵣ of encouragement will push you to dive deeper into friendships⸺ ⸺ɡ old and pursuing new. You'll feel seen and heard as Julie, Kendra, and ⸺ ᵢn pull up a chair at the table with you to show you the way to healthy and lasting friendships.

KARA-KAE JAMES, author of *Mom Up* and host of *Asking for a Friend* podcast

I recommend this book to anyone who has struggled to cultivate enduring friendships in the past. In these pages, you will be challenged, comforted, entertained, and equipped to be a good friend. With daily Scriptures to bolster your faith and everyday actions to strengthen your relationships, you will discover that true friendship isn't as elusive as you once thought.

SARAH KOONTZ, founder and Bible study author, Living by Design Ministries, LivingbyDesign.org

In this book filled with personal stories, Julie, Kendra, and Kristin demonstrate the power of friendship and the blessing of walking through life with those around us. Written with realness and vulnerability, *The One Year Daily Acts of Friendship* speaks to the ups and downs in relationships, the power of forgiveness, and generosity. I felt as though I was welcomed inside their friendship circle and suddenly had three sisters encouraging my heart as I turned each page. Regardless of your current friendship status, these daily reads will inspire you to grow your friendships and provide actionable challenges to find the friendships you long for.

What an honor to read these pages and understand the authors' passion for community, friendship, and sisterhood. I found myself saying "I'll just read one more page, and then I'll do the laundry." Let's just say the mountain of clothes still hasn't been touched, because I want to glean from the authors' wisdom. Their words have helped heal some friendship hurts in my life by providing new perspectives and possibilities to explore. I love when I find others with whom I can relate, and I'm thankful these three were willing to expose their hearts on these pages.

LINDSAY MAY, publisher of *Truly* magazine and founder of The Truly Co

An invitation to spend a year cultivating a variety of diverse and meaningful friendships? Yes, please! *The One Year Daily Acts of Friendship* devotional is a beautiful and timely reminder that friendship is all around us—if we'll only look for it, invite it, and embrace it.

RACHEL DODGE, author of *Praying with Jane: 31 Days Through the Prayers of Jane Austen* and *The Anne of Green Gables Devotional: A Chapter-by-Chapter Companion for Kindred Spirits*

The One Year Daily Acts of Friendship

Happy birthday to my — 2023
Wingman! :) Thank
you for always being
there — you could have
written this book — but
I knew you'd enjoy it!

THE ONE YEAR
DAILY ACTS OF

Love —
Angie

Friendship

365 Days to Finding, Keeping, and Loving Your Friends

Julie Fisk | Kendra Roehl | Kristin Demery

TYNDALE
MOMENTUM®

The Tyndale nonfiction imprint

Visit Tyndale online at tyndale.com.

Visit Tyndale Momentum online at tyndalemomentum.com.

Visit the authors' website at theruthexperience.com.

TYNDALE, Tyndale's quill logo, *Tyndale Momentum*, the Tyndale Momentum logo, and *The One Year* are registered trademarks of Tyndale House Ministries. One Year is a trademark of Tyndale House Ministries. Tyndale Momentum is the nonfiction imprint of Tyndale House Ministries, Carol Stream, Illinois.

The One Year Daily Acts of Friendship: 365 Days to Finding, Keeping, and Loving Your Friends

Designed by Eva M. Winters

Edited by Deborah King

Published in association with the literary agency of Books & Such Literary Management, 52 Mission Circle, Suite 122, PMB 170, Santa Rosa, CA 95409.

For information about special discounts for bulk purchases, please contact Tyndale House Publishers at csresponse@tyndale.com, or call 1-800-323-9400.

ISBN 978-1-4964-4101-0

Printed in the United States of America

26	25	24	23	22	21	20
7	6	5	4	3	2	1

Introduction

More than a dozen years ago, the three of us (Julie, Kristin, and Kendra) were among a group of women seated around a kitchen table. We were there at the invitation of Katrina, Kendra and Kristin's older sister and friend, but on that day many of the women—including Julie—were acquaintances only. Katrina had recently admitted to Kendra that despite being surrounded all the time by people in her church, neighborhood, and community, she was lonely. And with that in mind, she had invited these women into a Bible study in her home, determined to turn women who were mere acquaintances into friends.

Because of Katrina's invitation, those of us who pulled up chairs to her white-washed table and gripped mugs of coffee in our hands have gone on to live our lives intertwined—laughing and crying, arguing and forgiving, mourning and rejoicing over marriages, degrees, careers, cancer, deaths, adoptions, births, and everything in between. We have stood prayerfully in the gap for one another, held one another accountable, celebrated wildly over successes, sobbed over heartaches, assumed the best of one another, and laughed until our sides hurt. Doing life together has been a blessing those twentysomething girls could not have fathomed all those years ago, and as time has passed, we've learned how precious and critical it is to experience healthy friendships with others.

God created each of us with an undeniable need for authentic community, yet we often struggle to find true and lasting friendships. It's no secret that building community as women through all stages of life is important. But even though our lives are full to overflowing with people, many of us—an astounding number—would secretly confess that we still struggle with loneliness. Prioritizing friendships can get lost in the midst of busyness and responsibilities. Or sometimes, we lose sight of how to maintain healthy friendships rather than merely collect "followers" or social media acquaintances. We need encouragement, support, and fresh ideas for building and maintaining healthy relationships and community in small, everyday ways that carry relationship-rich impact.

Our prayer is that this devotional would offer a daily, encouraging nudge to reconsider how we live our lives among others, explore what genuine friendship actually means, and recognize how God amplifies what we find in healthy relationships in ways that are gloriously surprising and deeply satisfying. Each devotion concludes with an action step that is practical, doable, and relationally rewarding. As you read these words and act on them, may God draw you into deeper friendship with himself and with the people he has placed in your life.

Julie, Kristin, and Kendra

January

Be the Inviter

"You must love the LORD your God with all your heart, all your soul, all your mind, and all your strength." The second is equally important: "Love your neighbor as yourself." No other commandment is greater than these.

MARK 12:30-31

"I just don't understand! I'm the new woman in my neighborhood—shouldn't others be inviting me into their homes?"

The woman's question caught me off guard. I had just finished speaking to a group of women, encouraging them to look around at where they lived and find someone who may need a friend: in other words, look for ways to love their literal neighbors.

As I thought for a moment about her question, I realized it's one I secretly think as well. Why do I have to be the one to reach out? Can't others approach me first? Invite me into their homes? And then deeper questions, rooted in my own insecurity, surface: What if they say no? What if they don't like me? The fear of rejection will often stop me in my tracks as my mind quickly comes up with excuses for why I can't do it right now or how I'll get to it later.

And yet my excuses fall a little flat when I turn to Scripture, because although it is certainly nice to be invited in by others first, Scripture is clear that as Christians we cannot wait for an invitation. As followers of Jesus we are to be the inviters. We are the ones who include others. We are the ones who are to first show love, leaving our circles open to those around us. Jesus' greatest command may be simple to understand, but it takes intentionality to carry out. Love God; love your neighbor. There is no greater command. This is how I gently responded to the woman's question on that fateful morning. It's also the tender reminder I give myself when insecurity or fear rears its ugly head as I step out in faith to turn a stranger into a friend.

– Kendra

– Today's Act of Friendship –

Prayerfully consider one way you can invite
a literal neighbor into friendship.

Fearless Befriending

I was a stranger, and you invited me into your home.
MATTHEW 25:35

My tween daughter, Lizzie, is a fearless befriender. On the beach. In the airport. On the playground. If we are in a public space for any length of time, she is on the lookout for girls near her age. I've marveled at her boldness as she approaches girls she has never met with a confidence and ease I've never felt, despite being almost thirty years her senior.

Her conversations naturally turn into activity, and the newly minted friends are soon building sandcastles, jumping around on tide pool rocks as they look for tiny ocean critters, or pretending to be foxes on the playground equipment—there is no end to the creativity I've watched play out in these shared spaces.

Lizzie has discovered the joy in temporary companionship, in inviting others to join even though the likelihood of paths ever crossing again is between slim and none. She has the gift of hospitality, of putting others at ease and allowing them to belong, even if the belonging is fleeting and the community is only the two of them. I recognize this as practice, as skill building, as a training ground for when she has a home of her own to invite others into.

My daughter's befriending has also been an example I've started emulating. I now strike up conversations on subways while traveling and compliment strangers while we stand in the checkout line, realizing that Lizzie has it figured out. Hospitality comes in many forms, and we don't need to make it more formal or more complicated than it really is. We are to invite others into our sphere and into our life in the passing, temporary places just as we are to be inviting people into our homes and into our more permanent life spaces. And, truly, often our short-term hospitality leads to more permanent invitations to enter our homes and lives when our lives draw close in proximity.

— *Julie*

— Today's Act of Friendship —

Start practicing temporary hospitality in all the spaces you find
yourself, not worrying about whether or not your paths have
crossed for the moment or on a more permanent basis.

The Conversation That Changed My Life

Tell them to use their money to do good. They should be rich in good works and generous to those in need, always being ready to share with others. By doing this they will be storing up their treasure as a good foundation for the future so that they may experience true life.

1 TIMOTHY 6:18-19

"How about a little party—just a few people?" my husband, Tim, cajoled me one day.

Sighing, I turned to him. "Fine," I said begrudgingly as he cheered. Even as I agreed, I was already dreading it, envisioning the hours I would spend cleaning and cooking and corralling kids.

That pattern continued for the first several years of our marriage. While I genuinely enjoyed spending time with friends at our home, my introverted nature couldn't help but feel stressed in the weeks before each event.

And then, at a dinner party, we had a conversation that changed my life. Sitting in my friends' well-lit kitchen, sunshine streaming in the windows, we talked candidly about how often they hosted church events at their home. They seemed to have a revolving door of small groups and meetings.

One of my friends spoke up, and his words struck a chord deep inside. "It changed for me when I started thinking of our home as a resource," he said. "Rather than viewing it as something I needed to protect, it became something I could use."

The idea spiraled for me, as I underwent a radical shift—from thinking of my home, finances, and time as possessions to thinking of them as resources.

If my home is a resource, I can use it to invite others in. If my finances are a resource, I can share them with those in need. If my time is a resource, I can use it wisely to fulfill the calling God has placed within me.

Paul's words to Timothy remind us that being generous with our earthly resources is a way of storing up treasure for eternity. My friend's timely words to me were the perfect reminder that sharing our lives and homes with friends shouldn't feel like a drain on our resources; it should be a cause for celebration.

— *Kristin*

— Today's Act of Friendship —

List the resources you have that you can use to foster friendships with others, then utilize one of them.

Just Ask for Another Chance

The faithful love of the LORD never ends! His mercies never cease.
Great is his faithfulness; his mercies begin afresh each morning.

LAMENTATIONS 3:22-23

"I missed it," I sorrowfully stated into the phone as I pushed my too-full cart out the grocery store door and into the parking lot. "I knew I was supposed to get into that checkout line—I felt a nudging to do so—but I ignored it and just moved on to an open lane."

As I explained to my good friend Julie, when I looked over from the checkout lane a few down from the one I'd just finished paying in, I could see there was a problem: the couple over there was having trouble paying. I realized that if I had listened to that small voice telling me to get in that lane, I would have been the customer directly behind them, with an easy way to see their concern and offer to help. As it was, it would have been awkward from where I stood to somehow offer assistance. Feeling frustrated over my lack of listening, I said a short prayer for the couple and left the store, dialing Julie as I walked to my car.

Julie listened to my story and then offered me encouragement I still think about today: "Just ask for another chance, Kendra! God is gracious to give it to us. You messed up; it's okay. Ask God to give you another opportunity to make it right, and he will." As I sat in my car for a few moments after our conversation ended, I realized Julie was right. I quietly asked God to give me another chance—and the beautiful thing is, he has, many times over.

Julie's encouragement was just what I needed in my moment of guilt, and it reminded me of what Jeremiah tells us in Lamentations—God's mercies are without end, new every morning! When we mess up, miss opportunities, or even make mistakes, we can be confident in the faithful love and generosity of the Lord, who offers us a fresh start each and every day.

– Kendra

– Today's Act of Friendship –

Offer encouragement to someone who has been discouraged lately.

Unintentional Exclusion

*Make every effort to keep yourselves united in the
Spirit, binding yourselves together with peace.*
EPHESIANS 4:3

Kendra's text cut me to the quick: *Do you think she felt excluded?* And even as I read those words, I heard the truth of them resonate in my heart as I suddenly remembered Sara lingering nearby, trying to be part of the group but clearly on the outside of the circle.

Kendra is one of my most trusted friends. Our friendship has reached the comfortable point where silent presence is not weird, and where we have a tendency to gravitate toward one another in larger groups—seeking simply the comfort of being near one another in an unfamiliar setting.

And while there is nothing wrong with gravitating toward our friends, I've learned that my seeking the comfort of long-established relationships can result in the new girl being left to herself. It is not intentional, which makes my heart wrench all the more. In this case, there was someone new in the room who needed an invitation to join the conversation and camaraderie.

My stomach felt nauseous; I owed Sara an apology. And so I apologized—with sincerity and no excuses, owning up to being inadvertently hurtful because I chose to be comfortable instead of purposefully pulling her into our established circles. Tears spilled on both sides of that conversation, and we spoke honestly about how hard it can be to navigate relationships, even as adults.

As Sara and I have quietly started over, building a relationship premised on our love for Jesus and for the hurting and lost in our community, God has been doing a new thing, growing a new friendship, giving me a second chance to be in relationship with a remarkable woman of God. Recognizing when we've been hurtful and taking the steps to bring peace and unity back to that relationship is hard, in part because it requires us to be vulnerable and humble. But Beloved, it is so, so worth it. You don't know what God has in store for that relationship.

– Julie

– Today's Act of Friendship –

Take time to consider whom you may have excluded
unintentionally. Reach out in friendship to that person.

Hoarding the Fudge

The generous will prosper;
those who refresh others will themselves be refreshed.

PROVERBS 11:25

My grandma Jo was incredibly generous in a lot of ways. When my mom married my dad (Grandma Jo's son), my grandparents quietly altered their long-held Christmas Eve traditions to mirror my mother's own Christmas Day traditions. When our tired blue minivan would pull up to her small white house on Main Street in Rugby, North Dakota, Grandma Jo would put aside her tasks to play games with us kids for hours. And as a gifted pianist, she played weekly at her church and donated her talents to a local nonprofit for many years.

Despite her generosity, there was one thing Grandma Jo wasn't willing to share: her fudge recipe. Chocolaty, nutty, delicious—she brought it to church potlucks and funerals, showers and parties. Everyone raved. But anytime someone would ask her for her recipe, she would readily agree—and then promptly go home and write out a fake version to give to them.

My parents would roll their eyes and laugh a little, and my sisters and I were too busy licking our sticky fingers to care too much what the adults were doing. Years later, though, I asked my mom about the legacy of the fudge. Had Grandma Jo given us a fake version too? My mom was matter-of-fact: we had the real recipe—but it wasn't a secret anymore. Mom gave it out freely to whomever asked it of her. All that subterfuge of Grandma Jo's—and the subpar pans of fudge her neighbors and friends had made and been disappointed by over the years—had come to naught.

Proverbs says we'll be refreshed when we refresh others, and I believe that rather than diminishing our joy, sharing the things we love with others actually increases it. I've often wondered if my grandma would have gotten more enjoyment out of sharing the real recipe than she ever did over keeping it to herself.

– Kristin

– Today's Act of Friendship –

Share something of yourself—be it a recipe, gift,
or hidden talent—with someone else.

Grandpa's Buddy

Respect everyone, and love the family of believers.
1 PETER 2:17

My dad, Howard, was always a good friend to me. There was no question who the parent was in our relationship, but my dad also made sure that he spent time with me, did things with me, and listened to me as I grew. He was always genuinely interested in what I had to say and what was happening in my life. His example showed me what it means to be a good friend.

As a parent now, I find myself appreciating my dad's ability to extend friendship to my own children, especially my teenage son, Donnie. He and Donnie connect over hunting, fishing, and being outdoors. I watch as my dad engages Donnie, sincerely interested in his life, what he has to say, and his opinion on things.

Donnie, in turn, thinks the world of my dad. This has been especially valuable as Donnie has entered his teen years and my husband, Kyle, and I have had to make some hard parenting decisions, ones Donnie hasn't always liked. Knowing that Grandpa Howard is always there to listen and encourage Donnie, while also being supportive of our parenting, has been a godsend for each of us.

Parenting is sometimes hard, and having others around who can support us and our kids is invaluable. Parenting, like most things in life, is best done with the support of others. We weren't meant to carry the burden of raising kids all by ourselves. In a world of individualism, we are told that believers are family, and we are to love and respect others in the family, no matter their age. We can all look around and extend friendship to those in a different stage of life than we are, whether through offering a listening ear, teaching a new skill, or just spending time with them. It's one way that we support and love the family of believers around us.

— *Kendra*

— Today's Act of Friendship —

Look for someone in a different stage of life who may be struggling, such as a child or teenager. Extend friendship and support to them.

Celebrating Milestones

This is the day the LORD has made. We will rejoice and be glad in it.
PSALM 118:24

"Mom. Our neighbor was right, turning seven is THE BEST," my son said. He continued excitedly, describing a school day consisting of cupcakes, classmates singing "Happy Birthday" on repeat, and being celebrated everywhere he turned.

Celebrated. As we chatted, I tucked that stray thought away so I could pull it out and ponder it later.

My son and husband have birthdays only three days apart, and it was at the surprise party for my husband's milestone birthday that the theme surfaced again. My heart was filled to overflowing to see childhood friends and brand-new friends and friends from every circle of our lives gathered around the table, laughing as they gently teased my husband about his new decade. *Celebrated.*

It wasn't presents and cake that made my son's and my husband's birthdays over-the-top, extra-fun occasions—it was the people in their lives who paused in their daily routines to recognize and celebrate them. Life is far too short not to celebrate the good things, the accomplishments, the successes of those around us. We need cheerleaders, encouragers, influencers, and nudgers in our lives who will mourn with us, spur us on, and gently shove us into whatever new adventure we are contemplating. We need people who will celebrate with us.

God knew this, knows this. Scripture is replete with calls for believers to gather in community and unity, to ride to one another's rescue, to do life together. The first-century church is described as family, as parts of the same body, as being adopted into joint heirship with Jesus. It is a model for living that is God-breathed. We are called to stop and rejoice in the good—both in our lives and in the lives of others. God gave you the gift of this day, of milestones, of accomplishments—let's pause to rejoice and celebrate.

Let's not get so busy getting things done that we forget to celebrate loved ones and friends.

— Julie

— Today's Act of Friendship —

Consider whom you can celebrate. Take a moment to write a note,
start planning a party, or take that person out for an ice-cream cone.

Refusing to Take Sides

Let every person be quick to hear, slow to speak, slow to anger.
JAMES 1:19, ESV

"I'm right," I insisted, anger edging my voice. Hands trembling, I twisted the damp Kleenex in my lap. I paused and looked up at the women in my Saturday morning Bible study, who lined the edges of the living room.

Soberly, momentarily silent, they met my gaze. As I looked around, I had the sudden ugly, panicked feeling that maybe I wasn't right. And if that was true, then life as I knew it was about to change.

My husband and I had been talking about moving for months. At first, it was a passing thought, a wish and a prayer sent up on days when ice coated the highway or road construction added an hour or two to Tim's commute. But after a few years of driving hundreds of miles each day, he was convinced we needed a change. Me, not so much. I was comfortable where we were.

But voicing my anger and fears to women I trusted, the same women I saw every Saturday morning—women who knew me well—didn't give me the validation I had hoped for. Why was no one agreeing with me?

Finally, one friend handed me an extra tissue while another sweet friend spoke up: "I'm sorry, I know that's a hard decision. We'll be praying that God gives both of you the wisdom to know how to move forward."

Bewildered, I went home. My friends were quick to listen, but they hadn't taken up an offense on my behalf. Their own careful responses, in turn, gave me just the pause I needed to calm down and look at the situation from my husband's perspective.

Years later, I'm glad we ended up moving. We have a cozy home, wonderful neighbors, a church we love, and lifelong friends. It's humbling to me now, thinking of how in my righteous anger, I was so sure that moving was a mistake. I'm thankful that my wise friends didn't jump to agree with me that snowy Saturday morning. Even as they acknowledged my pain and uncertainty, their love and prayers pushed me to find the right answer—the God-given answer.

— *Kristin*

— Today's Act of Friendship —

Take the time to listen to a friend vent without
quickly offering your opinion.

Vulnerability in Friendship

This is my commandment:
Love each other in the same way I have loved you.

JOHN 15:12

"She was only twenty-eight when she passed away from cancer," I shared with the women sitting around the table with me. We had stopped for a meal on the way back from a dance competition, and I was telling them about my sister's death several years earlier and how hard it was during that season of loss (and even now, today). They listened compassionately, offering me support, and then after a moment of quiet, another woman began to share a hard part of her family's story. Again we all listened to and affirmed her, loved on her, and supported her admission of grief.

A year earlier I had first met these other moms as my daughter got more and more involved in dance. Slowly, we had begun to open up about our lives—not just the good parts, but the hard as well. The women sitting around the table had become more than just acquaintances over that first year; we had become friends.

Since that dinnertime talk these women have become even-more-trusted friends. But it didn't just happen by chance; it was my willingness to intentionally be vulnerable that opened the door to a deeper friendship. And once I did, it gave the other women permission to do the same.

Jesus commands us to love each other in the same way that he has loved us. To do this well requires us to be vulnerable and honest, loving and compassionate. Often, we can lead the way in friendships—whether old or new—by showing love in the same way we have received it from Jesus. This is the way to encourage deep, lasting relationships with others—ones that are rich and long-lasting. The kind that can weather hard times and misunderstandings. Jesus knew that to be in close relationship with others, we would have to love well—and we don't have to wonder how to do it. He led by example, and he is the model for our lives.

– Kendra

– Today's Act of Friendship –

Choose to be vulnerable with a close, trusted friend about something
you are experiencing or have walked through in the past.

Listening Well

*Confess your sins to each other and pray for each other so that
you may be healed. The earnest prayer of a righteous person
has great power and produces wonderful results.*

JAMES 5:16

Tears streaming down, I confessed that I had run ahead of God, had assumed I knew the plan, and now was watching as my best intentions resulted in chaos and failure.

My friend's response? A comfortable silence followed by a quiet, "Ouch." No attempt to smooth it over or to minimize the collateral damage my foolishness had wrought, just nonjudgmental companionship and a listening ear as I poured out the story.

There is something immeasurably valuable in the simple act of listening, something powerfully therapeutic in the gift of uninterrupted space to think out loud. My friend let me confess my mistakes without smoothing them over, without trying to minimize my actions. Her attentive listening gave me a safe space to reconsider exactly where I went astray, pinpointing the critical moment in which I publicly announced I trusted God in a situation while having a secret backup plan in reserve.

Having identified my need for control as the root cause of this particular disaster, we discussed God's character—his goodness, but also his tendency to accomplish his will in nonlinear, unpredictable ways so that we remember, always, that he is in control, and we are not. God does not share control, and that's sometimes a lesson I have to relearn the hard way.

As we parted ways, both having shed a few tears and having prayed over one another, I felt remorse but also hope, knowing where and why I'd stumbled, but having been put right with God and ready to get back to work. We desperately need spiritual brothers and sisters who will listen to our confessions and will prayerfully point us back to God, always.

– Julie

– Today's Act of Friendship –

Practice being a listener instead of a problem solver. Give other women
the gift of time to process their hard things aloud, gently pointing
them to God in prayer instead of attempting to fix their situation.

Refusing to Compare

A heart at peace gives life to the body, but envy rots the bones.
PROVERBS 14:30, NIV

Driving down the road with my mom, I couldn't stop crying. As the miles rolled by, taking us inexorably closer to a wedding shower for a childhood friend, I tried every trick in the book to get myself to stop. But despite my best intentions, the tears continued to roll down my cheeks as I stared blankly out the passenger window.

My mom, used to my tears, finally broke the silence. "Honey, you need to stop crying, or we can't go."

I knew it was true, and I was embarrassed at my lack of control. But I just couldn't help it. As a twentysomething college graduate, my love life was non-existent, and I was juggling three part-time jobs. I had plans for my life, and none of them were coming to fruition. Instead, life felt like it had temporarily stalled out.

Although I was a little jealous of my friend's happiness, I was mostly just ready for some happiness of my own. And though I eventually stopped crying, my self-induced pity party lingered.

It's been years since that moment of misery, but the temptation to compare myself with others remains. It's been said that comparison is the thief of joy, but when it comes to friendships, it robs us of much more. When we scroll through our social media feeds and find ourselves envious of other people's vacations, beauty, possessions, or seemingly perfect children or jobs, we hurt ourselves in myriad ways. Proverbs says that a peaceful heart—one that's truly content—is life-giving, while envy is like rottenness in our bones. Envy begins with us, but the ugly spillover often contaminates our relationships.

Do you feel like you're in a season of life where you're waiting on God or tempted to compare where you're at with someone else? Take heart and refuse the temptation to compare yourself with others, especially friends. Though we may have good plans, unless they are God's plans, they won't be the best plans. His timing is perfect. And unlike ours, his best plans never fail.

— *Kristin*

— Today's Act of Friendship —

When you're tempted to compare your circumstances with someone else's, resist the impulse, and meditate on God's goodness instead.

Made in God's Image

God created human beings in his own image. In the image of
God he created them; male and female he created them.

GENESIS 1:27

"Good morning, Jerry! How are you today?" I asked cheerily as I stopped on the roadside. I leaned out my window with a sandwich and water to hand to the man standing on the corner.

"I'm doing okay. Thank you for the lunch," he replied.

We chatted for another minute before I wished him a good day and waved goodbye.

"Do you know that man, Mom?" my daughter asked from the backseat.

"Not well," I replied.

I went on to explain how I'd noticed Jerry several months earlier standing on the corner near our neighborhood grocery store, sign in hand, asking for food. After that first sighting, anytime I would stop at the store, I would check to see if he was on the corner. If he was, I'd make sure to pick up lunch for him on my way out.

I explained how, as a Christian, this is one way I live out my faith, by noticing another human being, giving dignity by acknowledging him by name, and offering a little bit of help anytime I was able. I told her how Jerry knew my vehicle now and would begin to wave even before I approached, because he knew that I would stop. How we would often talk about the weather, how he was feeling, and on certain days, if he had a place to stay. I told my daughter I am careful to always be respectful toward him and not pry beyond what he wants to share. We may not have a deep relationship, but it is still valuable, because Jerry has value.

Every human being is made in the image of God and therefore has value—this is a core tenet of our faith. Living this truth out in our daily lives matters because showing other human beings respect reminds us of God's love for all of us. It's a small act that can be easily overlooked, but it is significant to our relationship with God and one another.

— Kendra

— Today's Act of Friendship —

Offer some encouragement and dignity to someone
simply because they are made in the image of God.

Knowledge versus Knowing

I am the good shepherd; I know my own sheep, and they know me.
JOHN 10:14

"Let me tell you about my friend," I said, launching into a description of Kendra—telling the room of women how Kendra became a foster, adoptive, and biological mother to five kids. I saw smiles from women who could relate to Kendra based on the information I was providing.

I paused before saying, "You all now know about Kendra through my eyes, through the carefully curated stories I have chosen to share with you, but you don't know Kendra. At best, you've heard Julie's version of Kendra. You are not in a personal relationship with her." Allowing the silence to stretch, I quietly asked the million-dollar question: "Do you know about Jesus, or do you *know* Jesus?"

If your relationship with Jesus is based solely on third-party testimony (sermons, books, podcasts, Sunday school teachings), no matter how theologically sound the messenger is, you know *about* Jesus; you don't *know* Jesus. Using third-party sources to learn more about Jesus is not a bad thing, but it can't be your only thing.

Just as we build friendships over little intimacies, careful disclosures, and long conversations that slowly develop into a deeply trusted relationship, we build our relationship with Jesus, our Good Shepherd, in much the same way. We spend time reading Scripture—lingering especially over those red words found in the New Testament, asking Jesus to reveal how we are to pattern our lives by reading about his. We talk to him—out loud, in our thoughts, or a mix of both—as we go about our daily tasks, as we have quiet time, as we drive down the road. We worship him when we pause to acknowledge the wonder of his creation in a tiny snowflake and when we acknowledge his sovereignty through song.

If we are committed to being women who live their faith out loud, then third-party knowledge of Jesus will not be enough. We need to know the Good Shepherd with the intimacy we reserve for our closest relationships.

– Julie

– Today's Act of Friendship –

Set aside ten minutes for reading Scripture and ten minutes for talking out loud to Jesus—not in traditional prayer, but as you would talk to a trusted mentor.

Inviting Others In

Live a life filled with love, following the example of Christ. He loved us
and offered himself as a sacrifice for us, a pleasing aroma to God.
EPHESIANS 5:2

"It's very different here," the woman said, shrugging. We were standing inside a mutual friend's cozy kitchen, and glancing outside at the snow-swept landscape, cold and icy with temperatures hovering just above zero, I thought perhaps she meant the weather. Or—considering the delicious, spicy soup and crunchy appetizers she'd brought to share—perhaps the cuisine.

But it wasn't those things at all.

I'd just met this dark-haired woman with the sparkling personality and penchant to laugh earlier in the evening. It was New Year's Eve, and we were spending it with old friends and new acquaintances, neighbors of the host couple. But as the women meandered into the kitchen, leaving the men chatting at the dining room table, the lighthearted conversation turned serious.

"In India, it was so hot that in the evenings, everyone would throw open their windows and doors. It was noisy and there were lots of kids around," the woman said. "Here, everyone is behind closed doors."

I found myself nodding in agreement. When Tim and I moved into our first home, I could count on one hand the number of neighbors I knew. Young and childless, we led busy lives and didn't spend much time thinking about our neighbors.

"It was very lonely, at first," she continued. "Because of my visa, I couldn't work or go to school. Then I met someone," she said, pausing to shoot a significant look at our hostess, smiling. "And now it's better."

As we left that evening, Tim and I marveled over how much fun we'd had visiting and playing games while our children shot Nerf guns and raced around, hollering and playing. Scripture tells us to live a life filled with love, but if I'm honest, it's too easy to shower that love on people who are already friends. Yet I'm struck by the idea that there are people in my town, perhaps in my own neighborhood, who feel as though they're cloistered behind closed doors, waiting for an invitation.

– Kristin

– Today's Act of Friendship –

Consider a neighbor or coworker you haven't met or spent
much time with who may be lonely. Reach out to them.

Restored Friendship

Be kind to each other, tenderhearted, forgiving one another,
just as God through Christ has forgiven you.
EPHESIANS 4:32

I'd had a falling-out with a friend several years back. It happened a bit unintentionally—I was in a season of grieving, and the pain I felt spilled out to those around me. It wasn't a pretty scene. I said and did things during that time that I later regretted.

The years passed, and we drifted apart, but I often found myself praying for this other woman. God would bring her to my mind, and I would feel conviction over the way I'd treated her. I began to pray that God would give me the opportunity to make things right between us.

Two years ago, I noticed her again as she joined a group I was a part of. I walked up to her hesitantly to greet her, and we engaged in small talk about our lives. I told her I was glad to see her again. After we left, I found and connected with her on social media. We began to talk whenever we saw one another until finally I invited her and her family to my house for dinner one night. Around the table, we shared about our lives, the things God had done over the years, and where we found ourselves now. When she left that night, I felt a peace about our relationship, thankful that God had made a way to redeem what had earlier been broken.

No friendship will ever be perfect, and we will all have times when we have to ask for and also receive forgiveness from others. Scripture reminds us in these times to be kind to one another, tenderhearted and forgiving, just as Christ has forgiven us. This friend extended forgiveness to me, allowing our friendship a second chance, and I am forever grateful. It is not always easy to be kind, tenderhearted, and forgiving, but when we are, we follow Christ's example.

— Kendra

— Today's Act of Friendship —

Is there someone you are holding a grudge against? Pray and ask
God to give you direction on how to forgive them. If you are the one
needing to ask forgiveness, reach out and say that you are sorry.

A Wise Investment

A man leaves his father and mother and is joined to
his wife, and the two are united into one.
EPHESIANS 5:31

"You are my best friend." I sighed the words as I reached for Aaron's hand.

We were driving to a local Italian restaurant to celebrate our anniversary, both of our birthdays, and his job promotion. After a season that had been too chaotic and without enough time carved out for one another, we were finally getting around to a date night to celebrate events that had taken place more than three months ago.

While it felt good to be spending time together, there was a part of me that felt genuine regret that we'd let so much time pass between date nights. I'd allowed my relationship with my best friend to fall into last place on the priority list, and it felt neglectful and wrong.

I have a perennial tendency to allow my calendar to fill up with things done for others at the sacrifice of my own schedule and, by extension, at the sacrifice of time set apart for my husband. And while sometimes it simply cannot be helped, I find myself carving out time to meet needs and take care of others without zealously protecting time for Aaron—arguably the most important person in my life.

Taking your spouse for granted is an easy trap to fall into. It's a slow, insidious slide from regular date nights and time set aside for deep conversation beyond kids and to-do lists into being roommates who feel like ships passing in the night.

A healthy marriage requires intentional, frequent investments of time and energy. Your commitment to one another, made before God, needs to be your priority because it profoundly impacts every other area of your life. God knows this, which is why he described the marriage bond as binding us together as a unit.

– Julie

– Today's Act of Friendship –

Set a regular weekly date (even if you don't leave the house) with your spouse. If you are not married, set aside regular time each week to invest in other important relationships in your life.

Words for an Aching Heart

*Death and life are in the power of the tongue,
and those who love it will eat its fruits.*

PROVERBS 18:21, ESV

I failed my first on-the-road driver's test. In fact, I made so many mistakes that by the time I narrowly avoided an oncoming ambulance, sirens blaring, that encounter was "the icing on the cake of my failure"—or so the instructor sniffed as he proceeded to fail me in a spectacularly cutting fashion.

Leaving the test center, I was in tears as I reached my mom's car. She took pity on me and offered to let me pick up my textbooks at school and return home afterward.

Back at school, the hallways were hushed, students busy in their classrooms with the exception of a few who loitered at the tables in the front entrance area. Although I tried to duck away from attention, my splotchy face was noticed by a boy I had dated briefly, an upperclassman who had a break during that hour. He walked me to my locker to see what was wrong, and when I told him, he doubled over with laughter—great, gasping whoops of laughter.

The shame I felt in that moment? That was the true icing on the cake of my failure. I wanted to cry all over again, and I escaped as quickly as I could.

Looking back, it was silly to cry over something as trivial as a driver's test. But in that moment of vulnerability, this boy's lack of empathy taught me a valuable lesson: I never want to make someone feel as bad as I felt then. The words we say bring life or death to the hearer's spirit, and what we choose to speak will resonate in someone's heart long after the conversation ends.

Now, when my children come to me with a trivial problem in school, I try to make them feel heard and important. When a friend tells me about a heart that's aching, I hold that in confidence. Because our vulnerability is what makes us human, and a true friend will never trivialize that.

— *Kristin*

— *Today's Act of Friendship* —

The next time someone comes to you with something
you consider trivial, don't dismiss it. Instead, show
the person that you value their vulnerability.

Coffee, Books, and Friends

Take delight in the LORD, and he will give you your heart's desires.
PSALM 37:4

It was more than eighteen years ago that I lived with my sister Katrina and her family. As a twentysomething recent college graduate, I moved in when her cancer returned for the second time and she needed extra help with her kids and home.

One morning Katrina told me that she was lonely. It was a surprising statement from her—she was always surrounded by people. She told me that she *knew* a lot of people, but then stated honestly, "I have a lot of acquaintances, but I don't have any friends."

She told me she'd been praying and had in mind some women she wanted to invite to her house for a weekly book study—a Bible study, of sorts. And even though she didn't know any of the women very well, she felt like they were the ones God wanted her to invite into her home.

A few weeks later, I was seated at her kitchen table with a cup of coffee in my hands and a plate of cookies and a new book in front of me. I looked around at the group of women—women I did not know, but who had all agreed to join my sister for her book club. I, being the younger sister, was included simply because of my relationship to Katrina and my proximity.

Something happened over those shared cups of coffee, chapters read and questions answered, prayer requests vocalized, tears shed, and joys celebrated—Katrina found the friendships for which she had prayed. And I, simply a bystander, found them too.

As I think back on that time, I realize that the legacy of my sister—the prayer of her heart—was not just for her, but for me as well.

There are times when we can wonder if it's frivolous to pray that we'd find friends, but Scripture tells us that if we delight ourselves in the Lord, he'll give us the desires of our heart. Katrina's longing for good friends wasn't shallow; God created us to be in community with one another, and I believe it's his desire that we'd have friends to encourage and support us, and we them.

— *Kendra*

— Today's Act of Friendship —

If you are lonely, pray that God would bring a good friend into your life.

The Bully in the Mirror

*Since we are his children, we are his heirs. In fact,
together with Christ we are heirs of God's glory.*

ROMANS 8:17

Be nice to my friend; I love her. My text message zinged off in response to my sweet friend's lament early one morning. She was frustrated, berating herself for grieving the loss of a pregnancy, determined that she should be "over it," and wanting desperately to feel only happiness for her pregnant friends instead of this mixed-up mess of simultaneous grief and joy.

She is a woman filled to the tippy-top with mercy and grace for those around her, and yet, on this hard morning, the voices in her head were unrelentingly cruel. I gently reminded her that life is almost always a kaleidoscope of grief, joy, fear, courage, and everything in between, and that there is no shame in quietly mourning while also outwardly celebrating.

My friend is not alone in allowing her inner voice to speak with viciousness. Every woman I've ever met, if she's had a chance to sit and quietly share her life's story, has confessed her inner bully.

That is not what Jesus has for us. We are not called to secret self-loathing. We are coheirs with Christ. We are the adopted children of God. When we trip up, the Holy Spirit offers gentle conviction, not shame and self-hatred. We must learn to recognize the difference so that when faced with our shortcomings, we are encouraged to do better instead of berating ourselves into exhausted defeat.

Words are powerful, especially the ones we speak over ourselves. When you see that girl in the mirror, extend to her the same grace you extend to your best friend, gently holding her accountable to change the things she needs to change and encouraging her to become the woman her Savior is calling her to be. Jesus loves that girl in the mirror so much that he willingly laid down his life for her. We don't get to bully the girl Jesus loves.

— Julie

— Today's Act of Friendship —

Every time your inner bully starts in with her cruel, snide
remarks, speak God's Word out loud and meditate on what
it means to be a child of God and coheir with Christ. If a
friend is struggling, encourage her in this as well.

Disciples and Friends

I no longer call you slaves, because a master doesn't confide in his slaves. Now you are my friends, since I have told you everything the Father told me. You didn't choose me. I chose you. I appointed you to go and produce lasting fruit, so that the Father will give you whatever you ask for, using my name.

JOHN 15:15-16

The men Jesus chose to be his disciples weren't—by modern standards, at least—obvious choices. Andrew, Peter, James, and John were fishermen with little power or influence. Matthew was a tax collector, and although he probably had more wealth than most, he was hated by many. Yet Jesus, in his wisdom, chose them to be part of his motley crew.

What if they were chosen specifically *because* of their lack of external trappings? Someone with great power or political leanings may have brought their own agenda to the table. And Jesus spoke many times about how wealth can be a burden that easily lures us away from our focus on him. Considering that, maybe it's actually not as much of a surprise to consider who Jesus chose.

I appreciate how John 15 gives us some insight into Jesus' intentional approach to friendship and what kind of friend he was to the disciples. First, he chose them. He didn't just stumble into his relationships. He was intentional in choosing the people who were in his inner circle. He also trusted them. Although the relationship may have started on unequal terms, Jesus didn't consider his disciples merely servants carrying out his will, but true friends he confided in. Finally, we see that they had common goals. Because they were all on a mission together—spreading the grace and truth Jesus brought to the world through his death and resurrection—Jesus knew they would continue on even after his ascension.

Jesus appointed his friends to carry out his work, in his name. He trusted them to relay the teachings he had given them and follow the path he'd set before them.

It's said that we mirror the five or so people we are closest to. Do your closest relationships model the example Jesus and his disciples set? If not, how can you work toward more intentional, trusting, on-mission friendships?

— Kristin

— Today's Act of Friendship —

Consider the five people you're closest to, then
spend some time praying for each of them.

Curly Hair Drama

Don't forget to do good and to share with those in need.
These are the sacrifices that please God.
HEBREWS 13:16

My daughter, Lizzie, has hair full of drama. Left on its own, her hair frizzes and tangles into a snarly mess and causes untold frustration when I try to tame it. There was a time when trying to manage her curls resulted in unending arguments and tense moments. She was a young lady who would much rather be climbing trees or reading books than fussing with product and who simply didn't care if her curls looked more street urchin than urban chic.

After a particularly harrowing morning hair battle, I waved the white flag of surrender and sought the advice of Ceena, my friend who has natural curls. Her hair is long, glossy, and black, with just enough curl to stir a quiet covetousness in women everywhere.

What I didn't know was that Ceena had struggled with and hated her hair until well into college. She explained the years of angst and experimentation until she stumbled upon the right products and a hair salon that specializes in curly hair.

I can't tell you the relief in my momma heart as Ceena's story echoed Lizzie's and my experience, and as she started freely sharing all her hard-earned knowledge about products and care routines for her bouncy curls. I cried tears of relief that evening as my phone started blowing up with images of every product on her shelves with specific recommendations for what products to try first.

In a culture that encourages women to hide the tips and tricks they've learned in an effort to appear effortlessly flawless or skilled in any number of ways, Ceena's generosity in sharing her curly hair knowledge saved us years of frustration and experimentation, and I often find myself grateful for her advice, even several years later.

Sometimes we assume that doing good, sharing, and making sacrifices that please God require grand gestures and huge expense. But sometimes it's the little gestures, the small efforts on our part that can radically change someone else's experience.

– Julie

– Today's Act of Friendship –

Share a tip or trick you've been concealing with a woman
in your circle, even if it's something that seems small.

What Gossip Reveals

Your kindness will reward you, but your cruelty will destroy you.

PROVERBS 11:17

"Wow, could she wear a little more makeup?" the coworker asked sarcastically, shooting a pointed glance over to a beautiful blonde woman in a cocktail gown across the room. "That stuff is caked on."

I attempted a semblance of a smile, uncomfortable in my attempt at politeness, but inside I cringed. The work colleague was often humorous, but sometimes what he meant to be funny came out as a thinly veiled criticism that felt a little vicious. We chatted for a few more minutes, then my husband and I escaped.

As we turned away, I murmured to Tim, "I wonder what he's saying about us."

The truth is, the people who gossip *to* us are the same people who gossip *about* us. Proverbs warns us that how we choose to treat others doesn't just have an effect on them, it impacts us as well. Gossip has a detrimental effect on our relationships and can potentially destroy friendships, while kind words build community and encourage all who hear them.

I'd be lying if I said I never listened to or spoke gossip. As humans, there's a part of us that loves drama, especially if it's someone else's drama. It's the reason people gawk at the aftermath of a tornado or can't help but slow down to stare at the car accident in the adjacent lane. It's the same reason that Tim and I watch shows like *The Bachelor* or I catch myself scanning tabloid headlines in the grocery store checkout. But while speculating on the lives of strangers can feel harmless, the lure of gossip can weave an insidious web around our hearts. If we choose to indulge in it, it will eventually erode our current friendships and dissuade others from becoming our friends.

In the case of the work colleague, his penchant for unkind gossip signaled to me that he couldn't be trusted—not as a friend and certainly not as a confidant. We must avoid gossip at all costs in order to cultivate fruitful and enriching friendships.

— *Kristin*

— Today's Act of Friendship —

Resolve not to speak gossip about anyone else, whether
that person is a friend or a potential friend. If a friend
starts gossiping to you, stop them in their tracks.

Welcoming the Stranger

He shows love to the foreigners living among you and gives them food and clothing. So you, too, must show love to foreigners, for you yourselves were once foreigners in the land of Egypt.

DEUTERONOMY 10:18-19

It was a cold winter day the first time we met our new-to-the-country friends, recently arrived from Somalia. We'd connected with them through a mutual friend and had several mattresses to deliver to their small apartment. When we walked in, we quickly realized they had very little. Rugs on the living room floor and a few dishes in their kitchen were all we could see. Even so, the family graciously welcomed us as we brought the beds in and asked where they'd like them to be set up.

Communication was challenging as they did not speak English very well, so we did most of it through hand motions and facial expressions. As we completed our task and put our shoes back on to leave, we asked if we could return to visit again. The family wholeheartedly told us to come back, and the next week we did just that.

We sat on their living room floor while the daughter made us smoothies to drink. Even though they did not have much, they were adamant that they wanted to share what they had with us. I felt humbled as I received their gift, knowing it came out of the little they had.

Over time, we have grown our friendship by inviting the family into our home, making them American foods while they've made us traditional Somali foods. We've shared about our cultures, families, and history. My husband, Kyle, has even been teaching the mother how to drive! It has been a rich relationship that is different from many of our friendships.

God reminds us that we are to show love to the foreigner living among us, meeting their needs. Kyle and I have realized that we've received from our new-to-the-country friends so much more than we've given. They've shown us what true friendship and hospitality look like by sharing what they have with us and always inviting us into their lives wholeheartedly.

— *Kendra*

— *Today's Act of Friendship* —

Extend friendship to someone new to your
community, church, or workplace.

An Unlikely Friendship

Since God chose you to be the holy people he loves,
you must clothe yourselves with tenderhearted mercy,
kindness, humility, gentleness, and patience.

COLOSSIANS 3:12

My son, Jonny, has a girl friend. And when I say girl friend, I mean a friend who happens to be a girl.

She is among the smartest in their class and is quiet and reserved. My son is loud, extroverted, and has a tender heart for those on the fringes of the elementary-aged popularity scene.

At some point during third grade, I started hearing Jonny mention Samantha's name more frequently during our after-school chats—they had started playing together on the playground and sitting next to each other during lunch. She told him that she missed him while he was on vacation, and I know he misses her when she is absent as well. Aaron and I gently encourage and protect this friendship because it is innocent and special. There is no crushing going on; this is simply a budding friendship between two slightly unlikely souls.

Friendships are excellent training grounds for learning mercy, kindness, humility, gentleness, and patience, especially for our children. We practice conflict management, compromise, compassion, and forgiveness in relationships, and having friends with personality traits and life experiences different from our own requires each of these skills. Jonny is learning what it is to be friends with a girl his age— an important life experience that Aaron and I are quietly helping him navigate.

Jonny isn't the only one in our household navigating friendship with someone who is nothing like him. Five years ago, I began to pray that God would send us friends far outside our comfort zone. As followers of Christ, we are sent to the world, and even living in central Minnesota has not limited God in expanding our friend circle. We are learning mercy, kindness, gentleness, humility, and patience in relationships that transcend nationality, religion, and language. And our lives are far richer for it.

– Julie

– Today's Act of Friendship –

Pray for God to send you friends who are nothing like the friends
you currently have, and seek ways to intentionally befriend
those who are different from you in significant ways.

Brave Friendship

For everything there is a season, a time for every activity under heaven. . . . A time to be quiet and a time to speak.

ECCLESIASTES 3:1, 7

We sat around the scuffed wooden table, the smell of pancakes and bacon redolent in the air. It was a chilly January morning, and our little group had chosen to meet up at a cozy restaurant for a weekend brunch. I had been the last to arrive, having made a slow haul along icy country roads, and I gave my friends breathless hugs before sitting down.

I expected the usual small talk, but I quickly realized that wasn't going to be the case. The mood sobered as one of my friends began to speak. "I've been feeling really down since my last baby was born," she said. "I would take him to a separate room to nurse so he wouldn't get distracted by my other kids, and my thoughts would turn dark. I wondered if my life really mattered." Six months before our meeting, she had decided she needed help and began seeing a counselor regularly.

"I wasn't going to put that all out there, and then—" She shrugged. "I thought, why not?"

Like dominoes, the other women seated at the table began to tell similar tales: of stress and anxiety, bouts of depression, family trauma, the intervention of medication or counseling. Each woman at the table could relate in some way to my friend's struggle, and her willingness to be brave gave each of us the courage to be brave too.

As we left that morning, I couldn't help but admire how courageous my friend had been to speak freely about her struggles. It would have been easy to fill the morning with small talk, but instead, I left feeling deep gratitude for rich friendships that give space and grace for the hard things in life. Scripture reminds us repeatedly that our words reveal our hearts—but only if we're willing to be honest with ourselves and with each other. There is a proper time to listen to our friends' concerns and also a proper time to speak of what we are walking through ourselves. As friends, let's support one another by providing the safe space needed to express our greatest joys and most vulnerable challenges in equal measure. It takes courage to admit the truth that life can be hard and good all at the same time.

– Kristin

– Today's Act of Friendship –

Tell a trusted friend about a struggle you're facing,
and ask them to pray with and for you.

Generous Friendship

Share each other's burdens, and in this way obey the law of Christ.
GALATIANS 6:2

My friend Krista is always quick to help others. I met her the first year my daughter Jasmine started dance, and she has been a gift to me over the years. She plans our hotel stays for dance competitions and organizes food, and she even helped me plan my daughter's tenth birthday party, offering to make the cake and set up the hotel room ahead of time—all to surprise Jasmine and make her birthday special. She's quick to ask, "How can I help?" and I've observed her on several occasions quietly stepping in to help without having to be asked to do so.

Krista's attitude of generously sharing her time and resources with those around her challenges me. Her ability to take time out of her own life and schedule to offer to carry another's load is convicting (in the best of ways!). Krista cheerfully follows Paul's encouragement to obey the law of Christ—meaning to love God and to love others. It's simple to understand but often takes careful thought to carry out. It takes intentionality and a slowing down of our own lives and busy schedules to notice another's burden and then offer a way to carry it with them. It's challenging, but also worth it.

When I ask Krista how she is able to help others so easily, she quickly brushes off the compliment, stating simply that she feels good when she can help someone else out. Krista easily offers her generous friendship to others, making life for her friends just a little lighter. I, too, want to live with my hands open like Krista does, willing to step in more readily when others need help.

— *Kendra*

— Today's Act of Friendship —

Notice someone who has a burden they are carrying
and offer to help them in some way.

Playdate Wednesday

Direct your children onto the right path,
and when they are older, they will not leave it.

PROVERBS 22:6

My father-in-law, Bill, chuckled as he told me that while his wife, Connie, had asked about academics during elementary school conferences, his focus had been on Aaron's social skills. As a newly engaged twentysomething, I'd never stopped to consider that social interactions might carry the same importance as academics.

I only knew Bill while he was in the midst of multiple battles with cancer, and he passed away a year after Aaron and I married. An exceptionally kind and thoughtful man, his funeral was packed. When the pastor invited people to share their stories of Bill, stories poured out about how, as a social worker, Bill went above and beyond in ways that forever changed the course of lives. I remember telling God that I hoped I could be someone who saw people with the same compassion and accuracy that Bill did.

As Aaron and I raise our own children, I've chuckled on more than one occasion at our own children's conferences. My first questions are about academics, and Aaron's are about the social interactions. Aaron inherited the very best qualities of his dad, and he has been, on more than one occasion, a strong advocate in our house for carving out time for playdates.

It is because of Bill and Aaron that Playdate Wednesdays became a thing. Wednesdays from immediately after school until approximately 4:30 are set aside for our kids to invite someone to our house. Is it inconvenient? Yes. Is it worth it? Absolutely.

Engaging in healthy conflict, compromising, and being trustworthy are relational skills that need to be practiced. Learning to wield those skills is as much a priority in our family as academics.

As Christ followers, we are specifically called into relationship with those around us. Giving our children the tools to have healthy relationships and allowing them time and space to practice the harder parts of friendship on a regular basis is part of our mandate to train up our children in the ways of God, just as our verse today reminds us.

– Julie

– Today's Act of Friendship –

Set aside regularly scheduled time for the children in
your life to have playdates with planned debriefings
to help them hone their friendship skills.

A Needed Text

Dear brothers and sisters, pray for us.
1 THESSALONIANS 5:25

We were taking one of our children back to the doctor. Over the past several months this child's mental health had been deteriorating, and it was at a point where we didn't know what else to do. Wanting to protect our child, we told very few people about the struggles we'd been facing, only sharing with a few trusted friends who we knew would be praying for us and our child.

The morning came for the appointment, and I left the house with our youngest to drop her off at my parents' house. As I walked to my car, I quickly texted Julie to let her know we were on our way and ask if she would please pray.

Within minutes Julie had sent a prayer back to me, through text. It read in part:

Heavenly Father, we thank you ahead of time for the work the Holy Spirit is doing already and will do this morning. Make this morning productive— regardless of what it might look like externally.
We love this child and are fiercely on their side, and we give them to you.
We pray peace for Kendra and Kyle. We pray for these relationships to stretch but not break, that they will snap back into close ties in the not-too-distant future.
We pray for healing, for trauma to be addressed so that healing may commence. We pray for second chances and mercy and grace to pour out in a deluge, that there is nothing that cannot be undone and then redone in a healthier manner.
We pray for anger to be addressed and faced and acknowledged, and that even as the anger is recognized, there is a turning toward you instead of away from you.
We pray for our dear sister in the teenage parenting trenches. Remind her of hope and give her exactly what she needs each day as she navigates the world's hardest job.
Amen. Amen. Amen. Go with God, friend.

Her words were the healing balm my heart needed right at that moment, and I am forever grateful for her timing. We are encouraged in Scripture to continue to pray for one another, and let's not forget how important prayer can be in friendship.

– Kendra

– Today's Act of Friendship –

Send a prayer to a friend who is facing something difficult.

The Grumpy Email

Whatever is in your heart determines what you say.
MATTHEW 12:34

When I got the email, my heart sank. What I had thought was a fun gift idea for a friend—ice cream from an online delivery service—had arrived on their doorstep a melted, sticky mess. In an email to the company, my friend detailed what had happened and ended by saying she didn't want a replacement and wouldn't recommend the company or their products.

I felt terrible about what had happened and immediately texted my friend to apologize. But inside, my feelings felt a little bruised. I wondered why she hadn't contacted me first, rather than simply copying me on her email. I felt hurt over what felt like a brusque tone of voice.

I've heard it said that hurting people hurt other people. It's true that I'm much more likely to lash out at others when I feel hurt. That's how I found myself turning snarky later that same week, when the company asked via email if I'd like a replacement. Rather than simply reiterate that my friend didn't want the item, I gave the shorthand version by saying the person was "grumpy" and asked them to ship the item to me instead. What I didn't realize was that my friend was copied on the email and saw my characterization of her response.

My heart sank—for the second time—when I got a text a couple of hours later. My friend apologized for being grumpy and explained how busy life had been lately.

Face flaming with shame and embarrassment, I apologized—again—for what had happened. I had no one else to blame for my thoughtlessness. Matthew warns that whatever comes out of your mouth is a direct reflection of what is in your heart. In this case, I'd let my hurt compound into resentment, which spilled over in an ugly way.

Relationships are hard. We can say things we don't mean, feel hurt by actions that weren't meant to be hurtful, or wrongly judge someone else's tone or intent. A gentle conversation would have gone a long way toward overcoming the hurt I felt and restoring a right relationship with my friend.

— Kristin

— Today's Act of Friendship —

Think of a time when you've responded with grumpiness rather than grace, then take one action toward restoring that relationship.

Frenemies

The righteous choose their friends carefully,
but the way of the wicked leads them astray.

PROVERBS 12:26, NIV

My daughter's recounting of her day included a story about a conflict between two classmates. After she labeled one of the girls a "frenemy" (slang for an enemy who sometimes acts like a friend), I gently interrupted her story, asking her what she thought the word "friend" meant, and whether a real friend would act as an enemy.

The question I asked my daughter lingered in my mind long after our conversation. Is it possible to be in genuine friendship with someone who, on occasion, intentionally acts in ways meant to cause mischief and hurt?

As I've invited others to walk alongside me, as I've opened my home and my life, as I've been hospitable to a wide range of people, I've also learned to be wise about who I invite into my most trusted, inner circle. Jesus has called us, as Christ followers, to be kind and generous. In fact, when we are told to love our neighbors as ourselves, no one is excluded—not one person. However, I am careful in choosing the women who will have full access to my heart, my thoughts, the hard things I carry. If I deem a woman unsafe, she is always welcome to be in peripheral relationship with me, but she will not be my friend.

What is unsafe? To determine this, I listen to how a woman speaks of others, and I pay attention to her reaction to conflict. Does she speak life over women who are not present, or hurt others with her tongue, as discussed in James 3? Does she dramatize conflict and drag unnecessary bystanders into it? If these traits are present during our first couple of interactions, I tread with caution about moving forward into a friendship with her.

Scripture is clear: while we are to love everyone, our friendship circles are to be carefully curated. Our friends shape us with their advice, and they have the power to push us either toward or away from God.

– *Julie*

– *Today's Act of Friendship* –

Consider whether you have frenemies in your inner circle that need to be moved into a less intimate relationship category than friend. If you've acted as a frenemy, pray about changes you need to make.

February

The Gift of Spring

Whatever is good and perfect is a gift
coming down to us from God our Father.
JAMES 1:17

On a whim, I grabbed a bag of hyacinth bulbs one fall while running errands at a big-box store, a fun idea swirling through my thoughts. Upon arriving home, I tossed the bag into the crisper of the garage refrigerator and promptly forgot about it.

I next thought of the bulbs on a chilly day in late December, and so I stopped to buy a small multitude of tiny vases at the dollar store. I returned home and gently placed each bulb on the top of a vase, allowing the bottom of the bulb to just barely kiss the water, lining them all up on the top of my buffet sideboard like small soldiers, before ignoring them again.

It wasn't long before the bulbs started shooting up the first hint of green, followed by narrow leaves. After several weeks, a tiny flower stalk appeared. I periodically topped off the water and rotated my vases, making sure the greenery was sprouting uniformly and that the flower stalks were straight.

I'm a girl with farming written into the very essence of her DNA, and it's in the depths of dreary winter that my soul cries out for the unfurling of new life. Even one flowering bulb brings me a joy that sinks deep—a God-given reminder that new life is right around the corner—in the physical world and also in my heart.

With my tiny bulb-soldiers showing the first hints of blossoming into intensely fragrant blooms in vibrant hues of purple, I deployed them into the lives around me, delivering them to women who, like me, needed a physical reminder that God is bigger, that winter ends, that there is new life at the end of hard seasons.

We all have giftings bestowed on us by God, things we are good at, whether baking homemade bread, wielding power tools, setting up budgets and spreadsheets, sharing insights into nutrition and exercise, or any other number of skills and talents. Let's use these things to encourage the women around us and bring them joy.

— Julie

— Today's Act of Friendship —

Use a skill or talent you have (e.g., gardening, baking, painting, doing home repairs, giving leadership advice) to brighten someone's day.

The Hotdish Fiasco

*Just as our bodies have many parts and each part
has a special function, so it is with Christ's body. We are many
parts of one body, and we all belong to each other.*

ROMANS 12:4-5

She left the church over a misunderstanding about hotdish. I'm sure that wasn't the only reason, but when no one set up a meal train after her newest baby was born, she decided to find a new church home.

Hearing about it later, while chatting with a friend, I was sympathetic. No one in a loving church community should feel left out. The woman and her family had been active in the church for years, hosting groups and volunteering their time. Since meal trains are often set up for families at the church, it's completely understandable that she would have felt hurt when her need was unintentionally overlooked. I would have felt hurt too.

But, if I'm honest, I was a bit flabbergasted as well. Why didn't she say something, rather than choose to leave? Why didn't she reach out and ask for help, rather than assume people should know she could use an extra hand? I can only imagine that she believed no one cared about her needs.

Misunderstandings can skewer community. Churches—like any other community or group of people—are made up of individuals who, through busyness or ignorance or perhaps even laziness, often fail. But as Paul writes in Romans, each person in the church is part of the body and must function together. We have a responsibility to each other to work together for the common good.

So how can we, as ambassadors of friendship, respond with generosity to such a messy situation? First, rather than dismissing the situation or gossiping about it with others, we can talk to the person to try to restore community or at least mitigate hurt feelings. Second, we can try to do better the next time. As members of the body of Christ, it's up to us to look for opportunities to help others who may be struggling—even with something as simple as hotdish.

— Kristin

— Today's Act of Friendship —

Extend friendship to someone by meeting a practical,
tangible need they have. Keep your eyes open for
someone others may have overlooked.

Workplace Friends

*There is no longer Jew or Gentile, slave or free, male
and female. For you are all one in Christ Jesus.*

GALATIANS 3:28

When I started working after graduate school, I was nervous. Having just completed my studies, I wondered if I'd have what it takes to do a good job in my first full-time position. On the day I walked into my new office, I met the two women who would become my closest confidantes and greatest support during my time there.

Trina and Tommy could not have been more different from me. Trina was from the South, single, ten years older than I, independent, and self-assured. Tommy was fifteen years older than I, a divorced mother with older children. On the surface, we may have looked ill-suited for becoming friends. But nothing could be further from the truth.

Over the couple of years I was at my job, these two were quick to offer a listening ear, answer questions, and encourage me when I was afraid. We learned all about one another's lives, listened through our struggles—both work and personal—and cheered each other on in everything. They did not belittle me or my insecurities but modeled their own confidence in a way that made me feel like I could be confident as well. They never laid out my weaknesses to others, and they were quick to come to my defense when necessary. I learned during my time there how to be in community with women in the workplace, and I am forever grateful to Trina and Tommy for being examples of welcoming others who were very different from them.

Often in our world today it is easy to spend our time with people who are just like us—who believe the same things, look the same, and are in the same stage of life. But Paul's reminder to the Galatians is one for us today as well—the reminder that no matter where we come from or who we are, we are all one in Christ Jesus. And often, these differences can make our lives and relationships richer.

— Kendra

— Today's Act of Friendship —

Reach out to someone who, on the surface, appears
to be different from you in some way.

When Obligations Get the Best of You

Always be humble and gentle. Be patient with each other, making
allowance for each other's faults because of your love.

EPHESIANS 4:2

"We'd love to have you volunteer!" the librarian told me cheerily. As an introverted, bookish teenager, I had thought the library would be the perfect location for me to help out. My heart sank as she continued, "Are you good with technology? Or perhaps you'd like to read to someone? We always need volunteers for that."

Since teaching technology wasn't my forte, I swallowed hard, pushing aside visions of solitary bliss amid stacks of books and halfheartedly agreeing to read to someone.

I met Rose a week later. Small and wizened, she welcomed me inside, bright eyes peering out from a face framed by soft, white hair. Introducing myself, I tried awkwardly to increase the volume of my soft-spoken voice as we got to know each other. She had lived nearly a hundred years and had interesting stories to tell, but I was ever mindful of my reason for visiting and impatiently moved the conversation forward, asking what book she would like me to read.

"Oh, anything," she said carelessly. We chatted for a few more minutes until I checked my watch, realizing with no small relief that our time together was up.

The next week I returned with *Treasure Island*. I'd never read it, and it seemed unobjectionable. But between the rhythm of my quiet voice and the snooze-worthy language of Robert Louis Stevenson, I quickly realized from Rose's not-so-subtle snores that she had fallen asleep.

I should have thrown out the book immediately and spent our time together in the weeks that followed asking about her life, but instead I slogged through several chapters before I ultimately stopped returning to visit at all. Looking back, I wonder what would have happened if I had followed my instinct to seek a genuine connection rather than pushing through a book neither of us were interested in.

Sometimes we feel duty bound to do something, and it spurs impatience in our hearts. We're called to be humble, gentle, and patient, but when we view relationships with people as obligations rather than opportunities, we miss out on experiences that could enrich our lives.

— Kristin

— Today's Act of Friendship —

Reach out to someone, not because you feel required to
do so, but because of your genuine interest in them.

Learning to Trust

*If one part suffers, all the parts suffer with it, and if
one part is honored, all the parts are glad.*

1 CORINTHIANS 12:26

Three of our five children we adopted from foster care. Two of them were older, having had life experiences with their birth families that were very different from our own. As one of our children began to struggle in life as a teenager, a mental health professional observed that this child had trouble trusting others. She went on to explain that it made sense, that many people who have been through traumatic experiences have trouble trusting—but then she challenged our child that the only way to do it, to trust, is to just start, even in small ways.

Later that week, we were discussing a few of this child's friends, and I asked whether or not they were trustworthy. Our child stated that they were, and I agreed. I then asked, "What if you told them just a bit of what's been going on with you this year? What if you were honest?" I was met with a deep stare, as if this child were pondering what would happen if they did. I quickly explained, "It's up to you to decide how much to say. You don't have to tell them everything, but what if you were honest just a bit with some of the things you've been dealing with?" My child looked at me and nodded, asking what I would suggest, and we role-played what to say. It may seem insignificant to some, but for this child, it was a huge leap of faith.

No one is meant to walk through life and faith alone. We need one another. Scripture reminds us that if one part of Christ's body suffers, we all suffer along with it—but for others to fully join in our suffering we have to be honest and let them know when we are struggling. Being able to trust a friend in our time of need can be challenging but can also hold some of life's greatest rewards as well. We do better when we mutually support one another in all of life's struggles and joys.

– Kendra

– Today's Act of Friendship –

Be honest with a trusted friend about something
you have been struggling with.

The Antidote to Fear

I am leaving you with a gift—peace of mind and heart. And the peace I give is a gift the world cannot give. So don't be troubled or afraid.

JOHN 14:27

"The American church is filled with fear; stop being so afraid."

My husband and I were at a luncheon for ministry leaders, and the pastor who was speaking had spent almost forty years in various African refugee camps—and his words held a truth I could not deny.

As I listened to him talk, I remembered feeling fearful when Aaron and I had recently attended a large Somali soccer tournament. I was one of the only women in attendance and was the only white woman. My fear was soon replaced with shame when I received kind, honoring treatment from the men in attendance—both from strangers and the young men we were there to cheer on. As we left, having had a lovely time with the young men Aaron has connected with over their mutual adoration of soccer, I pondered whether a Somali woman would have been similarly treated had she walked into a baseball tournament in my community.

In a community roiled by increasing cultural, religious, and racial tension, my family has befriended several young Somali men. My living room is often filled on Saturday mornings with teenagers who devour pancakes and egg bakes, who bring me the ingredients for Somali tea, who are polite and kind and hilarious and who love watching soccer as much as my husband does.

"Oh, Lord, forgive me my fear; forgive us our fear," I breathed as my mind returned and tuned in to the conversation going on around me at that small Saturday luncheon for leaders and a few tagalongs (my husband and I being among the tagalongs).

Fear cannot exist in the midst of friendship. When you draw near to someone, the what-ifs and unknowns have no room to fester and flourish. We are not called to fear. In fact, when we choose fear, we reject the gift Jesus gave us—the gift of peace of mind and heart. Fear paralyzes us, stopping us from being fully functioning children of God. The wonderful thing is that we get to choose, daily, whether we will accept or reject his gift of peace.

— Julie

— Today's Act of Friendship —

Consider whether you've allowed fear to prevent you from pursuing friendships with people whose cultural background differs from yours in some way. Choose to accept Jesus' gift of peace instead.

Cheer Each Other On

Encourage each other and build each other up,
just as you are already doing.
1 THESSALONIANS 5:11

Public speaking terrified me at first. I was a very shy child and young adult, and although I felt God nudging me to share with others, I still felt very anxious about speaking in front of a crowd. I let a few friends know about my nervousness and asked them to pray for me and my speaking engagements.

As I was preparing for one of my first events, one of my friends whom I'd asked to pray messaged me that she planned to come, just to cheer me on. She told me she was excited to hear what God had given me to speak, and she couldn't wait to join me. Her message was just the encouragement I needed as I continued to prepare for the event. Her excitement and confidence that God was going to use me gave me courage.

As I walked into the event a few days later, I quickly found my friend, who sat in the front, smiling at me the whole time I spoke. She was my cheerleader that morning, supporting me and reminding me that I could do the hard things God was asking of me. Her presence reassured me that I was brave and that I had someone who was for me.

We live in a culture that often tells us to go it alone, be independent, and get ahead for ourselves, but the Bible tells us that we are to encourage one another and build each other up. This is a complete shift in our thinking—but putting others first, listening as they share, and offering encouragement for what they are doing are some of the greatest ways that we can offer God-like friendship to those around us. It is uncommon, and people notice. My friend was Jesus in the flesh for me that morning, and her support was a reminder to me to do the same for others any chance I get.

– Kendra

– Today's Act of Friendship –

Send a friend who is trying something new some encouragement
to let them know you're thinking of them and are on their side.

Grace for Our Failures

You must be compassionate,
just as your Father is compassionate.

LUKE 6:36

It was Sunday night, and I felt completely overwhelmed by the prospect of Monday's arrival. The day had been fraught with troubles—squabbling children, a toddler who stripped naked and made a mess in her crib during nap time, and a husband who was out of town on business. By the time evening rolled around and I took a look at the next day's events, I wanted to cry from exhaustion.

I had a forty-five-minute drive one direction for a morning meeting, followed by an hour's drive in the opposite direction to pick up a delivery. Then I needed to go grocery shopping, race home for a late lunch, lay the baby down for a nap, and wake her up early to take the girls to swimming lessons. After a brief break for dinner, we'd head to gymnastics for almost two hours of mind-numbing practice, then race home to complete the never-ending bedtime circus routine.

Realizing that I had signed up to bring a meal to a new mom, I tried to factor it into my day. *Maybe I could get up really early and do it before the girls wake up,* I thought. *Or perhaps I could skip nap time and bring it then?*

Dissatisfied with the prospect of making a busy day even worse, I made the decision to message my friend and humbly ask if I could bring the meal the following day instead. "Of course," she said instantly, not seeming to mind at all.

Sometimes in friendship, we worry about disappointing others. We want them to think our life is smooth sailing, when in reality we're captaining a rickety boat that's leaking and listing to one side. Fostering true friendship means not just showing compassion to others—as Scripture calls us to—but being willing to accept compassion when we are in need of it too. The truth is, when we're honest with our challenges, most people will appreciate our willingness to be vulnerable and gladly overlook our perceived inadequacies. If they are willing to echo the grace we've received from Jesus, we need to be willing to receive it rather than condemn ourselves.

— Kristin

— Today's Act of Friendship —

Think of an area of friendship where you feel like you're failing, and
ask a friend to pray with you about it. And if someone is struggling
with meeting their obligations toward you, show them grace.

Keep Your Circles Open

*Don't forget to show hospitality to strangers, for some who have
done this have entertained angels without realizing it!*
HEBREWS 13:2

My community is filled with people whose ancestors immigrated to this area
well over a hundred years ago. And it's not just our community—all over central
Minnesota folks put down roots so deep that Aaron and I are considered outsiders
in our town, despite having moved here fifteen years ago and despite my having
grown up a mere thirty miles away.

It's been an interesting experience being the girl who belongs and yet doesn't,
who is a native but not a local, who understands the culture but is not part of this
particular group from this particular town. I didn't go to high school or college
in this community, and my extended family's ancestral roots—although deeply
rooted in this land—are deeply rooted ninety miles away, which might as well be
on the moon.

People who move to my community from afar often speak of struggling to
make friends with the locals and instead find themselves establishing relationships
with other nonlocals. How do you make friends with people who have no need
for friends, who hang out on Friday nights with their clique formed in elementary
school or every summer weekend with the cousins at the family cabin?

My local friends don't exclude the rest of us on purpose. It's just that their circles
are closed, and they have no need to do the hard work of establishing new friendships. Life is admittedly easier when lived with existing friendships, and there is no
need to seek out anyone else.

Closing our ranks to those who are new to our towns, our neighborhoods, or
our churches is simply not scriptural. And while it is an easy trap for us to fall into,
as followers of Christ we are commanded to be hospitable to the stranger. We are
commanded to keep our circles open, to allow space for newcomers, to be the ones
who take the social risk and move forward with an invitation. And, just maybe, when
we do so, we're inviting angels into our midst.

— Julie

— Today's Act of Friendship —

Look around for people who are new to your company,
neighborhood, or church. Don't let the sun set without
getting a coffee date with them on your calendar.

Down on the Farm

People were bringing little children to Jesus for him to place his hands on them, but the disciples rebuked them. When Jesus saw this, he was indignant. He said to them, "Let the little children come to me, and do not hinder them, for the kingdom of God belongs to such as these."

MARK 10:13-14, NIV

My cousin Joe works long hours at a local paper mill. Several times a year my family and I go up to visit the farm I used to visit as a child, where my aunt still lives. Joe and his family live right next door.

If Joe is home in the evening, he is sure to come by for dinner, and more often than not, he will saddle the horses and take my kids on rides around the yard. This is met with much delight, as my children love to ride horses and play at the farm. Joe has even been teaching my daughter Jasmine how to barrel race, patiently showing her how to guide her horse around the barrels and offering encouragement all along the way.

I watch as Joe never complains or grumbles but generously gives of his time and energy to bring others joy, even when I know he is tired from his long hours at the mill. He doesn't dismiss the kids because they're little but wholeheartedly befriends them, engaging with them to teach them something new and to inspire a love of animals and the farm. His actions show our kids that they are valuable and worthwhile, and because of it, I believe they will carry the memory of the farm well into adulthood.

In the book of Mark, the disciples were blocking people from bringing their children to see Jesus—perhaps out of a misguided attempt to preserve Jesus' limited energy. But Jesus was angry with them for doing so. He welcomed the children because he saw value in them, and so should we. Just like Joe does, we can befriend the children in our lives, teaching and encouraging them—it just takes intentional time to do so.

— Kendra

— Today's Act of Friendship —

Befriend a child in your life. Share something you love, teach them something new, or just spend time with them.

A Fatherly Example

*The LORD is like a father to his children, tender and
compassionate to those who fear him.*

PSALM 103:13

Every year on Valentine's Day, flowers arrived at school in the afternoon. Placed on tables and sorted by name, mounds of roses and carnations and daisies in glass vases sat in careful rows alongside bobbing balloons and teddy bears, waiting to be picked up. Shortly before school let out, names would be called over the intercom, letting students know that they should stop at their designated table to pick up an item.

Many of my classmates fretted over whether they'd receive something, but I never worried. Not because I was stunningly good-looking or was always in a romantic relationship, but because I knew my dad wouldn't forget. Every year, without fail, he sent me flowers for Valentine's Day.

My dad was my parent and disciplined me when I needed it, but he was my friend, too. In the mornings, he'd scratch my back—one of my favorite things in the world—to wake me up for school. While my sisters went clothes shopping with my mom, he and I would sneak off to Mr. Bulky's for candy. On Sunday nights, he made Norwegian pancakes that looked like crepes, served with butter and brown sugar, rolled up and eaten hot. We loved watching action movies together, especially classic James Bond flicks. He always praised my hard work at school, always talked up my reading skills to others, always asked when I was going to write my first book. He spent time with me, encouraged me, and loved me.

So when Valentine's Day rolled around, I didn't worry about it. My dad had proven that I could trust him. The Psalms tell us that the Lord treats us with tenderness and compassion, like a father with his children. And it's meaningful to remember that our parent-child relationship with God isn't simply a discipline-based one—it's a friendship. It's based on time spent together, on prayer, on seeing God at work in the world. Like my relationship with my own dad, it's one that, over time, proves trustworthy if we continue to seek him.

— Kristin

— Today's Act of Friendship —

Thank a parent or mentor for the example they gave you
of healthy ways to pursue relationships with others.

Calling Out the Lies

*Be alert and of sober mind. Your enemy the devil prowls around like
a roaring lion looking for someone to devour. Resist him, standing
firm in the faith, because you know that the family of believers
throughout the world is undergoing the same kind of sufferings.*

1 PETER 5:8-9, NIV

In a late-night email, she poured out her thoughts over a situation—thoughts of
self-doubt, recrimination, and accepting blame that, quite frankly, was not hers to
accept. It involved complex family dynamics that had her feeling defeated and at
fault for things beyond her control. As I read her words early the next morning,
indignation rose up within me for the lies she was believing.

I picked up the phone, catching my friend on the way to work, and gently but
clearly started dismantling the lies. I picked them apart, one by one, and, because
I know my friend well—both her strengths and her weaknesses—and am familiar
with the ongoing saga, I was able to point her to the truth in the situation, giving
her the freedom to rethink some of her destructive thoughts through the lens of
Scripture and Christ's grace.

Satan's lies are the most difficult to detect when they are mixed with a grain
of truth, and I'm convinced that those truth-lie hybrids are his terrible specialty.
Sometimes, we are so close to a situation that we need a spiritual sister to come
alongside us in objective observation. We need someone who knows the truth of
Scripture so well that she can sift the lies of Satan, gently holding us accountable
for the grain of truth while absolving us from his poison. These loyal friends are
our true sisters in times of need.

As desperately as we need such friends in our lives, we should be this kind of
friend in the lives of women around us. We should be women who are constantly
listening for those lies to be revealed in conversations with our friends, ready to spend
time and energy to be God's truth tellers cloaked in grace and love.

— *Julie*

— *Today's Act of Friendship* —

Look for ways to gently and compassionately call out the
lies the women around you are believing. Ask God if there is
someone in your life believing a truth-lie hybrid that needs to be
addressed, and then invite her out for coffee and a long chat.

Sacrificial Hospitality

*Work willingly at whatever you do, as though you were
working for the Lord rather than for people.*

COLOSSIANS 3:23

"Now remember," our pastor friend Carl told the group, "they're giving us their best. I don't care if you don't like it, you will accept it—and gratefully."

This reminder came as my husband and I were helping lead a youth mission trip to Mexico several years ago. We were going to be spending a week traveling throughout small villages, sharing about Jesus and encouraging the communities we were in along the way.

Carl went on to remind the teenagers (and us) that when we went into these villages and homes, people were giving us their best—their best food, their best drink, the best of the little they had.

It was a bit of a shock to realize that the simple dish they made likely included the only meat they had for that week, and instead of saving it for themselves, they had been quick to offer it to us. It was humbling and a little embarrassing, because we as Americans think so little about things like that. How much meat we eat in a week doesn't even cross our minds, but to the people we were visiting, giving up this meat was a huge sacrifice. And yet they did it, seemingly joyfully.

I came home with a new understanding of what hospitality really is. Beyond just being inconvenient, true hospitality can be sacrificial in many ways—placing others' comforts above our own.

I think often about the sacrificial hospitality displayed to us on that mission trip and still struggle to do it well in my own life. It seems our hosts understood what the Scriptures remind us: that whatever we do, we should do it as unto the Lord rather than people. If my giving is tied to my love of Christ, I won't be concerned about how much I'm sacrificing—because my goal is to simply honor Christ, who is worthy of everything I have.

– Kendra

– Today's Act of Friendship –

Show hospitality toward someone in a way that
requires a sacrifice of your money or time.

Friendship in Marriage

In the same way, husbands ought to love their wives as they
love their own bodies. For a man who loves his wife actually
shows love for himself. No one hates his own body but feeds
and cares for it, just as Christ cares for the church.

EPHESIANS 5:28-29

I love cheesy romance novels. Give me a sappy love story, witty characters, and a problem that's resolved in a satisfying way over a horror story any day of the week. Sure, it's predictable, but there's a comfort in knowing that no matter what happens, eventually I'll get a happy ending.

Real life is a bit more complex. All too often, we see the pressure that's placed on people to be romantic. From "promposals" to grand Instagram-worthy gestures, romance is placed front and center. But while keeping the spark alive is an important component in marriage, it's even more important to see the person you're married to as a friend—maybe even your best friend.

When things get tough, friendship in marriage can be the glue that binds a couple together. Recently, a colleague was experiencing problems in his marriage and seemed resigned to an eventual divorce. "I want to stay together for the kids," he told us. "But once they're gone, I'm going to just say to her—why are we together? You don't even like me anymore."

That sentiment is heartbreaking to hear. I don't want to just love my spouse; I want to like him too. My husband and I have individual hobbies, but finding places where our interests overlap fosters connection. For us, friendship happens when we cook or watch movies together. It happens when, every anniversary, we go through our highs and lows of the year and talk about what's on our bucket lists: Where do we want to travel? What house projects would be fun to work on? What didn't work this year and needs to change?

Ephesians directs husbands to treat their wives the same way they do their own physical bodies—by loving them and meeting their needs. Yet this isn't just a reminder to care for our spouse's physical needs—emotional needs are equally important. Going forward, let's resolve to not just seek a spark that can fizzle, but to foster deeper connection through friendship.

— *Kristin*

— Today's Act of Friendship —

If you're married, write down five ways you can cultivate
friendship with your spouse, then choose one to try.

When God Sends You a Friend

A friend is always loyal, and a brother is born to help in time of need.

PROVERBS 17:17

Jenna and I met online. We were both attending the same women's leadership conference, we needed a place to stay, and neither of us knew anyone else attending, so we decided to share an Airbnb. We thought we were merely saving money, but God had a better plan.

We were so excited to be in community with other women on fire for God and to make new connections that it never occurred to us that fellow attendees might not have a similar goal. It wasn't until I was sitting around a table with my assigned discussion group, making the obligatory introduction of my name and my hope for the conference with the words "I'm here to make friends!" cheerfully spilling off my lips, that I realized the extent of my miscalculation. By the looks on my tablemates' faces, they were not there to make friends, and if they were, I wasn't the girl they wanted to be friends with.

Mostly undaunted by my table's lack of enthusiasm, I forged ahead at the next break, striking up a conversation with a woman only to have her walk away from me mid-word when her colleague returned from the bathroom. Stunned by her behavior, I was momentarily reduced to the seventh-grade version of Julie, and all the insecurities of that younger version of me came crashing down in a tidal wave of rejection and hurt.

But, God. And Jenna. We sat together during the sessions and visited during the breaks. When we went out for dinner that night, we talked about the excellent information we were learning before the conversation turned quietly to our experiences with prickly women. It turns out that our fellow conference attenders weren't interested in being Jenna's friend either. And, somehow, that was comforting.

Realizing I wasn't alone in my experiences, I quietly thanked God for his foresight, for sending me a friend before I even knew how badly I'd need her.

— Julie

— Today's Act of Friendship —

The next time you are at a conference or other
gathering of women, invite a woman who is there on
her own to sit with you and join you for meals.

Missing Friendship

He will wipe every tear from their eyes, and there will be no more death or sorrow or crying or pain. All these things are gone forever.

REVELATION 21:4

When my sister Katrina died, the one thing that was particularly painful was how much I missed her friendship. I missed her listening ear when I'd had a hard day; I missed hearing her share about what had been happening with her life and children. I missed sitting together, watching our favorite TV shows, and going shopping at our favorite spots. I didn't truly realize all the life that we'd shared together, and how it wouldn't just be her person that I would miss, but all the things we'd shared together as friends.

I grieved the loss of time with her more than anything, and it's an ache I still feel today whenever she comes to mind. In some ways, as the years pass, it's even harder knowing that she isn't here to see her children grow into young adults, or that she wasn't here for the births or adoptions of any of my kids. I can't ask her about keeping a house or how she hospitably opened her home to others. I can't ask for any more decorating advice. It seems the little things are what I miss most. And although I take great comfort in the friends that God has brought to me, women who've become as close as sisters, I still wonder what Katrina would be doing today and what our lives would look like as sisters and friends.

I just miss her. And yet, I find comfort in Scripture. There is such great hope in knowing that Jesus will wipe away every tear that we have, death will be no more, and that all these things will be gone forever! What a promise. I can scarcely take it in! As we grieve the loss of loved ones, may this be our forever hope—this promise that we trust because he is forever faithful to each one of us.

— Kendra

— Today's Act of Friendship —

Spend some time reflecting on the life of a loved one who is no longer alive on earth. Then send an encouraging message to someone else who may be missing them as well.

Praying for Friends

*We are confident that he hears us whenever we ask for anything
that pleases him. And since we know he hears us when we make
our requests, we also know that he will give us what we ask for.*

1 JOHN 5:14-15

My husband and I moved to our current home in 2010. Though we loved our former community, my husband's patience with his hour-long commute was running thin, and as our family expanded to include children, we wanted to prioritize time together over time spent in the car.

That's how we found ourselves moving to a town that's a fraction of the size of our previous city, away from our family, in the dead of winter, with an infant at home.

Needless to say, we were a little concerned that opportunities to meet others would be few and far between. Individually, we had friends that we continued to lean on. But as a couple, we had only a few friends with whom we really connected, and none of them lived close to our new home.

Sometimes it feels like friendships should come easily or that we shouldn't have to put a lot of effort into "finding" friends. Yet as we settled into our home and community that winter, we realized that expecting friendships to fall into our lap wasn't going to work. Knowing that we needed to do something different, we resolved to start praying for friends.

Together, Tim and I began to pray regularly for godly, wise friendships with people we could count on. The Word of God says that when we come to him with our requests, he hears them. Within a few months, God answered our prayer in the form of two couples from the church we began attending in the spring of that year.

Nine years later, I consider these couples to be lifelong friends and a true godsend. We've prayed together, volunteered together, had fun together, and even traveled together. We've encountered challenges and celebrated the milestones of life. Yet I truly believe that those friendships may not have happened without our intentional prayers, whispered in faith to a God who sees and cares for us.

— Kristin

— Today's Act of Friendship —

Take the time to pray for friendships—either current ones you
already have or new friendships you may be seeking.

Unruly Tongues

No one can tame the tongue. It is restless and evil, full of
deadly poison. Sometimes it praises our Lord and Father, and
sometimes it curses those who have been made in the image of
God. And so blessing and cursing come pouring out of the same
mouth. Surely, my brothers and sisters, this is not right!

JAMES 3:8-10

The waitress, overhearing part of the conversation at our table, piped up as she brought our meals, "Oh, I heard about that event from people at my church!" We smiled and engaged her in small talk about the event but grew quiet after she left.

We were each thinking the same thoughts: *What part did she overhear? Did she hear us gushing about the myriad of positive things that took place? Or did she hear us lapse into complaining as we recounted a few of the negative remarks made to us by a tiny percentage of people in the midst of an otherwise wonderful experience?*

I lay awake that night praying about my unruly tongue. I asked the Lord to forgive me for letting it flap in a way and in a place that was not only unbecoming to myself but, more importantly, was unbecoming as a representative of him.

It is so easy to shift into gossip, into complaints, into words that tear apart instead of build up. After all, it's what we see and hear on TV, read online, and witness in our general culture. In the face of these cultural norms, it takes constant guarding, constant thought before we open our mouths and let the words spill out. James reminds us that our tongues are full of poison—and that we are just as apt to curse those God loves as we are to lift our voices in praise of God, sometimes in the same conversation.

We are called to consistency with our words—to be women who speak praises and blessings over others, and who zip our lips when we are tempted to engage in conversations that dishonor God and curse those he loves.

– Julie

– Today's Act of Friendship –

Ask yourself if the words you are about to speak are:
(1) kind, (2) helpful, and (3) necessary. If they don't
meet at least one of these criteria, zip your lips.

Don't Let Fear Stop You

Give all your worries and cares to God, for he cares about you.
1 PETER 5:7

I didn't know many of the women very well when I invited them to my house for a book club. I just kept having the thought that I should host a book club and invite a few of the moms from my daughter's dance studio.

I sent the message hesitantly, unsure if any of them would be interested in being a part of the group. My fears were quickly alleviated as several responses started coming in.

"Yes! I'd love to!"

"Thanks for inviting me!"

"What can I bring?"

All day my phone kept dinging with new messages. I quickly came up with a date that worked for most women and sent them the information on the book and the time we would meet.

At first I was excited, but as the month went by and the date began to loom closer, once again my own insecurities began to rise: *What if it's a flop? What if no one connects? What if this is just a terrible idea?* Each time I would combat the negative thought with the reminder that I'd been obedient to the small nudge from God to invite the women in and that they had willingly said yes to my invitation.

The evening arrived, and as each woman walked through my door, a little more of my anxiety went away. The ladies in my living room were kind and thoughtful, sharing honest stories and connecting over topics raised by the book. We ended the evening well on our way to friendship, and we promised we'd meet again for another book club soon. I closed my door after the last woman left, thankful that I hadn't let my fears stop me from inviting these new women into my home.

Scripture tells us to give all our worries and cares to God because he cares about us. When he asks us to do something, and we are obedient to listen, we can trust that he will be with us, no matter the outcome. Don't let your anxiety stop you from building new friendships.

– Kendra

– Today's Act of Friendship –

Reach out to someone in friendship when you feel a nudge to do so.

Joyful Friendship

Always be full of joy in the Lord. I say it again—rejoice!
PHILIPPIANS 4:4

We looked ridiculous. Ignoring good sense and a blizzard warning, my two friends and I had chosen to leave our husbands and collective children at home to go shopping at the Mall of America. Worse, we'd decided to leave our coats in the car so we wouldn't have to lug them along with us as we tromped through the mall.

Now, hours later, we faced the consequences as we awkwardly ran through the parking lot in subzero weather. One friend ran in front of me, the twelve-month-old footie pajamas she'd bought for her son flung around her neck like a scarf. Behind me, our other friend looked positively mummified by the way she'd stuck her arms backward through her five-year-old son's sweatshirt, yet she managed to smile even as her teeth chattered. Meanwhile, I was simultaneously using a new shirt as a scarf and chiding myself for wearing impractical boots on a day filled with ominous weather warnings.

But despite the cold and our silly appearance, all I could feel was joy. Laughing in great whoops that stole my breath, freezing my lungs from the inside out, I couldn't help but be grateful for the crazy loons whooping it up alongside me.

Friendship helps us in the valleys of life when hardships come, but it also makes the sweet moments of life that much sweeter. Paul reminds us in Philippians to rejoice and be full of joy. A cheerful heart really does make good medicine: laughter can reduce our stress and releases endorphins in the body. And who better to rejoice with than people who can see the humor and value of not taking themselves too seriously?

The two women I ran through the parking lot with have walked with me through parenting challenges, work hardships, and relationship struggles. They've seen me when my eyes are streaked with tears, but also when they are crinkled with laughter. My friends encourage me when I struggle and rejoice when I'm glad. A friendship established during the peaceful seasons of life can provide a bulwark later on, when troubles arise.

Let's be thankful for friendships that last through the good and the bad.

— Kristin

— Today's Act of Friendship —

Share a joke or two with a friend.

The Hidden Key

If someone has enough money to live well and sees a brother or sister in
need but shows no compassion—how can God's love be in that person?

1 JOHN 3:17

"I'll be there in a minute," I called as I tucked a key into a hidden spot outside. We were on our way out of town for a week, and I had an unexplainable compulsion to ensure that someone could access my house while we were gone.

It wasn't two hours later that I received a text from our neighbor. This woman and her family, including several children, had moved in eighteen months earlier. Aaron and I had prayed for years that more kids would move into our neighborhood, so this family was an answer to that prayer, and my heart swells up a few extra sizes when I watch our combined gang of kids biking, climbing trees, and building snow forts.

In her text to me that morning, she told me that her minivan wouldn't start and that she was in the process of finding a towing company. As we texted back and forth, that hidden key pushed to the forefront of my mind, and I remembered that our family car was sitting in our garage, filled with gas and with nothing to do for the week.

Silently thanking God for the persistent nudge to hide our house key that morning, I explained where it was, told her where my car keys could be found, and suggested she use our car as her backup plan. I sighed, knowing that no matter what was going on with my friend's van, she and her children would not be stranded and scrambling to find a solution on a cold wintry morning.

We are creatures who thrive in healthy community, and when we intentionally take care of those around us with our finances, our possessions, and our time, God brings it back to us in ways that are indescribable. Being obedient in generosity, in the big and the small, is an essential part of godly friendships and will reap rewards that are life-giving and soul-refreshing.

— Julie

— Today's Act of Friendship —

Ask God to show you someone in your circle who needs
some generosity, and then act on that revelation.

Embracing Those Who Are Different

Everyone who calls on the name of the LORD will be saved.
ROMANS 10:13

We looked around the sanctuary and realized within moments that this would be different from what our little family was used to. My husband and I had been sensing for a while that we were to start attending the church attached to a local shelter in our town, only two blocks away from our house. We walked there the first morning, not sure what to expect.

There were single men sitting off to one side of the room and elderly women in the middle. Several single moms with children and a few other families were interspersed throughout, people representing all races and walks of life. As the music began, I saw some stand to join the worship; others sat slumped as if beaten down by life. Children ran across the front—and all the while the pastor stood, smiling, while he praised God.

And I'm not sure why, but I couldn't stop the tears from falling. As I watched the people around me join in song about overcoming struggles and trusting God for everything, I got the sense that they understood the full meaning of the words they were singing, and it overwhelmed me.

My husband and I have continued to attend this little church every Sunday since. It's not what we'd previously known, but we've found budding friendships with those who are very different from us in this new space, and that just feels right.

When I look around at the varied people in our gathering space on a Sunday morning, I catch a glimpse of what God sees. Our differences don't matter—our backgrounds, our families, our races—*all of us* who call on the name of the Lord will be saved. We can create bridges with and embrace each other, knowing that God does the same for each one of us.

— *Kendra*

— Today's Act of Friendship —

Reach out to someone in friendship who, on the surface, seems different from yourself.

The Hallway Hug

*What good is it, dear brothers and sisters, if you say you
have faith but don't show it by your actions?*
JAMES 2:14

My sister Katrina was diagnosed with breast cancer when she was twenty-three. I was seventeen, still navigating the awkward social, emotional, and academic whirl that is high school.

I remember the day after the diagnosis. I was in first-hour concert choir, wrestling with the uncertainty of my sister being sick, when I suddenly felt like crying. Not wanting to make a scene, I quickly exited the room.

I managed to hold it in until I reached the hallway, which I thought was empty. Sobbing quietly, I hurried toward the restroom, nearly bumping into a boy named Aaron. He and I were in different friend groups that overlapped, but with a graduating class of fewer than two hundred, we knew each other.

Gripping my arms gently to stop me from bowling him over, he asked what was wrong. When I explained, he gathered me into his arms and gave me a huge hug. After a few moments, I thanked him and headed off to the restroom to finish restoring my red-rimmed eyes.

Neither of us ever talked about it again. In fact, he may have forgotten that it ever occurred. Yet I learned a valuable lesson: sometimes, all that's required of us to be a good friend is to truly notice those around us. Who do you know that is grieving? Who just had a major life transition? Who feels stuck in their job? Who is juggling the demands of being a parent to small children? Who is struggling financially? Who has received a diagnosis or deals with chronic pain? Who might be lonely?

James reminds us that our faith is made evident to others through our works. Meeting the tangible or emotional needs of others and going out of our way to respond with kindness and care is one of the best ways to make friends feel noticed and loved.

— Kristin

— Today's Act of Friendship —

Send a note to a friend who is struggling.

Breaking Rules

I was a stranger and you welcomed me.
MATTHEW 25:35, ESV

My husband's grin was infectious. Decked out in his soccer gear, he informed me he was joining the pickup game he had spotted some Somali guys playing at the park two blocks from our house.

I wondered at this bold move, remembering "The Rule" someone had told Aaron years ago as he played soccer one time with a group of international men: Somali men can jump into pickup soccer games with others, but no one jumps into Somali pickup games. Aaron obeyed that rule for far too long, thinking it was a rule from within the Somali culture that would be offensive if ignored.

When Aaron asked to join their game, he was greeted with a warm welcome. Soccer is a common language spoken the world over: there are hotheads and cool cukes, guys who dive at the slightest bump and guys who argue with the referee about a call. Aaron immediately recognized the soccer culture he knows and loves and found the camaraderie he missed as the language barrier and cultural differences faded into an unimportant background.

That evening of rule breaking turned into a pivotal moment in our house. Aaron returned home delighted that he had earned the nickname Coach, both because he was old enough to be a father to some of these young men and because his years as a soccer coach couldn't help but resurface. The majority of these young guys were self-taught, and that summer of pickup games slowly developed into mutually treasured friendships. Aaron now has a community of soccer friends—something he had missed intensely back when we first moved to central Minnesota—and they get an informal soccer mentor who can make gentle suggestions to refine their techniques and skills.

Loving our neighbor requires thoughtfully reconsidering which "rules" we have been obeying without thought, rules that ought not to be rules because they serve only to keep us from meeting one another and forming friendships that cross cultural and language boundaries. It is so, so simple. Why do we allow it to feel so hard?

— Julie

— Today's Act of Friendship —

What cultural "rule" do you need to reconsider and possibly
ignore? Prayerfully break it and watch God move.

Supportive Friendships

*We ask God to give you complete knowledge of his will and to give you
spiritual wisdom and understanding. Then the way you live will always honor
and please the Lord, and your lives will produce every kind of good fruit.
All the while, you will grow as you learn to know God better and better.*

COLOSSIANS 1:9-10

I'm part of a moms' group in my community. Each month the leaders gather to plan out the details of the larger gathering, study the Bible together, and pray for one another. I am privileged to be able to lead this group's Bible study portion each month and am always encouraged by the way that the women come together, share honestly, and support one another.

These women are real about their struggles and their joys; they cry with one another and cheer each other on. They listen well and seek to understand one another without judgment. They hold confidences while also committing to pray for one another. They leave each meeting knowing that they have been heard and affirmed, while also understanding that what has been shared will not leave that room. These are women of integrity, and I am honored to be a part of their fold. It is a gift, and I know not every woman is able to find friendships of this kind easily, since they can often take time to form.

God created us to be people in community, offering friendship and encouraging one another in our faith. Having friends like this will help us to grow in spiritual wisdom and understanding while helping us to live lives that produce every kind of good fruit because we will be spurred on in all that God has for us. Don't miss this part of friendship—the support and accountability we can find with others who are pursuing all that God has for them.

— Kendra

— Today's Act of Friendship —

If you are already in a support group, send a note thanking them.
If you are desiring this type of accountability, ask God to send
you someone you can start growing in your faith alongside.

Seeing the Stranger

You shall treat the stranger who sojourns with you as the native among you, and you shall love him as yourself, for you were strangers in the land of Egypt: I am the LORD your God.

LEVITICUS 19:34, ESV

"There's a new exhibit at one of the art museums," my classmate said offhandedly as we left class one night.

I finished shrugging into my backpack and turned to her, freeing my long hair from inside the collar of my heavy winter coat and pulling on my gloves.

"Would you like to go with me?" she continued.

Caught off guard, I hesitated, unsure how to respond. Between juggling a part-time job, a husband, a one-year-old daughter, and the never-ending mountain of homework I had to do for graduate school, I didn't really want to say yes. I lived forty-five minutes from campus, and the idea of scheduling a sitter and driving into St. Paul for an extra day seemed like too much work.

"I'm sorry, I can't," I said politely. "Maybe some other time."

I wasn't unkind, but in retrospect it was a time when I failed at friendship. Ji was from Tunisia, studying abroad for part of her degree and quite possibly lonely in the sea of busy grad students. Unlike undergraduate classes, where students lived on campus and associated with other students, graduate studies consisted of evening-only classes full of working professionals with busy lives outside of campus.

As a young adult, I had not yet learned the value of caring for others outside my small circle of friends and family. Given my inward-focused life, I had never considered the mandate from Leviticus to love sojourners as we love ourselves as something I needed to practice. I was too caught up in the fullness of my own life to see the emptiness of hers. Although she asked me to spend time together once or twice more, I always said no, and we remained acquaintances.

Ji contacted me earlier this year to say hello. In the eight years since I last saw her, my perspective on intentionally welcoming those who may feel isolated or out of place had changed significantly. I was glad for the opportunity to remedy my earlier mistake and responded readily to her message. It was just the reminder I needed to always keep the circle of friendship open, seeing the stranger whom we can welcome in.

— *Kristin*

— Today's Act of Friendship —

Ask someone you've turned down in the past to spend time with you.

The Importance of Proximity

Yes, I am the vine; you are the branches. Those who remain in me, and I in them, will produce much fruit. For apart from me you can do nothing.

JOHN 15:5

Sitting around the dining room table one evening, several women and I chatted amicably as our husbands oversaw the making of gourmet homemade pizzas in the kitchen. As mothers of teenage daughters, our conversation naturally turned to friendship, specifically the hard parts of friendship.

As I listened to the other women share stories of deep friendships lost somewhere along the journey of life, a theme started to emerge about the importance of proximity. On occasion, we were able to maintain long-distance friendships, picking up where we last left off despite big gaps, staying in contact despite time and distance. But many times even the closest friendships had faded when we moved—and I heard genuine regret in the voices of those gathered around the table for friendships lost as life paths diverged.

That conversation echoed in my head in the days after, and I felt a gentle nudge in my spirit, a whisper in my soul that turned my thoughts to my own relationship with Christ with a quiet question: *How often do I allow spiritual distance to slip between us, especially when life is relatively smooth sailing?*

I winced, recognizing the truth in the revelation and in the consequences of spiritual distance from Christ. Scripture is clear: our striving, our best intentions, and our good works are meaningless apart from God. If I want to be a woman whose life reflects Jesus, it is essential that I remain in close proximity to him. I need to be in intimate relationship with him in much the same way I am with my closest friends: by listening, spending time together (reading Scripture, worship), and conversation (prayer).

– Julie

– Today's Act of Friendship –

Examine your relationship with our Savior. Is it marked by
both reverence and intimacy? If it is not, start with a prayer
of repentance and carve out time for him alone.

A Welcoming Atmosphere

*A house is built by wisdom and becomes strong through
good sense. Through knowledge its rooms are filled
with all sorts of precious riches and valuables.*

PROVERBS 24:3-4

My family moved to a new town the summer before I started fourth grade. Luckily, that was the year everyone my age moved from third grade at Ripley Elementary to fourth grade at Wagner Elementary, so I didn't feel like such an odd duck. I was quiet and shy, but quickly became firm friends with a girl named Melissa.

My new friend lived in a beautiful home in the country. Her parents had both grown up in the area, and her dad was a hardworking farmer. As a result, Melissa had a large extended family, many of whom lived close.

I spent countless hours at their home. I remember playing in the rain in the spring, picking rocks out of the fields to prepare them for planting, cruising way too fast on a snowmobile in the winter, and playing games like Donkey Kong and Mario Kart year-round. We listened to music, talked about boys, and immediately rewound the VHS of *Clueless* to watch it over again. Melissa's lower-floor bedroom was a haven for me through all the awkwardness of middle school.

I loved spending time with my friend, but I also loved her big family. Her cousins made me feel right at home, even if I did worry that they would bounce me right off her trampoline. Her grandpa was gentle, her aunt and uncle were friendly, and everyone was always kind.

As a mom now myself, it's a great reminder to me of the influence I can have on my daughters' friendships. Proverbs says that our homes are more than just a physical location built from wood and concrete; they are built and strengthened by wisdom. Room by room, our homes become a haven to others when we fill them with the precious love and grace God so generously provides. In my mind, children and their friends are some of the most precious valuables who can enter our homes. The atmosphere I create in my home can reinforce love, respect, and care for others, or it can showcase indifference. Choosing to fill our home with love and friends is truly the richest way to live.

— *Kristin*

— Today's Act of Friendship —

Brainstorm ways to ensure that the atmosphere of
your home is welcoming to friends of all ages.

March

Walk with the Wise

Walk with the wise and become wise;
associate with fools and get in trouble.
PROVERBS 13:20

I wore a sunflower sweatshirt to my first middle school dance. It was my twelfth birthday, and my parents had agreed to host a slew of my friends for a sleepover that night. It's a mercy that I even had friends, considering the bulky sweatshirt and fish earrings I wore, combined with geeky glasses and Rapunzel-length hair. But, despite our dubious fashion choices and all the time we spent primping, we managed to arrive on time for the school dance.

I still remember the sweltering gym, the semidarkness punctuated by strobe lights, the thump of bass in the music. Teachers gathered on the edges as chaperones, while we middle schoolers awkwardly slow-danced or moved with wild abandon. I remember scoping out my crush, looking to see who was dancing with whom.

But, most of all, what I remember is the crying. Without fail—at that dance and every other middle school dance I attended in the next three years—some girl would end up crying in the bathroom over a relationship gone wrong. Sometimes it was over a friend; sometimes it was over a crush. No matter the reason, the lesson I learned early on was that it matters who you choose to let influence you.

Proverbs says to walk with the wise and become wise, because the alternative is bound to get you in trouble. Those drama-filled middle school years I'm thankful I never have to repeat? They were bearable because of my friends. I knew Katie, Kristina, Teresa, Tammy, and others were trustworthy. They worked hard in school. They cared about volunteering in our community, about advocating for our class-mates through things like student council. And they also cared about their friends, including me.

I still have a shoebox full of old notes from those friends, scribbled on college-ruled paper, folded in elaborate shapes. Those letters were amusing and encourag-ing, but they were also influential. They provided accountability for me, urging me in subtle ways to make good choices. Those wise friendships carried me through middle school dances, into high school and beyond.

— *Kristin*

— Today's Act of Friendship —

Ask a friend if you can be accountable to each
other in pursuit of a common goal.

Friendly Coaching

*Don't look out only for your own interests,
but take an interest in others, too.*

PHILIPPIANS 2:4

"This new group coming up is horrible!" my son Donnie lamented after dinner one evening following his first lacrosse practice of the season.

"Why? How do you know this?" I responded, trying to understand.

"Well, that's what the other players are saying."

We talked more about the younger boys coming up in the ranks and about how it felt when he was a freshman. We discussed what it means to be a part of a team, how making judgments based only on others' statements isn't really fair to the new players. Then Kyle and I challenged him this way: "What if instead of dismissing these younger boys, you taught them? How could you help them get better? How could you make your team stronger as a whole?"

Donnie nodded with understanding, while still unsure that it'd work. He agreed that he'd look for an opportunity to help a younger player in the following days.

Although I'd love for my son to include others and take the time to teach them, I know I have felt the same frustrations he's encountered. I've had jobs where others couldn't quite remember what to me seemed the most obvious of things; and even at home, I get annoyed having to remind my kids of their chores. I can be stingy when it comes to the time it takes to share knowledge or train my kids, and my son is no different. Sometimes it takes intentionally putting aside our own desires to help out someone else.

Paul encourages the Philippian believers to not only care about themselves but to look out for and take an interest in others as well. It's a challenge to us all to care about and build one another up instead of criticizing or withholding our knowledge and time. What better way to extend friendship and be generous with our talents than to share our knowledge with others?

— Kendra

— Today's Act of Friendship —

Take the time to teach someone a skill or offer guidance
to someone who needs a little extra help.

Seeing the Heart

Sympathize with each other. Love each other as
brothers and sisters. Be tenderhearted.

1 PETER 3:8

After a hard day spent in court as an attorney, I walked into the house that evening in tears. They were tears borne of unrelenting sadness, the kind that well up inside and then just quietly, unstoppably slip down your cheeks.

Dinner was already in progress as I walked in the door, so I wandered into the dining room, pulled up a chair between my preschool-age children, plastered a smile on my face, and asked them how their days were.

My son, Jonny, looked past my fake smile and straight into my heart. At almost three, he could normally be heard roaring like a lion and pouncing on his sister. He was—and still is—physical and active and tough, but he has a tender heart just like his daddy's.

Jonny pulled me in close for a hug and several slobbery yogurt kisses, asked if I needed a Band-Aid (because tears equal Band-Aids to the three and under crowd), and then invited me to snuggle with him on the couch. When I didn't move fast enough, he invited me again with a nudging, "Up, Momma!"

I caught my breath in wonder at his perception. How is it that my three-year-old was more aware of the secret tears of another than most adults are? How many people did I pass by today, oblivious that they, too, needed a hug and an encouraging word? How many times have I been so caught up in my own stuff that I've failed to reach out to a quietly struggling friend?

While I'm not there yet, I've often returned to this precious memory of Jonny as I strive to be sensitive to the whisper of the Holy Spirit. I'm quicker than before to check in with friends I haven't talked to in a while when I feel a tiny nudge in my soul or when a thought of them flits through my mind. We are called to look out for one another, to be there when life is hard, to see the heart behind the fake smile and cheery words.

— Julie

— Today's Act of Friendship —

Consider what friend the Holy Spirit might be nudging
you to check in with, and reach out right now.

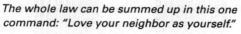

Puppy Motivation

The whole law can be summed up in this one
command: "Love your neighbor as yourself."
GALATIANS 5:14

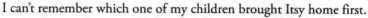

I can't remember which one of my children brought Itsy home first.

"Whose dog is that?" I asked, a little incredulous that someone would entrust their tiny, fluffy white dog into my children's grubby little hands.

"It's Sarah's grandma's dog," they said.

"That was nice of her," I said as the little dog jumped into my lap and snuggled in. "But if you're borrowing her dog, you should ask what her name is."

I found out for myself the very next day, after my preschooler gave me the slip. Realizing that she'd climbed up to open the garage door herself, I quickly raced down the driveway, only to see her a block ahead of me on her bike. As I trailed her down the street at a brisk walk, huffing the whole way, she saw me coming and started pedaling on her training wheels as fast as her legs could go. I caught up to her just as she rang the neighbor's doorbell.

Joyce, our new neighbor, was pleasant and kind, and quickly invited me and my capricious child inside. When I shook my head over how my trio of girls had borrowed her dog, she smiled and said that her hip hurts, so she doesn't mind them taking the dog for a walk.

As Ashlyn and I returned home a few minutes later, another neighbor called out to us from his garden and asked good-naturedly why I haven't just gotten my children their own dog. Shrugging, I smiled and countered, "Why, when they can live vicariously through the neighborhood pets?"

Though I didn't mention it, I couldn't help but think: *And why not, when they are making new friends?*

Scripture tells us time and again to love our neighbor in the same way that we love ourselves, yet it can be easy to overlook those who live closest to us. Tim and I hadn't taken the time to introduce ourselves and welcome our new neighbors to the area yet, but my gregarious children provided just the push we needed.

– *Kristin*

– *Today's Act of Friendship* –

Stop waiting for someone to befriend you. Instead, go out
of your way to introduce yourself or make conversation
with someone you've been meaning to talk to.

The Dinner Invitation

Cheerfully share your home with those who need a meal or a place to stay.
1 PETER 4:9

Last year we started a new tradition of inviting guests to join our family dinner one night each week. As my husband would constantly remind me: we are going to eat anyway, so why not invite others to join us?

Over the course of the year we invited single friends, young college-age neighbors, single moms, older couples, and families with small kids. Every week we would prayerfully consider who we should invite over, and each week God was faithful to bring someone to mind.

These dinners became not only a place for community and relationships to start but also for deep conversations about faith and family, heartache and joy to happen on a regular basis in our home. As the food was passed, there was often a comfort that came with the dish that was shared. It became my husband's answer to most problems: a couple was struggling in their marriage? Invite them to dinner. A young single mom was tired and discouraged? Invite her and her kids to come eat with us. A young family who was new to the country didn't know many people yet? Invite them over to get to know them better. Slowly we began to see how God was using our simple offering of time and food as a way to usher in peace and hope—a sense that neither we nor our guests were forgotten or alone. Hospitality doesn't have to be fancy or ornate; most people aren't going to care what you serve or how tidy your house is—sometimes a simple meal or food ordered in is the best!

Sharing our homes, whether by preparing a meal or putting clean sheets on the guest room bed, is an important way to show our deep love for each other—and to offer hope and peace, encouragement and joy as well. God shows up in our midst, and it is awesome to behold.

— *Kendra*

— Today's Act of Friendship —

Share a meal with someone new—whether you invite
them to your home or meet at a restaurant.

Accountability Partners

Wounds from a sincere friend are better than many kisses from an enemy.
PROVERBS 27:6

It was fully three seconds after dashing off an angry text to Kendra and Kristin that my phone rang. It was Kendra, and I knew why she was calling. We had just received a business email; I was seriously annoyed at the nitpicky comments we'd received, and my text to her and Kristin reflected my exasperation with a few frowny emojis tossed in for additional emphasis.

One of the things I appreciate the most about Kendra is that she is willing to lovingly confront me, even when I'm mad. She calls me out when I'm wrong, offers a different perspective to counter my assumptions, and gently reminds me that my faith calls me to grace. She isn't afraid to say the words I don't want to hear, and I listen because I know she has my best interests at heart.

Having a friend who loves me enough to correct me is not a blessing I take lightly, even if I'm slightly grumpy in the moment. It is far easier to not confront, to let things slide, to let friends do or say things that undermine God's calling on their lives than it is to gently hold them accountable. But I would far rather hear hard truth spoken in great love from my friends than listen to the fake sweetness of those who aren't truly on my side.

Knowing which words are hard truths and which are fake love requires wisdom on my end. I have to be willing to listen with an open heart, accept correction, and recognize that my friends are firmly on my side, even when they say things that might hurt. Sweet, empty words that smooth things over but leave unholy behavior unchanged is a trap used by the enemy of our souls to keep us from God's best.

– Julie

– Today's Act of Friendship –

Have you been ignoring the painful truth someone has shared
with you in good faith? Have you been avoiding a potentially
painful conversation with someone you love over unholy
behavior? Pray about how to have those conversations.

The "Small" Group

Let us think of ways to motivate one another to acts of love and good works.
HEBREWS 10:24

My coleader, Joy, and I had just finished preparing for our new church small group at my home. Low music was on, chocolate and beverages were out, and we were ready—or so we thought.

The doorbell rang. And rang. And rang. By the time I breathlessly finished answering the door and running back to the kitchen, fifteen women had arrived for our "small" group.

The night was rife with minor problems. There were a couple of well-meaning talkers who dominated the conversation, while others hardly got a word in. The discussion wandered off-topic no matter how many times we tried to steer it to the book. As I shut the door behind the last of them a couple of hours later and turned to my friend, we both looked a little shell-shocked.

The next week, only three people showed up. What had happened?

Like Goldilocks and her search for the perfect porridge, we'd run into the problems of being too large and then too small. In a too-large group, members might not think their voice or presence matters—after all, they might reason that others are waiting to take their place. A smaller group conveys intimacy and builds trust among members, and if someone misses a week, others notice. But a group that is too small can be intimidating and awkward. Unfortunately for us, and unlike Goldilocks, there really never was a "just right" group size, and we struggled the entire season.

Evaluating the dynamics afterward, I was forced to wonder: *How do we foster community in ways that encourage true connection?* The book of Hebrews encourages us as believers to meet together and motivate one another in our faith. Though mistakes happen and some things are beyond our control, I've come to realize that some of the responsibility rests on our shoulders. As leaders, we could have broken the original large group into two smaller groups, or sent personal messages to each member to make sure they knew how valued they were to us. As friends, we need to be willing to adapt, even when circumstances seem challenging.

— *Kristin*

— Today's Act of Friendship —

Consider adapting your behavior in a challenging
friendship or group to meet the needs of others.

Being Friendly but Firm

Bless those who curse you. Pray for those who hurt you.
LUKE 6:28

My daughter came home upset. Another little girl in her class was being unkind to her. It was not anything so extreme that I needed to step in, but just little unkind comments or looks—things that made my daughter feel slightly insecure. As I asked my daughter questions about the other girl—her life and how she treated others—it became evident that this girl may have had other things going on at home. It also became clear that my daughter was not the only girl in her class receiving comments and condescending looks: this girl treated many of the other girls in the same manner.

Once I realized this, the focus of our conversation began to shift to imagining what might be going on at home for this other child and why she might be speaking so unkindly to Jasmine and her other classmates. We then talked about not taking things personally, especially when we realize the behavior of another is not targeted only at us, and about how looking for ways to show compassion for another, even when they are mean to us, can shape the way we think about and interact with them. We ended by praying for the other girl and discussing ways that Jasmine could model good friendship behavior while also not letting the other girl continue to be unkind to her.

Jesus' command to respond to cursing with blessing is sometimes hard to hear when faced with a difficult person who has been unkind to us. I told my daughter that one way we respond to those around us is to resist the urge to act in the same manner as the person, and instead be friendly but firm. This means we do not have to subject ourselves to the abuse of others, but we can be loving in the way we respond to them. Then most importantly, we can pray for them, which is exactly what my daughter and I did for that little girl. It may not have completely resolved the situation, but it changed the way my daughter viewed the other girl, and that makes all the difference.

— Kendra

— Today's Act of Friendship —

Think of a way that you can respond in a loving way toward someone who has been unkind to you and then say a prayer for that person.

Seeing Past Stereotypes

*Do to others whatever you would like them to do to you. This is
the essence of all that is taught in the law and the prophets.*

MATTHEW 7:12

It wasn't until I was sadly descending the steps of Basilica of St. Patrick's Old Cathedral located in New York City, having discovered its massive wooden doors locked, that my stereotype of New Yorkers was shattered once and for all.

I'd started walking back down the sidewalk when I heard a suspicious "psst" from an older-model car parked on the street. I turned warily toward the car, where a stranger was pointing my family to a small side door tucked in St. Paul's stone walls at street level. He explained that we had about ten minutes before he had to lock up the building.

A bit stunned by the unexpected kindness of our new friend, I thanked him, and then my family slipped through the side door and down a quiet hallway. We reached the entrance to the sanctuary threshold, where we beheld a masterpiece of plaster and stained glass, fashioned circa 1808—a riot of color and Jesus and wonder so big that my entire family stood transfixed for several moments before we silently moved inside the sanctuary to explore.

You see, I had steeled my tender Midwestern heart for this trip to the big city, bracing myself for interactions with people who are brisk and without patience for gawkers from flyover country. I'd heard all the stories, and much to my chagrin, I believed them. I forgot for a moment that we humans are messy, nuanced creatures, not all good or all bad, incapable of accurate description by sweeping stereotypes.

And isn't that just like God? He confronts our wrong thinking head-on, acknowledging our mistaken assumptions even as we are reminded that God can use anything and anyone to accomplish his goals. Jesus didn't stereotype people. In fact, he routinely tore down stereotypes and embraced those rejected by polite society. Treating others as nuanced individuals, recognizing their humanity instead of stereotyping, seeing others as God sees them rather than as the labels we use to sort and dismiss—this is what Jesus did, what he is gracious enough to do for us, and this is what we are to do for others.

– Julie

– Today's Act of Friendship –

Reevaluate your stereotypes, considering how they might be holding
you back from the blessing of an unexpected new friendship.

Fatherly Friendship

Fathers, do not aggravate your children, or they will become discouraged.
COLOSSIANS 3:21

During my senior year of college, I moved home after Christmas break to complete my internship at the middle school in my hometown. I found myself in a bit of limbo—no longer fitting in with the college crowd but not quite part of the professional world. I didn't have many friends who lived in the area anymore, and I was lonely.

My ever-perceptive father picked up on this and, without making it obvious, began to ask to spend time with me. Over that spring semester we watched movies together and hung out, took bike rides and ate dinner together. He would engage me in conversation and was always genuinely interested in hearing about my day. Our relationship had shifted now that I was a young adult, and he became a good friend to me in a season when I needed one.

I often think of those months I spent back in my parents' home as I transitioned to adulthood. I didn't realize it at the time, but it set up the relationship we still have now—one based on friendship as adults. I still seek out my parents' opinions on things and share my joys and sorrows with them. They've proven to be some of my greatest supporters in life, and I value their friendship.

Relationships can change over time, and nowhere is this more evident than in the relationship between parent and child. As our children grow, we must allow them to develop independence from us—even when they make choices that may be different from our own—while also remaining engaged with them. In this way we can remain a positive influence in their lives as they become adults. Rather than frustrate our children with overbearing or protective behavior, we can encourage them with friendship. My dad did a lot of modeling of godly behavior—including how to be a good friend—that encouraged me in a season when I could have been easily discouraged.

— Kendra

— Today's Act of Friendship —

Think of a friendship that has changed over time and offer support and encouragement to your friend in the current season you are in.

Pray, Then Act

Don't just listen to God's word. You must do what it says.
Otherwise, you are only fooling yourselves.
JAMES 1:22

I sat down on the folding chair, smiling nervously at the two blonde girls next to me. It was the first meeting of the year for a faith-based organization that operated on my college campus of sixteen thousand students. As a girl who was feeling the forty-five-minute drive from home keenly, I had been praying for godly friends and hoped this might be one such opportunity to meet them.

The week before, I had heard a knock on the door of my freshman dorm room. I opened it, finding one of the leaders of Campus Crusade for Christ (today called Cru) standing there. She invited me to come to the meeting the following week, and with my desire for friendship in the back of my mind, I accepted gladly.

That's how I found myself milling with a couple hundred students in the large meeting space inside the student union. Groups of upperclassmen greeted one another with hugs, backslaps, and squeals of delight, while the younger set looked on awkwardly. After a few minutes, I decided to sit down. The two girls next to me had the same friendly smile, and it turned out that they were sisters. The younger sister, Steph, was new to our school.

Steph quickly became one of my best friends in college. Ours was a friendship that—along with two other friends, Stef and Tara—has lasted through more than fifteen years of job changes and moves, marriages, and a combined eighteen children. But beyond our college-girl love for *The Bachelor* and our current lives as wives and mothers, the tie that binds us is our love for Jesus. I know that, despite the physical distance, these friends wouldn't hesitate to help if I were in need.

I'd love to say that it was through my own efforts that I made such amazing friends. But the truth is, I first prayed for good friends and then seized the opportunity I was given. As Christians, we're told that we shouldn't just listen to the Word of God—we need to implement it. Our faith is what spurs us to action. Let's resolve not just to be open to friendship, but intentional in its pursuit.

– Kristin

– Today's Act of Friendship –

If you're in a season where friends seem scarce, ask God
to provide—then follow up on the opportunities he gives.
If not, send a note to someone who's been a friend for
a long time, thanking them for their friendship.

Grace-Filled Friendship

*Make allowance for each other's faults,
and forgive anyone who offends you.*

COLOSSIANS 3:13

"Mom, Charlie got mad at me today over nothing. He's too sensitive." Jonny's complaint came in the midst of his own frustration and sadness, certain he was a bad friend but unsure of what he had done wrong.

Charlie and Jonny have very different personalities, and Jonny's fun-loving exuberance is sometimes a bit much for Charlie's slightly quieter personality. They are learning to navigate each other's quirks, and that means sometimes they get frustrated. On occasion, I offer a wise word to help, and sometimes I let them wrestle through it on their own, secretly monitoring the conversation to make sure no one strays into inappropriate territory.

But this particular frustration was bigger than young boys learning to live in harmony, and a broader perspective is sometimes necessary when learning to be a godly friend.

"Honey, you know that Charlie's mom doesn't live with them, right?" I asked. Snuggling my son close, I spent the next several minutes talking with him about how Charlie's parents' divorce might be impacting Charlie—how Charlie might be feeling even if he doesn't verbalize it, how strong feelings sometimes spill out sideways into friendships, and how Jonny needs to be an especially good friend to Charlie right now, even if Charlie is more frustrating than usual.

Sometimes, we need a gentle reminder that we are not at the center of anyone else's story, and that godly friendship might require us to be more grace-filled and less easily offended when our friend walks through a particularly bad time. When we recognize that our friend's frustration is a direct result of external circumstances, and we just happen to be in the line of fire, we can set aside our own hurt and respond with love and grace, unoffended.

— *Julie*

— Today's Act of Friendship —

Consider who in your life needs extra grace from you and pour
an extra serving of unconditional love into that relationship.

Be Brave

God has not given us a spirit of fear and timidity,
but of power, love, and self-discipline.

2 TIMOTHY 1:7

I pulled into the preschool parking lot, drove to my usual spot, and paused before getting out of the car. It wasn't quite noon yet, and I was waiting for one of the other moms to open her car door so we could walk in together.

We weren't friends—yet—but we'd chatted more than once, and I had decided to be brave and ask her to have coffee. A couple of weeks earlier I had determined to try to catch her, but it never seemed to be the right time—which is what led to me sitting in my car, watching her car like a weirdo. When she finally opened her door, I quickly hopped out of my SUV and sped up a little until we were side by side.

"Hey, what were you up to this morning while the kids were in preschool?" I asked, feeling awkward. She paused for a beat before saying that she'd spent the morning volunteering in her older son's classroom.

"We should go for coffee some morning. I mean, if you're not busy," I added hastily. We agreed and exchanged numbers, and by the following week were sipping hot drinks together and having a friendly conversation. We agreed to meet again in the next few weeks.

The conversation I've described may seem like a normal occurrence. But for me, approaching someone I don't know is outside my comfort zone. When I was plagued by nightmares as a child, my dad had me memorize 2 Timothy 1:7 to remind me that God hasn't given us a spirit of fear. And although I'm no longer concerned about things that go bump in the night, that doesn't mean I'm immune to worries. Pain, humiliation, rejection, hurt feelings, ruined relationships, loneliness, and isolation are all fears I've faced. Yet God has called us to live a life of power, love, and self-discipline. Put another way, Paul encourages Timothy: "God doesn't want us to be shy with his gifts, but bold and loving and sensible" (MSG). God has wired us for friendship and community, and he wants us to be bold and loving and sensible in the pursuit of those connections—even when it requires a little bravery.

– Kristin

– Today's Act of Friendship –

Be brave! Approach someone you've been meaning to connect with and invite them to spend time with you.

When Love Comes as a Listening Ear

I am giving you a new commandment: Love each other. Just as I have loved you, you should love each other.

JOHN 13:34

An unexpected package came in the mail on an otherwise ordinary day. I held my breath as I opened the enclosed card. It was from Alissa, a friend of mine. She said she'd remembered the story I had told months earlier of purging my closet, and how in my haste I accidentally put a necklace I had just purchased from a fair-trade company in with all the things to donate. I was so bummed—I hadn't even had a chance to wear it. I stopped in at the secondhand store several times over the following month to see if it ever made it to the show floor, but I never found it there.

Alissa's note said she wanted to give me something just because—and as I opened the box, I saw the exact necklace that I had lost. She worked for the jewelry company and had the same necklace, and after remembering my story, wanted me to have it.

Tears filled my eyes, not so much because of the gift—although I certainly loved the necklace—but because she remembered something I'd said from months earlier and took the time to replace what I'd lost. She had truly listened to me, and in that moment, reading her words, I felt heard and seen.

Jesus commanded us to love each other, following his example of love. This can be challenging at times, especially in our fast-paced culture, but when we put aside our own agenda and take the time to listen to another—when we make them feel like they are known—we are loving like Jesus did. It may be a simple command, but it takes practice and intentionality to do it well.

— *Kendra*

— Today's Act of Friendship —

Really take the time to listen to another person and affirm that you've heard them in some way.

Family Friendships

"Don't sin by letting anger control you." Don't let the sun go down
while you are still angry, for anger gives a foothold to the devil.
EPHESIANS 4:26-27

It had been a long, cold month, and everyone in my house was suffering from a strong case of cabin fever. With the schools closed due to subzero temperatures, my children had been snappish with each other all day.

As the oldest of three siblings, I know how the game is played. Someone is obnoxious, someone retaliates, and then everyone runs pell-mell to mom in a race to tattle first. In a moment of mothering brilliance, I gathered my children together and sent them to their rooms with the following instructions: (1) I was no longer in the middle of their spat, and (2) they would not be leaving their rooms until they had worked out their disagreement with sincerity and love.

It wasn't long until I heard murmuring from upstairs. I snuck up the stairs a bit to make sure it was going well and had to suppress a secret smile. My children were sitting in their doorways, taking turns explaining what about the other person's behavior had been frustrating, listening with care, and sincerely apologizing for their individual roles in the conflict. Less than fifteen minutes later, they returned downstairs, friends once again, their disagreements resolved, asking if they could play together.

My mom frequently told my brothers and me that we would need one another's friendship as adults. She was right. I treasure my friendship with my brothers, and sibling friendship is an expectation I've set for my own children. Anger and frustration are inevitable as siblings grow up together, and learning to handle those emotions and resolve conflict in healthy ways is a skill to be learned and practiced. Scripture is clear: anger allowed to fester gives our enemy a foothold in our lives and relationships. We are commanded to deal with anger and the underlying conflict rather than avoid it or, worse, secretly feed it until it grows into a far larger problem.

Learning to handle conflict in a healthy way is a journey, not a destination. Teaching siblings (and teaching ourselves) to engage in healthy conflict will have successes and setbacks, but don't give up.

– Julie

– Today's Act of Friendship –

Consider how to incorporate a healthy conflict-resolution
habit into your family to strengthen the ties of friendship.

When Friendship Steps In

When God's people are in need, be ready to help them.
ROMANS 12:13

It was a Wednesday morning, and I had just finished getting my kids up and ready for the day when I got the phone call.

"Honey, I have some news," my mom quietly stated. "Uncle Jimmy had a heart attack last night—he's gone."

How? I thought. *What happened?* I was reminded of a similar call I'd received from my mom just a month earlier. Jimmy had been in the hospital; he'd had another episode with his heart. I'd told my mom that day, "It's going to be a sad day for me when Uncle Jimmy dies."

It was that day.

"Your dad and I are going up to the farm today," my mom said, bringing me back to the moment.

"I'm going with you," I hurriedly replied.

As I hung up, my mind was already planning how I would manage the day and be able to go along. I called my friend Terri, hoping her daughter Madi, a teenager who is great with my kids, would be around. But when I asked, Terri told me Madi was already babysitting for another family.

I burst into tears—something I had tried to steel myself against just moments before. As Terri asked what was wrong, I could hear the sympathy in her voice. I explained through my tears that my uncle had died, and that I was desperate to be with the rest of my family.

"I'll watch your kids," Terri said, without missing a beat.

"You don't want to watch my crazy kids!" I exclaimed.

"Yes, I do, I'm already on my way," she said.

As I hung up, I breathed a prayer of thanks for Terri's friendship. She quickly put aside her own agenda and stepped in to help me at the last minute, just as Paul tells us in Romans to always be ready to help others when a need arises. It can be a challenge to set aside our own schedules to help someone else, but it is one of the greatest gifts we can give to a friend.

— *Kendra*

— Today's Act of Friendship —

Look for a way you can assist someone in need.

The Silliest Contest

*Pay careful attention to your own work, for then
you will get the satisfaction of a job well done, and you
won't need to compare yourself to anyone else.*

GALATIANS 6:4

Are you ever intimidated by other women? I am. My insecurities stem from comparing the very best attributes of another woman with my own hidden worst parts—which means that I will never, ever stack up in this silly contest.

Silent intimidation is an insidious beast. We walk through life silently intimidated by some and silently intimidating others, causing untold damage to our hearts. Satan loves to use our insecurities to twist and tangle us up inside until we are so focused on our own inadequacies that we become ineffectual and useless. We become so consumed with our weaknesses that we believe we can do nothing, and so believing, we do nothing. We are our own worst enemies when we stop ourselves from using our gifts and talents before we've even begun.

Do not consider the woman next to you who appears to be saving the world and compare her accomplishments to your one small thing. Do not discount your one small thing. Our God is the God of the small things. I love that God uses those of us the world would consider the underdog, when it comes to talent and influence, to accomplish his will. That way there is no doubt who gets the glory and credit: God (see 1 Corinthians 1:26-29). If we show up offering him our meager resources, he will use us, and oftentimes he multiplies our humble offering into something far beyond our own abilities.

Scripture is clear: focus on what God has called you to do, not on the gifts he's given your spiritual sisters. Do not compare; do not discount the gifts God has given you. Stop allowing Satan to plant seeds of intimidation and comparison in your life, sowing discord into your relationships.

— *Julie*

— Today's Act of Friendship —

Seek forgiveness for the secret intimidation and comparisons
you've been allowing to take up space in your mind and
heart. Focus instead on what God has tasked you to do.

Cross-Generational Friendships

*One generation shall commend your works to
another, and shall declare your mighty acts.*

PSALM 145:4, ESV

"I just don't know if I'm needed," a friend confessed to our circle of leaders who run a local moms' group. Older than most of us by twenty years, my friend wondered if what she had to offer was still valuable to young moms.

The women around the table, myself included, looked at her as if we could not believe what she was saying. We immediately came to her defense, telling her that yes, she was valuable, that she had so much to offer all of us. We explained that we relied on her wisdom as a mom who now had adult children and appreciated her wise counsel when it came to raising older children and teenagers. She gave a timid smile as we sincerely sought to alleviate the doubt she was feeling and give value to her current station in life.

I've thought often about my friend and her concern that she may not be relevant anymore. It's a comment I've heard frequently from older people when it comes to mentoring and friendships, especially with a younger generation. I believe this is an absolute lie. We need friendships with those who are in a different stage of life! There is a richness in learning from someone who is a little further down the road of life than we are, just as there is in reaching back to those who are coming up behind us.

Scripture teaches that we should be telling the next generation how God has worked in our lives. Offering friendship to those older or younger than us allows us to do just that. My older friend can share from her own life the wonderful things that God has done, bolstering my own faith. And I, in turn, can tell a younger friend about struggles I have overcome. We were made to have friends of different ages and in all stages of life—they offer a unique richness and value to our lives that can't be provided by those who are in the same place we currently are.

— Kendra

— Today's Act of Friendship —

Think of a friend who is older (or younger) than you.
Tell them how much you value their friendship.

Messy Hospitality

*Live in harmony with each other. Don't be too proud to enjoy the
company of ordinary people. And don't think you know it all!*

ROMANS 12:16

"I'M SO ANGRY AT YOU!" My son's three-year-old voice reverberated through my house during a momentary lull in the adult conversation.

Aaron and I shared a glance before Aaron made a beeline for the gaggle of kids downstairs. I glanced around at the adults gathered in our living room, casting about for a way to revive the conversation as a slightly awkward silence descended momentarily.

Life is messy, and hospitality with children is oftentimes less than perfect. Add to that approximately fifteen people sharing a meal, and our house that afternoon could only be described as organized chaos. And yet, hospitality is the honest sharing of our lives, not the manufactured perfection we so often think is necessary, and *I love it*.

When my kids were young, my home was often filled with tiny princesses in flowing dresses darting between rooms and around visiting adults, boys shouting (mostly) in laughter as they played Sega racing games, and a poodle named Peanut hopping from lap to lap for quick snuggles.

We've lost the princesses and little boys' voices, but you can still find adults loitering in our kitchen, hands wrapped around mugs of coffee, talking about jobs and kids and the ups and downs of life. You find brokenness and breakthroughs, sorrow and joy, triumph and struggle in the lives of those who gather.

Give me a house filled with imperfect people, with chaos, with shouts of laughter, with quiet tears spilled over hard things any day over elegant dinners and small talk.

Jesus is found in the midst of messy hospitality, when we are vulnerable enough to let others see our imperfection even as we strive to be women who love God and love others. He's there when we are brave enough to admit that we are works in progress—that we don't have it all figured out. He's there when we invite others to walk alongside us without giving in to the temptation to put on our masks of perfection.

— Julie

— Today's Act of Friendship —

Consider who needs to be invited into the imperfect circles of your
messy life. Don't wait for a better time; invite that person now.

Keeping the Peace

Do all that you can to live in peace with everyone.
ROMANS 12:18

As I sat in the kitchen one afternoon, I overheard my daughter Jasmine talking to a friend on the phone. My daughter's whispered agreement and then not-so-very-nice comment about another girl in their class caught my ear. As she hung up, I asked if I could speak with her.

When I questioned Jasmine about the unkind comment she had made, I told her I was surprised, since it was out of character for my usually tenderhearted girl to talk ill of someone else. She shrugged her shoulders and with sorrowful eyes told me about some conflicts that had arisen between the girls in her class. Two of her friends had gotten into a fight, and one of them had told my daughter that she shouldn't be friends with the other girl anymore.

This was the same girl who, while on the phone, made unkind comments about the other. Jasmine felt pressure to join in, offering her own, albeit weak, unkind statement. As I sat and listened to her explanation of events, I saw immediate remorse in my daughter's eyes. I told her that I could relate to her and what she was going through, and that most of us have been in a similar situation at some point in our lives. We then went on to talk about friendship and boundaries and how she could be respectful while still advocating to be friends with both girls. We also discussed how joining in with another in talking behind someone else's back is never okay. We talked about the qualities of what makes a good friend: honesty, love, and kindness. We ended our talk by praying for both girls and for Jasmine to have wisdom in handling the situation.

Navigating friendship at any age can be a challenge. It can be difficult for any of us to offer support while not engaging in gossip or taking sides in relationships. We are reminded in Scripture to do all that we can to choose peace over discord. This is vital to having healthy friendships.

– *Kendra*

– Today's Act of Friendship –

When given the opportunity, choose to be a
peacemaker among your friends.

Simple Ways to Find Friends

Two people are better off than one, for they can help each other succeed. If one person falls, the other can reach out and help. But someone who falls alone is in real trouble.

ECCLESIASTES 4:9-10

Many years ago, while I was talking with my sister Katrina, she mentioned a woman she had seen across the room at church that morning. The woman had just moved to town for her husband's ministry position, and she and her family were new at church. Finishing up her description of the woman, Katrina said words that would ring in my head for years to come: "She will be my friend."

Katrina's intentionality in pursuing friends has remained important to me when I consider my own relationships and desire to pursue friendship with others. When seeking new friends, we can start where we are—with the neighbor we haven't met yet, or someone who has children the same age or who walks their dog the same time of day that we do. We can also reach out to acquaintances. If you attend the same church or work for the same company, you've already got something in common that you can use as a starting point for conversation. Similarly, places that foster community—church or community groups, groups that center around certain hobbies, or even the PTA at a child's school—are great places to find friends. Once you've pinpointed a potential friend, be brave in your pursuit. It took me a few months to work up the nerve and intention to ask an acquaintance at church out for coffee. She's since become a wonderful friend.

There have been numerous times when I've said internally or aloud to others: "She will be my friend." As Ecclesiastes notes, community with others is essential as two people together are better off than a person alone, because they can help each other out. Connection and community are integral parts of life—in fact, one study I read said that loneliness is as toxic to us as cigarettes.

Yet cultivating relationships is rarely something that happens by chance. Instead of simply purposing to leave our circle open, we must intentionally pinpoint people as a key part to cultivating successful friendships.

— Kristin

— Today's Act of Friendship —

Pay attention to those around you and purposely engage someone new in conversation with the goal of making them a friend.

Lifting One Another Up

When Moses' hands grew tired, they took a stone and put it under him and he sat on it. Aaron and Hur held his hands up—one on one side, one on the other—so that his hands remained steady till sunset.

EXODUS 17:12, NIV

I knew of Carol long before I knew her. I had watched her coordinate hundreds of volunteers, guiding them with wisdom and humility. I knew she was a leader who loved Jesus and loved others, and I prayed that I might draw close enough to learn by observing her.

One day, my phone rang. It was Carol. I was serving in her organization, but we did not know one another well. Her daughter was in the midst of a horrific divorce, and knowing my legal background, she was seeking to pray with someone who understood the system. And so that's what we did, weekly, for more than a year. We prayed as though we were the widow who would not leave the wicked judge in peace in Luke 18:1-8. We were persistent and consistent, and God continually showed up in big ways and small throughout that hard time.

Through that journey of prayer and support alongside Carol, I learned the importance of serving as Aaron and Hur did for Moses. In the biblical story, as long as Moses' hands remained in the air, the Israelites routed the enemy in battle, but as his hands grew tired and lowered, their enemy would gain the upper hand. It was only with the assistance of Aaron and Hur that Moses kept his arms aloft long enough for the Israelites to claim victory.

There is incredible strength in coming alongside a sister in Christ in quiet, fervent prayer over her hard things with no hidden agenda. There is no scarcity in the economy of God, and the success of another woman does not come at the sacrifice of our own. There is more than enough Kingdom work to keep us all busy, and we should be striving to serve as Aaron and Hur did at least as much as we are asking God to put us in the position of Moses.

— Julie

— Today's Act of Friendship —

Ask God to show you someone you can come alongside in sustained, prayerful support.

Neighbors and Friends

I recommend having fun, because there is nothing better for people in this world than to eat, drink, and enjoy life. That way they will experience some happiness along with all the hard work God gives them.

ECCLESIASTES 8:15

The winter days are short, but the deeply cold months can feel endless in Minnesota. By the time the snow disappears and the icicles fall off the eaves, our three daughters are more than ready to escape outside to enjoy the sun and warmer temperatures. To accomplish that goal, it's become a tradition for us in the past few years to create a summer bucket list—including a mix of at-home activities and day trips for new adventures. My children love the days when we eat breakfast in bed or have ice cream for dinner, as well as our trips to the biggest candy store in the state and to the park in Stillwater dotted with giant teddy bears.

Although we enjoy the out-of-the-ordinary pace of the activities and outings, our underlying focus is on relationships. While I love to experience adventures with my kids and spend time together as a family, I believe it's equally important to teach my children the value of prioritizing people over things. So, interspersed among "favorite foods day," family water balloon fights, and visits to art fairs are friend-focused activities. Some of these are more elaborate, like our neighborhood movie night (our cul-de-sac sets up an inflatable screen, and neighbors bring lawn chairs and snacks to share) or our grilling contests, where my husband pits his steak and ribs against the skills and flavors of his friends. Even when the adventure isn't expressly about friends, it's always more fun to include others. A scavenger hunt or a game of life-size Chutes and Ladders drawn in chalk on the driveway are more interesting when the neighbor kids join in, and a visit to a new park is better when we bring along friends to chat and play with on the playground.

The Bible reminds us of the importance of incorporating fun into our lives. There's nothing wrong with interspersing our hard work with experiences that help us appreciate both the toil and the joy of this life. When we use those adventures to foster friendship, we're twice as blessed.

– Kristin

– Today's Act of Friendship –

Come up with a list of fun ways for you or your family to include others in your lives, like hosting a bonfire, potluck, or movie night.

A Disgruntled Dinner Host

Where two or three gather together as my followers,
I am there among them.

MATTHEW 18:20

When an old friend called, my husband—ever the host—quickly invited him and his family over to our house for an evening meal. I was a bit disgruntled as I helped my husband prepare food and our house for company. But as soon as they entered our home, much of my bad mood lifted, replacing my annoyance with a feeling of peace and a sense that they were meant to be with us that evening.

As we shared a meal, we caught up on life and family. Then the conversation moved to faith—believing God for big things, experiencing changes of heart, and desiring nothing more than to be obedient to God's call. We talked about our plans to move out of our neighborhood into the heart of our city, something we believed and had peace that God was asking us to do. Our friends nodded in agreement with a shared understanding, and they explained how they'd been having similar conversations with God, very much mirroring our own.

The hours seemed to move by a little too quickly, and soon dinner ended. We shed tears as we spoke honestly to one another about things that were on our hearts that we had yet to share with anyone else, and we ended the night by praying for one another, encouraging each other, and agreeing to get together again soon.

Later, I lay in bed pondering our conversation. I was once again struck by how God knows our need, even before we realize it. How he often brings people to us at just the right time, when we need encouragement and understanding—even on the nights we think we don't want to host. I recalled Jesus' words that when two or three of his followers are gathered together, he is there too. It was a reminder to me that I don't want to miss the way that God will use friends to encourage me in doing his will.

– Kendra

– Today's Act of Friendship –

Invite a friend to dinner and share together what
God is doing in both of your lives.

Speaking the Truth in Love

Don't use your freedom to satisfy your sinful nature. Instead,
use your freedom to serve one another in love.

GALATIANS 5:13

It started with an unexpected message from a friend about a situation that had been weighing me down. Up until then, I was doing a good job of ignoring it, hoping it would go away. The text made it clear that this strategy had failed.

"What are you planning to do to resolve it?" she asked.

The innocent question rubbed me the wrong way. I'd been wrestling with the problem for a while, but no one had had the gall to call me out on it like she was doing. Reading her message, I felt a maelstrom of emotions, none of them pretty.

My abrupt response didn't deter my friend. She didn't get angry, but she also made it clear that she wasn't willing to drop it. And, the message implied, I should want the right thing done too. As leaders in the church, she pointed out, "we all have an obligation to the mission, unity, and health of the church over personal relationships." But that zinger was quickly followed by a dose of love: "My hope is that you can read through the words and know that they only come from a place of love and honor."

Seeing both the love and truth of her words, I agreed to work on resolving the problem. And, after further thought, I sent her a follow-up message the next day—this one, an apology.

As Christians, we're called to walk the line between "grace giving" and "truth telling." Too much grace giving leads to apathy over sin. Too much truth telling leads to a life marked by rigid legalism. As Christ followers, we're called to balance both ideals. Galatians tells us to use our freedom from sin to serve one another in love, and my friends' words—a hard truth—were also spoken in love.

— Kristin

— Today's Act of Friendship —

Think of one way to serve a friend, whether it's by speaking
to them about a hard truth or simply showing them love.

Choosing Friendship over Stuff

*Whatever you do, whether in word or deed, do it all in the name of
the Lord Jesus, giving thanks to God the Father through him.*
COLOSSIANS 3:17, NIV

"Whoa, what?!" Abe squealed as he started jumping up and down. Lights flashed on his arcade game, announcing that he had just won the five-hundred-ticket jackpot. "I won, I won!" he shouted, dancing a jig of excitement. We were at Dave and Buster's for Jonny's tenth birthday, and both boys were trying to earn tickets to redeem for goodies in the arcade store.

Jonny was exiting the bathroom as Abe started dancing, and he knew something awesome had happened. "What's going on? What did you win?" he asked, as he raced to Abe's side.

Five hundred tickets was more than double what either Jonny or Abe had already earned. As I watched the boys walk around the store, I could tell Jonny was trying hard to be happy for Abe but was struggling. The item Jonny wanted was two hundred points more than he had, and he was trying to find something within his point total. I watched as Abe quietly double-checked his own point total and picked out something that left two hundred points to share with Jonny.

"Here, Jonny. Happy birthday!" Abe said as he passed on the card with the extra points.

"Really? You're sharing some of your points with me? Thank you!" Jonny beamed as he gave Abe a hug.

"Of course. It's your birthday. Happy birthday, friend."

When we win a prize or are gifted an unexpected resource, it feels good, doesn't it? And it's normal that our first instinct is to keep it for ourselves. But God asks us to make our words and actions count for him—and choosing to share our unexpected blessing with a friend is a beautiful example of how to do that. When we thank him for blessing us with good things and share those good things with others, we reveal his love to the world.

— Julie

— Today's Act of Friendship —

Find a way to share an unexpected blessing with a friend.

Ask for Forgiveness

If you are presenting a sacrifice at the altar in the Temple and you suddenly remember that someone has something against you, leave your sacrifice there at the altar. Go and be reconciled to that person. Then come and offer your sacrifice to God.

MATTHEW 5:23-24

"I am sorry for what I said," I stated, eyes forward on the road. Julie and I were traveling to a speaking event together, and I'd been a little snarky to my friend earlier that morning.

"I know," she responded with a lopsided grin. "You were right to challenge me."

Although that may have been true, my heart was not in the right place when I had responded to her text. I spoke from a place of annoyance and anger, not love. I needed to apologize, not so much for what I said, but for my emotion behind it. My heart and mind were in the wrong place, and I knew it.

Although this was a small bump on the road of friendship with Julie, asking forgiveness of others is not something that has always come easily to me. There have been many more times where pride reared its ugly head and prevented me from apologizing, even when I knew that I was wrong.

But getting older and walking with God have made me much more tender to the Holy Spirit when he nudges me to make things right by asking for forgiveness, and this has benefited my closest relationships like little else.

Jesus did not mince words when he told us that we must be reconciled to those we've wronged before we can come to him in worship. If I am going to follow his teachings, then forgiveness in relationships must be central to my life. It may not always be easy, but I have never regretted mending a friendship through forgiveness.

– Kendra

– Today's Act of Friendship –

Ask God to show you if there is someone you need to apologize to. Pray for wisdom and then find a way to ask for forgiveness.

The Curse of Comfort

Let us aim for harmony in the church and try to build each other up.
ROMANS 14:19

Some of our dear friends from church disbanded their small group. Not because it wasn't going well, as I initially thought—but because it was going a little *too* well. All these people were great leaders who could lead their own group, my friend told me. And yet none of them would.

All too often, it's easy to become insulated by our own comfort. As an introvert who often feels shy in large groups, I can understand the impulse to avoid the discomfort of trying something new. These people weren't stepping out of their comfort zone because they didn't need to—no one was asking them to step up as leaders, so it was all too easy to stay in the proverbial nest. As believers, Romans admonishes us to seek peace and also to "build each other up." But how do we do that?

I remember a friend who once told me that some of the most life-changing words she ever heard were, "I can see that potential in you." Calling out the gifts and strengths of others is something that all of us can do to encourage them to step forward in faith. Of course, that requires us to take the time to recognize those strengths. I've heard it said that we should find the good and praise it. One of my friends is a homeschooling mom who does incredibly creative, Pinterest-worthy crafts with her kids. Another friend is the most encouraging person I've ever met—I leave every interaction with her with a smile on my face. Yet another friend is a wonderful listener who asks intuitive questions that always help illuminate my next step forward.

Although I see the potential in all of those friends, I don't always think to mention how much I admire the qualities they exhibit. Going forward, let's resolve to gently push our friends to use the strengths they already possess to step beyond the boundaries of their comfort zones. After all, an encouraging word from us may be just the push they need to take their next faithful step.

— *Kristin*

— Today's Act of Friendship —

Encourage a friend by telling her about a strength you see in her.

Sacred Friendship

*Ruth said, "Do not urge me to leave you or to return from following
you. For where you go I will go, and where you lodge I will lodge.
Your people shall be my people, and your God my God."*

RUTH 1:16, ESV

"I can tell you have a sacred friendship." The woman's words tumbled out before I prayed for her at a women's conference. I turned my head slightly to look at Kendra and Kristin, busy praying with other women.

Sacred? I paused in my response as a decade-plus of memories flashed past my mind's eye. Kendra, Kristin, and I were in our twenties when we met in a Bible study, and since then we've walked through all of the ups and downs of scary, exhilarating, exhausting, joyful life; all of it hashed over, prayed over, wept over, laughed over. Careers. Grief. Marriages. Death. Job loss. Anger. Adoption. Depression. New businesses. Master's degrees. Foster parenting. Medical stuff with kiddos, with parents, with us. Church launches. Cancer. Teenagers. Babies. Books.

We've cajoled and shoved one another out of our individual safe circles into circumstances requiring faith, requiring that we trust Jesus to come through. And then we've celebrated with wild abandon when Jesus showed up, as our faith grew, as our journeys took us on crazy new adventures with new opportunities.

These women continually point me toward Christ, and isn't that the very definition of sacred? As I prayed over the woman in front of me, asking God to bring her sacred friends too, the story of Ruth and Naomi came to mind. They walked through grief, anger, despair, doubt, trust, and ultimately redemption, and they continually pointed each other back to God. Their story is one of my very favorites in Scripture, and their friendship was sacred.

The beautiful thing is that sacred friendships aren't an exclusive club. It's not a closed circle. I am blessed with newer sacred friendships with women whose lives overlap with mine in other ways, in other spheres of my life. I would not be the woman I am today without my sacred friends; they have had a profound impact on my life, my faith, and my journey.

– Julie

– Today's Act of Friendship –

Consider who in your life needs a sacred friend—someone
cheering them on, praying for them, and pointing them
always back to Christ. Reach out to that person.

Marry Your Best Friend

Let no one split apart what God has joined together.
MARK 10:9

The conversation about how my husband and I met and started dating came up one night around the dinner table, and our kids wanted to know the story. I thought back to many years earlier when I was a young twentysomething living in the basement of my now sister-in-law's house. Her brother Kyle (my husband) would come home often, visiting his sister and inadvertently spending time with me as well. We became friends. We would spend time with his sister, sharing meals, playing games, watching TV, and over the course of time we got to know one another as friends—good friends.

When Kyle asked me out on our first official date, I knew how much I already liked and cared for him as a friend. I had watched him with his family, observed him interact with children, heard his passions, and knew his heart.

That night, after Kyle dropped me off, he sat on the front porch and wrote me a note. In it he detailed, among other things, that he knew he was going to marry me someday.

My daughter couldn't believe it. "How could you know that after just one date?!" she asked.

"Because I'd already spent so much time with your mom, I already knew her. We were such good friends—and when she said yes to a date, I knew I was going to marry her," my husband responded.

We went on to encourage our kids to not only marry, but date, someone you are friends with first. We told them that sometimes love and marriage are hard, but if you're good friends, it will help you weather relational storms.

Jesus tells us that no one should split apart a man and a woman whom God has joined together—and one of the best ways we've found to do that is to never stop being best friends with one another.

— Kendra

— Today's Act of Friendship —

Tell your spouse or a loved one why you're grateful for their friendship.

No One Should Be Left Out

*Don't be selfish; don't try to impress others. Be humble,
thinking of others as better than yourselves.*
PHILIPPIANS 2:3

"That's the kind of friend I want my girls to have," I told my husband as I closed the screen door firmly behind my daughters, watching as they hurtled pell-mell into the bright sunshine to be the first to reach their bikes, which were littered across the driveway, and race each other down the road.

Minutes earlier, standing in my quiet kitchen during lunch cleanup with my hands elbow-deep in dishwater, I had unintentionally overheard my outgoing daughter, Elise, and her new friend consulting about going to the other child's house, just a short walk down the road. They were busy tying their shoes and searching for bike helmets when the friend posed a question:

"Does Noelle want to go too?" she asked Elise. "I don't want anyone to be left out."

When Elise agreed, they hollered up the stairs to ask Noelle if she would also like to visit the friend's house. Noelle's yes was immediate, and her feet thundered down the stairs as she raced to slide on flip-flops and catch up with the two older girls.

I was struck by the fact that the other child's suggestion wasn't the result of half-hearted politeness or adult nudging—she didn't even know I was listening in the adjacent room. Instead, she spoke out of a true desire to be a good friend and include others within that circle of friendship. Philippians reminds us to be unselfish and think of others not just as our equals, but as our betters. That kind of bone-deep unselfish care for others and generosity of spirit provides the skills we need as friends to listen hard and love well. As a mom, that is the kind of friend I want my child to have—and it's the kind of friend I want to be, too.

— Kristin

— Today's Act of Friendship —

Think of someone who may feel left out. Do something
to help them feel more included, whether it's calling
them to chat or inviting them to an event.

April

Looking beyond Perfection

*The Lord doesn't see things the way you see them. People judge
by outward appearance, but the Lord looks at the heart.*

1 SAMUEL 16:7

When I first met my friend Samantha, I was a little jealous. While I sometimes felt like I was floundering in life in general and motherhood in particular, she seemed to have it all together. Our second children were born just a few weeks apart, and I can still recall how she showed up at my door with a meal for our family—her hair done, dressed in a cute outfit and boots, looking bright-eyed and ready for adventure, even while her own toddler and infant were waiting in the idling car. Meanwhile, I was in hastily donned stretchy pants, my unwashed hair hanging in my face, while my newborn hollered prodigiously in the background.

What made it all worse was that my friend was so—well, nice. In fact, she was one of the absolute nicest people I'd ever met, always ready to lend a hand or a listening ear. I appreciated her friendship, but deep inside I held some misgivings—if she hadn't been so darn nice, that teeny-tiny part of me would have disliked her, just a little.

While I knew objectively that my friend wasn't perfect, I still felt intimidated by her—until one day, to my surprise, she got up in front of a large crowd and told the story of how she had battled anorexia in her youth. Sitting in the crowd, I wept unashamedly as I listened to my beautiful friend reveal her "imperfections," the hard-won battle she'd fought to emerge healthy and whole.

Isn't it funny how what we see as weaknesses are instead reminders of the strength and mercy of our God? In 1 Samuel, the Lord tells Samuel that while people judge by outward appearance, the Lord looks at the heart. It can be all too easy to judge others based on their outward appearance—but God reminds us throughout Scripture that it's our heart that truly reveals who we are. If I had continued to judge my friend based only on her seeming perfection rather than the radiant heart inside of her, I may have missed out on a deeper relationship with someone who has become one of my closest friends.

— *Kristin*

— Today's Act of Friendship —

Make a list of people you've judged solely based on their outward
appearance. Pray for God to forgive you for the judgments
you've made and to help you see the true hearts of others.

Cross-Cultural Friendship

Don't look out only for your own interests,
but take an interest in others, too.

PHILIPPIANS 2:4

"What do you need?" I asked my new friend, Faduma, as I looked around her sparse apartment.

"Oh, nothing," Faduma said shyly.

"Are you sure?" I responded. "What about more dishes or bedding?"

She simply shrugged and smiled, responding that she was happy just to have a safe place to sleep.

Faduma is new to this country after having spent twenty years in a refugee camp. Every time we shared a meal, she told me how much she wanted to find a job and how many places she'd applied to work. When I asked what else she needed, she was quick to say that she was okay, but I wondered how it could be true.

Finally, after several visits, Faduma said she'd love a bus pass so she could go to English classes. I might not have been able to fix everything for her, but this I could do. I stopped the very next day to purchase a bus pass so she could get to English classes.

When I dropped off the pass, she was incredibly grateful, and I was struck by the dogged resilience of this woman and her children. Even though her situation seemed overwhelming, she continued to pursue her dreams and await the future with hope. Since giving her the bus pass, my family and hers have spent more time together, sharing meals and listening to one another's stories. Her friendship has been invaluable to our family, teaching us all about the courage it takes to start anew.

As I think about my new friend, I am struck by how easy it would be for me to go about my days relatively unaffected and unaware of the needs of others in my community. I have the luxury of living my life with little thought toward the concerns of others, if I so choose. But that is not what God asks of us. As Christians, we are called to see to the needs of those around us, rather than focusing on just our own. We should be showing kindness toward others, remembering that sometimes love looks like a bus pass for a new friend who has become so dear.

— *Kendra*

— Today's Act of Friendship —

Extend the hand of friendship to someone
overlooked in your community.

Orphan Easter

No one lights a lamp and then puts it under a basket. Instead,
a lamp is placed on a stand, where it gives light to everyone in
the house. In the same way, let your good deeds shine out for all
to see, so that everyone will praise your heavenly Father.
MATTHEW 5:15-16

Easter that year initially felt a bit sad. With our extended family either traveling or living too far away for a weekend gathering, it was going to just be me, my husband, and our kids. Instead of withdrawing into our own little Easter celebration, I began reaching out to friends, international college students, and neighbors with an invitation: anyone without family nearby or anyone who'd never been part of an American Easter celebration was welcome to join us. The invite went out to the friends of my friends, and we ended up with a crew of around thirty "Easter Orphans" on Sunday afternoon.

Knowing we'd have international guests in the mix—Muslims, atheists, and Christians—I prayerfully pondered what Easter should look like. I'd spent decades secretly despising the silly traditions around bunnies and eggs that consume and overshadow the resurrection of my Savior, but this year the Holy Spirit told me to co-opt those silly traditions for Jesus. And so I did. I bought the traditional Easter candies, boiled dozens of eggs for dying, and prepared a Farkle tournament with chocolate bunnies wrapped in gold foil for trophies.

It was my favorite Easter ever. We laughed over how disgusting Peeps taste and discussed best egg-dying techniques. We enjoyed steak and lamb after my husband spoke a blessing over all of us, recognizing God and inviting him into our gathering. Two of our guests received the Golden Bunny Farkle trophies, and I later learned they stashed them in the freezer because they liked them too much to eat them.

We did life together, and Jesus was in the midst of it all. His presence was in my house, wrapped around my guests, regardless of whether they knew him yet or not. It's important to show Christ's love with no strings attached, praying we'll have an opportunity to share words about him in time. And showing love requires proximity, a drawing together, an invitation into our homes and our lives.

— *Julie*

— Today's Act of Friendship —

Plan a concrete way to show others the love of Christ this Easter
season, considering whom you might invite into your celebrations.

The Gift of Remembrance

Be happy with those who are happy, and weep with those who weep.
ROMANS 12:15

I'm officially older than my oldest sister. If that sounds odd to you, it feels strange to me, too. My sister Katrina died from breast cancer at the age of twenty-eight, and at thirty-five, I'm now several years older than she was when she died.

I often wonder how our relationship would have changed over the years. I'd like to think that our friendship would have grown stronger, as it has with my sister Kendra. I wonder what Katrina would think of my children, whom she never got to meet. I also wonder what she'd think of me. She wasn't perfect, but she was just so likable. She was warm and funny and fun. So often, I feel myself trying to measure up to my memories of Katrina. Even though I know she wasn't perfect, in my mind, she's become that way: Saint Katrina, keeper of coffee and lost causes.

That's not true, of course. I know that she was only human, but I loved her heart for others and the spiritual maturity she exemplified. Since she died, I have missed her wisdom. More than that, I simply miss the sound of her voice and her laughter.

I know that because of Katrina's faith in Jesus, someday I will see her again. Until then, I'm comforted by the thought that she will live on in my memories. One of the sweetest things a friend of mine did was turn quietly to me one day and ask, "What would Katrina think of that?" My throat tightened with unshed tears, but in my heart I felt so grateful.

My friend's invitation to speak openly about a sister I grieve felt like an unexpected gift. Too often, we shy away from approaching topics like death and grief because we're unsure of what to say, or we worry about making someone uncomfortable. Yet the beauty of friendship is that we are called to not simply share in our friends' joy but to enter their grief with them, coming alongside in all circumstances and seasons of life. My friend's question wasn't an imposition; it was a relief. I felt honored when she posed that question so casually, as if to say, "Of course what Katrina would think now still matters." Because, in my heart, it does.

– Kristin

– Today's Act of Friendship –

Ask a friend to recall memories of a loved one they are grieving.

Letting Go of Anger

Everyone should be quick to listen,
slow to speak and slow to become angry, because human anger
does not produce the righteousness that God desires.

JAMES 1:19-20, NIV

I was angry and I couldn't shake it. Someone was intentionally speaking ill of a good friend of mine, and I wanted nothing more than to defend her. I knew that what was being said about her was not kind or even correct, and I wanted to put this other person in their place. I found myself thinking all sorts of not very nice things about this other person, imagining arguments I would like to start with them, and all this was happening nowhere else but in my own mind.

As the days wore on, I began to see how my anger toward this person was taking away from my own peace. I knew in this specific instance it was not my place to step in and say something. My role was to supportively listen to my friend and pray for her and the situation. I felt convicted over my harsh assessment of the other person and began to pray for God to do a work in her heart and life. As I prayed for both women, my heart softened. I remembered the humanness of the other woman and the fact that I am not perfect and am often in need of grace myself. Slowly my anger began to dissolve.

James reminds us not to let our emotions quickly escalate into anger, but to take the time to listen and consider the circumstances. We're even given the reason why: because human anger does not produce the righteousness that God desires; it doesn't produce the kind of fruit that shows others that we love God. And when we respond from a place of anger, we will often do and say things we'll later regret. I know this truth all too well. I've also learned that if I bring my anger to God first, I respond to others in a much better way than if I quickly spout off. It allows for relationships to remain intact that could otherwise be damaged by my quick and harsh words.

– Kendra

– Today's Act of Friendship –

Have you been holding a grudge against someone for
what they've done to you or a friend? Instead of thinking
negative thoughts about the person, pray for them.

Joining Her Cause

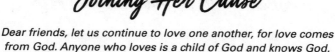

Dear friends, let us continue to love one another, for love comes from God. Anyone who loves is a child of God and knows God.

1 JOHN 4:7

"Cadbury eggs are expensive! And I need a lot of them this year," I told my friend Myndee. It was a passing comment—not even a complaint—in a conversation about my Easter plans. I was telling her about how our family had hosted an Orphan Easter last year—a gathering at our home for those with nowhere to go for the holiday—and that we loved it so much that we were going to do it again this year.

Two days later, my phone pinged. "Are these the Cadbury eggs you were needing?" Myndee texted me, attaching a picture of the eggs in question, clearly snapped in the middle of a store aisle. She bought me the eggs and two gold-foiled chocolate bunnies to serve as the trophies for the Farkle tournament at our gathering.

My first instinct was to protest—I didn't mean for her to buy the eggs, and it never occurred to me that she'd consider my passing comment, a small part of our evening of wonderful conversation, as a need she could fill. Pausing, I realized she was giving me a gift far greater than eggs and bunnies; she was giving me the precious gift of partnership.

We all want people to join our causes, but how often do we tangibly partner in our friend's cause, with a joyful heart, before she has even asked? How often do we invest financially in the support of something close to her heart without the pitch ever being made?

The gift of eggs and bunnies reminded me that my friend sees me, hears me, and knows my heart in ways that go far beyond the monetary value of Easter candy. Her love for Jesus, for me, for the quiet ways Jesus is working is wrapped up in those eggs and bunnies, and it's a gift I will treasure forever.

— Julie

— Today's Act of Friendship —

Ask Jesus to reveal ways you can shower friends with love by partnering in their heart causes, and then follow through.

What My Mom Taught Me

*She is clothed with strength and dignity,
and she laughs without fear of the future. When she speaks,
her words are wise, and she gives instructions with kindness. . . .
Her children stand and bless her. Her husband praises her.*

PROVERBS 31:25-26, 28

My mom is one of my best friends. Of course, there are a few topics we don't discuss in the same way that I do with my other girlfriends. She also doesn't want to know about any shenanigans I got into as a teen, even though they happened nearly twenty years ago. But despite those omissions, I still consider her a close friend. We talk on the phone frequently, and we usually have coffee once a week.

I've learned a lot about friendship from my mom because she is a good friend herself. And now that we're both adults, the same qualities that make her a good friend to her peers have held her in good stead as she and I navigate this season of our relationship.

Although the challenges I face now are a little weightier than what to wear to prom, the lessons I've learned from my mom have helped me be a true friend to others. From her words and example, I learned not to gossip. Even as a teen, I could tell my mom about friend drama and never worry that she'd whisper about it to someone else's mom. She rarely gossips, and I trust her because of it. She also taught me to not offer unsolicited advice. Some of the most hurtful words I've heard regarding my parenting or career choices happened when someone tried to offer "helpful," unsolicited advice. When I do ask my mom for input, she offers it in a careful, loving way. Finally, she taught me never to use guilt or manipulation to influence others. My mom doesn't betray the trust I've placed in her by loading me up with guilt, and relationships that use manipulation are not healthy.

Both my mom and the woman described in Proverbs 31 demonstrate wisdom and kindness, two traits I value. Her model for relationships is one I hope I'm teaching to my daughters.

— Kristin

— Today's Act of Friendship —

Consider what your parents or other trusted mentors taught you about friendship. Thank them for a lesson you learned from their example.

Second Chances

Do to others as you would like them to do to you.

LUKE 6:31

Two years ago, my daughter encountered cruel words and cliquish exclusion from some of her peers—typical "mean girls" who make themselves feel good by putting others down. As we talked about the hurt she felt, I gently reminded her: hurt people hurt people.

One young lady I desperately wanted to label and dismiss as a "mean girl" was a child caught up in difficult life circumstances. While my anger on my daughter's behalf was justified, I also felt a tug of prayerful sympathy as I remembered my insecurities at that stage of life. And while this girl's actions weren't okay, understanding the larger context deflated my indignation and gave me an entirely new perspective—her "mean girl" behaviors were a way to shield herself from further pain.

Jesus is for that girl just as fiercely as he is for you. And when we see people as Jesus sees them, our hearts soften, our perspectives shift, and we stop taking their words and attitudes and behaviors personally. That doesn't mean that we are doormats, allowing others to abuse us; however, we can respond with mercy and grace rather than with harsh words of our own, and we can teach our children to do the same.

Lizzie did not retaliate, and she did not try to turn their social circle against the other girl. We talked about boundaries she could set, and I monitored the situation closely in case I needed to have a conversation with their teacher. We found ways to minimize contact with this other girl while increasing contact with friends outside of that social circle to give Lizzie a safe place. Fast-forward two years, and both girls remain in the same social circle and have established a new, tentative friendship. There are no more harsh words, no more exclusionary games. While Lizzie and I discussed carefully moving forward, we realized that a once-enemy had crossed over into the beginnings of friendship because, in part, Lizzie did not treat her like an enemy, even when she could have.

The golden rule has seeped out of Scripture and into our general culture for a very good reason: treating others as you want to be treated is a teaching so valuable and so true that it can turn enemies into friends.

– Julie

– Today's Act of Friendship –

Reevaluate how you interact with women you've labeled and dismissed as "mean girls." Create a plan for both grace and boundaries.

Seeing the Whole Person

They kept demanding an answer, so he stood up again and said, "All right, but let the one who has never sinned throw the first stone!"

JOHN 8:7

We sat across from one another, coffee cups in hand. We'd had a misunderstanding and instead of avoiding one another or assuming what the other might be thinking, we decided to sit down face-to-face and talk it through. It felt awkward at first, but as the morning went on, my friend and I came to understand where we were each coming from. Forgiveness was given, allowances were made, and a bond was forged more strongly than it had been before.

It can be easy to make snap judgments about others or their intentions, especially when we are not with them in person. When we take the time to look someone in the eye and speak with them, we are seeing the whole person. We see their pain, their joy, their insecurities, their strengths, and their value—we see all of who they are—and it can often change the way we perceive them. We are more than the opinions we hold, and we can be friends with those who are very different from us when we see their humanity.

Jesus modeled this so well for us. In the story of the woman caught in adultery found in John 8, Jesus could not have been more different from the woman brought before him. The men who cast her before Jesus could never have anticipated his response. Instead of demonizing her based on one sinful act, he saw her for the whole person that she was and then told her accusers, "Let the one who has never sinned throw the first stone!" Although Jesus did not condone her behavior, he looked past it to her heart, offering compassion and freedom to live another way. I believe he challenges us to do the same. Can we see past behaviors to the hearts of those around us and offer friendship to someone who may really need it?

— Kendra

— Today's Act of Friendship —

Think of someone you've been judging lately. Ask God
to help you see them as a whole person, and choose
to extend friendship toward them instead.

Providing Wise Counsel

A friend is always loyal, and a brother is born to help in time of need.

PROVERBS 17:17

"I need to talk to you about a divorce," Sheila whispered, her words faint across the phone line.

As a practicing attorney, I didn't find those words particularly shocking, but I was dismayed to hear them nonetheless. Sheila, a friend from church, was in the midst of several hard parenting years, and she and her husband were struggling. Their teenage son had arrived home after a misstep of epic proportions, and her husband had not handled it well.

After Sheila finished, my questions began. I asked about physical and emotional abuse, about what else might be happening behind the scenes. Once I had confirmed that no abuse was occurring, it became clear that Sheila's call was a direct result of her son's mistake. Sheila was reeling from her son's actions and was in crisis; her husband was also in crisis; and their son was actively driving a wedge between his parents—whispering into his mother's ear that she should divorce his dad.

I gently asked Sheila whether she was talking to two other trusted women in our circle and whether she had told them how badly she and Joe were struggling. As fellow Jesus followers, wives, and parents, I knew they would give Sheila godly advice. Over the months that followed, these women repeatedly spoke truth to Sheila, pointing her back to God and praying with persistence over her entire family.

Now, several years later, Sheila and her husband are happily married. Their son is thriving, having survived his teen years despite some bad decisions along the way. With the help of godly counselors, Sheila and Joe came out of the crisis having grown closer rather than apart.

When Shelia wanted to hear that it was okay to walk away from her marriage, her friends loved her enough to tell her the truth. Then they wrapped around her, Joe, and their entire family with love and support. Sometimes, the best thing we can do for a friend in crisis is to speak loving truth as we also meet their needs through offers to watch kids, meet for coffee to listen without judgment, and anything else to help navigate a difficult season.

— Julie

— Today's Act of Friendship —

Most of us know someone who is struggling in their marriage, with parenting a teenager, or with some other difficult life circumstance. Actively wrap this friend in encouragement and support.

Grateful for Friendships

Whatever you do or say, do it as a representative of the Lord Jesus, giving thanks through him to God the Father.

COLOSSIANS 3:17

My pastor once talked about how a thank-you that goes unexpressed gives the impression of ingratitude. When he said it, I felt so guilty. Too often, I have had every intention of sending a thank-you note to a friend or family member but, over time, simply forgot about it. It's not that I'm ungrateful—just forgetful. I'm ashamed to admit that I have even taken the time to handwrite thank-you notes and still failed to send them. I'm pretty sure there are a few stray thank-yous tucked into my bedside table, lost in the depths of outdated paperwork and half-read novels.

Praising God and thanking him for his blessings is a priority for me. And it's easy to remember to thank someone who does something tangible, in the space of a moment—a friend who drops off a meal, a neighbor who loans you a book or tool. But what about the friend who texts me prayers when she knows I'm having a hard day? How about the sister-in-law who tells me what a good mom I am? Or the friend who takes the time to genuinely interact with my children at church instead of bypassing them to talk to other adults? These are moments that I hold dear to my heart, but it's rare for me to speak my gratitude aloud—and if I don't do it right away, I'm much more likely to forget to send a message or note later on.

Can gratitude transform the way in which we approach our lives? Paul reminds us in Colossians that all our words and deeds should be done with thanksgiving and the remembrance that we are representatives of Jesus himself. Since we are his ambassadors, our thankfulness is an outward expression of the internal change in our lives, a reflection of God's love for us.

— Kristin

— Today's Act of Friendship —

Think of one or two specific people in your life whom you can thank for an act or word of encouragement. Send them a message or give them a call to express your thanks.

I Want to Be Her Friend

Worry weighs a person down;
an encouraging word cheers a person up.
PROVERBS 12:25

A few years back, I was the emcee for a women's event where one of my friends was going to be sharing her love of decorating on a budget and the creative ways she'd learned to use and reuse things to beautify her home. I supported her during her time onstage by asking questions and engaging the audience.

My friend did a lovely job sharing, and as she did, I commented to the crowd that the first time I met her, I knew that I wanted to be her friend. She smiled shyly as the conversation continued.

After the session was completed, and as we were putting things away, she told me how struck she was by the comment I had made about wanting to be her friend. To me, it wasn't a big deal, but to her, it was huge. She went on to explain that as a child, she always struggled with friendship and wondering whether she belonged. My words, unbeknownst to me, struck deep into that place in her heart that still at times felt insecure about friendships with other women.

I stopped what we were doing and looked her in the eye. "Those weren't flippant words," I said. "I really did want to be your friend the first day we met."

She nodded and smiled as we moved on to other topics, but I left the conversation thinking about how important our words are to others. We never know the past wounds someone else may be carrying, and our encouraging words have the power to bring comfort in ways we may never know. We can be the supportive friend someone else desperately needs; it just takes a little intention on our part.

— Kendra

— Today's Act of Friendship —

Offer encouragement to a friend for no reason other than you just
want them to know that you care and are thinking about them.

Supporting Our Sisters

An open rebuke is better than hidden love! Wounds from a
sincere friend are better than many kisses from an enemy.

PROVERBS 27:5-6

"Honestly, you are one of the only white women I trust. You listen and try to do better instead of getting defensive or minimizing my feelings."

Hearing my dear friend's heartfelt words, I clutched the phone a bit tighter, trying to make up for the thousands of miles stretched between us, wishing we were face-to-face. My friend is a woman of color, and we were having a deeply honest conversation about race, interracial friendships, and what it was like for her to live in my Midwestern community's predominantly white culture before moving to a diverse area of Washington, DC. Our friendship has given me a tiny glimpse into how frequently people react differently to her than they do to me, based solely on our skin color. I've learned to listen carefully to what she has to say about the ways in which our predominantly white society makes my life easier, even as it makes hers more difficult.

My friend explained that white women often say that they support women of color, but when offering support becomes uncomfortable, white women frequently say or do nothing. And because white women are part of the dominant culture, we can walk away, abandoning our sisters of color to navigate difficult situations alone.

As I reconsidered our conversation the next morning, I asked God if I was guilty of downplaying hurtful words because the speaker might not have intended to be racist, or brushing aside a racist joke or an insulting descriptor for a group of people because the person is "just that way." Have I stepped back from the discomfort of conflict, avoiding correction because I literally don't have skin in the game?

The conviction of the Holy Spirit is gentle but firm, calling us to repentance without shaming us for our sins, and I confess that I've abandoned my sisters of color a multitude of times in order to avoid even mild conflict with someone I love or people I work alongside.

My friend's words about racial inequality have sometimes been hard to hear because their truth is undeniable, and her loving rebuke is well deserved. More and more, I hope to become a trustworthy friend to my sisters of color, defending and supporting them regardless of whether they are in the room.

– Julie

– Today's Act of Friendship –

Ask the Holy Spirit to reveal ways in which you've abandoned your faith
sisters of color, and pray through how you will confront racist statements
(overt or otherwise) from coworkers, family members, and friends.

Helping a Friend in Need

Share each other's burdens, and in this way obey the law of Christ.
GALATIANS 6:2

A couple of quick raps on the hospital-room door announced we had a visitor. Tim and I called out a greeting, and the door opened quietly to admit Phil, one of Tim's friends from CrossFit. An hour earlier, Tim had ruptured his Achilles during a 5 a.m. exercise class. A friend from the class had driven him home, and after Tim woke me up, I took him to the hospital, where we were now waiting to have his leg examined.

Rummaging through the plastic bags he'd brought in with him, Phil pulled out an extra T-shirt, a pair of pants, breakfast sandwiches, muffins, and a sports drink. "I grabbed everything I could think of," he said. "Everything I needed but didn't have when I got hurt."

Over the next hour, Phil chatted with us, made us laugh, and offered to drive Tim around if he needed it. Phil's compassion for Tim and his situation was motivated, in part, by a shared experience. He knew what it was like to be the person in the hospital bed, uncertain and facing surgery. He also recognized that in our early-morning haste to get to the doctor, we likely hadn't had the time or forethought to eat breakfast or bring extra clothes.

Though we love celebrating with our friends, the apostle Paul reminds us that we're called to share in their hardships as well. It's easy to empathize with someone who is in pain or offer to pray for them, but how often do we take the extra step of providing actual, tangible help? As friends, it's important not just to support the emotional needs of the people we care about, but to consider their physical needs as well. Jesus demonstrated the importance of meeting the needs of others when he fed more than five thousand people with two loaves of bread and five fish. As Christians and as friends, it's our responsibility and privilege to do the same for those around us.

— Kristin

— Today's Act of Friendship —

Find a tangible way to support a friend in need, whether it's by bringing them a meal or offering to run an errand for them.

It Doesn't Have to Be Perfect

*Cheerfully share your home with those
who need a meal or a place to stay.*

1 PETER 4:9

Recently Kyle and I started having our neighbors over for a game night, and it makes me wonder why we didn't throw our door open sooner. We have the absolute best time! Even as I wonder, I know many of the reasons that used to hold me back: my house isn't clean; I don't know what to serve them; my kids will act up; our friends may not have fun—on and on the excuses rolled through my mind, allowing me to push off an invitation.

Once I got over the initial excuses, I came to realize that none of those things mattered. Our neighbors just liked being included in our family, and they were honored to be invited in. Never once have they commented on my kids' behavior (and they can and do act crazy), the cleanliness of my bathroom, or the kind of food I serve (chips and salsa is our go-to snack). They comment only on the fun they have and the warmth they feel while in our home. And the truth is, that's what I feel too.

Sometimes we put too much pressure on ourselves when it comes to hospitality and inviting others in. As Christians, we should gladly open our homes to others, and the Bible doesn't share any other requirements—there's no mention of how fantastic the meal has to be or how lovely our house needs to look. Often it's our own expectations that get in the way of inviting others in. Opening our homes can be as simple as buying some snacks, pulling out some old games, and including others around our tables. A perfectly clean house is optional!

— Kendra

— Today's Act of Friendship —

Invite someone into your home, either for dinner or a game night,
and see what kind of friendship can be forged in the process.

Pen Pals

Walk with the wise and become wise.

PROVERBS 13:20

Everyone needs an Aunt Claire. My favorite memory of her is of a middle-aged woman roaring like a sea monster as she emerged from the lake with a pile of seaweed on her head and arms stretched high—before bursting into gales of pure-joy laughter.

In retrospect, I cannot help but smile at her audacity, but as an insecure middle schooler, I was one part horrified at the thought of wearing seaweed as a wig and one part awed. In my aunt I recognized the kind of woman I hoped to be someday: a woman so secure in her identity that she is unafraid of looking foolish in the name of fun.

Life races by, and as I draw nearer to my own middle age, I continue to want to be the kind of woman my Aunt Claire exemplifies. She is a woman of deep and abiding faith, having lived through hard seasons and deep tragedy without losing her hold on Jesus, always sharing him freely with those around her.

She and I became pen pals this past year. In a time of text messages and Instagram, my aunt is decidedly old school and off-line, and I initially struggled with how to go about an off-line, long-distance relationship. Writing a letter is harder than dashing off a quick text and a photo. Stamps misplace themselves, and my handwriting looks ugly and uneven as I pour out stories across the pages. But Aunt Claire has been all grace and forgiveness over my stops and starts, my delays, and my clumsy attempts at the new-to-me art of letter writing. She tells me stories of the faith warriors in our family and entrusted me with a letter and photo of a great-aunt who prayed faith into our bloodlines. Aunt Claire writes of her faith journey and encourages me in my own faith. She provides perspective and wisdom as a holder of my family's lore, and I look forward with anticipation to her letters in my mailbox.

– Julie

– Today's Act of Friendship –

Take time to consider relationships that might require a different type of time investment from you. Do not overlook the joy of deep friendship with aunts, uncles, or other extended family members.

Honesty in Friendship

The LORD detests lying lips, but he delights in those who tell the truth.
PROVERBS 12:22

In one of his sermons, my pastor said that every yes we give is a no to something else. I've gone through seasons of life where I felt like every yes given—even for good things, even for great things—was a no to family, to sleep, and to sanity. Navigating work-life balance can be exhausting.

Yet even among close friends, my pride can get in the way of admitting when I'm in a season of difficulty. Though I've read the proverb that talks about how God loves our truthfulness, it's only when I manage to recognize and lay down my pride that I can fully experience the power of honesty to foster true, authentic friendship.

Mindful of that call to honesty, the next time I found myself struggling, I chose to mention it. One day, as I was sitting with friends, a coffee cup in hand and children running rampant, I decided to be bravely, painfully honest.

I told them I was stressed out; I needed to say no more often.

I told them I felt overwhelmed as a wife and mother.

I told them this season of hardship felt unending.

As my friends paused—to squeeze my shoulder, to pass me a Kleenex—I found myself profoundly grateful for the power of honesty. As I swallowed the lump in my throat, I was comforted in knowing that my friends care about me, that their kind words are a balm to the soul. Their careful consideration is a reminder of the truth that calls to me even amid tiredness and stress and an endless stream of diapers and dishes: God is love. And he loves us, just as we are.

The quiet comfort of these essential truths, like dappled sunlight moving across my living room floor on a cold winter day, wraps me in warmth. It's a reminder that this too shall pass. And if I'm willing to be honest with trusted friends, I'll never walk through it alone.

— Kristin

— Today's Act of Friendship —

Choose to be honest with a friend about a challenge you're facing.

APRIL 18

A Common Bond

Don't be concerned for your own good but for the good of others.
1 CORINTHIANS 10:24

My mother loves to sew and quilt. She has made quilts for all her children and grandchildren, and she invests a great deal of time and care in the things that she makes. Last year, she was asked if she wouldn't mind teaching women who are new to the country how to sew, as this could be a practical skill for them to learn as well as a marketable experience for potential employment opportunities. My mother is not a terribly outgoing person; she tends to be rather quiet and shy. But even though she was a bit nervous about stepping into this new role, she still agreed to help teach.

Each week she gathers with a small group of ladies who want to learn to sew, as well as several other instructors who are helping to teach the women. Through the group, she's gotten to know one young woman who lives close by quite well, even giving her a ride to their weekly meetings. The two women are friends on opposite ends of life's cycle: one young, just out of high school with dreams for her future, and the other a grandmother with years of life experience to look back on. My mom has been able to offer this young woman motherly advice, not just in how to sew but also in how to find employment and navigate future plans. The two women have forged an unlikely but significant bond.

As followers of Jesus, we should consider others' needs as just as important as our own. My mother could have very easily dismissed the opportunity to help other women learn a new skill and gone on with her life, but she felt compelled to look out for the good of those who were in need of assistance. In turn, she has not only been able to teach women a practical skill but has now forged a new friendship that she would have missed if she hadn't stepped out to help others, even though it was a little intimidating at first.

— *Kendra*

— Today's Act of Friendship —

Ask God to show you someone to come alongside,
to teach a new skill or encourage in life.

Distracting Interruptions

Tune your ears to wisdom, and concentrate on understanding.
PROVERBS 2:2

An old friend and I hadn't seen each other for several years. As she welcomed me into her cozy home on a crisp spring morning, I enveloped her in a hug and told her how glad I was to see her. She gave me a quick tour of her home, and then we settled into the living room, coffee in hand, to talk about how much life had changed since the last time we'd met.

The conversation was pleasant, but as our time together went on, I became more and more self-conscious. Every time I would open my mouth to speak, my friend would attempt to finish my sentence. It wasn't just a word here or there; it was every single sentence!

I'm soft-spoken by nature, but I don't really think of myself as being painfully slow to speak. Yet her constant interruptions made me hyperaware of my voice and what I was saying. Was I not talking quickly enough? Were my stories too boring? Was there something wrong with me? The persistent interruptions made me feel tongue-tied and clumsy, and I found my thoughts becoming more and more scattered.

As our time together drew to a close, I felt equal measures of guilt and relief. Although I was genuinely happy to see her, my self-confidence had taken a hit because of her newfound habit. Proverbs reminds us to focus on listening and understanding others because those habits foster wisdom. Since that coffee date, our friendship has faltered because I felt like my friend wasn't really hearing me and didn't care enough to listen.

Even though I try not to finish other people's sentences, I'm still sometimes guilty of failing to listen well. How often have I waited impatiently for someone—a friend, my child, the person at the checkout—to finish speaking or relaying a long story so that I can hurry on with my day? Listening deliberately is a skill that needs to be nurtured with practice and patience. May we always choose to listen well to those around us and gain the wisdom we seek.

— *Kristin*

— Today's Act of Friendship —

Remind yourself to listen well. When someone tells
you a story, choose to ask additional questions of them
rather than turning the attention back to yourself.

Crabs in a Bucket

Their mouths are full of cursing, lies, and threats.
Trouble and evil are on the tips of their tongues.

PSALM 10:7

As my middle schooler broke down in tears, confessing that they'd avoided working on assigned math homework for months due to classmates' mockery, my heart broke.

Lord, help me! I pled silently, enveloping a smallish body in a bear hug. As we pulled apart, I cupped their no-longer-tiny face in my hands and whispered with hot conviction, "Do *not* let them steal your future. They are telling you lies."

It was time to tell my baby adult the story of the crabs in the bucket. It goes like this: if there is only one crab in the small bucket, it can climb out and escape. However, when there is more than one crab in the bucket, they focus on pulling down the others attempting to climb out. The result? They all wind up on the dinner plate when they could have otherwise easily escaped.

Some people are like the crabs in the bucket, emotionally pulling down everyone around them because of their own insecurity and pain. While I am desperate for my children to generously show love to such hurting people, I also want them to be wise and discerning, recognizing the metaphorical crabs in their circles.

As my child and I talked, I explained that when they avoided math due to embarrassment, they gave their classmates significant power to impact their future choices and potential careers in mathematical fields. Given the opportunity, our enemy will sneakily hijack the hurtful words of others in an attempt to derail God's intended plans for us. This is a lesson that goes far beyond a middle school classroom. How often do we allow others to drip poisonous lies into our ears that change the trajectory of our lives?

Being women who love and follow the way of Christ requires us to recognize the lies offered by a hurting, insecure world. We can be kind, compassionate people who at the same time do not allow the words of others to steal our future choices.

— Julie

— Today's Act of Friendship —

Ask God to help you distinguish holy correction and discipline, sent through sincere hearts and lips, from pure poison sent by our enemy.

When You've Made Mistakes

*The LORD is merciful and compassionate, slow to
get angry and filled with unfailing love.*

PSALM 145:8

I knew that I had messed up. Tempers had flared, and I'd spoken in anger to one of my children. Although we spent time afterward talking and resolving the situation, I went to bed frustrated with myself for once again allowing my child's behavior to ignite an angry response in me.

As I turned off my light, I shook my head and let out a big sigh. Kyle looked at me with compassion in his eyes and leaned over to pull me into an embrace. He knows how I will replay what I said and how I could have approached things differently over and over again in my mind. I have a tendency to berate myself for not doing better. As he reached for me, he whispered in my ear truth about my mothering, our child, and the good I was doing. Tears flowed as his words soothed an ache over my own shortcomings and even mistakes. I hadn't done things perfectly, but my husband's compassionate response was just what I needed in that moment.

Kyle's tenderness to me when I'd made a mistake reminds me of how God approaches us all. The Lord is so full of mercy and love. He doesn't lose patience with us, even when we deserve it. This, to me, is the perfect example of what a good friend should be. Being able to accept apologies from others and love them through their mistakes is one of the greatest ways that we can be a friend to those around us. None of us are perfect—we will all need a little mercy and compassion from time to time, and that's okay. In a world that often wants to point out others' flaws and failings, we can be the ones who come alongside to encourage others, especially after they've messed up.

– Kendra

– Today's Act of Friendship –

Offer encouragement to a friend who has recently made
a mistake or is downtrodden or discouraged by life.

Trouble Talk

*The tongue can bring death or life; those who love
to talk will reap the consequences.*

PROVERBS 18:21

Many of us women love to talk—myself included. In fact, I often have to curb my impulse to gossip. I'm never trying to be malicious; I just want to know what's going on. Call it the latent reporter in me.

To me, gossip can sometimes fall into the category of "trouble talk," a term coined by linguistics expert Deborah Tannen. It's the idea that, as women, we share our troubles as a way to connect with other women. It strengthens our friendships. It makes us feel closer to one another. In fact, according to Tannen, if I were to share something difficult in my life, and the woman I was confiding in either ignored the problem or was unable to sympathize, it would damage our budding friendship. As friends, we instinctively know that our friend is seeking empathetic trouble talk, so if they tell us about a hardship, and we have nothing to contribute in return, we end up telling them a similar story about someone else—a friend or family member, a neighbor or community member, perhaps even a Hollywood star—all in an attempt to let our friend know she's not alone.

Yet the Bible reminds us time and again that the words we say possess both power and consequences. Words can be life-affirming or cutting, encouraging or harmful. As Christians who seek to emulate a loving God, we need to be careful that our well-meaning desire to support a friend doesn't devolve into gossip or slander of another person. Perhaps next time someone trouble talks with you, you can opt for a life-giving way to affirm them. For example, offer empathy for the feeling itself without offering someone else's story in return. Saying something like, "I can see why that would make you angry," lets them know that you care without crossing the line into gossip.

If you do choose to use someone else's story to trouble talk in return, keep the people involved anonymous. Sometimes, it really can be helpful to let someone know they aren't alone by talking about someone who overcame a similar challenge. However, avoid the impulse to include details that might identify the person or persons you're speaking about.

— *Kristin*

— Today's Act of Friendship —

The next time someone tells you something difficult,
listen and respond without gossiping.

Letting Her Go

Tell God what you need, and thank him for all he has done. Then you will experience God's peace, which exceeds anything we can understand.

PHILIPPIANS 4:6-7

The story tumbled out over sandwiches and coffee: a friend close enough to be a sister, the maid of honor in her wedding, and now . . . nothing. Facebook friends with no interaction, lives once closely intertwined now lived separately. I heard sorrow, regret, and quiet bewilderment in her voice, even all these years later.

She has reached across the chasm dividing them on more than one occasion over the years, and her friend runs hot and cold, wanting to rekindle their friendship one moment before disappearing for several more years.

The silence stretched between recounted stories of the closeness they once shared. Then she quietly confessed, "God asked me what my life would be like with her friendship in it."

My eyes widened slightly at the unexpected statement. "What would it be like?" I whispered.

"Chaotic." A long beat of silence followed her reply.

I leaned in slightly with the next question: "Can you handle chaotic right now?" "No."

We sat in contemplative silence. She is a professor, a mom of tweens, a woman in ministry, a wife to a man in ministry. Her life is full of juggling people and obligations, and she is working hard to keep all the balls in the air and all of her loved ones on track. Her emotional load is currently full, and a complicated, chaotic friendship right now would likely put her over her emotional weight limit.

Sometimes, we have to let someone go. Sometimes, someone lets go of us. God is big enough to hold our grief, our anger, our utter confusion over complicated, messy, hard friendships. He is safe to wrestle with, to shake a fist at, to hold us during seasons of lament. When we take our hard things to him in prayer, we are promised peace in his presence, regardless of the storm swirling around us.

— Julie

— Today's Act of Friendship —

Take time to turn to God about hurts from past friendships. Pray for healing, for peace, for a quiet revelation of how you might have hurt another.

Secure in Christ

I know the LORD is always with me.
I will not be shaken, for he is right beside me.

PSALM 16:8

Not long ago I had the privilege of being a part of a conference with a group of women that I love. One of the special pieces I got to participate in was a video that shared women's stories before each session. In the video, I talked all about how fear has overwhelmed and ruled much of my life, and yet ever-so-slowly, God has begun to walk with me down the road to face my fears.

Afterward, a woman on our team came up to me during a break and told me how my story encouraged her. She said, "I never would've guessed that you struggled with fear and insecurity—you always look so put together."

And all I could do was smile and say, "Isn't that always what we think when we look at others?"

The truth is that sometimes I walk into a new situation and feel like I did when walking into a new school in seventh grade. All the old insecurities flood back in, and I think, *This is just so awkward.* But the older I get, the more I realize that things haven't necessarily gotten easier for me; I've just learned how to mask my insecurities better. And I've noticed that others often feel just as insecure and awkward as I do.

No matter how insecure we may feel, we can be secure in the Lord's constant presence and the fact that he is always with us. This truth has allowed me to find freedom in being honest with others about who I am, instead of always trying to hide behind some facade of what may look good on the outside, but doesn't really represent the truth about who I am inside. Because no matter if other people walk away from us, God never will—of this we can be sure.

– Kendra

– Today's Act of Friendship –

Be honest with a friend about your own insecurities while
also remembering how secure you are in Christ.

The Perennial Struggle

If one person falls, the other can reach out and help.
But someone who falls alone is in real trouble.
ECCLESIASTES 4:10

"Why do I struggle so much with this?"

I paused before responding to her text, praying how best to respond to my friend's familiar spiral of feeling not good enough.

She is immensely talented: intelligent, compassionate, and a superstar in her profession. Her perennial struggle is one of unworthiness, and she falls periodically into the trap of trying to prove her worth, to be perfect. I know this about my friend, and the moment I start to hear an undertone of unworthiness creep into our conversations, I slam the proverbial brakes and U-turn our conversation back to God's grace and our inability to ever be deserving of what he so freely gives.

Perennial struggles—we all have one or two. We all have something we return to again and again, causing us to veer off course. The enemy of our soul knows about our struggles, and these are the weak spots he goads repeatedly, trying to get us to doubt the promises of God, trying to tempt us into sin, seeking a foothold with his lies.

The people closest to us can typically see us slipping into harmful thought cycles and behaviors before we can realize or see it for ourselves. Something as small as a simple word or nudge from someone who loves us and has our best interests in mind can remind us of God's truth. Ecclesiastes reminds us how much we need people who pick us up—spiritually and physically—when we're slipping into our perennial struggle. We're not meant to walk through life on our own, never relying upon anyone else. The truth is that we are stronger when we are in a spiritual community, in friendship with other Jesus followers.

— Julie

— Today's Act of Friendship —

Ask God to reveal your perennial struggle and the perennial
struggles of your closest friends. Make a plan for how you
will support them when they are tempted to believe lies
and resolve to reach out when you start to struggle.

Friendship Is the Theme

Live a life filled with love, following the example of Christ.
EPHESIANS 5:2

A number of years ago, I wanted to get to know several women in my neighborhood, but I wasn't sure how to go about doing it. I decided to host a chocolate-tasting party in my home and invited some friends as well as the neighbor women. As I googled chocolate-tasting-party tips, a plan easily developed for the night.

I enlisted the help of friends and my husband to prepare food and set up my house for the small event. As the women came and we began the evening, conversation flowed easily. The women talked about the different chocolates and began to find out about one another's lives and families as well. Even though the evening revolved around tasting sweet treats, the true objective was to simply get to know the other women better.

If you're a bit introverted like me, hosting people in your home can feel intimidating and awkward. I've found that planning a party around a theme can be one easy way to develop friendships, as the theme provides a ready topic of conversation. Since that first gathering, I've held several themed parties, from wooden-sign-making parties to book clubs to game nights, realizing that when you utilize a theme or activity, it allows you to get to know others while engaging in something fun.

After I host a party, people will tell me that what they enjoyed most was not the theme or activity but the kindness they felt while participating in the event. The friendships and conversations that begin to take shape are the most meaningful part of the night and encourage me to live a life filled with love. I've come to realize it really doesn't matter what the theme is, since it's just a vessel to encourage us all to spend some time getting to know others better. Friendship is the real purpose for (and gift of) the gatherings.

— Kendra

— Today's Act of Friendship —

Plan a themed party and invite a few friends and
acquaintances you'd like to get to know better.

Working Together

All of you together are Christ's body, and each of you is a part of it.

1 CORINTHIANS 12:27

I got the call on a Thursday morning while I was visiting my parents' home. My husband was far away, and he sounded discouraged, his voice strained. As my children flitted around me like so many butterflies, unaware of the danger of a coming storm, I sat down on my mother's couch, gripped my phone tightly, and held on.

Something had happened at work, a situation beyond our control. Although I knew things could and would work out, in that moment, I felt crushed in the talons of fear's unrelenting grip.

When the call ended, I looked up to see my sister and mom staring back at me sympathetically. The three of us prayed and talked, and I smiled—but inside, I felt sick with the worry and the waiting.

It was on my way home that I gave in. Feeling brokenhearted and brave, I pulled the car into a parking lot and posted a message on our church ladies' Facebook page, typing through my tears to a group of women whom I consider friends:

My family could really use your prayers today. I can't give more details but would covet prayers for peace and wisdom, especially in the next twenty-four hours.

And then, miraculously, the outpouring began. My phone began to ding repeatedly with more than fifty texts and Facebook messages from friends, each one a prayer, an expression of love and concern. And every time I heard another message from a friend arrive, I felt the cloud of misery dissipating a little bit more. I felt the hard-won peace I had pleaded for edging out circumstances that, on their own and within my own power, felt overwhelming and insurmountable.

God designed us to live in community. We are not meant to function alone, struggling to face the challenges of life by ourselves. Instead, together we represent the collective body of Christ, part and parcel of a whole that must work together in concert to accomplish his will. As friends who form a faith community, we are stronger together.

— *Kristin*

— Today's Act of Friendship —

Reach out to a friend in your faith community, thanking them for the contributions they bring to the collective body of Christ.

Living an Inviting Life

A glad heart makes a happy face; a broken heart crushes the spirit.
PROVERBS 15:13

It was on a dreary day in the middle ground between winter and spring that Kendra and I set off for a rare day of junking, coffee, and just hanging out together as we dreamed about the repurposing possibilities for all the funky stuff we stumbled across.

As we approached the cash register with our small purchases in a farmhouse-turned-cute-antique-shop, we struck up a conversation with the woman running the till. She had overheard our rambling conversation as we wandered throughout the house, and as she wrapped the cute glassware Kendra had bought, she teasingly said to us, "I wish I was your friend." Without a pause, we laughingly told her that we are always on the hunt for new friends and that we would totally be her friend. We all laughed as the sale was completed and said a merry goodbye as we headed off for the next store.

It wasn't until we had all parted ways that her words sank in a little deeper. We were in a town hours away from where we lived, so actually becoming friends wasn't a practical possibility; however, the clerk saw something in Kendra and me, something in our interaction with one another and with the strangers around us, that drew her into our circle, if only for a few minutes.

Oh, Jesus, that's the woman I want to be all the time, I quietly prayed as we walked down the sidewalk. I want to be a woman who walks into the grocery store, the gas station, and all the ordinary places with an invitation for others to belong, even if just for that moment. I want to be the kind of woman who makes others feel comfortable, welcome, and included—even if I never see them again. I want to be a woman of whom others whisper, "I want to be her friend."

Women are hungry for community, for relationship, for friendship—even if it is just a warm smile and small talk. What an easy way to spread the love of Christ as we walk through our days.

— Julie

— Today's Act of Friendship —

As you walk through your day, create space for others
to belong, even with just a smile and a greeting.

A Listening Ear

The LORD is close to the brokenhearted;
he rescues those whose spirits are crushed.

PSALM 34:18

We sat across from one another on her well-worn couch, the sound of our kids playing in the basement in the background. She twisted her hair around her finger as she told me of the pain she felt from the recent separation in her marriage and the struggle her children now faced as they dealt with their own pain brought on by her husband who chose to leave his family.

We talked honestly about the pain and trauma kids face, of counseling and medication, of family support and faith. I told her of my own children's experience with trauma and walking through hard times. Her pain was evident and raw, and instead of turning away, I sat with her in the middle of it, listening as she laid her heart bare, for her and her kids. I nodded in understanding of what she was sharing, without offering platitudes that would do little to help her current state. And somehow, through the process of talking and listening, hope began to spring forth. As I rounded up my children to go home, we smiled at one another, understanding that even when nothing can be truly fixed in the moment, just being able to share is enough. As my family walked out her door, I told her I'd be praying, and we'd meet again soon.

The Lord is close to the brokenhearted, and therefore, I believe we should also be. Often in our fast-paced world it is uncomfortable to slow down and sit with those who are hurting, but to be a good friend, that is exactly what we will need to do at times. The question we need to ask ourselves is if we are trustworthy people whom others can count on when times get hard. Do we pray for our friends and offer encouragement without denying their pain? Can we sit with the hurting just as Jesus does? It's never too late to start.

— Kendra

— Today's Act of Friendship —

Pray for a friend who you know is going through a hard
season and then ask if you can be a listening ear for them.

Worthy of Friendship

Such love has no fear, because perfect love expels all fear.
1 JOHN 4:18

"Thanks for putting up with me!" In loopy cursive, I finished writing the message in the high school yearbook and signed my name with a flourish.

I handed it back to the girl who sat next to me in concert choir, the same chairs we'd both sat in for the last four years. Though we weren't close friends, after so many hours together, we were on amicable terms.

Glancing at my message, she looked me in the eye.

"Why do you always say that?" she said. Confused, I looked at her again. "'Thanks for putting up with me'?" she said, the question clear in her voice, eyes grave. "I don't sit next to you because I have to. I sit here because I want to."

I had meant it in a joking way, but when she put it that way, it made me wonder—did I really think that my friends were just putting up with me, or did I think they liked me for myself?

I could chalk it up to teenage angst and insecurity, but sometimes I still think that way, even as an adult. The excuses are varied:

"I don't want to impose."
"They aren't my friends; they're Tim's friends."
"We only hang out as a group, not one-on-one."
"We're just friends with the same people."

No matter the reason, the true heart of the issue is whether or not we truly believe we're good enough.

While it's true that some relationships form due to proximity, most friendships are created by choice. When insecurity sneaks in, we can combat it by recognizing that, as John says, there's no place for the darkness of fear within the light of love. Fear has no place in our relationships, and recognizing that our insecurities are rooted in fear is the first step toward walking with confidence in the loving relationships Jesus has called us to.

— *Kristin*

— Today's Act of Friendship —

Consider whether you truly believe that you're worthy of the friendships you have. Spend time praying that God would show you how to see yourself as worthy and loved, the same way he sees you.

May

God Has This

*When we get together, I want to encourage you in your
faith, but I also want to be encouraged by yours.*

ROMANS 1:12

"God has this," I whispered over the phone to my dear friend. She and her husband had uprooted themselves from central Minnesota and moved to Washington, DC, so she could take an unpaid legal fellowship with International Justice Mission in a crazy adventure completely at odds with their usually steady personalities.

Saying yes to God in obedience often involves unexpected detours and trusting him even when the situation feels like it has spiraled out of control and cannot possibly be what he intended. In this case, my friends fully believed that God had opened the doors and was providing a way for Ceena to combine her legal degree with her passion for advocating for human rights—but the road was rocky as they traded stability and a law firm job for no jobs and a nightmare apartment. There were days when her texts were a lament about how hard everything felt. She wondered why following God would have so many roadblocks.

As Ceena's friend, I was privileged to have a front-row seat to their journey. There were many conversations in that waiting place when things were hard and doubts assailed my friend. There were times when she was so buried in the thick of it that she couldn't see, and I, as the friend, had the perspective and distance to see how God was working. When she couldn't see clearly, I pointed her back to God, praying boldly over her and Jordan and encouraging her to continue trusting before yet seeing.

The end of the story is the stuff of wildest dreams, with Ceena receiving a full-time, paid job at International Justice Mission. But the importance of godly friendship during this journey was not lost on either of us—our faith grew during this journey; hers because God made the impossible possible, and mine because I got to journey alongside her through all of it and not just hear the glossed-over, happy ending.

Having a praying friend who points us continually back to God when we are in the middle of the story is so important. When we live lives intertwined with one another, letting each other see the whole story, we are both encouraged to grow deeper in our faith in ways we would not grow alone.

– Julie

– Today's Act of Friendship –

Think of a friend who is in the waiting place, obediently
trusting God. Find a way to encourage her.

When Parenting Looks Different

[The Lord] said, "My grace is all you need. My power works best in weakness." So now I am glad to boast about my weaknesses, so that the power of Christ can work through me.

2 CORINTHIANS 12:9

I met someone a few years ago who made me rethink parenting. She's an amazing mom. She is calm. She does not yell to be heard. And she has that rare ability to let silence reign for a little while and not feel a need to fill the space, but just lets it breathe.

Yet she's not a "perfect" parent. Her kids eat junk food for breakfast and loathe vegetables. They go to bed later than I do and sleep in longer, and no, they are not teenagers.

And it could be easy to think, *Why isn't she making them eat veggies before they have that cookie? If she doesn't wake them up soon, they're going to miss half the day!*

But I don't. Because she is a great mom. And when I met her, she was also homeless.

In the summer that she and her kids stayed in our guest room, I felt convicted. On days when I had the freedom to spend four or five hours playing with my daughters, she would spend four or five hours calling to find a place to stay long-term. On days when I worried about making meals or finishing piles of laundry, she scoured online job postings and worked on craft items to sell at local venues for extra cash.

As our friendship deepened despite our differences, I realized that at the end of the day we are both good moms. And we are simply doing the best we can.

It's okay that we're not perfect. In fact, our weaknesses are simply opportunities for greater faith. It's in our weaknesses that the power of Christ can work through us. If we had it all together, we wouldn't need grace. If we knew all the answers, there would be no need to look beyond ourselves. And if we could always stand alone, we would spend no time on our knees.

— Kristin

— Today's Act of Friendship —

Make an effort to befriend someone who approaches something differently than you do, whether it's parenting, work, or the way they mow their lawn.

The Gift of Presence

*Since God chose you to be the holy people he loves,
you must clothe yourselves with tenderhearted mercy,
kindness, humility, gentleness, and patience.*

COLOSSIANS 3:12

My friend Sara never seems to be in a hurry. Wherever she is, she will stop and talk to other moms, recalling details of their lives and the names of their children. Sara shows care for others in the way that she remembers them.

I first met Sara a few years ago when our daughters ended up on the same dance team. Sara engaged easily in conversation with me about my family while also sharing details of her own. We quickly became good friends, and I've watched as Sara brings everyone into her circle. She is quick to welcome a new person, and I've never seen her leave anyone out. She is someone who notices others and makes them feel welcome. And although she would brush off her ability to do this, I believe it is a gift to be able to make others feel comfortable so effortlessly.

When someone needs a hand, Sara is there to help. When someone needs a listening ear, Sara is quick to sit with them and slow to leave. And even though I know that Sara's life and work are very demanding, and her schedule is often full, you never get the sense that she doesn't have time for you. She has mastered the skill of being present with those around her, and it is a benefit to all who know her.

In a world that can be very fast paced and busy, we are meant to demonstrate the qualities that God values, traits such as mercy, kindness, humility, gentleness, and patience—and to do this well will take our time. It will take us being willing to slow down and see the people in front of us. This is a skill that takes intentionality, but the results will be, as my friend Sara knows, a deeper connection to those around us.

– Kendra

– Today's Act of Friendship –

Notice someone who needs you to be present with
them and set aside your to-do list to be a friend.

The Ministry of Soccer Fields

"Love the Lord your God with all your heart, all your soul, and all your mind." This is the first and greatest commandment. A second is equally important: "Love your neighbor as yourself."

MATTHEW 22:37-39

Pulling my car onto the shoulder of the gently curving road, I scanned the fields containing a hundred soccer players, searching for Aaron. He was easy to spot, his pale skin and blond hair highlighted beside the Somali players running around him—a visible reminder of the cultural and religious differences between us.

Aaron and I live in a community whose racial and religious tensions have been exposed in a series of hateful incidents, and we have long pondered how to engage our large Somali community through genuine friendship. But friendship requires trust, and when trust is hard to find, we must be the ones willing to step outside of our comfort zones instead of inviting others into our safe spaces.

For Aaron, moving outside of his comfort zone meant taking the risk of asking to join a group of young Somali men in their pickup soccer game. Those games in the nearby park then morphed into a fathering/coaching/mentoring relationship with the young men he played alongside. Many of them arrived in the United States after years in refugee camps, often in households headed by single moms. Now, these young men gather periodically in our home on Saturday mornings for a pancake breakfast before they head downstairs to shout encouragement at their favorite Premier League soccer team on the TV and tease those rooting for the opponent.

I cannot help but smile as I listen to the good-natured teasing in two languages whenever a goal is scored, because I'm reminded that we have finally figured out how to be bridge builders after a number of well-intentioned failures.

Loving others requires proximity, and it often requires us to be bold, uncomfortable, and vulnerable. As believers, we are the ones called to carry the risk of rejection as we move forward with an offer of friendship, trusting God to do the rest.

– Julie

– Today's Act of Friendship –

Ask God to show you how you might take the risk of rejection when reaching out to a people group who look, think, or believe differently than you, rather than asking them to walk into your comfort zone.

When You're on the Fringe

Give all your worries and cares to God, for he cares about you.
1 PETER 5:7

Paging through the contents of my daughter's pink school folder, I glanced at a drawing, then paused for a longer perusal. The title at the top read "My Wishes." Underneath, she had drawn several cartoonlike figures depicting herself and the various things she wished were true.

"Be popular," was the caption of the second wish, and my heart sank a little when I read it.

"Honey, why do you want to be popular?" I asked.

She hesitated briefly, then said, "Because I feel lonely at school."

My heart ached as she explained that no one was mean to her; they simply had friends they preferred and played with, so she was often left out. We talked about what healthy friendships looked like, some ideas for reaching out to friendly faces at school, and how being popular doesn't always mean having deep friendships.

But later, lying sleepless in bed, my heart worried over the topic. My husband and I have spent time talking to our children about noticing those on the fringes and inviting them in. But what happens when we're the one on the fringe? I wonder if my daughter's desire to be popular isn't one we all secretly have. Don't we all want to be liked? Admired? In community with others?

In the days that followed, I leaned in even more than usual, spending time with my sweet girl. When she came home with a bracelet that a friend from another class had made for her, I smiled and cheered a little. When she told me how a girl in her class played with her in gym, I squeezed her tightly. In the same way my daughters bring their worries to me, the Bible reminds us to give all our concerns to God, our Father. As a mom, I can't fix everything for my child. But I can pray with and for her to find a good friend. I can help foster friendships that are blossoming. I can be by my child's side as she navigates the uncertainty this life brings. And I can always direct her to God, who knows her needs and cares for her.

— Kristin

— Today's Act of Friendship —

Reach out to someone who you think may feel left
out or isolated and could use a friend.

Intentional Friendship

Don't forget to do good and to share with those in need.
These are the sacrifices that please God.

HEBREWS 13:16

Last spring, I had the unexpected chance to show friendship to some neighbors who abruptly had to move out of their rental house. We'd noticed a few weeks prior that their vehicles were gone, the house was dark, and no one was around. Disappointed that the family might have left before we could say goodbye, I found myself watching at the window, waiting for a chance to connect with them, hoping to see them one more time.

My opportunity came a few mornings later as I made a lunch for my daughter. I peered out the window and noticed their car in the drive, trunk open, loaded with household items. For a moment, I hesitated, looking at all the lunch items out and thinking it was too inconvenient at the time. But just then, I remembered a gift card sitting unused in my wallet. I quickly wrapped the card in a note with our phone numbers and went to say one last goodbye to our neighbors.

As we talked, they told me how hard the past couple of weeks had been and how sad they were to leave our neighborhood. We hugged as I gave them the gift card, wished them well, and asked them to please call if there was anything we could do to help. I walked home feeling encouraged that I hadn't let the opportunity to connect pass me by.

The writer of Hebrews tells us that when we find ways to serve those around us, it's really sacrifices that we are offering to God. Being a friend to others, even those we do not know well, is not always convenient. Being willing to stop and listen to the small nudging from God to step in, to do or say a kind word in the moment, will almost never feel timely and is often sacrificial. But I think that's the point. Let's not miss the little ways we might extend friendship to someone else today who may need it.

– Kendra

– Today's Act of Friendship –

Take time to extend friendship toward someone
else, even when it's inconvenient.

I See You

Suppose you see a brother or sister who has no food or clothing, and you say, "Good-bye and have a good day; stay warm and eat well"—but then you don't give that person any food or clothing. What good does that do? So you see, faith by itself isn't enough. Unless it produces good deeds, it is dead and useless.

JAMES 2:15-17

"Thank you for seeing me."

As I read the text message, I paused over those words.

Our friend is walking through what feels like an impossibly difficult season, and while most of the time Aaron and I feel helpless in the face of his struggles, knowing there isn't a single thing we can do to fix it, we've been supportive with bits of help and small kindnesses. We've tried to lighten his proverbial load in physical, practical ways, and we've been praying alongside him—which is far more powerful than any of us can understand this side of heaven.

Still, I was a bit taken aback by his words. We'd been simply helping our friend—someone we care deeply about—and I'd not considered it much beyond that, especially when what we do is small compared to the mountain he faces.

Since then, I've thought about that text message frequently. In a world of constant distractions, we all long to simply be seen. We can give others our undivided attention, caring enough to come alongside them in an attempt to ease the burden, sticking with them during the journey, even if we cannot fix their problems entirely. It is oftentimes less about what we do and more about the fact that we take the time and energy to do *something*—to show God's love in tangible form.

As people of faith, we are called to more than words; our internal faith must be manifested by our external actions. We are not saved by our works; however, our works reveal our faith—or lack thereof. When we come alongside someone with a listening ear, with an offer to watch their kids, with physical assistance in some way, we are the hands and feet of Jesus. And it is by being his hands and feet that we reveal the love of God to the hurting world around us.

– Julie

– Today's Act of Friendship –

Come alongside someone struggling by
meeting a physical need in some way.

Who's Listening?

Too much talk leads to sin. Be sensible and keep your mouth shut.
PROVERBS 10:19

Typing quietly at my computer, I immediately noticed when she entered the coffee shop. Adorned in the latest exercise clothes, corkscrew curls, and a high-wattage smile, she walked confidently to the counter with a couple of similarly attired friends.

I recognized her, but she didn't seem to recognize me, so I returned to my work without thinking much about it. We had met at a mutual friend's annual event but never had a lengthy conversation. As she and her friends snagged their coffee drinks and settled into the cushy brown chairs behind me, my ears perked up when one of her friends mentioned our mutual friend's name.

I didn't mean to eavesdrop, but she made no attempt to modify her volume, her words carrying clearly across the room.

"Oh, she's trying another exercise program," she said carelessly. "I mean, she's always trying something new, but her eating habits are terrible." As her friends hummed their agreement, she continued, "She's not going to lose weight if she doesn't fix that."

A little stunned, I felt my ears burning. Didn't she realize that other people could hear her words? Hadn't she thought about the fact that someone else might know the person she was talking about? I had thought that the two of them were friends, but what kind of friend criticizes another in such a thoughtless way—and in public, of all places? I knew my friend would be hurt if she knew what the other woman had said.

Proverbs reminds us that words can trip us up if we're not careful and some things are best left unsaid. Not only did the words reflect poorly on this woman, but they made me consider the times I haven't been careful enough with my own words. Have I repeated gossip? Have I had unwise conversations about others when I'm talking on the phone in front of my children? Have I cloaked criticism of someone else's actions with a falsely pious prayer request to a group? In all of these situations, silence is our best and most kind option. May we always strive to say helpful, not hurtful words, ever mindful of who might be listening.

— *Kristin*

— Today's Act of Friendship —

Refuse to gossip about anyone.

When You Are Known

You know when I sit down or stand up. You know
my thoughts even when I'm far away.
PSALM 139:2

Kyle and I adopted three of our five children from the foster care system. They are amazing kids with incredible resilience, and yet there are traumas from their past that continue to affect them today. We have sought advice and help from professionals, understanding that we aren't able to do this alone. After a particularly hard season of parenting where we felt very much alone, we signed up for a parenting class specifically about adopted kids and trauma. It's humbling after parenting for so many years to recognize that you still don't always know what to do, but we love our kids too much not to humbly seek out help.

The first night of class we sat in small groups around tables, and each person shared their story of adoption. We listened as others laid out concerns, and I found myself nodding along, often with a whispered, "Me too." We were then given tools by the trainer to help us in our parenting, as well as reminders and explanations of the effects trauma has on our children and how we can show them compassion. Kyle and I left feeling like we had hope again in our parenting. As we drove home, we both commented on how nice it was to be with people who understood what we were going through. It felt good to be known.

It is wonderful to feel known by other people, but even when we are not, Scripture tells us that God knows us. He knows the smallest details, even when we sit or stand. He knows what we're thinking at all times. He understands our struggles and our joys, and he is there for us no matter what we are facing. Do we see God as our friend? Do we have others around us who have walked through trials similar to ours? The truth is, you are not alone, and you are meant to be known.

– Kendra

– Today's Act of Friendship –

Seek out support for what you are walking through, first by finding
Scripture to let you know God is near, and then with others around
you, whether it's a group, class, or even just a close friend.

A Toxic Friend

No one can tame the tongue. It is restless and evil, full of deadly poison. Sometimes it praises our Lord and Father, and sometimes it curses those who have been made in the image of God.

JAMES 3:8-9

"I chose to protect my son by ending the friendship," my friend said, sighing. Her comment was both sad and firm.

Her son, Sammy, is a tenderhearted elementary schooler. Brandon, his usually polite and well-mannered friend, nevertheless had a habit of making hurtful remarks to her son and then tracking her down to repeat those hurtful complaints directly to her.

For a year, my friend regularly had Brandon over for playdates with Sammy and, at first, worked to simply redirect the conversation with Brandon when he approached her with critical comments about her son, assuming they arose out of frustration from a minor conflict the boys were having.

Eventually, my friend began to realize that the comments were not based in frustration or annoyance but were a learned behavior. Brandon's running negative commentary had been absorbed from someone important in his life, and he was learning to do friendship with the same unhealthy habit.

How do we balance loving others well and avoiding relationships with potentially toxic people? My friend struggled in prayer for months over her son's friendship with Brandon. She knew that while another child might be able to handle Brandon's imperfect friendship without internalizing his negative comments, her son—with his gentle heart and tendency to internalize and meditate on hurtful words—could not.

Sometimes, boundaries are necessary. Tongues left untamed and untrained drip poison. Just as we should not allow others to drip poison continually into our own ears, as parents, we are responsible for establishing healthy, protective boundaries for our children until they are old enough to do so on their own.

— Julie

— Today's Act of Friendship —

Set appropriate boundaries with people who drip poisonous words and do the same for the children in your life.

Old Friends

How good and pleasant it is when God's people live together in unity!
PSALM 133:1, NIV

I've known Lindsay for as long as I can remember. Growing up, we lived next door to each other. With just a year between us, we quickly became inseparable. In fact, a lot of my early memories involve Lindsay: the snow tunnels her dad engineered, the celery her mom always added to our lunches. How, whenever we played post office or school, her fake name was always Jenny and mine was Judy. When I moved several hours away at the age of ten, I'd still get to see Lindsay a few times a year when she visited her grandmother. We had a fun girls' weekend in college, were part of each other's weddings, and birthed our oldest children just a few months apart.

What I love best is the ease of our friendship. Not that we've never had disagreements—I remember epic battles over Barbies in which I showed a lot of maturity by stomping out of her house—but, overall, it's an easy relationship. I think it's because she accepts me, just as I am, and I do the same for her. Although we have different temperaments, parenting styles, and giftings, each of us recognizes the good things about the other person instead of subtly trying to compare.

The last time Lindsay visited, I enlisted her help in preparing goodie bags for an event, stopping only to make a late-night custard dash to Culver's. At first, she complained good-naturedly about getting roped into a chore, but then she proceeded to tirelessly spend hours helping me finish the bags. The strength of our long friendship meant that there was no need for me to apologize for asking her to do a thankless task and for grabbing fast food rather than wining and dining her during her visit. Instead, the pleasure of our mutual company provided all the fun we required.

As friends, we find our sweet spot when we learn how to live in harmony with one another, as the Psalms suggest. In a world of constant criticism and comparison, may we always be friends who choose to see the best in others and in ourselves. Only then will we find true ease in friendship.

– Kristin

– Today's Act of Friendship –

Call or message an old friend today, someone who accepts
you for who you are. Thank them for their friendship.

Obey the Nudge

As for the rest of you, dear brothers and sisters,
never get tired of doing good.

2 THESSALONIANS 3:13

Can I pray for you in any way?

Kate's text pinged as I stared at myself in the bathroom mirror, contemplating how particularly hard today seemed, how I felt like a failure as a parent after a chaotic, angry morning in my house before everyone was out the door to catch the bus.

Kate always seems to sense when something is sliding sideways in my life. Her texts are often synced to whatever hard thing I'm facing. I smiled through tears as I read her message, loving both her and Jesus in that moment. It is no coincidence that Kate seems to read my mind: she listens to the nudging of the Holy Spirit and is particularly gifted at reaching out in compassion and care to those around her. Her perfectly timed texts remind me that I am not alone, that God sees me in the hard spots, and that he loves me so much that he nudges my friends to reach out.

In my life, it is uncanny the situations I step into with just the right prayer or word of encouragement when I obey God's nudge. Obeying the Holy Spirit is going on mission with Jesus, serving as his tangible hands and feet in the lives around us. It requires listening to that still, small voice that wells up often, almost as a feeling in our souls and being willing to set aside time in our busy days and to-do lists. It sometimes requires us to be inconvenienced. But it is always worth it. There is rarely a to-do list that cannot be rearranged, but an opportunity to be ambassadors of Christ is something of eternal importance that is fleeting and time sensitive. God continually invites us to be doers of good, to be people who reveal his love and his presence in tangible ways. Let us not get so distracted by the temporal that we ignore the eternal.

— *Julie*

— Today's Act of Friendship —

Ask the Holy Spirit to nudge you on behalf of others, and then practice obeying that nudge. If you've failed, ask for a second chance. We serve a God of second chances.

A Generous Mindset in Friendship

The Holy Spirit produces this kind of fruit in our lives: love, joy,
peace, patience, kindness, goodness, faithfulness, gentleness,
and self-control. There is no law against these things!

GALATIANS 5:22-23

I serve as part of a leadership team with other women in my local community, and my team studies a different topic from the Bible each year. This year we've been exploring what it means to have a generous mindset in relationships with others. We've discussed God's generosity toward us, loving difficult people, giving our resources of time and money, having the attitude of Christ, and finally being generous in our relationships with other women.

At one of our meetings, we spent part of the morning sharing about our histories with other women, and many told stories of old wounds from past friendships. We talked about what that was like and how we could move ahead in relationships with wisdom, but without letting old hurts hinder us from lasting friendships now and in the future. Many of us began to recognize how we'd let things in our past affect our current relationships, and we prayed for one another, that we could move past these unhealthy patterns of thoughts and actions toward others.

Scripture tells us that if we are going to have a generous mindset toward others, then the fruits of the Holy Spirit must be evident in our lives. I ask myself often, do I live in and generously give out love, joy, peace, patience, kindness, goodness, faithfulness, gentleness, and self-control? And if not, why? What is stopping me from being generous in all these areas of life? I found that as I looked at these fruits and how they were evident in my life, my relationships and friendships with others began to improve as well. Generosity is not just limited to topics of money or time but applies to the way that we think about and approach those around us as well.

— Kendra

— Today's Act of Friendship —

Choose one of the fruits of the Spirit that you think you
could incorporate more within your current friendships,
and consider one way you could begin.

Modeling Friendships

*Imitate God, therefore, in everything you do,
because you are his dear children.*

EPHESIANS 5:1

"Mom, we're basically twins," my daughter's voice bubbled from the backseat of the car. "We both like pink and unicorns and JoJo Siwa and Dork Diaries. We have so much in common!"

Smiling to myself, I listened as Elise continued to enumerate the qualities of her friend on our drive home. Her Girl Scout troop had worked on a friendship badge that evening, and the two friends had spent time talking about themselves in order to celebrate what they had in common. As the newest member of the troop, Elise was excited to experience camaraderie with the rest of the group.

I love to witness my children's uncomplicated approach to friendship. Although the social waters are getting a bit murkier as my daughters race toward middle school, overall, things are still straightforward. Elise is often outgoing and doesn't hesitate to reach out to others; Noelle's soft personality innately draws others into her circle; and Ashlyn's cheerful disposition and expressive face openly show her delight with others.

Even so, their moments of elation or disappointment over friends always serve as unique reminders to assess the friendships in my own life. In Ephesians, we're told that we should strive to imitate God. After all, we are his children, adopted into his family. In the same way that I seek to follow the gracious and merciful example of my heavenly Father, I want my own example of healthy friendships to be something my children can reflect into the world without hesitation. Do I showcase empathy and genuine care for those around me? Do I speak negatively about others or wisely choose kind words of encouragement? Do I demonstrate the qualities it takes not just to attract friends, but to keep them?

As a parent, I have a responsibility to model healthy relationships, including friendships. Our gracious God began the good work of showing us what loving relationships are like. Let's be conscientious about demonstrating those same admirable qualities to the children in our lives.

— Kristin

— Today's Act of Friendship —

Take time to talk to a child in your circle of
influence about healthy friendships.

Doing Life Together

Do not neglect to show hospitality to strangers.
HEBREWS 13:2, ESV

Road tripping has become a Memorial Day weekend tradition in my family—with a twist you might not expect. For the past few years, we've invited Chinese teachers who are here for a year or two as part of an exchange program to join us on our travels. Together, we set off for a nearby destination that's doable in a three- or four-day weekend.

One of my favorite such weekends was our road trip to Rapid City, South Dakota. We stayed in a tiny cabin and explored Mount Rushmore, fed carrots to the donkeys in Custer State Park, and took photos astride the jackalope at Wall Drug, where we laughed so hard, we almost wet our pants.

Doing life together: it is one of my favorite things. And taking international friends on vacation with us quickly became a cherished pattern in my life. There is nothing quite like road trips and kitschy tourist traps (thanks, Wall Drug!) to replace polite small talk with the stuff real life is made of: discussing cultural differences within the safe context of friendship and building memories as our children turn somersaults in the warm sunshine on the freshly mowed lawn of the small mom-and-pop campground.

If you are mentally ticking off your family's unique quirks and thinking to yourself that such an adventure would never work, please believe me when I say that my family is not perfect. Inviting others in doesn't start with a four-day road trip to the Black Hills looking for buffalo and jackalope. It starts small and tentative over bonfires and potluck dinners. It starts with being bold and brave enough to reach out to a stranger instead of hiding in the comfortable circle of your best friends.

Our colleges are filled with students from all corners of the world, many of whom are here on their own and would love to be adopted for American holidays, cultures, and customs. And our cities and neighborhoods are filled with new arrivals, people craving connection beyond our polite but often distant and dismissive small talk. Let's invite them in.

– Julie

– Today's Act of Friendship –

Consider who you might invite into your circles: the single mom two doors down, an international student, a new coworker? A warm spring day is the perfect time to ask someone over for a glass of lemonade on the back patio.

God Is My Friend

You saw me before I was born. Every day of my life was recorded in your book. Every moment was laid out before a single day had passed. How precious are your thoughts about me, O God. They cannot be numbered!

PSALM 139:16-17

I grew up in a church that taught me from a young age that I could talk to God anytime and anywhere. It trained me to believe that most of the thoughts that would spin around throughout my day were really just conversations with God. To me, prayer wasn't something that I needed to set a specific time aside for—all my thoughts could be conversations with God. Because I grew up believing this, it was easy for me to think of God as my friend, as someone who cared about all of me, about the big and small things in my life.

I realize not everyone believes this. I've come to understand that what we were taught as children, as well as our own life experiences, can affect the way that we view God. But the Bible is very clear about the character of God. No matter what we were taught or believe, we can always hold it up against the Word of God to know if it is true. I have often had to combat some false assumption about God based on the truth of his Word, and that is a very good thing, because what the Bible says is so much better than what I could believe on my own about God!

Do you struggle to see God as your friend, or as someone who is interested in all areas of your life? Psalm 139 tells us that God is interested in every moment of our day, that he cares about all of it. We are constantly on his mind, and he is thinking good thoughts toward us! What better friend could we have than him?

— Kendra

— Today's Act of Friendship —

Rejoice in God's friendship with you, and meditate on Scriptures that teach this truth.

Buckets of Grace

You must be compassionate, just as your Father is compassionate.

LUKE 6:36

Sighing in frustration, my friend confided that there had been conflict between her daughter (the bride) and her daughter's future mother-in-law as the wedding ceremony loomed. "I just wish she would remember that my daughter is in her early twenties; she's still figuring this out," my friend said. She is a wise and mature woman, someone who has spoken life over me repeatedly as I raised children just a step or two behind her.

I don't know what the conflict was or what had caused the hurt feelings, but I took mental notes for my own potential son- and daughter-in-law, as well as for the other friends in my life who are still figuring things out as they enter new stages of life: first-time parenthood, raising teens, empty nesting, career restarts, medical diagnoses, and any other number of new experiences.

Those of us with more life experience under our proverbial belts are called to show grace and compassion when those coming behind us misstep, snub us inadvertently, and stumble. We should support our friends when they make newbie mistakes without even realizing it.

Jesus' words in Luke 6 bring to my mind an image of a child's red plastic beach bucket and of Jesus using that bucket to soak me in grace and compassion as he upends it over my head. Liquid grace and compassion, running in rivulets, covering me from head to toe. Jesus whispers that I should take up my own plastic bucket and pour that same grace and compassion over my relationships, especially over the women who are still working out what it means to be in a new season, doing a new thing, learning a new skill set.

When I'm tempted to take offense, Jesus is there, reminding me that I was once the new bride, the new girl in the office, the new mom—and gently reminding me of my own missteps as I entered an unknown season of life. And then I think of the red plastic beach bucket and what it has meant to me, and what it would mean for her.

— *Julie*

— Today's Act of Friendship —

Imagine the pouring out of liquid grace and compassion
when you are tempted to be irritated with a friend.

The Richness of Friendships

True godliness with contentment is itself great wealth. After all, we brought nothing with us when we came into the world, and we can't take anything with us when we leave it.

1 TIMOTHY 6:6-7

For the past couple of years, I have been drawn toward a more minimalist lifestyle. On the one hand, as a mom with three young daughters, I can feel my anxiety rising in tandem with the amount of clutter in my home. On the other hand, I adore shopping. Nevertheless, I'm trying to make slow changes toward buying less and living with intention and contentment.

As I move into my midthirties, I'm realizing more and more that the consumption of my twenties has evolved into a renewed focus on rich relationships. I would much rather fill our home with people, not stuff. Paul reminds us that true contentment is found when we choose not to focus on filling our homes and lives with possessions that are temporary and will ultimately leave us unsatisfied. After all, the possessions we treasure will end up as dust, yet loving others well can provide us with riches beyond measure.

This truth was brought home for me the day I witnessed my sister's funeral. She died at age twenty-eight after a five-year battle with breast cancer, but her hope and faith throughout her cancer battle inspired many. Sitting at the front of the sanctuary on that cold November day, I was astonished to see people packed into the church, standing in the back and spilling into the hallways. Katrina had learned the value of rich friendships, and her legacy was there, standing on the carpeted floor of the church building.

My sister's gracious and welcoming nature drew people in, and she and her husband entertained frequently. Her hospitality has encouraged even me, an introvert, to invest in authentic friendships. For that reason, we've had single moms and their kids stay in our house for months at a time. We've hosted weekly church small groups, thrown big Super Bowl parties, and had sprawling outdoor barbecues and smaller, intimate dinners. May we always seek to be content with what we have, and resolve to fill our homes with people, not stuff.

– Kristin

– Today's Act of Friendship –

The next time you feel tempted to buy an unneeded product for your home, use the money to treat a friend to coffee or a meal.

Noticing Others

Dear friends, since God loved us that much,
we surely ought to love each other.

1 JOHN 4:11

I recently read an article in which the author explained that there are two types of people in the world—ones that walk into a room and say "Here I am" and others who walk in and say "There you are!"* As I thought more about this, I began to consider what kind of person I am most often. If I'm really honest, I'm not always a "there you are" person. Many times my own insecurities, especially in a new setting or situation, can make me someone who waits for others to approach me. But honestly, I don't like this about myself. I want to be a more welcoming, friendly person.

Even though my natural tendency is toward shyness, I can still work to be different, to be a more open and inviting person, and this is something I am beginning to encourage myself to do more often. I am pushing myself to be a "there you are" kind of person as I walk into a room, making others my focus in the way that I ask questions, listen, and take the time to get to know and be friendly to those I come in contact with. I am putting my phone away more often (I tend to take it out when I'm in slightly uncomfortable situations) and spending time with the person who is in front of me. I am making connections and actively befriending others, and it feels right.

God loved us enough to send his Son for us, and if he did that, then surely we can cross a room to show love for one another. As believers, we've been given so much that it should overflow to those around us. One of the easiest ways to love well is to start by seeing others, acknowledging them, and welcoming and befriending them. Whether we come by it naturally or not, we can all work to be a "there you are" kind of friend.

— *Kendra*

— *Today's Act of Friendship* —

The next time you walk into a gathering of people, think about how you can be a "there you are" kind of friend instead of a "here I am" one.

---

* Jill Savage, "There You Are!," Proverbs 31 Ministries, April 8, 2016, https://proverbs31.org/read/devotions/full-post /2016/04/08/there-you-are.

Southern Hospitality

*Let us think of ways to motivate one another
to acts of love and good works.*
HEBREWS 10:24

Several years ago, Kendra and I left behind our crisp Minnesota fall to experience a weekend of breakfast grits, sweet potato desserts, and even sweeter Southern hospitality.

It was our first experience at a writers' conference, and it was a little nerve-racking. As we tucked ourselves into the front seat of the hotel shuttle bus, we casually listened to those around us telling their stories. Listening to the amazing accomplishments of the poised, polished women, I could feel my eyes widen and my heart drop.

What are we doing here? I wondered to myself. *We are way out of our league!* Some of the women had eye-popping social media followings, while others had numerous book deals under their belts. One of our roommates even had her DIY house featured in *Country Living* magazine. How could we possibly compete with all that talent?

But once we got past the fancy résumés, we realized that we were in a safe space. Over salads and sweet tea and even into the wee hours of the night, we talked to our new friends about health troubles and herbs, babies and teenagers, communities in need of help and social justice causes we cared about. Once I pushed my own insecurities out of the way, what I found was that each woman we encountered was real. Each woman was flawed, each woman doubted herself and her talents, each one worried about finances and parenting. Each one loved, lived, and dreamed just like us, and the weekend was proof that despite their shiny, polished images, each one needed encouragement just as much as we did.

Dreams are something most people don't ask about, something you strive for in stolen moments late at night or in the cracks of the day, alone. Scripture encourages us to motivate one another to acts of love and good works, but that's only possible if we can overcome our own insecurities in order to cheer on those around us. Let's resolve to be women who cheer wildly for others, spurring them on with love and friendship.

— Kristin

— Today's Act of Friendship —

Encourage a friend in their pursuit of a dream.

Mr. Freeze

A cheerful heart is good medicine.
PROVERBS 17:22

My husband's hands get colder than those of anyone else I've ever met, and he thinks it is hilarious to sneak up and stick his frigid fingers on the back of my neck or the small of my back "to warm them up," especially if my own hands are busy doing a dinner-related task and I cannot readily protect myself.

Rather than get mad when his icicle hands try to steal my warmth, I shriek loudly and engage in evasive maneuvers, invoking the help of our children from every corner of the house. Our family descends into momentary chaos, with everyone chasing through rooms until I've been dogpiled by a husband and two children with varying motives of either helping dad or mom, and we are all breathless with laughter.

This ritual sounds a bit ridiculous, but it is so, so important. Raising children, pursuing careers, and keeping a household running can slowly and insidiously turn spouses into roommates and into people who are always responsible and dull as dull can be.

In the midst of responsible adulting, there is nothing quite like a short game of chase to restore a twinkle to our eyes and humor to our marital relationship. Play is good for the soul, and it is good for our marriage and our family. It allows us to laugh together, to release responsibilities for a few minutes of living entirely in the present, to reconnect with everyone in our family with loving—albeit cold—touch.

Playfulness is something we tend to set aside as beneath us instead of recognizing the emotional, spiritual, and physical benefits that come with setting aside our grown-up responsibilities and just having fun, even for a few minutes. Cheerfulness and joy are found in play, and they are good medicine for ourselves and for those in relationship with us.

– Julie

– Today's Act of Friendship –

Cultivate a habit of play in your relationships. Revel in your inner ten-year-old from time to time instead of being prim and proper.

The Dinner Invitation

Dear children, let's not merely say that we love each other; let us show the truth by our actions.

1 JOHN 3:18

I met Cindy when we started attending a local church in our neighborhood that was also attached to a homeless shelter. Cindy was the children's church leader, and every Sunday she would plan activities with lots of care to teach the children about loving God and loving others. As my youngest child was shy and didn't want to be left alone in the class, I became Cindy's weekly helper, passing out papers, answering questions, and quieting children who got a bit too rambunctious. Week after week, I watched Cindy teach simple lessons with passion and conviction, and I marveled at how well she loved the children in the class, despite her lack of a home or security for her future.

One Sunday, as we were eating lunch after the kids' program, I asked Cindy if she and her boys would like to come to our house for dinner that week. She readily agreed. On Thursday night we shared a meal of tacos, and as our boys went off to play, she told us how she came to live at the shelter, how she grew up in foster care, and about the plans she had for her future. We told her about the foster children we'd cared for and our own adopted kids. We talked about the struggle of raising children and providing for a family. We realized we had more in common than not, and the hours quickly passed until Cindy and her family finally had to get back to the shelter before curfew. As we said goodbye, we made promises to meet again soon, grateful for how Cindy had blessed our family with her teaching and grateful for the opportunity to bless her in return.

As Christians, we're called to show love not just with words but with what we do. Even though Cindy was living in a shelter with her children, she led well with love in the children's program at church. In turn, we were able to show her and her boys kindness by inviting them into our home. Mutually supporting one another in love is one way we walk in friendship with others.

— *Kendra*

— Today's Act of Friendship —

Reach out to someone who is loving people well through their actions and let them know their hard work is not unnoticed.

Community over Competition

*Make me truly happy by agreeing wholeheartedly with each other, loving
one another, and working together with one mind and purpose.*

PHILIPPIANS 2:2

Leaving the gathering, I walked out into the soothing crispness of twilight, a sunset of brilliant pinks and oranges fading into dappled hues of violet and blue. My car exited the small town, and I turned up the music as I headed out on the two-lane highway.

As my car dipped through rural hollows, I reflected on the value of community: how these friends—fellow writers and ministry-oriented women who have passions and goals that I love to witness—have silently passed me Kleenex to dry my tears, given hugs that squeezed the breath from my lungs, and laughed about everything from children to procreation, old lady jokes to hashtags.

These women span generations and cultures, but together they volunteer with a statewide women's ministry organization to put on conferences for single moms, female leaders, and women from all walks of life. As a collective, they work with a united purpose, urging one another on from good things to even greater things. They embody the idea of community over competition.

Driving down the highway, I couldn't help but think about how this unity among friends is fostered by my friend Carol, the director of the ministry. Carol leads as a servant in many ways. She excels at helping people find their niche and gives them space to lead their own area well, without micromanaging the details. Once Carol has placed someone in a position of authority, she goes out of her way to find the good—and praise it. She encourages those around her rather than focusing on her own accomplishments. And when things go awry, as they so often do with large-scale events, Carol's classic phrase is, "That's just the way we like it." She has made adaptation a way of life, and she's taught us to approach situations with grace and people with compassion.

Carol's leadership calls out the innate, unique gifts of each person around her so they can work in harmony for Christ's glory. How much could our church groups, friend groups, neighborhoods, schools, and communities benefit from incorporating that kind of servant leadership? As followers of Christ, let's resolve to take the lead in fostering this friendly sense of community, coming together to love and work for the benefit of all.

— Kristin

— Today's Act of Friendship —

Invest in a community of friends working toward a
common goal. Help others find their niche, praise their
efforts, and adapt when things don't go as expected.

Pearls in the Pigpen

Don't waste what is holy on people who are unholy. Don't throw your
pearls to pigs! They will trample the pearls, then turn and attack you.
MATTHEW 7:6

My daughter has a gift for storytelling, and she has been working hard on a fictional tale of a girl named Ashley. One day she asked my husband to print a draft of her story so she could take it to school with her the next day.

The next morning I found the manuscript forgotten on the hall table in my daughter's haste to get to school. A handwritten note was written across the top: "I hope you like it." I went about my own busy day with those words bouncing around in the back of my head until I finally paused to consider why that note was bothering me.

When she got home from school that afternoon, I casually asked why she had written those particular words across the top of her story. Her answer was as I suspected; she'd intended to show it to a group of girls who had been giving her a hard time that school year. I gently asked what response my daughter had been hoping for from her classmates, and we walked through a variety of reasons why their response to her story might not be positive. We talked about why we should be discerning in our vulnerability—choosing carefully the women we seek advice or input from, understanding that not everyone has our best interests at heart.

As my daughter and I were talking, I could feel the Holy Spirit reminding me that this conversation was as much for me as it was for Lizzie. How often do we offer up our budding talent for the approval of people who do not have our best interests at heart? How often do we throw our pearls before the proverbial swine, hoping that they will finally affirm us instead of tearing us down? Let us be wise in our vulnerability, seeking guidance from those who love us, even imperfectly. And let us be safe women who hold another's vulnerability as the precious gift it is.

— Julie

— Today's Act of Friendship —

Have you been casting your pearls before swine? Are you guilty of
being one of the pigs in the pigpen? Ask the Holy Spirit to show you
if you have either habit and what steps you might take to break it.

Unlikely Friends

Now I am giving you a new commandment: Love each other.
Just as I have loved you, you should love each other.

JOHN 13:34

For the past several years I've been an organizer and co-emcee for a statewide single moms' retreat. When I first heard about the retreat, I just knew I'd want to be a part of it, but I was also hesitant. What would I have to offer? I'm not a single mom. I really didn't have many close friends who were single moms. How would I be able to help? And would others think I didn't belong?

But when I shared my fears with Carol—the main organizer of the event—she quickly smiled and told me that sometimes God uses people in places and ways they never thought possible. And so I agreed to do it, in part because I had also gotten to know Julie, the other organizer for the retreat and my co-emcee for the event. Julie is a single mom herself and is one of the kindest people I know.

In the end, the weekend went beautifully. We laughed together. We cried. We were honest. We had fun. We bonded. We became friends. And here's what I keep thinking about: *What if I had missed this opportunity? What if I had let my insecurity or ideas about how I'm different or have nothing to offer be a reason not to participate? What would I have missed?* Now the single moms' retreat is one of my absolute favorite weekends out of the entire year. You couldn't pay me to miss it. I love this mission, this sisterhood of women.

Is there something outside of your comfort zone that you feel called to do? Maybe, like me, what's holding you back is what you perceive as your differences. Maybe God is planning to use you in spite of those differences. We were meant to love those who, at least on the surface, look very different from us, obeying God's command to love others as he has loved us. Sometimes friendship is created in some of the most unlikely places.

— *Kendra*

— *Today's Act of Friendship* —

Commit to participate in or attend an event or gathering
with people who are different from you.

Well-Seasoned Words

Let your conversation be always full of grace, seasoned with salt, so that you may know how to answer everyone.
COLOSSIANS 4:6, NIV

It was Silly Day at preschool. My four-year-old was wearing pajamas, one silver shoe and one ladybug shoe, and oversized floral sunglasses that accompanied numerous wild buns in her bright blonde hair.

As we stepped from the cold outside into the warmth of the hallway, I peeled off my daughter's coat. The mom next to me straightened from where she crouched over her son, removing his coat and hat. But as she stood, I realized her son was wearing regular clothes. For a moment I panicked. Did I get the wrong day? "All ready for Silly Day!" I blurted, trying to cover my discomfort.

The mom next to me looked at her son, then at my daughter. I could see the dawning realization that she'd forgotten to dress her son for the occasion.

Noticing the look of ire the mom was now directing my way, another mom stepped in. "I think it's all week," she offered casually, offhand.

"You can do it Thursday or Friday," the first mom told her son. But as she followed us into the bathroom to supervise her son's handwashing, I felt the weight of her stare. How had I gone from Awkward Mom to Judgy Mom?

Our natural response to uncomfortable situations is often to simply fill the space with words in an effort to hide our own awkwardness. How many times have I said something foolish to mask the fact that I had no idea what to say? How often have I unintentionally hurt another in order to cover up my own failings? Colossians admonishes us to be gracious and thoughtful in our conversations. Our well-seasoned words can go a long way toward nurturing loving relationships.

As the woman's son and my daughter headed into the preschool room to hang up backpacks and find their name tags, I offered the other mom a hesitant smile. A small gesture of apology. A silent plea for grace. My feelings of inadequacy should never be a reason to undermine someone else. Instead, those moments should be seen as opportunities for grace—for them and for me.

– Kristin

– Today's Act of Friendship –

Apologize to someone for thoughtless words you've spoken to them.

My Sister from Another Mister

*Be kind to each other, tenderhearted, forgiving one another,
just as God through Christ has forgiven you.*

EPHESIANS 4:32

"Remind me why I am lying on your dirty floor?" Kendra joked, peering up at me.

I looked down at Kendra, lying on her back next to my fireplace, painting the brick under the hearth as I perched uncomfortably on a step stool, painting brick above the mantle. We'd been painting for what seemed like forever, and we were completely over our initial enthusiasm for the project, even as an hour or so remained before we would be done.

Why, indeed? I didn't have an excellent answer for why one of my dearest friends had agreed to help me paint my monstrosity of an ugly brick fireplace, but she had and here we were, covered in paint and slightly cranky because the project was taking longer than we had anticipated. It's the sort of thoughtfulness she shows me on a regular basis, entering into the dirtiest, most uncomfortable parts of my life.

Kendra is like a sister to me. She knows my faults, has seen me at my worst, and loves me well despite that knowledge. She daily shows me the kindness, tenderheartedness, and forgiveness described in Ephesians. I am safe to share my hardest struggles, my deepest fears, and my wildest dreams with her, because she will hold those vulnerable pieces of my life with compassion and care, while challenging me to be a better woman when I've fallen short of the mark.

In a world of "you do you" permissiveness with a heaping side of snark, we need to be women who embody God's kindness, tenderness, and mercy to our friends as we stand firmly on scriptural truth. Whether we're painting an old fireplace or offering words of compassion, we can reflect the love of Christ to a cynical, disillusioned world and stand out as women who have something different to offer. We offer Jesus, and friendship with us should reflect that.

– Julie

– Today's Act of Friendship –

Ask God to reveal one person in your life who needs an extra dose of kindness, tenderness, and mercy, and extend it to them.

Taking Time to Be Friendly

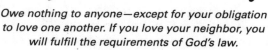

Owe nothing to anyone—except for your obligation to love one another. If you love your neighbor, you will fulfill the requirements of God's law.

ROMANS 13:8

My husband and I moved into a different area of town two years ago. It's an old neighborhood with wide sidewalks that span blocks as far as you can see. Kids race up and down the sidewalk, with parents hurrying behind. Elderly couples shuffle by, and single professionals with their dogs make a usual route of our street. When we noticed all the foot traffic, we decided that sitting outside on our front lawn in the evenings would be a perfect way to get to know others in our neighborhood. Our kids soon saw what we were doing and decided to join us by playing in the yard, enjoying the warm summer evenings.

This habit has been a wonderful way for our family to not only connect with others in our neighborhood but also with one another. We've developed budding friendships with those who live around us and are slowly getting to know others in our neighborhood, while also strengthening our family bonds.

When we love our neighbors, we are fulfilling the requirements of God's law. Although our neighbors are not limited to those who live close by, it certainly includes them. As followers of Jesus, we should be some of the most loving and hospitable people in our neighborhoods and communities. Our homes should be such places of peace that others feel safe and valued. We don't have to make a lot of grand gestures or do elaborate planning to make others feel loved: just setting up a couple of chairs, sitting outside, and starting conversations with those who might come across our paths is all it takes. You never know what friendships could develop when you take the time to be friendly.

— Kendra

— Today's Act of Friendship —

Spend time in your yard and see if you can start conversations with others in your neighborhood.

Remembering Who You Are

My old self has been crucified with Christ. It is no longer I who live, but Christ lives in me. So I live in this earthly body by trusting in the Son of God, who loved me and gave himself for me.

GALATIANS 2:20

As a people pleaser, I'm often tempted to confuse my labels with my identity. It's as though I have a report card for relationships, and instead of earning grades in math and English, I'm earning grades in daughter, wife, mom, and friend. I spend way too much time wondering, Are my parents pleased with me, thereby making me a "good" daughter? Is my marriage picture-perfect, thereby making me a "good" wife? Are my children intelligent, compassionate, perfectly behaved angelic creatures, thereby making me a "good" mom? Am I a woman who meets all the needs of my friends, never failing them, never disappointing them, thereby making me a "good" friend?

The truth is that I control—at best—one half of a relationship. I cannot control my parents' thoughts, feelings, or actions; I cannot control my husband's thoughts, feelings, or actions. I cannot control my friends, and I am slowly losing my illusion of control over my children as they grow into their own personhoods. It is unhealthy to use my children, husband, parents, and friends as my report card, and doing so can lead to dysfunction in those relationships.

Paul teaches us in Galatians that our identity is in Jesus. Embracing that truth is life-giving for us and for those around us. When I am able to remain rooted in that truth, my relationships with my parents, husband, children, and friends are healthier. I am less prone to attempts at manipulation and power struggles when I am not defining myself through the lens of those labels.

— *Julie*

— Today's Act of Friendship —

Ask God to reveal where you might be finding your identity in your relationships and how that might be adding unnecessary pressure on you and on the other people involved.

Delighting in Friendship
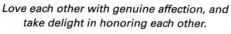

*Love each other with genuine affection, and
take delight in honoring each other.*

ROMANS 12:10

Of all my children, my oldest, Elise, has the ability to believe everyone else is exactly like her. For instance, a little girl named Kara, who has Down syndrome, is one of her favorite friends to play with at church. Elise doesn't mind the frequent hugs and touches Kara bestows, and when you see the two of them together, they are usually laughing uproariously or racing around the gym.

One day after church several years ago, one of the children's leaders approached me to tell me that Elise doesn't always understand the idea of compromising when she and Kara want the same coloring page. Although I promised the leader I would speak to Elise, I found myself struggling to communicate the idea to her. You see, Elise looks at others and sees commonalities, not differences. She didn't understand the need to adapt her actions for her friend's benefit because, in her mind, they are the same.

Elise takes to heart the Scriptures' admonition to love others with affection, and delights in honoring Kara's fun-loving nature. Her attitude is one that challenges me, as an adult, to do better. How many times have I fallen into the trap of thinking that someone else's parenting style, worldview, hobby, or personality is too different from my own? What if, instead, I focused on the special, unique qualities of that person and chose to delight in them?

At the heart of it, we are all made in the image of God, precious and worthy and loved. Though I found myself inexpertly explaining things to Elise that day, I've realized that my children don't need me to have all the answers. Instead, they need me to model the heart of Jesus, being filled with mercy, compassion, and an appreciation for all the things that make us unique and beautiful.

— Kristin

— Today's Act of Friendship —

Think of someone you've considered too different from you to be
a close friend. Make a list of five traits that are special about them,
then find a way to honor and celebrate those unique qualities.

Deep Friendships

Ruth replied, "Don't ask me to leave you and turn back.
Wherever you go, I will go; wherever you live, I will live. Your
people will be my people, and your God will be my God."
RUTH 1:16

Not long ago a good friend of mine admitted that she was so thankful for our small group of friends that had developed over the past year because, prior to that, she'd never really had girlfriends. I looked at her, a bit stunned by her statement. I was surprised to hear that she didn't have other good friends since she is one of the kindest and friendliest people I know. When I mentioned this, she just shrugged her shoulders and said she'd had a few friends in high school, but marriage and kids took priority, and friendship was put on the back burner to manage more pressing concerns.

Although I certainly understood what she meant about other things getting in the way, I also know how important it is to have good friends in all stages of our lives. It can happen to any of us: life gets busy, and although we may know a lot of people, we can miss having real and deep friendships with others until one day we realize we don't have any really good friends. If this is where you find yourself, you can have hope in knowing that you don't have to remain there.

The story of Ruth and Naomi portrays one of my favorite friendships in the Bible. Ruth and Naomi loved and supported one another and walked through all of life together. In a beautiful statement of vulnerability, Ruth made a commitment to her friend to go with her wherever she might go. There may be many reasons for the book of Ruth in the Bible, but one, I believe, is to show us the power of community. Ruth and Naomi's example teaches us to start by spending time with other women, sharing life with them, and then opening up honestly about the good and hard things we are facing. It may not happen all at once, but just one little step at a time grows deep friendships.

We have a lot we can learn from these two women. All is not lost if we find ourselves in a season of not having close friendships. We each have available to us the ability to reach out to someone today and make friendship a priority.

– Kendra

– Today's Act of Friendship –

Reach out to someone with whom you want to
either maintain or deepen a friendship.

June

What's Your Friend's Name?

All of you should be of one mind. Sympathize with each other.
Love each other as brothers and sisters. Be tenderhearted,
and keep a humble attitude.

1 PETER 3:8

From my cozy bedroom armchair, I could hear clattering schoolbags and shuffling feet as my children entered the main-floor mudroom. My two older daughters had participated in a community education swim-and-movie event that evening with other children from the area, and they had just returned home. Hair still damp, they shucked their coats and shoes and hollered out a hello.

"Mom, I made a new friend!" Noelle, my seven-year-old, said with a smile on her face as she entered the room.

"You did?" I asked. "What's your friend's name?"

"I don't know," she said, shrugging. As she wandered off to get ready for bed, I couldn't help the smile that tugged at my mouth. As an adult, I can't imagine claiming someone as a friend without asking their name. Yet this isn't the first time that one of my children has told me about a friend they spent hours with but hadn't bothered to ask their name.

As an adult, I often ask people for their names, occupations, and information about their family. Yet how often do my questions truly dip beneath the surface? I'm ashamed to say that there have been many times when my conversation doesn't progress beyond small talk. Even though my children may not know their new friend's name or how to contact them, they've spent time asking more thought-provoking questions. They can tell me that their friend loves sausage pizza but loathes pepperoni, thinks their older brother is annoying, and has a mutual love for unicorns.

As Christians, we're told to sympathize with one another, but that depth of feeling only occurs when we are willing to ask the more profound questions—after all, you can't truly love or be united with someone you don't know well. By taking a genuine interest in others, we reflect Christ's love into the world and our relationships deepen. It's only by engaging with others beyond the surface level that we will experience the true richness of friendship.

– Kristin

– Today's Act of Friendship –

Ask a friend questions, listening to their response without
turning the conversation to focus on your own answer.

Taking Down Fences

This is how God loved the world: He gave his one and only Son,
so that everyone who believes in him will not perish but have eternal life.

JOHN 3:16

We moved into our new neighborhood in the spring, and immediately my husband formed plans to take down the large privacy fence that blocked off our yard from the alley behind it. A few weeks later, on a warm, early summer morning, we began the work.

Shortly after the fence came down, we wanted to host a neighborhood party to get to know the other people living on our block. Kyle took invitations around with our kids, and we planned for the party we'd host in our backyard. Several neighbors came through the alleyway, easily accessing our backyard now that the fence was gone.

As the evening went on, we started a bonfire, and as people began to settle in and move past the nervousness of small talk, one neighbor mentioned to my husband, "We knew you'd want to be our friends when we saw the fence come down." My husband affirmed his statement that yes, we wanted to be friends.

Our neighbor's offhand statement has stuck with me, even today. How often do we erect fences, either physical or metaphorical, to keep people at a distance? John 3:16 is a familiar verse to most of us, but do we fully understand the text, "This is how God loved the world"? This verse teaches us that God loves everyone, not only those we naturally love, but also those we don't. He didn't give his Son only for those we want to invite into our lives, but also for those we'd rather keep at a distance. God gave his only Son for all of us, indiscriminately, and if we are his followers, we must be willing to love others in the same way. Because although there's nothing inherently wrong with having fences in our backyards, we must be careful about the fences we erect in our hearts.

— Kendra

— Today's Act of Friendship —

Consider who you may have kept at a distance and find one
way you can extend friendship toward that person.

The Gift of Grit

Moses' arms soon became so tired he could no longer hold them up. So Aaron and Hur found a stone for him to sit on. Then they stood on each side of Moses, holding up his hands. So his hands held steady until sunset.

EXODUS 17:12

It was at the midpoint in our hike to the summit of Black Elk Peak that I promised our daughter a break upon reaching a fork in the trail that was surely just around the next bend. She and I plodded along slightly behind the rest of our group, peering longingly around each curve, both looking forward to that promised break and a little snack I had tucked into our backpacks.

When we finally got to the fork, I reached for my pack, grateful for the opportunity to rest before tackling the steepest part of our journey. But my daughter, upon reading that the summit was one-fourth of a mile up the trail, turned to me and said, "We made it this far without stopping, let's keep going! I want to reach the top without resting!"

Um . . . what? I watched as she disappeared up the rocky trail before I continued as well, pondering how having companions and encouragement can help us press through hard things we'd otherwise be tempted to quit. I pushed my daughter, and then she pushed me, each of us having the energy and motivation at different points during the hike to keep the other one moving forward.

Merriam-Webster defines *grit* as "firmness of mind or spirit; unyielding courage in the face of hardship or danger." This quality can be an internal strength of character or a powerful external coming together as a community of believers. We see grit in the story of Moses, Aaron, and Hur. Moses was tasked with keeping his arms raised so that the battle below against a much larger army would be won, but it is only with the help of Aaron and Hur that the Israelites were victorious that day. Aaron and Hur gave Moses the gift of grit—the courage to continue until his work was done.

We were never intended to go it completely alone, relying only upon ourselves. My strength is multiplied in my community of family and girlfriends who refuse to let me quit, who give me gritty encouragement, even during my moments of whiny argument about why it is too hard and too uncomfortable.

— Julie

— Today's Act of Friendship —

Which of your friends may need gritty encouragement?
Encourage her, even as you find a way to ease her burden.

Longing to Be Popular

Obviously, I'm not trying to win the approval of people, but of God. If pleasing people were my goal, I would not be Christ's servant.

GALATIANS 1:10

My husband and I pulled up to the small-town Eagles Club on a Saturday night.

"Ready?" I asked him, taking a deep breath as we opened our car doors. I stepped out, tottering briefly on high heels, smoothing the back of my shirt as I straightened my shoulders. Walking slowly toward the building, I entered a gloomy entryway lit with neon signs. It was my high school class reunion.

On the way to the event, my husband joked that it wasn't too late to go to a movie. I'll be honest; I was tempted. Although I enjoyed high school and had great friends, I now realize how often I compared myself to others and found myself lacking. As an adult, I have no desire to return to that version of myself. Yet as we circled the room filled with old classmates, I felt my innate shyness emerge, and it frustrated me. I felt unsure about who to approach or what my reception would be like. In my current friendships, I rarely feel that kind of pressure. So why was I letting my insecurities get the better of me?

Tim and I visited with old friends for a few hours, said our goodbyes, and headed home. In the darkness of the night, my husband dozed while I drove, and I found myself engulfed in a mix of emotions. Although I enjoyed the event and caught up with friends I hadn't seen in the past decade, the evening was marred by my own insecurities as I wondered if my life seemed too boring or if who I had become lived up to others' expectations.

It's human nature to want to feel well liked, but Scripture reminds us that getting others to think well of us is not our primary aim in life. Instead, God's good opinion should be our highest goal. As friends, let's encourage others to embrace their God-given identity instead of falling victim to the false idol of comparison. And if we choose to compare ourselves to anyone, may it be our friend Jesus.

— Kristin

— Today's Act of Friendship —

Prioritize friendships that encourage you to focus
on God's approval, rather than those that foster a
competitive striving for the approval of others.

Supporting Others' Parenting

A troublemaker plants seeds of strife;
gossip separates the best of friends.
PROVERBS 16:28

My son came home one evening after spending time with friends and began to tell me about all the fun they'd had while they were out together. As I listened, he went on to complain about one of his female friend's parents, who, in his mind, was giving her a hard time.

"Her mom was so rude," he stated. "She told her she had to come home right then and didn't even give a reason." As he took a breath to continue speaking ill of his friend's mom, I felt a small smile tug at the corners of my mouth.

I raised a hand to interject. "Honey," I replied, "I don't know if her mom was being rude or not, and I also don't know how your friend was speaking to her mother. But I will tell you, I am not going to throw another parent under the bus. Sorry, but parenting is hard enough and I'm not going to speak ill of someone else."

He nodded begrudgingly at my response as our conversation moved on to other topics.

I thought later about how often I feel the pressure to parent well and the desire not to be judged by other parents. Despite all the benefits of social media, one downside is the pressure it can place on parents to always do and say things perfectly. The reality is that we are all human and will make mistakes, and this includes our parenting.

God does not mince words when he tells us that gossip pushes friends apart. The last thing I want to do to my friends who are parents is plant seeds of strife. I want them to be confident that I will not belittle their parenting to anyone, including our kids, and I know they'll do the same for me. We can often wonder if we're parenting correctly, disciplining appropriately, and teaching our kids the right things. Knowing we have other parents as friends who can support us and our parenting is so helpful.

– Kendra

– Today's Act of Friendship –

Offer encouragement to a friend who is in a
challenging season of their parenting.

Opposites Attract

*There are different kinds of spiritual gifts, but the same Spirit
is the source of them all. . . . God works in different ways,
but it is the same God who does the work in all of us.*

1 CORINTHIANS 12:4, 6

Lizzie, Jazzy, and Addi. Our girls, born six months apart to two besties, have been hanging out with one another since before they could crawl. I once hated the unfairness of arbitrary school boundaries that zigzagged between our houses resulting in our girls attending different schools. But sometimes, we cannot see God's immense blessing until far later, until one day, we realize that our repeated lament was a blessing in disguise and that God knew exactly what he was doing.

Because our girls have gone to different schools, they've had the freedom to define their friendship without the interference of classmates and school hierarchies that often make middle school friendships complex. They are learning to cheer one another on in their wildly different strengths and to be young women who are secure enough in their friendship to release one another into other friendship circles. Having a strong friendship circle outside of classmates has been life-giving for my daughter, and it has given me a new appreciation for the importance of different groups of friends.

Several of the girlfriends I hold closest to my heart know one another only tangentially. They hail from different seasons of my life and different social circles that my husband and I move through, and they have a vast array of skill sets and strengths very different from my own. The family of God is diverse in a thousand ways, but it is the same God in all of us, and he has gifted each one of us uniquely. He is the unifier, the glue that pulls his diverse family into community.

I'm only now beginning to understand the immense blessing of an inner circle of girlfriends who are varied and diverse, each of whom challenges, loves, and supports me in different ways. Finding friendship with women who are different from you and who hail from different backgrounds and experiences brings a richness and depth to life that you do not want to miss.

— Julie

— Today's Act of Friendship —

Pray that God would send you a diversity of deep, new friendships
and then watch for the women he puts in your path.

Establishing Boundaries

We are each responsible for our own conduct.
GALATIANS 6:5

It happens every spring when we emerge from the long, cold Minnesota winter. As soon as the snow starts to melt and the temperature tops 50 degrees, my children hurtle headlong outside, usually barefoot and coatless. But, also without fail, I find myself having to randomly quiz them on our expectations for interacting with neighbors. The rules are simple:

Talk to Mom before you go to someone's house.
Play outside, rather than inside, with friends.
If your friend isn't home and you decide to visit another, tell Mom first.
Share with others, and clean up any messes you contribute to making.
And, because they once knocked on a neighbor's door, flashed pitiful, puppy-dog eyes at her, and told her she "forgot" to give them a granola bar: don't ask for food (you can eat at home).

Our neighbors are incredibly kind and have likely overlooked many a faux pas, but that doesn't mean we aren't trying to teach our kids manners. Our rules aren't meant to stifle our children; they are meant to help them understand the need for healthy boundaries.

Likewise, the rules that govern friendship are complex. Yet in the same way that a few rules help maintain positive relationships with our neighbors, establishing boundaries is equally important for maintaining healthy friendships. This includes things like refusing to indulge in gossip, accepting responsibility for mistakes, asking for forgiveness, sharing information in an appropriate way (not under or over-sharing), not compromising our core values, and knowing how and when to say no when it's needed (as well as accepting no from our friends).

Galatians reminds us that we are each responsible for how we behave. As people of God, our goal should be to maintain the healthy boundaries we've established while still conveying love and grace to those with whom we are in relationship.

— *Kristin*

— *Today's Act of Friendship* —

Make a list of healthy boundaries. Resolve to work on establishing (or renewing) a boundary for maintaining a friendship.

Let's Be Real

All of you, dress yourselves in humility as you relate to one another,
for "God opposes the proud but gives grace to the humble."

1 PETER 5:5

We were getting ready to host a party, and I was feeling a bit nervous. A large group of people were coming, and we had a lot to do. One of our young single friends came to help. As she saw my husband and me interacting, she noticed our anxiety, and stated, "Oh, I'm kind of relieved to see that you're nervous."

"Why is that?" I asked.

"Because now I know you feel nervous too when you're having people over."

"Of course we do!" I responded honestly.

The party came and went just fine, and as we were cleaning up, I found myself thinking about my younger friend's comments. I was a bit embarrassed in the moment that she saw us when we were stressed out, but afterward, I was glad she had. I didn't want her thinking we have it all together all the time.

Too often we can try to present a perfect appearance to others, giving the illusion that we have it all together or that nothing ever causes us stress or anxiety. When we do that, we don't show people who we really are and can create the expectation that they have to be perfect as well.

But this is not what God would have us do. As we interact with our friends, we can choose to wear a humble spirit, remembering that God opposes those who are proud but gives grace to the humble. I would not have done my young friend any favors if I hadn't humbly let her see our weaknesses. She would most likely have left feeling discouraged by her own shortcomings. Instead, she was encouraged by us to pursue the things God was asking her to do, even when she was afraid, because she knew that others were doing the same thing. Our showing her our own insecurities gave her boldness to step out in faith.

— Kendra

— Today's Act of Friendship —

When you feel the pressure to put up a facade with a
friend, choose to be honest with them instead.

Assuming Good Intent

*Stay alert! Watch out for your great enemy, the devil. He prowls
around like a roaring lion, looking for someone to devour.*

1 PETER 5:8

It was the end of an exhaustingly long week, and Aaron and I were taking a few minutes to catch up over a warm cup of tea after the kids had gone to bed. As I started bellyaching about a small, ongoing irritation I had with a friend, his words brought me up short: "Assume good intent."

Well, *humph*. A flood of irritation swept through my body at his gentle admonition, but even as I scowled at him, I knew he was right. I mentally replayed the irritating situation— assuming good intentions by my friend in the scenario—and found my hurt fading away. My friend wasn't being purposefully hurtful, and when I gave her the benefit of the doubt, I could see the situation through the lens of love and friendship instead of offense and hurt.

Satan wants to destroy our closest relationships: our marriages, our friendships, our family relationships. He wants us pitted against one another so that he can pick us off, one by one, destroying us with lies underpinning layers of hurt and offense. If we walk through life angry and hurt, we'll not reach the fullness of the plans God has for us. And that's his goal: if he cannot convince us to deny the existence of God, he tries to render us useless and impotent, unable to be used by God to further his Kingdom purposes. Carrying hurt and offense and unforgiveness will tie us up in knots, keeping us from God's best for ourselves and those around us.

One of the best ways to protect our relationships from Satan's wily attacks is to practice assuming the best of those we love—always working from the assumption that they love us, that they have our best interests at heart, that they are unintentional when they hurt us. Don't let Satan tear apart your relationships; choose to strengthen them with a loving response.

– Julie

– Today's Act of Friendship –

When you are feeling irritated or angry, hurt or offended
by a loved one, pause to reconsider the situation,
attributing good intentions to the other party. Then pray
over whether and how to speak with them about it.

A Compassionate Heart

"When you put on a luncheon or a banquet," [Jesus] said, "don't invite your friends, brothers, relatives, and rich neighbors. For they will invite you back, and that will be your only reward. Instead, invite the poor, the crippled, the lame, and the blind. Then at the resurrection of the righteous, God will reward you for inviting those who could not repay you."

LUKE 14:12-14

My dear friend Susie loves to befriend those who are homeless in our community. She doesn't just serve them once and then leave, but truly builds relationships with them over time. She gives rides and offers other practical assistance when she can, and she also listens to their stories, prays for them, and believes God has called her to love them well.

Some people have been critical of Susie's relationships with her new friends. They worry that she is putting herself in unsafe situations. Although she understands their concerns about her safety, she is not unwise in the way that she approaches others who, to her, are not a project. She sees each one as a whole person, valuable in God's eyes, and sees her actions as more than just ministry or service to others. She's actually doing life with people, befriending them and supporting them along the way.

When I hear Susie share about her friends in the community who are homeless, it challenges me in the way that I think about and interact with others. Susie has a very clear understanding of God's love for the homeless, and she is passionate about seeing them know and experience that love through her words and actions. It reminds me of what Jesus said in Luke, that we should not invite just our friends and family and well-off neighbors into our homes, but instead invite those whom society might look down upon. When we do, God sees our actions to care for those who have nothing to give in return, and he will reward us.

– *Kendra*

– Today's Act of Friendship –

Extend a hand of friendship toward someone in your community who is homeless by giving them something to eat, supplying a piece of needed clothing, or offering an encouraging word or smile.

Invited In

It is good when you obey the royal law as found in the
Scriptures: "Love your neighbor as yourself."
JAMES 2:8

We moved into our current home on our oldest daughter's first birthday—a neutral two-story house with a secluded backyard and a light, airy feel inside that I adored. It was winter when we moved onto the quiet cul-de-sac, but as it turned the corner toward spring, we quickly met our new neighbors.

At our previous home, we spent time with two couples but didn't take the time to get to know anyone else. Now that we had a child, we really wanted to make more of an effort to become involved with the people who lived around us.

We realized right away that we had moved into a great neighborhood. There were kids and adults of varying ages and stages of life, and they had already established traditions that they invited us to join. One couple invited us to their annual Halloween party. Another neighbor across the street organized Secret Santa and brunch for all the ladies. Our neighbors waved as I drove past, chatted with me at the mailbox, and crossed their yards to say hello as I walked by.

As the years went on, they spoke kindly to my three children, who pestered them at every turn, asking if they could play with their pets or their lawn toys. They've invited us to birthday parties, just-for-fun parties, and graduations. As a collective group, we've sent flowers when someone was grieving the loss of a parent and gone on a dinner cruise on Lake Minnetonka. We've watched children grow up, listened to pounding hammers as new houses went up and new families arrived, and witnessed how our neighbors embraced those new arrivals too.

Scripture often reminds us to love our neighbor as we do ourselves, and I'm grateful our neighbors did this for us. They invited us into the community they'd already established, not seeing their traditions as reasons to exclude others, but as opportunities to invite them in. Through their example, I have become much more likely to extend a hand of friendship to those around us over the years. Because of their kindness, I don't just consider those who live close to me as simply neighbors; I also consider them friends.

— Kristin

— Today's Act of Friendship —

Reach out to a neighbor and invite them to join you in
either an established tradition or a new venture, whether
it's a book club, bonfire, or neighborhood cookout.

A Shared Burden

Two people are better off than one,
for they can help each other succeed.

ECCLESIASTES 4:9

I sat around the table and listened as each woman took a turn sharing her most recent prayer request. We each nodded and wrote down a note, offering sympathetic looks and encouraging words. I was struck by the deep concerns they shared, especially those centered on parenting amid hard issues their kids were facing. I left the moms' group meeting determined to keep these women and their children in my prayers.

The next morning as I thought once again of the other moms, I realized that I could never have guessed what each mom was facing prior to her disclosing her deep pain. When I see them out around town or on social media, they look like they are completely put together. I don't mean to imply that they are somehow being fake—they are some of the sincerest women I know—but I think it's a fact of life that we can all carry burdens that others may not see or know about unless we tell them. I started thinking about how often I cross paths with friends who are struggling with a concern that I know nothing about and how often we hide our pain from others with a simple "I'm fine" when we're asked how we're doing.

The moms' group reminded me that we need to share and carry one another's burdens and heartaches. We are not meant to go through trials alone. God gave us friends so that we'd have support and encouragement, reminding us that a companion can lift us up when we are struggling. God designed us to be in friendship with others because he knew we'd need to both receive support and give it in order to be successful in life. It's not a weakness to need others; it's actually one of our greatest strengths.

— Kendra

— Today's Act of Friendship —

Reach out to a friend who you know is going through
a hard time and offer them support through a listening
ear, prayer, or just being present with them.

Forgive an Offense

Make allowance for each other's faults, and forgive anyone who offends you. Remember, the Lord forgave you, so you must forgive others.
COLOSSIANS 3:13

At least once a day, my youngest daughter tells me I'm not her friend. Although she is usually cheerful and easygoing, like most four-year-olds, she doesn't like to be told no. It usually happens after I tell her she can't have any more afternoon snacks or that it's time to stop playing with Barbies so we can leave for preschool. Although I patiently tell her that words have power and what she said was hurtful, internally, I brush it off. I know she's at a developmental stage where she wants more control in her life, and the words she speaks are one of the ways she tries to assert that control.

If I'm honest, we live in a world where it's easier than ever to decide that someone is no longer our friend. If someone shares too many political posts on their social media or sends us one too many messages about a product they're selling, we'll likely unfollow or unfriend them. In real life, we might decide it's easier to screen their calls or stop returning them, or perhaps even stop attending the same gym, group, or church. In that sense, my four-year-old is a lot more honest about her feelings than many adults.

In a world of imperfect people, conflict is unavoidable. Yet admitting we got our feelings hurt can make us feel weak, vulnerable, angry, or disappointed, and confronting someone makes us nervous. Instead of seeking reconciliation, we back away. Yet Scripture reminds us of how important it is for us to give and receive forgiveness. Though our attempts to avoid someone who hurt us may provide a temporary fix, they don't address the pain that remains under the surface.

In the case of my daughter, it helps if I acknowledge her feelings as well as my own. Talking through the pain first helps us to move on to find a resolution. When I openly offer my daughter forgiveness for the hurtful words she's spoken—asking her if she'd like a hug—she usually burrows her small head into my neck and tells me she's sorry, unprompted. The apology comes naturally once she realizes that she's hurt my feelings. As friends, let's work hard to address the hurt we feel or have caused in others in order to move on to true forgiveness and restored relationships with those around us.

— *Kristin*

— Today's Act of Friendship —

Be honest with a friend about your feelings,
then actively work on forgiving them.

Trusted Advice

The heartfelt counsel of a friend is as sweet as perfume and incense.
PROVERBS 27:9

"Carol, I need your advice," I said, pouring out my current parenting conundrum to her over the phone as I sat one early morning in the parking lot of my law firm. Carol was a mother of adult children, grandmother to children who are in their teens, and she was just the woman I needed in the midst of an ongoing power struggle with my toddler. She loved Jesus and loved me and had experienced the full parenting spectrum—something the women in my peer group lacked. And, most importantly, she was gentle and encouraging in her advice to me, never making me feel less than.

Parenting comparison is an especially insidious trap, at least for me. I want so desperately to be a good mom that I'm particularly vulnerable to self-doubt and recrimination in my parenting, silently and internally exaggerating my weaknesses while minimizing my strengths so that I cannot always see clearly. Because this is an area where I trip easily into comparison, I've learned to be exceptionally careful about whom I turn to for parenting advice. I need women who love my children, who love me, and who can accurately reflect the situation back to me when my internal lens is distorted. What I don't need is advisers who exacerbate the problem.

To whom do you turn when your internal lens is distorted? Do you confide in women who play into your distress, making themselves feel better as they make you feel worse? Do you confide in women who always rush to your side, justify your feelings and position, and affirm your distorted lens—even if you're not demanding blind loyalty?

As I learn to recognize where my weaknesses lurk, I reserve conversations about those areas for women who listen carefully, who ask clarifying questions rather than rush to advise, who never blame or shame, who always turn me back to scriptural truth and lead me to the feet of Christ. I seek out women whose wisdom leaves me feeling encouraged and strengthened, whose words—even in gentle admonishment—are life-giving and filled with the sweet perfume of hope.

— Julie

— Today's Act of Friendship —

Where do your comparison weaknesses lurk? Ask God to reveal them to you, and then to reveal which women in your life can be trusted to give you an accurate assessment when your perspective is distorted.

Don't Listen to the Lies

*The thief's purpose is to steal and kill and destroy. My
purpose is to give them a rich and satisfying life.*

JOHN 10:10

We were getting ready for a large event in our community, and I was helping to coordinate the program. The week leading up to the gathering of women was filled with last-minute details and texts to make sure everything would be ready to go. Throughout the week, a small voice was whispering in the back of my mind, saying things like, *You're not really needed there; no one would notice if you didn't help out; they've got other people more qualified.* On and on the negative thoughts continued. I brushed them aside, but the feeling of inadequacy and insecurity lingered.

On the morning of the event, we gathered together as a leadership team. As we mentioned prayer requests, I shared honestly about the thoughts that had been assailing my mind all week. The coordinator of the event listened intently and then looked me in the eye. "Those are lies meant to discourage and distract you," she stated. "You are needed and wanted here. Don't listen to those lies." Suddenly, her words affirmed what I knew to be true but had a hard time believing when I was by myself. Community made all the difference.

Our enemy, the devil, is always scheming to tear us down. One way he accomplishes his purpose is by isolating us and making us feel like we are all alone, because that is when we are most vulnerable to believing the lies he tells us. When we are in community with one another and can honestly share the things we are struggling through, our friends can offer us truth and encouragement in the midst of all we are facing—reminding us of the abundance Jesus wants to give us. Sometimes we need to get around other people to hear what is true.

— Kendra

— Today's Act of Friendship —

Reach out to a friend who seems to be struggling and remind
them of the truth of who they are and their value in Christ.

The One-Upper

If I must boast, I would rather boast about the
things that show how weak I am.

2 CORINTHIANS 11:30

She's what we like to call a one-upper. "Your garage is almost as big as mine," she told Elise one day. "We travel a lot for BMX competitions. I've been on so many airplanes!" she said a little later on. Listening to their conversations, I hear my daughter trying to find things they have in common, but eventually she gives up. There's just no topping a perpetual one-upper.

With adults, bragging is often less overt, but it still happens—especially on social media. We share about our perfect homes or fun events, tropical vacations or glamorous selfies—all in an effort to showcase our lives in the best light. Like my daughter's one-upping friend, who is generally a pleasant child, it's never meant to be malicious. But to those who are watching, it can become glaringly obvious who has the most or the best, and who doesn't.

I can rejoice in others' good fortune, yet the stories I appreciate most are from friends who balance their ups with a behind-the-scenes look at their downs as well—the friends who talk about how they've had a hard time adjusting to being a new parent or are trying to make healthy food choices or are struggling to overcome mental health challenges. On days when I feel worried or sad, that level of authenticity helps me remember I'm not alone.

It takes great courage to admit our weaknesses. But as Christians, we know that it's in the challenges of life that we can most often marvel at the faithfulness of God. Paul even reminds us to boast in our weaknesses rather than trying to mask the challenges we're facing. When I look back through old Bible studies lined up on the bookshelves in my office and see the prayer requests jotted in the margins, I am encouraged by how God was ultimately faithful even in circumstances that felt impossible.

Our willingness to admit our vulnerabilities to our friends can affirm who we truly are in a way that one-upping never will. It's when we can honestly say, "There's no way I could have done this on my own" that we demonstrate the greatness of God and his ability to use us regardless of our shortcomings. And while tropical vacations are objectively beautiful, weaknesses affirm our authenticity and inner beauty—and that will always be something to boast about.

– Kristin

– Today's Act of Friendship –

"Boast" to a friend about a weakness you possess.

Standing in the Gap

If two of you agree here on earth concerning anything you ask,
my Father in heaven will do it for you. For where two or three
gather together as my followers, I am there among them.

MATTHEW 18:19-20

"After two weeks in NICU, my son is going home today." Her voice cracked on a sob, and I clutched my phone a little tighter as my own tears started streaming down. There was still a myriad of appointments in their future, still a journey of healing to walk, but we could not help but weep with joy at the first glimpse of normality.

My friend lives two thousand miles away: too far away to hug, too far away for me to storm the hospital with takeout food and chocolate as she grapples with all that comes along with new motherhood, complicated one hundred times over by a baby hooked up to tubes and wires. As my friend slipped into motherhood the hard way—living alongside her son in the NICU for two weeks—I stood in the gap for her, weeping and sometimes shaking my fist at God, praying with anger, praying with hope, praying as I wept for healing, for provision, for rest in the midst of chaos and uncertainty.

I told my friend that I would be her advocate before the gates of heaven, praying with persistence like the widow in Luke 18. I sent some of my prayers via text so my friend could be encouraged, knowing with certainty that she and her husband were surrounded by others praying in accordance with Matthew 18. Some prayers were between just me and God.

Just as I don't need to understand why flipping a light switch makes my lights turn on, I also don't need to understand how prayer works. I trust God, and I trust what he says to be true. He tells us that gathering together in unified prayer changes outcomes, and that promise has become my practice. I pray over my friends, over their children, and over their marriages with fierceness and consistency. If I love someone, I am praying for that person—it is just a part of being in friendship with me.

– Julie

– Today's Act of Friendship –

Pray for your friends consistently, standing in the gap for them.

Trying Something New

*I am about to do something new. See, I have already begun!
Do you not see it?*
ISAIAH 43:19

"If you are free tomorrow, you could come and work out with me. It's so relaxing," a new friend texted one evening as I was coming home from an event. *Why not?* I thought as I texted her back asking for more details. When the morning came, I was excited but also filled with trepidation. I'd never been to this facility before, and I wondered what the other women would be like. I made my way to the studio and was greeted by my friend. We entered the facility and she began to show me around. As other women came in, she introduced me and started small talk among us. We worked out together (she was right, it was very relaxing!) and then afterward we visited with the other women for a few more minutes before saying our goodbyes.

As I left the studio, I was struck by how often I go about my daily routines and rarely step into a new space or activity, by how little I engage in trying new things or meeting new people. Or when I do meet new people, it's in a context where I already feel very comfortable—at moms' group, at my church, or in my neighborhood. This experience encouraged me to pursue more unfamiliar opportunities, because even though it was slightly uncomfortable, it was also fun to try something I hadn't done before.

God spoke to Israel through Isaiah to say that he was going to do something new, that in fact it was already in process—but he questioned if the people could see it. God, I believe, does not change; what he spoke in Scripture is still true today. He is always doing something new, but do we see it? Do we try new things? Do we open ourselves up to new experiences or people? Who knows the friendships that could be formed if we'd step out of our comfort zones and into unknown places.

— Kendra

— Today's Act of Friendship —

Take a friend to try something you've never done—whether it's
a new coffee shop, a new route home, or even a new activity.

Concrete, Hopes, and Dreams

Encourage each other and build each other up,
just as you are already doing.
1 THESSALONIANS 5:11

Aaron and I became friends with Jason and Christa years ago when we invited them to our house for dessert. As the evening was winding down, Aaron and Jason were in the family room while Christa and I settled into cozy chairs in my living room. Christa is the kind of woman who quickly moves past small talk, and we were soon laughing and crying as we talked about hopes, dreams, and the hard things in life.

After I hugged my official new friend at the end of the evening, Aaron and I gently shut the front door and they disappeared down the sidewalk. Moving toward the kitchen for a quick cleanup, I asked what he and Jason had been talking about for the hour or so that we had separated into different rooms.

"Concrete," Aaron replied.

I paused, certain I had misheard. "You talked about concrete?" I asked, slightly incredulous.

He suddenly looked a bit uncertain. "Umm, yeah? What did you guys talk about?"

"Umm—we cried over hopes and dreams . . ." I trailed off, now wondering which conversation was weirder for a first evening with new friends.

Both slightly confused at the wild difference between our respective conversations, we couldn't help but laugh at the difference between male and female friendships.

That memory is the perfect reminder for me that my husband tends to grow and bond with new friends in physical ways—often over a task or activity—while my relationships tend to grow deeper through coffee and conversation. I intentionally keep that difference in mind as I encourage Aaron to set aside time and space for activities with his male friends—whether that means watching a soccer match, playing a sport, or even chatting while manning the grill. My husband needs the encouragement and support found in godly fellowship as much as I do, and I actively seek to support him in this effort.

— Julie

— Today's Act of Friendship —

Find a way to support the friendships of the men in your life, taking into consideration how their relationships may look different from your own.

JUNE 20

Our Original Friend

*I no longer call you slaves, because a master doesn't
confide in his slaves. Now you are my friends, since I
have told you everything the Father told me.*

JOHN 15:15

My sister Katrina died from breast cancer when she was twenty-eight, just two days after I turned twenty-two. The sibling squabbles of our youth had developed into a deep friendship after high school, and I counted her among my closest friends.

Katrina was fun and funny, and her death left an aching chasm in my life. There were many days when I would be caught off guard by how much I missed her. I'd hear the sound of her voice on her home answering machine or drive by T.J. Maxx (her favorite store) or see someone wearing chartreuse (her favorite color) and feel grief rise up like a mighty wave to swallow me whole. It seemed incomprehensible that life could continue to go on around me without pause.

But it was in those early days of grief, when my family members and I practically lived in each other's pockets, that I began to experience the friendship of God. From a young age, he had been my Savior. Yet it was only now, in that place of quiet desperation and sorrow, that I began to recognize him as Lord. As I prayed, the truths spoken in the Word of God echoed in my heart. That he had plans for me. That he was the same yesterday, today, and forever. That he would provide a place of rest. That when I felt weak, he would give me strength. That he would give me his peace. That no power could ever separate me from his love.

They were verses I had memorized as a child. But now, as an adult, they became lifelines. In the book of John, Jesus explains that we are not slaves, but friends. This is an important transition: rather than simply expecting us to follow orders, he makes us his trusted confidants. As our original friend, Jesus wants to comfort us when we mourn and celebrate with us when we are joyful, yet he can only do so if he has been invited. Like any true relationship, friendship with Jesus is never a one-way street.

— *Kristin*

— Today's Act of Friendship —

Thank Jesus for his friendship. If you don't consider him a friend
yet, pray that he will reveal himself to you as your original friend.

Friend-Filled Vacation

Keep on loving each other as brothers and sisters.
HEBREWS 13:1

My sister-in-law April is a very hospitable person who takes every opportunity to invite others into her life and day. On her most recent family trip to a resort, only an hour from our town, she invited my family up for a day of swimming and games. While we were there, she told me that she had another mom coming up with her kids the next day for a much-needed day of fun and how they'd welcomed other families to join them as well.

We spent the afternoon swimming in the pool, eating pizza, and playing bingo, and as we made the drive home and all my kids fell asleep quickly in the backseat, I considered April's hospitality. I thought about how easy it would have been for her to just spend the time with her family and not include others, and then I thought about her reasoning—she wanted others to experience the same joy, fun, and time away from daily tasks that she and her family were enjoying. It was a reminder to me that any occasion in our lives can be an opportunity to invite others in, build closer relationships, and offer others a little happiness.

April's example reminds me of the encouragement we receive in Hebrews to show love to others as if we were brothers and sisters. We are to think about and keep on loving others in all areas of our lives, and we can include them in activities like vacations, birthdays, or even holidays—things usually reserved just for family members. When we invite others to join us, like we would brothers or sisters, we can offer them the reprieve they need. It seems like such a small thing, but it can make a world of difference to someone going through a hard time. When love is our primary goal, we will see every moment as an opportunity to love others well.

– Kendra

– Today's Act of Friendship –

Ask God to show you an area of your life where you could invite someone else to join you, treating them with the loving welcome you might show a brother or sister.

Reaching Out

Kind words are like honey—sweet to the soul and healthy for the body.
PROVERBS 16:24

Kristin's text arrived as I was curled up in my hospital bed awash in pain, waiting for scans to tell me what was wrong. The pain had come on suddenly and with an intensity I'd never encountered, and I was secretly scared about what the doctor might find. I reread the prayer Kristin sent me as my tears almost blurred out the question at the end of her message: "How can I help?"

Those four simple words felt so important in my moment of uncertainty and fear. I was putting on a brave face for friends and family, and her question reminded me that I'm loved, that I'm seen—even while waiting by myself after sending Aaron home with a firm plea to keep the kids distracted and calm. She also let me know she was willing to change her plans if there was something she could do to help me out.

I was released from the hospital several hours later with a diagnosis of kidney stones, some medicine, and the assurance that everything would be fine, but Kristin's simple prayer and offer of help stayed with me. While there wasn't anything she could do to help me in the moment, her genuine offer bolstered my spirits and pointed my thoughts back to Jesus as I reread the prayer she prayed over me. My body may have needed the medicine and the doctor's care, but my spirit needed Kristin's kind words to lift me up.

It's hard to watch friends struggle while we wonder how to help and whether there is anything we could do that would make a difference. Proverbs reminds us that kind words are good for us—body and soul. Offering prayer and encouraging words is always a great first step, but simply asking the question "How can I help?"—like Kristin did—is another wonderful way to respond.

— Julie

— Today's Act of Friendship —

Try adopting Kristin's "How can I help?" response
with a friend facing a hard week.

Practical Friendships

When God's people are in need, be ready to help them.
Always be eager to practice hospitality.
ROMANS 12:13

Maybe it's because I'm a parent and know how much work it is to put dinner on the table every night, or maybe it's because I don't actually love cooking, but I adore practical friends. You know what I mean—the friends who hear that you're sick or struggling in some way, and immediately offer to drop off a meal for your family or run an errand for you? Those kinds of friends.

I always appreciate it when people offer their thoughts and prayers or tell me to let them know if I need anything, but the practical friends who skip the asking and move straight to the doing are the ones to whom I'm eternally grateful.

Recently, my husband ruptured his Achilles and had to have surgery to repair it. A friend messaged me to say that she would be praying for us and then followed up her prayer with action. *"What's a good day for me to drop off a meal this week?"* she asked. Although I have a hard time asking for help, I felt so grateful. Being tasked with all the errands, housework, and child-rearing—in addition to a couple of looming work deadlines—had left me feeling stressed out and at my wits' end. My friend's practical action helped ease the pressure and let me know that I wasn't alone.

Scripture reminds us to be ready and willing to jump in and help a friend. Those words aren't a suggestion; they are a command. As Christians, we are meant to be the hands and feet of Jesus in this world. Helping those in need—be they strangers or friends—is ultimately a reflection of the love and care Jesus showed to us. May we always choose to be people who don't just hear the word—or halfheartedly offer to help—but find actual, tangible ways to reach those in need.

– Kristin

– Today's Act of Friendship –

Do something tangible (make a meal, drop off coffee,
or run an errand) for a friend who is struggling.

Up Close and Personal

*This is my commandment: Love each other
in the same way I have loved you.*

JOHN 15:12

My friend Christa and I were catching up after months of busy lives, holidays, and travel, and her face glowed as she talked about her family's recent trip to Haiti. Stories tumbled out about the little girl their family was sponsoring at a small school, about how curious children swarmed the guys as they completed basic construction projects. She talked of the school administrator who welcomed visitors with the kind of hospitality that we Americans rarely encounter in our own culture.

As she took a deep breath, my friend's eyes suddenly welled up. She asked if I had heard about the civil unrest sweeping that tiny country. Tears fell down her cheeks as she shared about recent events, about flaming tire barricades on roads that blocked supplies, about families running low on water and food. She spoke of the people's anger and frustration toward the government—anger that was swelling toward violence and sweeping up the students, their families, and everyone associated with their school into chaos and danger.

"Julie, these people are my friends; I love them. And there is nothing I can do to help them." Her whispered words held the pain of someone who loves deeply and personally.

This is the beauty of friendship. We pray differently when our hearts are involved. When we've shared a meal, walked alongside, and entered into relationship with someone else, our prayers reflect that love. This is the kind of love Jesus loves us with—the close-up, personal love found in friendship. When we love others the way Jesus loved us, our prayers well up from the depths of our souls until they pour out of us with a desperation born from the knowledge that without God's intervention, there is no hope. We turn from lukewarm prayer wimps into unstoppable prayer warriors who will not accept no for an answer. Christa is an unstoppable prayer warrior for her friends in Haiti, and because I love Christa, I am too.

– Julie

– Today's Act of Friendship –

Consider who in your workplace, church, neighborhood, or
community God may be calling you to draw closer to, and
ask God how you might pray differently for that person.

Taking My Cue from the Golden Rule

Do to others as you would like them to do to you.
LUKE 6:31

I was sitting in my office making notes one afternoon when a recently hired social worker came in and asked if she could sit down. I obliged and asked how she was doing. She told me she was fine, but she had a question for me: How did I get along so well with everyone at work? She went on to explain that she had been talking with a seasoned coworker who told her that if she wanted to know how to navigate relationships in the workplace, she needed to talk to me because I seemed to get along with everyone.

I was a bit taken aback by her statement, although I appreciated the compliment from my older and wiser coworker. While I certainly did not engage in relationships perfectly at that workplace, I tried hard to be friendly to everyone. This meant that I was intentional not to gossip, backbite, or get sucked into any cliques, and I was quick to offer help to others when asked. I did these things, not only because I am a Christian and believe this to be a way to live out my faith, but also because I understood that I might need my coworkers one day, and I wanted their help and friendship when the time arose.

I told my coworker that I just tried to be kind, friendly, and follow the Golden Rule, and that was how I had been successful in relationships at work. She thanked me and said she was going to try to do the same.

On the surface, treating others the way we would want to be treated sounds easy enough, but imperfect people (ourselves included!) can make this command challenging to follow. It takes self-sacrifice to approach others as we would like to be approached—in the way that we love, forgive, or show compassion and help (even to people we don't particularly care for). And yet, the reward is great: healthy, blossoming relationships—even friendships—where we might not have expected them.

— Kendra

— Today's Act of Friendship —

Think of ways that you can treat others how you would like to be treated, whether with friends in the workplace, at home, or in your community.

Friends to Count On

*Reliable friends who do what they say are like cool
drinks in sweltering heat—refreshing!*

PROVERBS 25:13, MSG

My dad got a new job when I was in elementary school. As soon as he finished his training, we moved from a city of forests and hockey to one with farmland and fewer trees. The house I had lived in since birth was situated on the edge of town, but I quickly fell in love with the location of our new rental home, positioned just two blocks off of the main street.

I spent the summer riding my bike up and down the streets around our house, memorizing their names: Sibley, Marshall, Holcombe. It wasn't long before my explorations led to finding kids around the same age who lived close by. Lisa was kitty-corner from our house, Rachel was across the street, and Lauren and Erin were a block and a half away.

I missed my old friends, but these new friends made me feel less alone. As we played in the giant lilac bush in my backyard or watched movies in the coolness of a friend's basement, I stopped worrying about entering a new school and focused on getting to know the neighbor kids.

One day, we rode our bikes down to Handi Stop, a local gas station, to purchase slushy drinks. We raced back to Lauren and Erin's house and scampered up to an overheated attic, where we dared each other to endure the sweltering heat as long as we could with only our icy drinks to alleviate the burn. That lasted until their mom realized what we were doing, kindly scolded us, and made us come down to the main level.

In the same way that those brain-freeze-inducing slushies were a welcome relief from the heat, Proverbs tells us that reliable friends also bring refreshment to our souls. Even after I started school in the fall—and despite not being in class with any of the neighborhood girls—I still felt comfortable, knowing that those friends would be there after school, ready to play. As the new girl, the reliability of their friendship was a gift from God when I needed it most.

— Kristin

— Today's Act of Friendship —

Take the time to thank a friend who is reliable.

A Secret Mentor

Cheerfully share your home with those who need a meal or a place to stay.
1 PETER 4:9

"Oh, it's the UPS man, Pete!" my friend Christa exclaimed as she peeked out the window and down the long driveway. It was dinnertime, and she had a houseful of guests laughing and catching up over pizza. She flung open the door, greeted Pete as though he were an old friend, and invited him in for a slice of pizza. To my astonishment, Pete was at the end of his route, so he shucked his shoes at the door and came in for a quick slice.

That's Christa. Always welcoming, always inviting, always making room for someone else around her table, in her house, in her life. Is Christa perfect? Of course not, and she'd never claim to be. But I watch the way she invites others in, including them in her circles. I watch her because she's really good at it, and I want to emulate her in the way I live my life. I view her as a hospitality mentor, even if I never tell her so directly for fear that it would make her self-conscious.

Christa isn't the only one. There are several women in my life whom I secretly view as a mentor in one area or another. I love picking up new ways of welcoming others from the women around me because they have skill sets and experiences different from my own, and they inspire me in their creativity.

Because I want to be more hospitable, more inclusive of those standing on the edges, I draw close to women who are already skilled in these areas, who are already doing it, and learn from them. Being hospitable is a skill set that can be learned, and while I can't replicate Christa's natural giftedness in this area, I'll develop my own, and God will use my unique style of hospitality for his purposes and his glory.

— Julie

— Today's Act of Friendship —

Find some hospitality mentors and draw near
to them, looking for ideas you can use.

Neighborly Friendship

The whole law can be summed up in this one command: "Love your neighbor as yourself."

GALATIANS 5:14

Often on weekends, we invite a few of our neighbors over for dinner and games. We'll grill steaks and potatoes, while they'll bring some fancy dessert that we'll savor while we sit and play a lively game of cards. These young men are the unlikeliest of friends—they're much younger than us, single, in college, and from other countries—and yet they have become so important to our family. We have sometimes wondered if they would think we were too old to be friends with or that we wouldn't have anything in common. However, as we've gotten to know them better, they have commented on how much they like being around our family and children. They miss their own families who are not currently residing in the United States, and being with our family reminds them of home. They have come to treat my husband and me like older siblings to seek out wisdom and advice from, creating bonds between us in unexpected ways.

When it comes to friendship, it can be easy to associate only with others who are like you. Although there's certainly nothing wrong with that, we also don't want to miss the richness of community that is found with those who are different than we are, whether it be in age, race, culture, or class. We're commanded to love our neighbor as we love ourselves, and Jesus puts no boundaries or limits on who qualifies as our neighbor!

I often wonder what we would have missed if we hadn't gotten to know these young men, and it makes me sad to think how easily we might have dismissed this opportunity for friendship if we'd been guided by outward appearances. These young men are our unlikely friends, it's true, but our family has been truly blessed by their friendship.

— *Kendra*

— Today's Act of Friendship —

Begin to look for and grow friendship with someone who is different from you.

Raising Up Girls

Let everything you say be good and helpful, so that your words
will be an encouragement to those who hear them.

EPHESIANS 4:29

Watching my daughter, Lizzie, from across the room, I knew the moment she gave up hope.

We were at a friend's house, painting canvases just like the Paint Nights advertised all over town, but this event was under the loving tutelage of Terri, who happens to be one of the gentlest, wisest women I know.

As I watched Lizzie struggle with her canvas, I struggled with my role at that moment. Should I swoop in? Should I not swoop in? I had opted for a weird middle ground of periodic background hovering with little bits of help. Because I can't paint, I can't say that my help did my daughter any particular favors. And once things got messy, I didn't know how to fix them.

As my daughter quietly left the room, I trailed behind. "Let's go get Terri; she'll know how to fix this," I whispered, and we struck off in search of her. As I knew she would, Terri came through for us. She cheerily helped Lizzie restart while chatting about how wonderful painting is because you can just wipe it off and start over. The gift of a redo and encouragement from an artist was all Lizzie needed, and her next painting turned out beautifully.

My daughter is coming to an age where she needs the community of other women who love her well. She needs women who speak words of life and encouragement over her, who believe as deeply in her as I do. She needs women who will see glimpses of who she will be at age twenty, thirty, and beyond and who will call it out in her tween and teen years. When my girlfriends co-mother my girl in this way, it is a priceless gift. Watching as another woman comes alongside my daughter with encouragement and instruction brings tears of joy to my eyes and a prayer of thankfulness to my lips.

— Julie

— Today's Act of Friendship —

Watch for the tween and teen girls in your circles, considering
how you can actively encourage, cheer on, and mentor them.

Fitting In

Don't copy the behavior and customs of this world, but let God transform you into a new person by changing the way you think. Then you will learn to know God's will for you, which is good and pleasing and perfect.

ROMANS 12:2

Growing up, I often became a chameleon to fit into my surroundings. I tried playing basketball but was so timid that I never had a foul called on me during the entire season. I played the clarinet for years—and spent hours practicing, despite not really enjoying it—so that I could participate in marching band and take trips with my friends during high school summers. I was a statistician for wrestling—a sport I knew nothing about—because my boyfriend was a wrestler. I cut my hair like Rachel from *Friends*, wore Doc Martens look-alikes, and taped songs off the radio like all my friends did. Later, I wore studded bracelets and black T-shirts to punk-rock concerts because my college boyfriend liked the music.

It's not that I ever fully altered who I was—I was still the same bookish girl who loved reading, action movies, and academics—but I often found myself subtly changing my preferences to suit those around me. Though I always had one or two close girlfriends to ground me, I floated among a few friend groups and enjoyed identifying with more than one group of people.

The problem was that I would oftentimes only let people see parts of me—the parts of me that were acceptable to them. In Romans, we're told not to worry so much about fitting in with the world around us, but instead to focus on God's truths and how they influence who we are and who we're becoming. The truth is that in our ever-changing, always-striving world, the person the world tells us to be is constantly shifting. Jesus, in contrast, is unchanging—he is the same yesterday, today, and forever. Transformation can only come when we recognize our identity as beloved children of God.

When it comes to friendship, true friends admire each other, not for their changeability, but for their authenticity. Claiming our heritage as children of God and letting him transform us from the inside out is one of the best ways we can deepen our friendships.

— Kristin

— Today's Act of Friendship —

Thank a friend for their authenticity, and be honest with them in return.

July

Seeds of Peace Instead of Strife

A troublemaker plants seeds of strife; gossip separates the best of friends.
PROVERBS 16:28

A close friend of mine went through a challenging season with her oldest son. Although he was hardworking and loving, he was also rebellious at times. Like a lot of teens, he didn't like his parents' rules and couldn't wait for the day when he didn't have to listen to their instruction. This caused friction between my friend and her husband and their son, often putting a strain on their relationships.

At the same time, this young man had a good friend he spent a lot of time with. He also became good friends with the parents of his friend. Over time, he began to share with his friend's parents the things that he didn't like about his own home—their house rules and family guidelines. And these other parents, instead of being respectful of my friend and her husband, agreed with their son, siding with him that their rules were too strict and unfair.

My friend was angry, but more than that, she was hurt that another parent, when given the opportunity to speak truth and compassionately point her son back toward his family, did just the opposite—they sided with him against his family, increasing the friction that was already present and adding more strife to an already strained relationship.

Over those difficult teen years, my friend learned to rely on God and his wisdom in relating to her son, but she also determined that she never wanted to be someone who created more stress for another family. My friend vowed to always lovingly encourage and listen to her children's friends while also being an ally to their parents by being respectful of their rules and guidelines.

As I think about my friend, I'm reminded that I want to plant seeds of peace rather than strife among my children and their friends. I'd love for others to know that they are loved but also that their families will always be supported in our home and conversations. And I've been sure to let our friends who are parenting know that I will always speak well of them in our home. As a Christian, I want to be someone who plants seeds of peace, not strife.

— Kendra

— Today's Act of Friendship —

Be intentional to plant seeds of peace among your friends
and let them know you are supporting them.

Mentoring Friendships

Don't look out only for your own interests, but take an interest in others, too.
PHILIPPIANS 2:4

I fell into journalism. It wasn't a career path I had envisioned for myself. In fact, I pursued a mass communications minor for the sole purpose of making my English degree more marketable.

Despite my initial misgivings, I quickly fell in love with the industry. Coworkers like Kate, Maggie, and Aleisha welcomed me and made me feel like part of the team. I enjoyed the busyness of the newsroom, the feeling that there was always something exciting happening. I enjoyed working as a copy editor, reading the newspaper from cover to cover each night. It felt good to be part of the daily miracle of creating content that mattered to our community, packaging it to perfection, and sending it to the press by 1 a.m.

But for someone who had taken only a few measly courses in journalism and worked for the college newspaper, transitioning to a daily newspaper felt like a giant leap. As a new employee, I worried about whether my skills were lacking. Although I was familiar with the editing process, my new role also involved page design, which was foreign to me. I struggled to find my footing.

Thank goodness for mentors. I can still recall the uncomplaining patience that Ryan, my boss, displayed. I felt compelled to show him all of my pages and ask endless questions. Finally, at my first review, he kindly pointed out that I needed to trust myself more. I was doing just fine. But inside, I knew that all the skills I was learning wouldn't have been possible without Aleisha's serene poise, Kate's perfect memory, or Maggie's creative genius. My coworkers were excellent teachers, and it was through their encouragement that I gained confidence. As time went on, I considered them not just coworkers but friends.

The willingness of my coworkers to mentor me made all the difference in my ability to succeed. A true friend will recognize areas where we need to improve and spur us on to accomplish them, a characteristic that requires each of us to consider the needs of others just as often as we consider our own. As Christians and friends, may we continue to seek out mentoring friendships that serve to make both people stronger as they work together as a team.

— Kristin

— Today's Act of Friendship —

Consider taking on a mentoring role for a coworker or another friend.

A Sweet Friendship

As iron sharpens iron, so a friend sharpens a friend.
PROVERBS 27:17

Ellie, quiet and a little shy, was assigned to sit by Isaiah during lunch. Being the opposite of quiet and shy, he struck up a conversation about her pet cat that first day. The next week he invited her to join the game he and another friend, Landon, were playing, and their friendship slowly grew from there. They now sit at the same lunch table every day, work together in class, and spend recess together on the playground. At the end of the school year, their teacher posted a picture entitled "The Three Musketeers." It showed Ellie, Isaiah, and Landon sprawled together on the playground grass.

We live in a culture that automatically romanticizes friendship between young boys and girls. It happens innocently enough with cute jokes about a preschooler's "boyfriend" or "girlfriend" and continues with snarky comments anytime our youngsters mention a classmate of the opposite gender one too many times. And yet we do our children a tremendous disservice when we teach them that relationships with the opposite gender can only be romantic ones, and we do their future spouses no favors either.

Isaiah and Ellie's friendship is just that: a sweet companionship—no crushing, no romance. As their moms watch friendship flourish between these two classmates, they are careful not to tease them because they don't want to tarnish the camaraderie they've developed. Ellie is one of the smartest kids in class, is compassionate and kind, and is a steady, calm voice in Isaiah's life. Isaiah is a natural includer whose gregarious personality draws out Ellie's quieter one. They sharpen each other, drawing upon the strengths of the other as they learn what it means to be good classmates and friends.

— Julie

— Today's Act of Friendship —

Resolve not to tease or make careless comments about the
boy-girl friendships you see the children in your life developing
in preschool, elementary school, and even beyond.

Friends on Mission

*He makes the whole body fit together perfectly. As each part
does its own special work, it helps the other parts grow, so that
the whole body is healthy and growing and full of love.*

EPHESIANS 4:16

"We will be back in time to come over for the BBQ!" Julie texted one beautiful afternoon. "What can we bring, and how can we help?" she asked.

Relief flooded me, since I'd just told her earlier that day that I was feeling a bit overwhelmed. We had a party we planned for that evening, and I was wondering if we had enough space for fifty people. I quickly sent back a reply with a request for additional chairs and tables, along with gratitude that they'd be around to join us. The evening started with Julie and Aaron and a few other friends helping us set up, get food ready, and greet people as they arrived. It's a task they instinctively know to do, circling among the guests, making sure everyone feels welcome and included.

I am grateful for friends who come alongside and help us. We intentionally invite others into our home and lives alongside friends who understand that this is one way to share the love of God. Building relationships with people takes time, and our close friends are on mission with us to love those around us well. We each support one another and the relationships we're developing beyond our faith community.

We are meant to work alongside others to reach those who may be far from God. As believers, we are a part of one body, and each part has its work to do while also complementing and supporting the others. We need one another and our gifts to live with meaning and purpose—and besides, it's just more fun to do it with friends!

— Kendra

— Today's Act of Friendship —

Throw a party with close friends and invite others
you are trying to get to know better.

A Time for Interruptions

*Your love has given me much joy and comfort, my brother, for
your kindness has often refreshed the hearts of God's people.*

PHILEMON 1:7

I was mentally running through the lists of tasks I needed to accomplish that day when the doorbell rang. My slippered feet slid on the newly swept floor as I skidded over to the door to open it. Calling out a hello to my friend and her son, I swiveled to grab the item they had stopped to pick up.

But when I turned around, I saw them placing their shoes on the mat and laying aside their coats. Realizing that the brief hello I had anticipated was going to turn into a longer visit, I quickly adjusted my plans and invited them into my kitchen for a cup of coffee.

As the visit turned into one hour, then two, then three, I could feel my internal clock ticking. I had so much to do that day! I kept a smile firmly on my face, but I couldn't help but think of the hours of productivity slipping from my grasp. Yet as the day wore on, I resolved to put aside my desire to check items off my list and simply focus on my sweet friend's presence. By the time their hats and coats were collected and I closed the door behind them later that afternoon, my heart felt lighter. In seeking to make my friend feel comfortable and put her needs above my own that day, I was the one who ended up feeling refreshed.

As women juggling numerous tasks and roles, it can be hard to allow ourselves to be interruptible. Our to-do list is often so full that the thought of adding in coffee with a friend or a long phone call to catch up feels impractical at best and irresponsible at worst. Yet when we feel the Father's nudge to connect, and willingly lay aside our tasks in favor of intimate community with others, God honors our desire to follow his calendar over our own. When we do, we'll often find ourselves marveling over the joy and comfort we've received from our friends when we least expected it.

– Kristin

– Today's Act of Friendship –

When a friend or coworker stops by or calls, allow yourself
to be interruptible and connect in a deeper way.

Being a Friend to Yourself

*See how very much our Father loves us, for he calls
us his children, and that is what we are!*

1 JOHN 3:1

I realized several years ago the unkind way in which I talked to myself at times. I said things that I would never say to someone else, things like, *Why can't you just lose these last ten pounds already?!* or *You really said the wrong thing there.* I replayed conversations or actions in my head and picked apart things I could have done differently or better.

This became exhausting. My inner critic had me so tightly wound that I had a hard time enjoying my own life. I was fearful in most situations and was anxious about doing new things, concerned that I would fail or make a fool of myself. But the more I read Scripture, the more I realized that these thoughts did not originate with God. These were not things he would say to me, so why was I saying them to myself?

One day I stopped and thought about what I was saying to myself and decided: *It's time to stop being so mean to myself.* I started a list of all the things that God said about me: I am loved, made in his image, called his child, created to do good works, and on and on. Every time a negative or critical thought would come, I reminded myself of the truth found in God's Word. Over time, I began to develop a certainty about who God said I was, and my inner critic began to quiet down. I was gentler in the way that I spoke to myself.

If we are loved dearly by God, enough that he calls us his child, then we are valuable to him and therefore shouldn't belittle or put ourselves down. Learning how to be a friend to yourself and speak God's truth over yourself is often the first step in being a good friend to others.

– Kendra

– Today's Act of Friendship –

When a negative or critical thought comes to mind,
replace it with the truth of what God says about you.

Together on Mission

*The human body has many parts, but the many parts make
up one whole body. So it is with the body of Christ.*

1 CORINTHIANS 12:12

"Ack! I need two cans of black beans—anyone have black beans?!" My text message zinged off to Kendra, Samantha, and Alissa, my American friends, as I made the final preparations for a picnic in our backyard that would be attended by more than twenty international visitors. Aaron and I love to host, and we especially love to invite people originally from far-flung places into our backyard, into our home, and into our lives.

We've discovered that the simple act of sharing a traditional American meal often results in conversations about culture that leave both sides with a deeper understanding, with secret fears ebbing and being replaced by newly formed friendships. We've also learned the importance of cohosts—inviting other families who love Jesus to join us in cultural bridge building. When we allow them to help prepare food, set up tables, lead their own conversations, and share both the joy and the burden of hosting, then Aaron and I don't find ourselves trapped in the kitchen or in front of the grill for the entire event.

Asking my friends to scour their pantry for a can of black beans is just one tiny example of how my faith friends come alongside Aaron and me on the missions God has given us, just as we come alongside them on the missions God has given them. Our husbands regularly serve as the grill masters for one another's neighborhood gatherings, allowing the man of the house to spend his time with his neighbors instead of flipping burgers. We cohost baby showers together, one woman hosting and the other three or four handling the decor, the food, the devotional, and the games. We fill in the gaps for one another, becoming a team whose whole is greater than the sum of our parts. We combine our individual gifts and skills and talents in cooperation with one another, doing far more together for God's glory than we can do on our own.

— Julie

— Today's Act of Friendship —

Be a friend's cohost for her next event, offering to handle the
prep and cleanup so your friend can mingle with her guests.

Grace for Our Weaknesses

That's why I take pleasure in my weaknesses, and in the insults, hardships, persecutions, and troubles that I suffer for Christ. For when I am weak, then I am strong.

2 CORINTHIANS 12:10

Growing up, I had a classmate who cried a lot. It seemed as though every time I looked her way, her eyes were welling with unshed tears or her head was buried in her arm to stifle them. Even though I was never unkind, inwardly I vacillated between pity and embarrassment.

It wasn't because I thought she was weak; it was because her crying reminded me of something I didn't like about myself. You see, I have always been a crier too. My friends and I have a running joke that if I'm in the room, they'll never cry alone. I cry when I'm happy, sad, angry, or frustrated. I cry when I watch sappy movies or when others talk about difficulties. Tears are the release valve for my emotions. But even though I can joke about my penchant for crying, that doesn't mean I like it. Crying is messy and often makes other people uncomfortable, and I would much rather be the person who passes out Kleenex than the person who needs the tissues.

In friendship, sometimes we must extend grace to others whose weaknesses are similar to our own. Whether we struggle with tears or anger, talk incessantly or are painfully shy, all of us have qualities we perceive to be weaknesses. Yet as Christians, we are reminded that our weaknesses aren't a cause for embarrassment, they're something that can be used for the glory of God. Or, as Paul says, "When I am weak, then I am strong." When we see the qualities we struggle with reflected in others, as I did with my long-ago classmate, it must be our aim to extend grace in even greater measure. Because we know the struggle the other person experiences, we are uniquely positioned to sympathize and love the person who struggles in a similar way.

— Kristin

— Today's Act of Friendship —

Pray wholeheartedly for a friend whose weakness mirrors your own.

No Tearing Down

Don't use foul or abusive language. Let everything you
say be good and helpful, so that your words will be
an encouragement to those who hear them.
EPHESIANS 4:29

When I was a child, I had a conversation with my dad about friendship. I was telling him about a friend of mine at school who wasn't always nice to me and would sometimes tease me in front of others. My friend thought this was funny, when really it was just hurtful.

My dad listened and then told me about his good friend George. Even though he and George were very different, they had a shared understanding that they would never make fun of one another for their faults or shortcomings and that they would always be respectful of one another.

"Sometimes even adults use humor in a way that puts someone else down instead of building them up," my dad told me. "I decided when I was still young that I didn't want to be that kind of friend, because a good friend shouldn't cut you down." He shared honestly, telling me about a few times when people's supposed humor had been at his expense and it was hurtful to him. He advised me to talk to my friend about what he was doing and how it made me feel.

The wisdom my dad shared with me as a child has had a profound impact on the friendships I've developed both then and even now as an adult. I still think about that conversation and my dad's healthy view of friendship and realize his advice is just as valuable today as it was back then. When I hear people around me saying things to put others down or to compete in unhealthy ways, I recognize these aren't the things I want to define my friendships. Rather, I want everything I say to be good, helpful, and encouraging in order to build strong and lasting friendships. That is the very definition of what makes a good friend. Let's work to build one another up, not tear each other down.

— *Kendra*

— Today's Act of Friendship —

Use your words to encourage and uplift a friend.

Coming Together

Love the sojourner, therefore, for you were sojourners in the land of Egypt.
DEUTERONOMY 10:19, ESV

It was the Muslim holy month of Ramadan, and Sarah was hosting her third annual Ladies-Only Iftar—an interfaith evening for women to gather together to break the Ramadan fast, with each woman bringing food from her cultural background. I attend the iftar every year, bringing my grandmother's rhubarb dessert to share, because I believe in the importance of showing up. I leave overflowing in heart and stomach after the nonstop conversation and a culinary cornucopia of dishes passed down from other grandmothers originally rooted in Africa, the Middle East, and Asia whose daughters are now firmly rooted here.

My community has been ripped apart by religious and racial tensions as thousands of refugees have made a home in a land that has been predominantly white and culturally Christian for generations. Race, language, and cultural differences often drive a deep chasm between refugee Muslims and the locals in our community, which used to leave me bewildered about where to even begin with outreach. And yet, I knew that our Savior expects those who follow him to reject such attitudes of tension and fear, choosing to show love instead.

I began praying that God would open doors and bridges into our refugee community in ways that showed respect while also not asking me to hide or minimize my faith. Sarah's house is one of those bridging places, a space where I am invited as a Christian woman into community with others who are from vastly different places and backgrounds.

Muslim, Jewish, and Christian women gather yearly in Sarah's suburban house. We laugh as we ask one another's names yet again even as we make no promises that we'll be able to remember them next year, and we talk excitedly between mouthfuls about the cultural importance behind the amazing variety of dishes covering the table and every inch of counter space. Friendships are slowly forming in this middle place, a place where fear slides away as we rediscover the humanity of ordinary women under the labels.

God did not give us a spirit of fear, and he explicitly called us to welcome the newcomers and refugees among us. It is possible to be bridge builders without forsaking or hiding our faith, and when we pray for the opportunities, he will swing open the doors.

— Julie

— Today's Act of Friendship —

Ask God to reveal to you the newcomers in your community,
especially those from other countries. Pray for bridging opportunities,
and then prepare to respond with a yes to those invitations.

Long-Lost Friends

Every time I think of you, I give thanks to my God.
PHILIPPIANS 1:3

I opened the hotel-room door and gasped at who I saw passing in the hallway. "Kelsie!" I said. "I didn't know you'd be here!"

We were hundreds of miles from our hometown and hadn't seen each other in a decade, but I would have known her anywhere. She had the same sandy brown hair and friendly smile as always. Not wanting to be late for the wedding we were both attending, I swallowed my surprise and climbed into our car to head to the venue. As rain spattered the windshield, I marveled to my husband Tim over the presence of a friend so far from home.

Kelsie and I met in fifth grade. We lived on opposite ends of a long block dedicated to our local schools, and we spent junior-high summers taking leisurely walks around the neighborhood in the hopes of glimpsing cute neighbor boys playing basketball. We even dressed up with our friend Melissa and pretended to be members of a wedding party, lip-syncing "Wishin' and Hopin'" from the movie *My Best Friend's Wedding* in front of our classmates. It felt ironic that now, years later, we were picking up where we'd left off at an actual wedding. Her husband was a groomsman, and Tim and I had become friends of the couple after he joined the CrossFit gym they owned.

After the outdoor ceremony, we headed inside to find a table. Now a successful career woman, Kelsie had married her high school sweetheart and had a young daughter. As the evening wore on, I listened to her talk about the medical challenges they'd faced with their child and found myself wiping away tears. Those moments of sadness were offset by laughter and the joy of shared happy memories.

As friends, it can be easy to lose touch. Life gets busy, people move, or sometimes we simply drift apart. Seeing my old friend reminded me of how grateful I'd been to have her in my life growing up. As people of God, let us practice gratitude whenever we consider our friendships, old and new.

— *Kristin*

— Today's Act of Friendship —

Reach out to a friend you haven't talked to in a
while, and make up for some lost time.

A Foundation of Laughter

Most important of all, continue to show deep love for
each other, for love covers a multitude of sins.

1 PETER 4:8

Grandma Connie leaned across the dinner table, addressing my children with a conspirator's grin. "Do you think your daddy ever gave Aunt Amy a hard time during dinner?"

Giggles broke out all around as we answered in unison with an exuberant "Yes!" We'd heard the stories, told with affection and laughter, of how little-brother Aaron hassled his beloved older sister. Adult Aaron smiled wryly, acknowledging his pesky younger days.

Despite being the pesty younger brother, today Aaron often calls his sister for a quick check-in while walking the dogs, staying in touch in the midst of the busy parenting years. "Love you, bud," he says affectionately as he signs off. I do the same with my two younger brothers. We text and call regularly, gently giving one another a hard time, offering advice, or simply listening as we catch up on one another's lives in three different states.

Does this mean that we never have conflict with our siblings? No. I'm certain both Aaron and I have been irritating in a hundred different ways as adults. But our siblings love us deeply, just as we love them deeply in return, and we practice forgiveness, assuming the best of our siblings just as they assume the best about us.

I want the same sweet blessing of sibling friendship for my own children. And while there are some things Aaron and I can do to foster this, the truth is there is simply no perfect formula for raising our children to be friends as adults. Families (in most cases) are assigned, not chosen, and I have friends who are not close to their siblings for a variety of reasons.

The best advice I've received in this area as a parent is that adult-sibling friendships are built on a foundation of laughter and fun developed by playing together as children. If they have enjoyed one another's presence in childhood, loving deeply and practicing forgiveness even in the midst of disagreements and bickering, they will have the skills necessary to build a friendships as adults.

— *Julie*

— Today's Act of Friendship —

Encourage laughter, fun, and forgiveness among the young siblings in your life—helping them to build the foundation for future friendships.

Modeling Friendship

*Direct your children onto the right path, and when
they are older, they will not leave it.*
PROVERBS 22:6

"Make sure you are including Beth," my friend Sara whispered to one of her girls while a bunch of children gathered around the pool at a recent event. Sara caught my eye and smiled as she sent her daughter off to play. I observed her daughter talking with the other little girl as she invited her into the group that was playing together in the pool.

Sara is someone who includes everyone, and she is teaching her daughters to do the same. She intentionally notices someone who is new or would be left out and works hard to invite them into a group. She does it naturally, and I appreciate her tender approach to welcoming others in. She is modeling this behavior, not only for her own daughters, but for mine and our other friends as well.

I want my children to learn what it looks like to be a good friend, not just from me but from the women I am around as well. We all have strengths and traits that come more naturally to us than others, and it is good to raise our kids in community with others who model things we want our own children to learn. How much better will it be if they can learn healthy skills in friendship at a young age?

We know that we are to direct our children onto the right path, and when they are older, they will not leave it. It doesn't really matter if you are a parent or not, modeling behavior for others in friendship is something we can all do. You have strengths in friendship that others around you lack, and we need one another to encourage us in areas where we are weak. Maybe you are a good listener but aren't always quick to offer help, or maybe you are quick to offer a meal or a ride but don't always notice a new person. In whatever ways you are strong, set a good example while also noticing and learning from others.

— *Kendra*

— *Today's Act of Friendship* —

Thank a friend who has modeled friendship well for you
and tell them what you appreciate about them.

Pursuing Peace

Never pay back evil with more evil. Do things in such a way that everyone can see you are honorable. Do all that you can to live in peace with everyone.

ROMANS 12:17-18

Several years ago, an acquaintance of mine and her best friend, a male, were watching a movie together at his home when the woman's husband suddenly slammed his way through the back door, barreling into the room. The enraged husband had felt sure that he would find the two friends in a compromising position instead of at opposite ends of the living room, crunching on popcorn.

As the woman related the episode to several of us later that week, I didn't say much, but I felt sympathetic toward the husband. His uncertainty over his wife's friendship with another man was likely fueling his response toward the situation, but instead of taking his concern seriously, she seemed dismissive. Rather than responding in a way that helped defuse the situation and address his fears, she seemed to think he was being ridiculous—and told him so.

I don't mean to say that she shouldn't have been friends with someone of the opposite sex—in fact, there is a lot of value in having friends of both sexes. Whether they are coworkers, neighbors, or friends from church or the gym, friends who have varying perspectives on life can bring many benefits to our lives, regardless of whether they are men or women. But if you are married, as my friend was, it's imperative to have open communication with your spouse and establish boundaries around friendships that you can both agree to follow. That way, there are fewer opportunities for misunderstandings—especially ones that can billow out of proportion.

It's only when we are willing to openly shine a light on all of our friendships that we can live in peace with one another. My friend likely had the best of intentions in handling all of her relationships with integrity; she simply didn't think her friendship warranted oversight from anyone else. But as Christians and friends who actively seek to notice the needs of those around us, we should always strive to consider the validity of others' emotions, even if they differ from our own. Being sensitive to the needs of those around us is an essential ingredient in friendship, whether we are married or single.

— Kristin

— Today's Act of Friendship —

If you are married or dating, have a discussion with your
significant other about healthy friend boundaries.

Being Okay with Messy

Jesus stood up again and said to the woman, "Where are your accusers? Didn't even one of them condemn you?" "No, Lord," she said. And Jesus said, "Neither do I. Go and sin no more."

JOHN 8:10-11

"When I woke up this morning, I didn't anticipate having to spend most of my afternoon tucking my drunk friend into bed before dinnertime and watching her three young children who were left to fend for themselves until their dad got home," my friend Carrie stated sorrowfully. "She's one of my best friends, and today I found out she's a closet alcoholic."

I offered prayers for Carrie and her dear friend while also sitting with the unspoken and unanswered questions: What do we do when things get hard? When we find out about our friends' struggles, how do we respond?

I found an answer as Carrie continued: "Alcoholism is messy. Secrets in friendships are hard. But I love her. I love her kids. These are the moments Christ fills the gaps of friendship. During the shock and disbelief that a friend could do 'something like that,' there is the whisper of Christ telling me how to love her, how to still call her my friend, how to lean in." Carrie is not hopeless. She is trusting that Jesus will lead her in the ways to lovingly help her friend through this time.

As I sat thinking about Carrie's words, I was reminded of the time the woman caught in adultery was brought to Jesus. The people asked him what should be done with her after her obvious sin. They expected Jesus to condemn her, and yet he didn't. He protected her, and when her accusers had left, he told her he didn't condemn her either, that she was free to go and sin no more.

Such wisdom and goodness from our Savior. In this life we're certain to rub up against one another's imperfections and even sins when living in true community. How should we respond in those times? With shock and disgust? Or with compassion and love? Although boundaries are sometimes necessary in relationships, we cannot let our desire to remain comfortable or safe keep us from loving others well in the middle of their mess.

— *Kendra*

— Today's Act of Friendship —

If you have a messy friendship, choose to offer that person love and support during this time.

Peanut the Poodle

This is real love—not that we loved God, but that he loved us
and sent his Son as a sacrifice to take away our sins.

1 JOHN 4:10

Peanut is a scruffy little brown dog, a doggie senior citizen who is blind and going deaf, but who hasn't let either of those facts stop him from happily roaming our house seeking snuggles and warm places to nap.

Peanut's favorite human is my daughter, and his snuggly presence has been a constant in Lizzie's life since just before kindergarten. It is into his furry ears that she has poured out her heartaches and dreams, yearnings and jubilation, and worries and successes as she has navigated her entire elementary school career. And it is on her bed that he sleeps every night, hogging most of her pillow.

Theirs is a friendship that runs deep, transcending species and language. On hard days, his wholehearted, unconditional doggie love has comforted and soothed her, sometimes in ways that even the unconditional love of Mom and Dad—who are human and therefore imperfect—has not been able to. There is something about the always-happy-to-see-you, I'll-lick-you-when-you-are-sad-no-matter-what presence Peanut provides for Lizzie that gives me the tiniest glimpse of God's agape love that says, "I love you, no matter what."

I sometimes wonder if pet-human friendships are a better reflection of God's unconditional love for us than our own human relationships are. Peanut's love is not complicated with expectations, and it is unhindered by the baggage we tend to drag into human marriages and friendships. Peanut loves Lizzie. There is no comma, no qualifier added to that sentence.

God's love for us is the same, increased a million multitudes of times. Unconditional. Unwavering. Unstoppable. And, frankly, rather unfathomable given our fickle hearts and wayward behavior. As I asked God what that crazy kind of love looks like one quiet afternoon, my mind's eye saw Peanut and Lizzie. While that might sound crazy to those who don't own pets, it spoke to my heart in a powerful way. And now I'm reminded of God's love for me as I watch Peanut seek out Lizzie.

— Julie

— Today's Act of Friendship —

Ask God to reveal tiny glimpses of his agape love for you in
your daily life, so that you would have a constant reminder
of his unwavering, unstoppable, unfathomable love.

Pioneer Girls

Timely advice is lovely, like golden apples in a silver basket.
PROVERBS 25:11

As a child, I was always part of the church kids' program. It didn't hurt that sparkly jewels placed on a treasure chest were the reward we obtained for memorizing Bible verses—their shining hues of amethyst and emerald were an incentive for me to work hard to remember my verses.

When we moved to a new town just before I entered fourth grade, my family joined a new church, and I attended a new kids' program. Pioneer Girls was steadfastly led by a gentle, loving woman named Ann, who was a local teacher and a family friend. Each week I would show up on Wednesday nights for activities and songs and crafts, as well as the once-a-year highlight of a Friday night sleepover at the church. I loved it.

As I continued to climb grade levels, my leaders changed. But the person in charge was always a mother or grandmother willing to pour her life into the young girls who attended each week.

Years later, when I returned for an event at the church, I had a conversation with an older woman named Shirley who had been one of my leaders during those tender years. She recalled a memory of me, one I'd forgotten, and commented fondly about my shy nature and childhood mannerisms. As we talked about who I was then and who I was now, I could hear the pride in her voice. At that moment, I felt profoundly grateful for just how much she and all the other women of the church had poured into me, how much they had cheered me on. Now, after many years' absence, they celebrated the woman I'd become.

The mentoring friendships of the older women in my church—the hours they spent leading discussions with my grade-school friends and me, the Sunday mornings they spent interacting with me through junior high, the conversations we had that affirmed me through high school—all of those spoke life and wisdom into my heart. The care these women showed me reflected the love of Jesus. As women and as friends, may we always be open to pouring into those following behind us.

— *Kristin*

— Today's Act of Friendship —

Go out of your way to celebrate the success
of a friend you've mentored.

The Messy Middle

*God chose things despised by the world, things counted as nothing at all,
and used them to bring to nothing what the world considers important.*

1 CORINTHIANS 1:28

"I've been creeping on you these last two years," she said, before quickly adding, "in the very best way, of course."

She had approached me in the local coffee shop, and I set aside my laptop so I could listen to her story—one of trusting God during a scary career change. She emerged from that experience, having found peace and joy and abundant life by making choices that were best for her family—without regard for how our culture defines feminine success.

It turns out she and I were on a similar journey of quitting long-term careers for a completely new thing at the same time. I had publicly shared part of my story while I was in the midst of the journey, never pretending that I had it figured out, or that God had snapped his fingers and moved me from point A to Z with no struggle on my end. Through hearing my story, she found encouragement in her own journey. We spent several minutes comparing notes and acknowledging the immense goodness of God until her friend arrived and we parted ways.

Vulnerability. I hate that word. I hate being asked to allow others to see my imperfections and my struggles. But I've watched God move mightily through the hardest parts of my story so many times that I no longer fight it. I've learned that we are all sick to death of pretending that nothing is ever hard or wrong or broken, and that others find encouragement when they realize they are not the only ones secretly struggling.

There is a careful balance to be struck. While I would caution against broadcasting every weakness to the whole world (the Scripture about not casting your pearls before swine comes to mind), we have to be willing to share some of our hard stuff when the Holy Spirit nudges. After all, God uses us when we are weak and small to bring himself glory. I find the messy parts of my story are encouraging to other women in their own messy middles, and we strengthen our faith, our friendships, and our community when we share these things.

— Julie

— Today's Act of Friendship —

Ask the Holy Spirit to show you what messy middle he wants
you to share with someone who is struggling. Come alongside
her in support and community and faithful encouragement.

Hidden Opportunities

The LORD said to Samuel, "Don't judge by his appearance or height, for I have rejected him. The LORD doesn't see things the way you see them. People judge by outward appearance, but the LORD looks at the heart."

1 SAMUEL 16:7

In the midst of a sea of glittering dresses, my friend noticed another woman across the cruise ship deck. She was admittedly beautiful, but in my friend's estimation, her blue sequined dress was a little too tight and short, the bodice a bit low-cut. Dismissing the woman as someone she would have little in common with, my friend sought other people to talk to during the cocktail hour.

She didn't think much of it until she ended up seated next to the woman for dinner. Initially hesitant, she quickly found her perceptions turned upside down. The woman was a homeschooling mom who loved Jesus and was passionate in her pursuit of him. She radiated sweetness. As the conversation continued, my friend felt ashamed. She had pegged the woman as too flashy to be a woman of substance.

As humans limited by what we can see and hear, it's second nature for us to pigeonhole others based on their appearance or speech. We assume our surface observations allow us to fully understand the content of their character. Yet it's in moments like these—even on the rolling deck of a cruise ship—where we recognize how untrue our perceptions can be. Unfortunately, our desire to neatly categorize others can result in missed opportunities to find true friends.

As people of God—and women seeking authentic friendships—let's lay down our desire to close our circles and our hearts against those who may look or act different from us. Instead, let us be openhearted and open-minded, choosing to view people the way God does. Let us intentionally view others with love and mercy as we seek to understand the true content of their character.

— Kristin

— Today's Act of Friendship —

When you are tempted to judge someone based on their appearance, give them the benefit of the doubt and choose instead to pursue a conversation.

Closer than a Sister

There are "friends" who destroy each other, but a
real friend sticks closer than a brother.

PROVERBS 18:24

Everyone needs a Jenny in their life. Supportive, steady, with a secret competitive streak over board games and daily step counts, Jenny (and her husband, Carl) have run to our rescue more times than I can count.

Since we have no family nearby, we've added Jenny's name and phone number to our children's emergency contact forms. Whether it's driving hundreds of miles to rescue my husband stranded on a Wednesday night with a blown engine, or delivering a spare key after I locked the kids and myself out of the house early on a Monday morning while Aaron was traveling, Jenny's family has shown up in some of our most desperate moments and has been a part of some of our happiest memories.

We've traveled together. We've acted as sous-chefs and grill masters during one another's parties so the hosts could focus on mingling instead of cooking. We've walked alongside one another through heartaches, serving as a listening ear and a safe place to unpack complex emotions as we decided next steps.

Jenny and Carl have been family to us in the good and the bad, through the funny and the hard, and their friendship is both precious and sacred. That does not mean that our friendship has always been easy—we fight for it at times, choosing to believe the best of each other, choosing to navigate each other's imperfect moments, understanding that we bring both strengths and weaknesses to our friendship because we are humans who sometimes miss the mark.

The friendship of someone who sticks closer than a sister is to be clung to, held sacred, and fought for, because that kind of friendship is precious and rare. It often takes years to develop, with shared moments of hilarity and sadness. It grows as you live everyday life alongside one another, over cups of coffee and game nights and backyard BBQs. It involves making time for each other and understanding that the rhythm of friendship will sometimes require you to give more to make the friendship work, just as sometimes it will require her to give more during your season of need.

– Julie

– Today's Act of Friendship –

Think of a friend who is closer than a sister. Send her a note
or text letting her know how much she means to you.

Telling Whoppers

*It is not that we think we are qualified to do anything on
our own. Our qualification comes from God.*

2 CORINTHIANS 3:5

Glasses and silverware clinked, their bell tones muffled slightly by the striped place-mats gracing the table. My husband and I were finishing up dinner with another couple, and as we served dessert, the conversation turned to our friend's work. As a church staff member, she spent a lot of time with the youth group and had a number of humorous stories about the teenagers with whom she interacted daily.

But she paused, sobering, as she reflected on one student in particular. He was generous to a fault and extremely good-natured, she said, but he had a problem: he told whoppers. Obvious, unable-to-cover-the-untruth whoppers. He would pretend that he already knew someone he'd never met before, or "talk" to distant family or friends on his phone with no one on the other end of the line. When the other students realized his untruths, they would sometimes tease or ignore him.

My friend seemed frustrated. "I wish he knew that he didn't have to pretend," she said. "He's so likable as himself."

Later on, I reflected on that conversation. I don't think I tell outright lies, at least most of the time. But how often have I conveniently left out an unflattering bit of information during a conversation, or untagged myself from a social media photo I didn't like? One time I pretended that I had eaten squab in the past so that I didn't look foolish in front of a waiter at a fancy restaurant—something my husband has teased me about mercilessly.

Many of us fall prey to the idea that, in friendship, a little more or less explanation might make us seem more palatable to others. We're worried that who we are by ourselves might not be good enough. Yet we know that, in God, we can have a holy confidence. He made us with intention and has called us to accomplish very specific tasks. He does not make mistakes. Let us resolve to live out that confidence in the friendships he has provided for us, knowing that we need not pretend to be anyone other than who we are.

— *Kristin*

— Today's Act of Friendship —

The next time you are tempted to give a half-truth
about an aspect of your character, don the holy
confidence of God and choose honesty instead.

The Brave Call

Instead, we will speak the truth in love, growing in every way more and more like Christ, who is the head of his body, the church.

EPHESIANS 4:15

Christa had gotten the call in the midst of the worst storm of her five-year marriage. She was in a season of struggling to remain faithful—a too-busy life with too little time together had whittled her relationship with her husband down to a shadow of what it had once been, creating the perfect environment for her feelings to be pulled elsewhere.

Understanding the desperate place Christa's marriage was in, a good friend took a chance and contacted Christa—she wanted to be able to understand what was happening. Christa explained to her friend what was really going on, acknowledging that she didn't like where her marriage was either.

"She told me she wanted to hear my side of the story and that she loved me. She was praying for my marriage to be restored," Christa told me on the phone as we were talking about the value of friendships in our lives. She explained that her friend offered no judgment, only support for her and her husband. Christa said it was one more confirmation from God that she needed to pursue her husband and work to restore her marriage. The woman who reached out has become an even closer friend to Christa through the situation. She spoke up when others wouldn't, and Christa now knows she can depend on her no matter what.

After I said goodbye to Christa, I thought about what a brave call that was for her friend to make. She must have been unsure about how Christa would respond, but wanted to understand and reach out in love, while also speaking truth to her in that hard place.

I've often heard it said that we are to speak the truth in love, but many times people use this as just another way to tell others what they really think, without much love to be found. Christa's friend is a wonderful counterexample of what it looks like to speak truth to someone, while also completely loving and showing compassion toward them. It's a challenge to each of us when we see things that need to be addressed in our friendships—can we approach them with a balance of love and support?

— Kendra

— Today's Act of Friendship —

Don't put off a hard conversation with a friend. It may be just the support they need, but make sure you are really speaking the truth in love.

Attack of the Louse

God has not given us a spirit of fear and timidity,
but of power, love, and self-discipline.
2 TIMOTHY 1:7

My toddler had just emerged from the bath, squeaky clean and chattering happily as I grabbed the comb, ready to give their little head a quick brush. Noticing movement, I squinted my eyes, wondering if I had just seen a strange little bug dart through thick blondish locks.

Um . . . my sleep-deprived brain worked overtime to categorize what I had just seen. Not a wood tick. Not a mosquito. Was that—my entire body froze in sudden horror at the thought—*lice*?

I sent an overwhelmed, freaking-out text to Terri—mother of five, therapist extraordinaire, hairstylist, and dear friend. She is a woman of wisdom who is rarely ruffled and has received any number of freaked-out texts from me over the years because she is just a step or two ahead of me in the parenting journey.

Within thirty minutes, she was standing on my doorstep, and her calm, almost nonchalant demeanor immediately began to calm my storm of swirling emotions. Her confirmation that my beloved toddler had lice was said with the same even-keeled emotional intensity she might have used if we were discussing where to meet for lunch or coffee. Her matter-of-fact tone soothed my frayed nerves in a situation that felt overwhelming and slightly shameful.

Terri's gentle, practical approach in my moment of parental panic is one I have tried to emulate for the newish moms (and women in general) in my own circles. She actively seeks to dispel fear, speaking truth and love over the situation. Where another mom might be tempted to showcase her parenting competence during another's obvious struggle, Terri instead uses her wisdom and experience to gently come alongside with encouragement and discernment, approaching the challenge with a spirit of power, love, and self-discipline. In a culture filled with anxiety and self-doubt, it is easy to adopt a spirit of fear, and we desperately need women who stand alongside us in God's truth.

— *Julie*

— Today's Act of Friendship —

Seek to intentionally dispel the anxieties you sense in women
around you in the workplace, in motherhood, and in your community
by speaking words of power, love, and self-control instead.

JULY 24

When Friendship Takes Action

*I have been a constant example of how you can
help those in need by working hard.*

ACTS 20:35

My sister Katrina was diagnosed with breast cancer at age twenty-three. At the time, she had a young daughter and had just started radiation therapy when she found out she was pregnant with a son. My sister adored her children and spent time with them whether or not she felt well. But over the next five years, as she continued to battle cancer, Katrina would have periods when she was healthy interspersed with times when she was very sick.

As a young mother, Katrina's cancer battle was exponentially more exhausting. Not only did she have to juggle potty training, temper tantrums, and preschool pickup but there were also times when she became so sick that she couldn't get out of bed. Although she had a wonderful group of friends who prayed with her, encouraged her, and brought meals, one friend in particular offered a very practical gift. For many months, Carol volunteered to clean Katrina's home from top to bottom, spending several hours once a week on the task.

If I'm honest, there are many days when cleaning my own home feels like a sacrifice. I hardly want to scrub my own toilets or fold my own laundry, much less do someone else's. Yet Carol's decision to be the literal hands and feet of Jesus removed some of the burdens my sister carried in a tangible way. The hard work Carol put into cleaning tubs and tile, scrubbing the kitchen floor, and vacuuming bedrooms was a gift that lasted long after she returned to her own home. Her actions are a good reminder to me that, as a friend, I can support others simply through my own hard work. God doesn't ask us to use money we don't have or talents we weren't given to help others—he asks us to utilize the things we already possess. And sometimes, all it requires is the use of our own two hands.

— Kristin

— Today's Act of Friendship —

Brainstorm a task or action you can take that would
help a friend in need. Then, follow through on it.

215

Spiritual Aunties

We are many parts of one body,
and we all belong to each other.
ROMANS 12:5

It's an unlikely friendship, seeing as how she is three, and I'm parenting children three times her age. She periodically spends an hour or two with me in the middle of the day when her mom has a meeting, and we've struck up a friendship based upon our mutual love of gardening and my dogs.

RaeRae is short for Areala, and she is a delightful young lady who has decided that I am a delightful oldish lady. I've started keeping a stash of her favorite snacks and making a few simple plans when I know she'll be around, and she arrives with a hug and laughter and the adorably mangled English of a toddler.

RaeRae also brings with her the gift of living in the moment. With my to-do list and work set aside, I get to delight in experiencing the world through her eyes. In the spring we've planted seeds, examining the remarkable differences between the various types while I stealthily help her practice her counting. We go for walks to see the "castle house" down around the corner, pausing to admire the turrets and ponder if they allow birthday parties to be held there. We "train" my dogs, meaning RaeRae hands them treats for just being dogs and loving her. And we talk about all the things a three-year-old girl wants to talk about and a few of the things a fortysomething woman wants to talk about.

Friendship transcends age, and I am delighted by my young friend's companionship and joyful enthusiasm, even as I come alongside her mom by temporarily caring for RaeRae and being a loving adult in her daughter's life. I'm a spiritual auntie, and both RaeRae and I are blessed by our relationship.

We were never meant to go it alone. We are called the body of Christ because we are knit together in a spiritual relationship, called to encourage one another in what it means to follow Jesus. We all need spiritual aunties—women who are a few years older, a bit more seasoned, who show us how to walk in Jesus' footsteps.

— Julie

— Today's Act of Friendship —

Look around to see who Jesus may be calling you to be a spiritual auntie to, whether a young bride, a new mom, or a neighbor child.

Share Your Gifts

*In his grace, God has given us different gifts for doing certain
things well. So if God has given you the ability to prophesy,
speak out with as much faith as God has given you. If your gift is
serving others, serve them well. If you are a teacher, teach well.*

ROMANS 12:6-7

I met my friend Valerie a few years ago. We were both part of a leadership team for women in our community. I knew immediately that we would be friends. She's kind, funny, and relatable, but what I love most about her is that she is not afraid to share the hard things that have happened in her life, and she has a passion for teaching others by walking alongside and sharing the challenges she's faced.

Valerie has a way of talking about difficult things while still offering hope. Her words are always rooted deeply in the Word of God. She knows in whom she believes, and she clings to him even when her own life doesn't always look like she'd planned or hoped. And because of this, she leads others well by pointing them to Jesus in their own lives and struggles. She is a compassionate teacher with a heart for women to find freedom in Christ regardless of what their lives may look like at the moment. I am so grateful for her willingness to teach. It is a gift from God and a blessing to anyone who hears.

God has given each of us gifts to use to encourage and build up one another. We don't have to be ashamed of our gifts or make them out to be less than they are. I believe that God wants us to walk in humble confidence in all that he has called us to do. In fact, Scripture tells us that whether our gifts are serving, teaching, or any other thing, we should use them well. Valerie is a wonderful example to me and to other women of someone who walks confidently in the gifting that God has given her, and it is a huge blessing to those around her. Don't be afraid to share your gifts with those in your community—they need your talents, just as you need theirs.

— *Kendra*

— Today's Act of Friendship —

Encourage a friend by telling them how much you appreciate
a gift that they share with others, and ask God to show
you what gifts he would have you share with others.

Working Together

*Let us think of ways to motivate one another to acts of love
and good works. And let us not neglect our meeting together,
as some people do, but encourage one another, especially
now that the day of his return is drawing near.*

HEBREWS 10:24-25

When I first met and married my husband, we ate a lot of chicken and white rice—not because we particularly liked the bland combination, but because it was all my husband knew how to cook. I didn't know how to cook at all—I had never boiled an egg, never made anything more complex than grilled cheese. I basically survived on Pop-Tarts and cold cereal in college.

But by the time we moved into our current home on our oldest daughter's first birthday, I had mastered a number of dishes and developed an interest in making more things in our home from scratch. Luckily, I had several new friends who were much more accomplished in cooking, baking, and making things than I was, and they were generous in sharing their knowledge. One friend gave me a SCOBY to start making my own kombucha, while a second friend offered to pass along some sourdough starter. Another friend offered up a natural cleaning solution that helped remove my child's ink stains from the wall and gave me long-lasting woolen balls that replaced our dryer sheets. Several friends and I pooled our resources and spent a fun evening making soap, bath salts, sugar scrubs, and lip balm. And, to this day, my friend Joy's granola recipe is a mainstay in our household.

Although I began with a limited skill set, my friends were eager to help and never made me feel self-conscious about my shortcomings. Instead, they simply stepped in and offered their own tips and tricks for accomplishing the tasks I had set out to do. They motivated and reminded me of how God loves it when we encourage one another. Days spent with children running amok or evenings that end around a crackling fire can help foster a solid foundation of friendship.

As the years have passed, I have had the chance to pass on some of my own granola recipes to other friends who needed a boost. I'm so thankful that encouraging, wise friends helped me when I needed it and demonstrated how I could do the same. We are always, always better together.

— *Kristin*

— *Today's Act of Friendship* —

Share your knowledge or expertise with someone else.

Open Up Your Circle

*Accept each other just as Christ has accepted
you so that God will be given glory.*
ROMANS 15:7

"Mom, can we see if Addi and her mom want to meet us there?" Jasmine asked as we were making lunches and getting ready to go to the beach.

"Of course," I responded.

Jasmine quickly dialed her friend's number to invite her along.

Inviting others along on day trips and vacations has become a common occurrence in our home. Our adopted son's older brother often comes on vacations with us, and there is always an extra family that comes to spend the day when we vacation every summer with my husband's side of the family. Keeping our circles open and looking for those we can include has become one of the greatest lessons we want our kids to learn. Just the other night, as we were planning to go out for dinner, my husband asked our children, "Who could we invite to join us?" And my five-year-old will often tell me when it's been too long since we've made a plan to visit our elderly neighbor, Al. She doesn't want us to go too long without seeing him. It's encouraging to see how quickly our children pick up on our example.

My husband and I didn't always have open circles—when we first started dating, most of our friends were in the exact same place in life that we were. It's something we've learned to do over time as we've studied the Bible more and grown deeper in our faith. Now we often ask ourselves, *Would Jesus welcome this person?* If the answer is yes, he would, then we know, so should we.

As believers, we are to accept each other just as Christ has accepted us so that God will be given glory. When we welcome others in and are willing to start new friendships, God is given glory in the way that people see our love for one another. It's a beautiful thing when we open up our circles.

– Kendra

– Today's Act of Friendship –

Think of someone in your community but outside of your immediate circles. The next time you go out for dinner, invite that person to join you.

A Seat at the Table

Since we are surrounded by such a huge crowd of witnesses to the life of faith, let us strip off every weight that slows us down, especially the sin that so easily trips us up. And let us run with endurance the race God has set before us.

HEBREWS 12:1

As we walked into the room, a sea of beautifully set tables awaited us. With black tablecloths and tulip centerpieces, they were ready for the hundred or so leaders who would be joining us for our leadership luncheon.

I wove across the room, looking for my spot at the head table as the event's emcee. Looking to put down my event notes and get settled, I glanced over and read the name card next to mine: Reserved for Lizzie Fisk.

Sisterhood Leadership is an offshoot of Bridging the Gap—a women's ministry organization that blankets the state of Minnesota, focusing on encouraging, empowering, and equipping women in leadership roles. The women involved are a living part of that great cloud of witnesses set forth in Hebrews, women who cheer one another on in the individual faith races God has given us to run.

For months, our leadership team had pondered how to start pulling our daughters into this faith community of women—women we wanted our girls to be among. I had emailed Carol, our leader extraordinaire, saying that I'd like to have Lizzie tag along to volunteer in small ways. I explained that we planned to sit together at a table off to the side, where I could still get to the stage, rather than at the traditional emcee spot at the head table. Carol's response was immediate: Lizzie would sit next to me, and I would sit at the head table.

My daughter had no idea that her seat next to me that night meant another woman was asked to sit elsewhere, but I immediately grasped the significance of that reserved seat. My daughter was being invited into our community of faithful women, allowed to watch and learn from the coveted front row instead of being placed in the back of the room where her youth and inexperience would normally relegate her. It was a visible, tangible welcoming of my daughter by my community of faith leaders, and it moved me to tears and reminded me to go and do the same for other daughters.

— *Julie*

— Today's Act of Friendship —

As you seek to notice and encourage the daughters of your friends, deliberately include them in your community.

God Is for You

Don't be afraid, for I am with you. Don't be discouraged,
for I am your God. I will strengthen you and help you.
I will hold you up with my victorious right hand.

ISAIAH 41:10

I was talking with a friend just the other day about our perceptions of God. If they are off, even just by a degree or two, over time that will very much skew what we believe about him and what we believe about how he feels about us, others, and the world at large. My friend made the point that it is so important to seek out Scriptures that tell us who God is and about his heart toward each one of us, and I wholeheartedly agreed.

If we struggle to believe that God loves us, then we need to look for Scriptures about his love. If we struggle to believe he is good, then we need to look for Scriptures that tell us he is good. If we don't know if he will protect us, stick with us, or be consistent—we can find Scriptures that will tell us the truth of who he is in all circumstances. He does not hide from us, but too often we believe lies about his character and don't try to combat them when they arise. They may seem so small, but over time, even what seem to be little lies can grow into deep caverns that create distance between us and God.

This is not at all what I believe God desires for us. I believe that God wants to be our very best friend. He wants us to turn to him when we are lonely or afraid or angry. He longs for us to know how much he loves us. Isaiah reminds us that we don't have to be discouraged, because he is with us. He will strengthen us and hold us up, and we don't have to be afraid. We can confidently know and believe that God is for us.

— *Kendra*

— Today's Act of Friendship —

Combat an untrue perception you've held about God
as your friend with the truth found in Scripture.

Gathered Together

Where two or three gather together as my followers,
I am there among them.

MATTHEW 18:20

We met on Sunday nights at the local coffee shop, arriving separately to grab strong coffee or steaming tea, settling weary bodies and souls at the scuffed wooden table. As one after another arrived, those already gathered offered welcoming smiles and hugs, asked about work and kids, and spoke quietly about the week ahead. Then, as one, we joined together to pray and spend the next hour talking about faith working in our lives.

Over the years, I've participated in countless women's groups. Ones that were held in coffee shops, homes, or the side rooms of churches. Playgroups where my children climbed high on someone else's backyard swing set and snatched muffins off picnic tables. Moms' groups where we dropped off kids with volunteer childcare workers and spent an hour chatting about a book on anger or marriage. Park groups where I spent the better part of the hour chasing toddlers and sweating profusely. Quiet, early Saturday morning Bible studies with trusted friends ringing a living room. And reflecting on each of these circumstances, every iteration, I have to marvel. There's something sacred about gathering together with other women of God. My deepest friendships, my greatest confidences, my heaviest prayer requests have often been revealed or strengthened at women's groups. Because it's in those moments—through the quietly voiced fears and anxieties and praises of those in our midst—that God reveals the state of our hearts to us and offers us the safe space to unburden them.

Friendship is fostered when we seek authentic community with one another, and gathering together corporately is one of the ways we experience this truth. When we invite our Savior into our living room, our backyard, or our local coffee shop, he is near, and his power is at work among us. Do not underestimate the power of women who gather together to seek God.

— *Kristin*

— Today's Act of Friendship —

If you aren't part of a larger community of women
or Bible study, consider joining one.

August

Join the Club

Two people are better off than one, for they can help each
other succeed. If one person falls, the other can reach out and
help. But someone who falls alone is in real trouble.
ECCLESIASTES 4:9-10

I'm part of an online group of writers that includes seasoned, published authors as well as those just getting started, some who are finishing books or still in the dreaming phase or anywhere in between. We come together on a social media platform daily to exchange information, ask and answer questions, and share encouragement freely.

It has become a safe place for me to talk about my journey, hopes, and dreams and then listen as others share theirs as well. It's a place of community built on respect and a common love of story and creativity. And although writing can appear to be an individual profession, I've realized through this group that even the most successful writers have teams of people who guide and encourage them.

My online writers' group is a constant reminder to me that we all need support. We all need people who can encourage us and our dreams. When we are stepping into a new venture, it is good to look around (whether in real life or online) and find others who are pursuing similar goals. Finding others who are walking the same path that we are, who can give and receive information and advice, will keep us going when we're discouraged or ready to quit.

This truth is affirmed throughout Scripture. We are meant to be there for one another and help each other succeed. And if one person falls, the other can reach out and help. What a beautiful picture of friendship! God designed us to support one another; we weren't meant to walk through life or pursue our dreams alone. We were meant for community, and I have found that we go a lot farther together than we do all alone.

— *Kendra*

— Today's Act of Friendship —

Find a friend or group of friends (either in person or online)
to encourage you in a dream or interest you share.

Sisters and Friends

*Love each other with genuine affection,
and take delight in honoring each other.*
ROMANS 12:10

As children, the three of us didn't always see eye to eye. My two older sisters, Katrina and Kendra, were two years apart and had a close relationship. But as the baby of the family, born four years later, I sometimes felt like an afterthought.

Kendra and I didn't really get along until she left home for college, but looking back, I'm sure the fault was mainly mine. After all, I did sometimes snoop through her closet, and I swiped her jeans countless times. Yet even with the way we occasionally sniped at one another, there were moments of sweetness. We played games and watched movies together, and there were many mornings I woke up to find her asleep on my floor after watching a scary movie with friends. And though the three of us could fight among ourselves, heaven help the outsider who spoke a bad word about us—my dad called Kendra "defender of the weak," and she lived up to the strength of character and will that designation implied.

But with the advent of adulthood, marriage, and babies—and the loss of our sister Katrina—my relationship with Kendra has gotten sweeter. We don't always agree, but we love and respect each other. I admire the way she's chosen to live her life, the things that matter to her, and the woman of God she's become. She is fierce, in all the best ways.

To love and honor one another can sometimes be a challenge, especially when navigating complex family relationships. Now that I am a mom of three daughters, my friendship with my sister has become a comfort and an encouragement to me. I pray that the ties that bind my own children together will one day deepen into the sweetness of friendship, as they have for me. One way we've already begun to cultivate that is by always refocusing on love: when my daughters fight, I ask them to pause and say three things they love about their sister. Choosing to see the best in others can lead all of us to deeper, richer friendships—with sisters, family members, or other people who fill those roles.

— *Kristin*

— Today's Act of Friendship —

Thank a sibling (or cousin, another family member, or
someone who feels like family) for their friendship.

The New Girl

*If you are kind only to your friends, how are you different
from anyone else? Even pagans do that.*
MATTHEW 5:47

As I slipped into the empty pew before the service, I sighed. Aaron and I were newlyweds, just graduated, and had moved to St. Cloud for our first "real" jobs. There had been a lot of change in a very short period of time, and knowing almost no one in the community, we were still finding our footing amid all the newness. A drummer for most of his life, Aaron had quickly been recruited for the worship team, and so here I sat alone, the new girl in the empty pew.

Until Katrina. Beautiful and poised far beyond her twentysomething age, she drew people to her like a magnet. And one Sunday, she blew into my otherwise empty pew and my life with an introduction, a twinkle in her eye, and an invitation to come sit with her, followed quickly by an invitation to join her Bible study on Tuesdays.

The rest, as they say, is history. I spent hundreds of Tuesdays with a group of fellow twentysomethings gathered around her kitchen table, wrestling with our faith, crying and celebrating over babies, marriages, school, careers, and everything else. Those formative years bonded us deeply, and we became spiritual sisters—women who loved one another fiercely and ran to one another's rescue even as life tugged our daily routines in different directions.

I could not fathom the gift God was sending me when Katrina extended her invitation, and I've taken that lesson to heart. I try to be always on the lookout for women I jokingly call My New Best Friend. Because I was once the new girl, I now strike up conversations with new girls, trying to ease the awkwardness of being alone in a new place, inviting them into groups, and intentionally including them.

God's girls are inviters—women who are kind and quick to reach out beyond our comfortable circles of established friendships, always looking to include the new girls.

– Julie

– Today's Act of Friendship –

Ask God to help you be an inviter—especially if this is not a natural part of your personality—and strike up a conversation with a new girl.

Playing Old Tapes

You will know the truth, and the truth will set you free.
JOHN 8:32

I was listening to a friend lament a hard situation she was facing. She and I had walked through many years of life together, and as she shared about her current situation, I heard some lies she'd believed long ago begin to resurface in response to what was happening now. I waited until she had a chance to finish, and then I stated, "I feel like these are old tapes being played again."

She listened as I explained that it sounded like a lot of old lies were trying to rise up to deceive and discourage her. She nodded in agreement as she considered the thoughts she'd been having. She told me she could see that it was true, and that she didn't want to go back to listening to old lies. Together we prayed for her current situation and for the truth to be evident.

Since that conversation, my friend has told me she often thinks of that phrase "playing old tapes" when she's facing new challenges in life. It helps her to identify if she is reverting back to believing lies about life and God, or if she is combating them with what she knows to be true today.

The funny thing is, I didn't even really think about what my words meant until they were already out of my mouth. Any understanding or wisdom my friend gained was from God, not me. One thing I do know: God often uses us to encourage and speak truth to one another in love. Jesus said that when we know the truth, it sets us free. Sometimes we see the truth for ourselves and sometimes we need friends to help us see it. Either way, that truth can lead to freedom in our lives.

— Kendra

— Today's Act of Friendship —

Encourage a friend who has been discouraged lately with
the truth of who God is and the hope of his promises.

Waiting Places

Wait patiently for the LORD. Be brave and courageous.
Yes, wait patiently for the LORD.

PSALM 27:14

My assistant popped into my office to tell me about Ceena, the lawyer the law firm had interviewed and hired while I was on vacation. A recent law school graduate, Ceena was passionate about human rights and would be joining in our medical malpractice legal group.

I felt my eyebrow twitch in surprise at the information—what was a human rights attorney doing practicing in central Minnesota instead of the East Coast, and why would the firm hire her to defend medical malpractice cases? It made zero sense.

Neither Ceena nor I remained at that law firm. She is now in Washington, DC, working for International Justice Mission, and I am writing books and teaching college courses, my law license on inactive status. We are both on mission for God, together in friendship but separate in the paths he has set our feet upon.

Our time spent as coworkers totaled just over eighteen months before we went down wildly different roads, and yet those eighteen months were a lesson in why waiting for God's timing is always better than jumping ahead of him and trying to do it ourselves. We both credit that relatively short period of time as a God-ordained, God-designed intersection of our individual lives. We developed a deep and abiding spiritual sisterhood before our orbits flung us apart, possibly forever.

Prior to Ceena's hire, I had been struggling. Unhappy in my legal career, I found myself waiting on God, asking him to make my next steps clear, praying that I would not act ahead of his timing in an attempt to resolve my discontent. Had I jumped ahead of God's plan, in my anxiousness to get out of the hard waiting place, I would have missed meeting Ceena and the precious gift of friendship God was preparing.

Wait patiently for God's plan to unfold; do not rush through hard places ahead of him. Be brave. Be courageous. God has something far better than what we would have dreamed for ourselves—and it just might be a new friend.

– Julie

– Today's Act of Friendship –

As you wait patiently on God, watch for who he
might be sending to intersect your path.

Common Interests

No one has ever seen God. But if we love each other, God lives in us, and his love is brought to full expression in us.

1 JOHN 4:12

Kyle and I have been married for fifteen years. Initially, we enjoyed many separate interests and hobbies. After we started having children, we realized we weren't spending as much time together as we had before kids, and we wanted to change that, so we started thinking about activities we could do together. My husband enjoyed cooking, so I would sit in the kitchen and visit with him while he cooked. We both loved being outdoors, and so we would go for walks or cross-country ski together. We were mindful to begin and continue to do things together, creating a habit of friendship and showing one another love through shared experiences, even during the busyness of family life, work, and everything else.

Incorporating this practice has made all the difference in our marriage. We wanted to be intentional with our friendship, remembering that it's not always the over-the-top romantic feelings and gestures (as portrayed in movies) that make love last. Truthfully, there's nothing all that interesting about what we do or how we do it—but this practice is the foundation that keeps our relationship strong, and that is everything to us. It has also been an example to our kids of what loving another person looks like through every season of life.

All relationships take some time and intentionality to cultivate, whether it's a marriage, family, or other close friendships. When we do this, we are following the Scripture that tells us that when we love each other, God lives in us, and his love is brought to full expression in us. This allows our children, our families, and those we come in contact with to see God's love because it's expressed through our intentional acts of loving one another.

– Kendra

– Today's Act of Friendship –

Show love and care for someone close to you by inviting them to join you in a common interest.

Sufficient in Christ

Each time he said, "My grace is all you need. My power works best in weakness." So now I am glad to boast about my weaknesses, so that the power of Christ can work through me.

2 CORINTHIANS 12:9

A close friend once dated my ex-boyfriend after he and I broke up. To be fair, she asked if it was okay beforehand, and I agreed. It wasn't her fault that I was lying about how I felt. But as time went on, that seed of unforgiveness took root and began to flourish. Our friendship, once strong, faltered. I started spending more time with other friends and didn't make as much of an effort with my old friend. And, as a result, we drifted apart.

I have a few regrets in my life, and that lost friendship is one of them. How foolish to give up a precious, trusted friend because of a temporary relationship. How stubborn to continue in my dishonesty—lying by omission—rather than owning up to the hurt I felt. I squandered a friendship that spanned years, all for a boy I had dated for a few short months.

With the wisdom of hindsight, I now understand why that season felt hurtful—my hurt was rooted in the lie that I was not good enough. It's a lie that even today I struggle to conquer. I've held on to bitterness when someone critiques my parenting skills. I've felt resentment toward those I perceive as smarter, more talented, or more beautiful. I've masked my authentic self in the hope of impressing others—all because I'm afraid I don't measure up.

Scripture teaches us that as Christians we are called to something more, something better. As beloved children of God, we can experience holy confidence in who we are and who he has called us to be. Because we know that his grace is all we need and his power is made perfect in our weaknesses, we can experience the freedom Jesus offers by letting go of the resentment, bitterness, and unforgiveness that seek to entangle us. May we instead recognize our value in Christ and have the confidence to pursue true, honest, and authentic friendships.

— Kristin

— Today's Act of Friendship —

Choose to forgive a friend for a hurt they caused, whether knowingly or unknowingly.

Seasons of Lament

For everything there is a season, a time for
every activity under heaven. . . . A time to cry and a time
to laugh. A time to grieve and a time to dance.

ECCLESIASTES 3:1, 4

Women I love, who love Jesus, have walked through impossibly hard things, through seasons of deep lament, and I've found myself being extraordinarily careful in my responses. Long ago, I stopped promising that everything was going to be okay. I stopped telling women that God wouldn't give them more than they can handle. I stopped saying all the empty, clichéd encouragements about cancer, hard-to-parent children, and bone-crushing grief and disillusionment—things we are inclined to say when faced with the discomfort of not knowing what to say and wanting to smooth over the awkward moment.

I believe wholeheartedly in the goodness of God, in his authority over everything, and in his ability to work extraordinary and ordinary miracles. But I've also watched while God has seemingly stood by in the midst of crisis, with the brilliance of his handiwork made clear only years later. And sometimes we have no answers to our questions this side of heaven, and we must simply trust.

Instead of inadequate platitudes spoken with the best of intentions, I've learned to offer the precious gift of listening. Providing a quiet presence in which someone can wrestle out loud with God and simply sitting alongside them in that hard place is therapeutic. And lingering alongside them in lament without trying to fix things often results in their finding God's peace in a hard place—which is far more useful than anything we can provide on our own.

Life is filled with times of jubilation and sorrow. We don't get to opt out of the hard stuff, and in fact, God often does his deepest, most holy work through those hard seasons. Let us be women who are good friends during the times of weeping and grief.

– Julie

– Today's Act of Friendship –

Who is in a season of lament? Invite that person into your
home for coffee and do far more listening than talking.

Don't Judge

God alone, who gave the law, is the Judge.
He alone has the power to save or to destroy. So what
right do you have to judge your neighbor?

JAMES 4:12

I worked for two years as a social worker at the Veterans Affairs hospital in my community. During that time, I was assigned to the chemical dependency and mental health treatment program. Veterans would enter treatment for approximately a month and a half and live on campus while working hard at getting their lives in order. I would come alongside as a therapist and care coordinator to listen to their experiences, help them set goals, counsel them, and encourage them to start new, healthier habits. Before I began working there, I had the unspoken assumption that the veterans coming for help were very different from me and the people closest to me. After all, I'd never dealt with a severe mental illness or addiction.

I am a bit embarrassed to admit this now, because I quickly realized that nothing could have been further from the truth. The men I met reminded me so much of those closest to me—mostly my husband and father. They had similar senses of humor and protective feelings over their loved ones. They were hardworking and kind and compassionate, wanting to do right by their families.

It didn't take long for me to realize that we were not that different, although they may have experienced things I never had. We all desired love and belonging, all wanted to find meaning in life and pursue goals and dreams. The whole experience changed my perception of people and friendship and showed me just how harmful it is to judge others without really knowing them.

God alone is the Judge. And therefore, we have no right to judge our neighbor— it's not our place. Although there may be times we need to confront a friend's unhealthy behavior, I've learned that without knowing someone's story or experiencing it personally, I can't be sure how I would respond if put in a similar situation. It's my job to love others; I'll leave the judgment to God.

– *Kendra*

– Today's Act of Friendship –

Think of someone you have been quietly judging and plan to
extend God's love and friendship toward them instead.

An Honest Mistake

Love prospers when a fault is forgiven,
but dwelling on it separates close friends.
PROVERBS 17:9

Good friends of ours had confided that they were going to be moving away, and my husband, Tim, was upset. Later that week when he encountered a mutual friend, he assumed the man also knew our friends' news and mentioned it casually in conversation.

"I'm really bummed that they're leaving the community," Tim said.

The problem was that he wasn't supposed to tell anyone. Our friends had asked us to hold their words in confidence. And, by assuming that the mutual friend knew the news as well—rather than asking our friends about it first—he unwittingly broke that confidence.

At home, having realized his mistake, Tim wrestled through the situation. As he called our friends to apologize for speaking out of turn, his remorse and regret were heartfelt. The breach of trust had been accidental, but it still had real-life consequences. My husband couldn't have foreseen how a few innocent sentences would spiral into a larger conflict that impacted our friends' livelihood and their standing in the community. Unfortunately, the damage was already done.

Our friends responded with gracious forgiveness, but the painful lesson stuck, never to be forgotten. Many times, the words friends confide to us may not have far-reaching consequences, but they still matter on a smaller scale. How well we keep those confidences is a measure of our trustworthiness. As friends, we must honor the vulnerability displayed in a friend's request for privacy. Similarly, the way my friends responded with grace to my husband's mistake is a reminder of how I always want to strive to respond when someone disappoints me. When we respond with grace, we reflect the mercy that God has shown to us as well. Earning and rebuilding trust is not an easy task, but if we remain committed to friendship, love and trust will eventually prosper.

— *Kristin*

— Today's Act of Friendship —

Analyze how adept you are at keeping others' words in
confidence, and resolve to not speak out of turn.

We're in This Together

Kind words are like honey—sweet to the soul and healthy for the body.
PROVERBS 16:24

Not long ago, I joined an online group of women entrepreneurs to gain support and knowledge for my business. What I did not know when I began was that this group of women not only shared tips and advice but also encouraged one another in their businesses on a daily basis. They are constantly reminding each other that the work they do is valuable and worth a decent wage. I smile every time I see the women in the group, who otherwise wouldn't know one another, cheer each other on, problem-solve difficult situations, and affirm one another.

It's astonishing to find such community (and not competition) among women who are all in a similar profession, but it works so well. There is an unspoken understanding that we are all in this together, even though we each work on our own. Our group has a shared camaraderie: we want everyone to be successful.

Proverbs teaches us that kind words can do our souls and bodies just as much good as healthy food—and that is what I see in my online friends. This group of women exemplifies more than just good business sense; they are modeling good friendship qualities by bringing life and health to each other through the words that they speak. Everyone in the group knows she belongs, she is valuable, and what she offers is worthwhile. In essence, we each matter.

The truth is that whether we own our own businesses or not, we all need friends who will encourage us and remind us of our worth. We all need friends who make us feel like we aren't alone. My online group has been a reminder to continually uplift and encourage other friends in my life. You can never share too many sincerely kind words with others. They really are sweet to our souls.

— Kendra

— Today's Act of Friendship —

Thank a friend who has come alongside and encouraged you in your
dreams and pursuits, or send a friend a note of encouragement.

The Gift of Baked Goods

*The generous will prosper; those who refresh
others will themselves be refreshed.*

PROVERBS 11:25

Upon finally confessing to myself that baking does not bring me joy, I gave away my springform pans (never having used them) and bought a wok. By contrast, Alissa—my friend who lives five houses down—is an amazing baker. She loves it, knows I loathe it, and so periodically sends one of her kiddos around the cul-de-sac with a plate of something deliciously homemade to share with my family.

If I were to guess, Alissa would say that those plates of sugary goodness are a small gesture, an easy thing, no big deal—but they are a big deal to me. To me, those plates are love—reminding me that I'm not alone in my parenting, that I'm not alone as a woman, that I'm noticed and cared about enough to be baked for. Alissa supplements my mothering with a skill set I don't have, showering my family with love in a way I've finally acknowledged I'm not good at. I deeply appreciate her baking because I treasure the love and caring conveyed by that deceptively simple plate of cookies.

God places individualized gifts and talents within us so we can reach the world around us. I know women who can envision what each element of a kitchen remodel will look like before a hammer has been swung, women who are organizational mavens, and women who know all the apps and tech questions to ask when raising preteens. I've benefited from their advice and insight, just as other women have benefited from my own skill sets and life experiences. That's the thing: what feels easy and relatively small to us is enormously helpful to someone else. We bless others out of our own strengths, even when they feel insignificant and unimportant, because they are valuable to someone else. We reveal the love of God by being open-eyed and openhearted to those who are weary or struggling around us, and in doing so we find ourselves refreshed.

— Julie

— Today's Act of Friendship —

Use one of your gifts or talents to unexpectedly bless a friend.

Do You Know How Much I Love You?

His unfailing love toward those who fear him is as great
as the height of the heavens above the earth.
PSALM 103:11

"Do you know how much I love you?" I asked my son Abe one night as I tucked him into bed.

"How much, Mommy?" he replied.

I had to think for a minute about my rhetorical question, not actually expecting to need to explain how much, a bit unsure about where to even begin. *How much do I love this boy?*

"Oh, buddy, I love you more than this bed, more than our house, more than even food," I said. And he laughed—not a giggle, but an all-out, throw-your-head-back belly laugh.

I smiled. "How much do you love me, honey?" I asked.

Grinning, he told me, "I love you more than my bed, my toys, and my clothes."

"Wow, that's a lot," I said.

This became our thing. He'd ask me, "Do you know how much I love you?" and I'd reply, "How much, Abe?" Then he'd list all the things he loved me more than, and I in turn would do the same.

One summer, while on vacation, my son asked me this question as we walked to our cabin from the pool. As I responded to him, I heard God speak softly to my heart: *Do you know how much I love you?*

"How much?" I whispered.

I love you more than this creation, more than you love your children, as much as my own Son.

And my thoughts stopped, just for a moment. I was in awe of just how much God loved me, just as I do my own children. Loving me enough to sacrifice his own Son. Reminding me that he is a good Father and friend to all.

God compares his unfailing love toward us to something so vast we can hardly understand it—the distance from the earth to the stars. Such great love is humbling and comforting. Even though our lives may take unexpected turns and things don't always work out the way we planned, the one thing we can always depend on is God's love.

— *Kendra*

— Today's Act of Friendship —

Make a list of all the ways God has been a faithful friend
to you, then give him thanks for his great love.

The Bad Boy

This is what you must do: Tell the truth to each other. Render
verdicts in your courts that are just and that lead to peace.

ZECHARIAH 8:16

My friend's new boyfriend seemed like a bad influence. He was wild and partied on the weekends, was crass and loudmouthed. In fact, he seemed like her complete opposite. I didn't understand why she found his bad-boy nature appealing, and I worried about the choices she might make because of his influence—so I decided to intervene.

After talking to another concerned friend, the two of us devised a strategy to create distance between my friend and her boyfriend. And it worked. But it also failed epically, because her next boyfriend—the one we advocated for as an alternative to her current boyfriend—ended up being worse in ways we couldn't have anticipated.

My friend never knew about my intervention—but I did. I knew I had broken the trust she'd placed in me, and I didn't think she would forgive me if I came clean.

Afterward, I berated myself. *Why hadn't I talked to her about it instead of being deceptive?* I wondered. After all, we had been friends for years. She trusted me, and even if she disagreed with my perception of her boyfriend, our friendship was strong enough to withstand a single hard conversation. Instead, I took the coward's way out. Not only that, my guilt over how the ugly situation had spiraled out of control made me an even worse friend. I became afraid to speak the truth in future situations after having already ruined things so thoroughly.

Perhaps the only good thing to result from the experience was the lesson I've never forgotten. The next time I was tempted to intervene in a friend's life, I thought long and hard about the honest conversation I'd need to have. And, more importantly, I prayed and asked for wisdom beforehand. Friendship requires bravery—and honesty. Speaking hard truths, being vulnerable, and admitting the mistakes we make are all part of deep, authentic friendships. Our good intentions are never a replacement for honest conversations.

— *Kristin*

— Today's Act of Friendship —

If you are putting off an honest conversation with a
friend, be brave and speak with truth and love.

Taking Time to Remember

God blesses those who mourn, for they will be comforted.
MATTHEW 5:4

"You know, one of the greatest things someone did for me was to send me a card anonymously each month for an entire year after my dad died," my friend Rachel said one day as she talked about what it was like to lose her dad. "They wanted me to know that they were still thinking of and praying for me, and that meant so much over the course of that first year."

As I thought about what Rachel said, I realized it was such a simple task and yet one that would have taken intentionality and reminders to do over the course of an entire year. My friend Rachel had no idea which one of her friends made the commitment, but she was incredibly grateful for the support the cards brought her in that first year.

She explained that you're always shown a lot of compassion at first, but then life just goes on for people. "It was nice to know someone was still praying for me well beyond when other people had stopped mentioning it," she said with a smile.

As she spoke, I thought about how nice it is to be remembered. It reminded me of a friend of mine who still sends me a message and a prayer each year on the anniversary of my sister's death. She wants me to know that she still thinks of Katrina and of my loss. Her kind words bring comfort like little else does on that day.

I find hope in the promise that God will comfort those of us who grieve, and one of the greatest ways we can show up for a friend who is grieving is to continually offer them comfort, even if it looks like everything is okay. We must understand that grief is a continual process, one that doesn't end after the funeral. Long after the prayers and condolences of most have dwindled, it is comforting to have someone remember you and your grief.

– Kendra

– Today's Act of Friendship –

Reach out to a friend who is grieving and let
them know you are praying for them.

Fostering Friendship

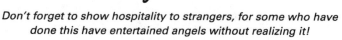

Don't forget to show hospitality to strangers, for some who have done this have entertained angels without realizing it!

HEBREWS 13:2

When Aaron and I enrolled our children in the Chinese immersion program, it was with thoughts of using Mandarin someday in the faraway future. We had no idea God was planning to bring China to us in our central Minnesotan community. But he has, and we've loved it.

One evening each August, we host a backyard picnic to welcome visiting Chinese interns, also inviting other families to come. Children perch in our climbing tree, dig in the sandbox, and dart between adults as they chase and play. Their parents chat with our new interns over burgers and brats, comparing cultural notes over the food, answering questions about the grocery store, the bus system, and other practicalities. Aaron and I mingle, making sure the interns leave with the seeds of friendship planted—though not necessarily with me.

As much as I treasure the individual friendships I've found with the interns, I'm also passionate about fostering friendships on a larger scale. Our interns need an entire community of families who invite them into their homes and into their lives; my family cannot do it all. Practically speaking, this means the more experienced families mentor other American families in connecting with our visitors. We help them set up WeChat accounts (the Chinese version of Facebook) ahead of time so we're communicating via a platform familiar to the interns. We preplan an online calendar of fun events hosted by various families, encouraging others to add additional excursions throughout the year. After the picnic, we invite everyone on a road trip to Chicago's Chinatown over a long weekend and then make sure there will be a mix of Americans and interns in the cars so they can chat on the way.

And then I ask God to do the rest. I pray for him to fan the flames of friendship, to put people with similar interests together, to knit hearts together as only he can, and to create lasting relationships even after our interns return home. Befriending people from other cultures has been so good for our family, and God tells us to do exactly that. When we show hospitality to strangers, God sends the most interesting, amazing new friends into our lives—perhaps for only a short period of time—and that is a blessing beyond measure.

– Julie

– Today's Act of Friendship –

How might you create a space for others to find friendship?

Side by Side

*Understand this, my dear brothers and sisters: You must all
be quick to listen, slow to speak, and slow to get angry.*
JAMES 1:19

My sister Kendra told me once that if you want to have an honest conversation with someone, go for a drive. There's something about sitting side by side, not having to make eye contact, that makes people open up about the challenges they're facing while the landscape scrolls past the window.

Side by side is a strategy that works with my children, too. At night, I often snuggle next to my oldest daughter in the top bunk bed in the room she shares with her sister. At nine, she has a whole host of worries that my youngest, at four years old, can't even begin to fathom. Those quiet, sacred moments at the end of the day are when she'll tell me things she would never dare say aloud in the light of day with her sisters bouncing around her. Instead, side by side is where she finds the courage to confidingly tell me who hurt her feelings, why school felt hard that day, or what someone said that she didn't understand.

Side-by-side conversation in a car provides connection yet removes the burden of eye contact. As the person focused on staying within the white lines while driving, we can be intentional to listen well, speak slowly, and pause when our friend needs a break. As the person in the passenger seat, we can find the courage to say words we couldn't imagine spilling out of our mouths face to face.

Yet that side-by-side posture isn't just the practical, physical manifestation of the way we feel comfortable communicating with those we love—it's also an indication of the way we should approach friendship. In friendship, we choose to come alongside our friends, sharing the joys and hardships of life. Side by side isn't a posture of supplication or confrontation; it's the decision to turn shoulder to shoulder with someone, united in the pursuit of common goals. As friends, let's resolve to face the ups and downs of life side by side, listening and loving well.

– *Kristin*

– *Today's Act of Friendship* –

Spend some time side by side with someone,
whether it's a friend or Jesus.

Circles of Friendship

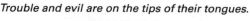

Trouble and evil are on the tips of their tongues.
PSALM 10:7

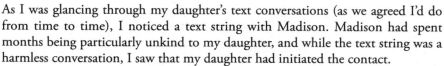

As I was glancing through my daughter's text conversations (as we agreed I'd do from time to time), I noticed a text string with Madison. Madison had spent months being particularly unkind to my daughter, and while the text string was a harmless conversation, I saw that my daughter had initiated the contact.

Gently probing into why she had reached out via text to Madison, I asked Lizzie whether she thought Madison was a safe person. As Lizzie equivocated, I pressed for a firm yes or no, forcing her to stop and think through her response before answering honestly. I explained to Lizzie that by initiating that text conversation, she gave someone who has been intentionally cruel unlimited access to her in places and spaces Madison previously could not reach.

This is not just a lesson for my daughter. I can think of several occasions on which I allowed someone unlimited access to the vulnerable parts of my life, despite knowing she did not have my best interests at heart. Those decisions resulted in unhealthy relationships and situations, causing me deep hurt.

I have learned to hold my friendships in concentric circles—with the tightest circle closest to me reserved for women whom I trust implicitly. These are the people who get to see the vulnerable parts of me, the rawest version of myself, because—even when they hurt my feelings—I know they want the very best for me.

The women I have deemed unsafe can still be in relationship with me because I believe, always, in the redemptive power of God, but their access to my most vulnerable side is limited until I see a sustained change in how they approach relationships.

We are to be discerning in whom we allow unlimited access to our lives. Listening carefully to how someone talks to and about others is one of the best ways to determine how much access they should have. The words we speak often reveal our heart's condition.

— Julie

— Today's Act of Friendship —

Evaluate your relationships, determining if there are women who might need to have limited access to the most vulnerable parts of your life.

Build One Another Up

Encourage each other and build each other up,
just as you are already doing.

1 THESSALONIANS 5:11

We'd left the gathering, and I could tell Kyle was upset. When I reached across the dash of the car for his arm and asked what was wrong, he gave me a pained expression.

"I really didn't like it when you made that offhand joke about me," he stated.

"I am so sorry," I replied. "I was only teasing. I would never have said it if I knew it would hurt your feelings. Please forgive me."

He nodded acknowledgment and gave me a little smile.

This type of misunderstanding, although not a common occurrence in our relationship, is one that we try to resolve quickly. Kyle and I, since we first started dating, have had mutual respect for one another and an understanding that we would never intentionally make fun of, belittle, or hurt the other person. We've seen too many couples use their words to cut one another down, and we determined early on that we would always use our words to build one another up. Although we don't do it perfectly, it's a promise we still hold to today. Of course, we've definitely said and done hurtful things to one another, but we always believe the other person did not do so intentionally. And when it does happen, apologies flow quickly and easily between us.

We've all seen people use sarcasm and humor to cut one another down. Or we've known people who appear to always be competing with those they're in relationships with, whether at work, in their families, or even among friends. But Scripture tells us over and over again that we are to love one another well, giving clear direction on how to do so. For example, we should use our words to encourage and strengthen others. If we do this consistently (not that we do it perfectly!), we can create and maintain deep and lasting relationships with those around us.

— *Kendra*

— Today's Act of Friendship —

Send an encouraging text to a friend, building
her up in a specific area of her life.

Seasons of Friendship

He heals the brokenhearted and bandages their wounds.

PSALM 147:3

We became good friends toward the tail end of high school, strengthened our friendship in college, and continued it into young adulthood. Yet by the time my first daughter was born and my second was on the way, we'd drifted apart. Our messages to each other—once frequent—were few and far between; her promises to visit the next time she was in the area never materialized.

Even as I felt the weight of our disconnect, I saw her posting with other mutual friends on social media: talking about their birthdays, seeing them when they were home on holiday, attending their weddings, or holding their children. When I saw those posts on my feed, I hurriedly clicked "like" and scrolled past in an effort not to feel the full weight of envy and sadness. At the same time, I reasoned with myself that I was an adult and could rise above the hurt I felt. I rationalized why time and distance had separated us. And I tried to move on, as I felt she must have moved on.

It's one thing to have a friendship end suddenly, but the slow slide back into acquaintanceship is another kind of grief. I struggled through anger, bitterness, and sadness before finally arriving at acceptance. The progression was gradual, but remembering the friend I have in Jesus helped heal my hurt. When we are in pain, he is near. With grace and mercy, he bolsters our flagging spirits and smooths the rough edges of our wounds.

It took me many years to realize that while some friends are truly lifelong relationships, many others are present only for a season. Though I still care for my friend and would love to catch up sometime, I've quit longing for the closeness we once had. I appreciate the influence she had in my life during that season, recognizing how her friendship was a gift. Her strength, independence, and fearlessness helped me to be brave. Her sense of humor rescued me in the depths of my grief over my sister's death. Her friendship was a treasure then, and it's a treasure now—even if it's just a part of the memories I hold dear.

– Kristin

– Today's Act of Friendship –

Reflect on friends who were in your life for a season, thanking God for the gift of that friendship when you needed it most.

Undoing Unease

Do to others whatever you would like them to do to you. This is the essence of all that is taught in the law and the prophets.

MATTHEW 7:12

As I visited with a new acquaintance at an event, I noticed a woman across the room who looked particularly ill at ease. Having been the secretly insecure new girl more than a time or two, I'd learned to recognize the signs in others, especially when the mingling involved slightly intimidating circumstances. I wrapped up my conversation and then approached the woman, introduced myself, and invited her to join my table during the event's dinner.

Was it awkward? A little. Small talk with strangers is not my strong suit, and there have definitely been times when my friendly overtures have been rejected. I know very few people who love talking to strangers, especially when other, safe-from-rejection options are available. But I'm practicing the art of noticing unease and being the one to intentionally dispel it.

Do you know what I have discovered as I practice this uncomfortable (at least for me) habit? Interesting people with fascinating stories. When we part ways, I almost always find myself pausing to genuinely thank God for allowing me to hear that woman's particular story or glimpse her particular journey. I usually walk away from the conversation enriched in some small way, finding a blessing of my own even as I try to bless someone else.

When we go about our lives trying to treat others how we want to be treated, we are both a blessing to others and blessed ourselves. It is so often in the pouring out of ourselves that we are filled up. I so love this truth about God, especially in a culture that touts self-care and self-love almost exclusively as an inward focus. While there are times and seasons in which pulling inward is healthy, I find God's biggest blessings tend to come through the pouring out.

– Julie

– Today's Act of Friendship –

Start actively looking for a woman on the fringes of whatever event or group or place you are in, and engage her in conversation.

Worth the Risk

A gossip goes around telling secrets, but those who
are trustworthy can keep a confidence.

PROVERBS 11:13

Just the other day, we posted on one of our social media accounts about friendship among women—what we love about it and what is challenging. We asked the women who read the post to tell us their stories of friendship over the years. Many women shared times of joy where friends were there to cheer them on, stories of encouragement and loving others well, but just as often women shared painful memories of times they'd been wounded or hurt by women in friendship, often starting in childhood or as teenagers. One woman stated that she has a hard time being vulnerable in friendship with women for fear that, if down the road they are no longer friends, the other women will share her secrets with others.

This concern, although valid, shouldn't stop us from forming deep friendships with women around us and being willing to share vulnerable parts of ourselves with others. It is true that sometimes friendships don't last for a variety of reasons—seasons of life change, someone moves away, or interests change—but we can still be women who love well and hold one another's stories in confidence.

As Christians, we should be the first to avoid gossip, to hold another's secrets in confidence, and to be dependable in our friendships. If we make it our goal to love others in this way, whether or not we remain good friends won't change the way that we treat them or talk about them, even if the friendship ends. We will keep their secrets and wish them well even if we are no longer close. As Christians, whose goal is to love others, we should do this well. Let's be women of whom no one would ever have to ask, "Is it worth the risk to be friends with her?"

— Kendra

— Today's Act of Friendship —

Determine to lovingly listen to your friends
and hold their stories in confidence.

Look for the Best

Too much talk leads to sin. Be sensible and keep your mouth shut.
PROVERBS 10:19

I worked in a women's clothing store during my college years. My manager was kind and flexible about scheduling around classes, and I've always loved clothes. There was a singular satisfaction to be felt in unboxing new shipments, pulling the slippery sheets of plastic away, and hanging the clothes to perfection. Though some days the constant folding and straightening could be monotonous, overall I enjoyed working with customers to find items that flattered their unique shape and personality.

For the most part, my coworkers were amiable, with the exception of one. She was my age, slim with blonde hair and a sharp laugh. I didn't mind chatting with her on most days—she was funny, and her quick wit always made the time pass quickly—but some days she seemed a bit more on edge. On those days, I'd watch her buzz from one coworker to the next, asking about their problems and anxieties. It wasn't because she wanted to commiserate—rather, she simply seemed to love the drama. She thrived on it. It didn't matter if it was her own or someone else's—her face would light up at the prospect of a problem to be hashed out, picked apart, and gone through with a fine-tooth comb.

If the situation was something outside of the store, it rarely resulted in anything but a gossipy conversation. But if the issue of the day involved a misunderstanding with another coworker, it inevitably led to more disunity and disgruntlement. The girl's pot-stirring amped up the situation even more, and coworkers who normally saw themselves as friends found themselves digging in on opposite sides of minor disagreements.

The girl's preoccupation with drama inevitably resulted in a second consequence— a harsher, less patient, less pleasant attitude. The words she chose to speak not only influenced others and how they viewed minor irritations, they also affected her own relationships with coworkers who might otherwise have been friends. The lesson she unwittingly taught me is one I haven't forgotten. Whether it's at work or in the community, it can be easy to get pulled into drama. Instead, let's resolve to be friends who believe—and look for—the best in others.

— *Kristin*

— *Today's Act of Friendship* —

The next time you hear a friend gossiping, choose not to participate.

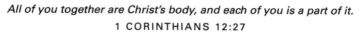

Variety in Friendships

All of you together are Christ's body, and each of you is a part of it.
1 CORINTHIANS 12:27

"I'm going to Fred's again this Friday night if you don't mind," Kyle said after dinner one week.

"Of course not," I replied. I've gotten used to his frequent Friday nights with his good friend Fred, whom he's known since childhood. We've learned over the years that it's important for each of us to cultivate friendships beyond just each other. Kyle is my best friend, but he also needs male friends who listen to and encourage him in life, and I support him in that. Kyle, in turn, supports the time I spend cultivating friendships with encouraging women. My girlfriends will say things to me and respond in ways that Kyle never would think of. It's not that one type of friendship is any better than the other; both are valuable in different ways.

Spouses are great friends, but they should not be our only friends. We all need a community of people around us. I recently heard a speaker say that we need all kinds of friends with different personalities and qualities to fill our lives—we need those who'll make us laugh, others who'll listen to us cry, someone who's adventurous, and another who challenges us. And when we have this, it creates a beautiful network where everyone supports each other with their strengths and giftings.

Have you tried to get all that you need from only one relationship? No one person is meant to fill our every need. I love the picture painted in Scripture of Christ's body being made up of all of us collectively together. No one operates alone—we need the unity found in all the unique ways that we were made to come together to live out our faith. Community with others through friendship is one of the greatest ways we show the world we are followers of Jesus and a part of his body.

— Kendra

— Today's Act of Friendship —

Support your spouse or close friends by encouraging them to
continue to develop close friendships beyond your own.

A Burden Lightened

Share each other's burdens, and in this way obey the law of Christ.
GALATIANS 6:2

I felt a terrifying lurch as the car began to fishtail on the rural dirt road, loose gravel pinging off the doors. Spinning once, twice, then again, it finally slammed to a halt on its side in the ditch. Hanging from the lap belt that crossed my hips, I knew from the blinding pain in my spine that something was very wrong.

Two ambulance rides, one spine surgery, and seven days in the hospital later, I was finally released—the two vertebrae I'd broken in the accident held together with metal and a bone fusion, a back brace encasing my chest and the upper part of my hips. My body was healing, but the fun summer I had envisioned was irrevocably altered. I couldn't be part of the marching band or take the weeklong band trip with my friends. Cheerleading wasn't possible, either. I couldn't even drive. To a seventeen-year-old, that felt like the kiss of death.

Thank goodness for friends. Several of them visited me at the hospital and my home to cheer me up, but my friend Lynn was a lifesaver. On hot days when she wasn't working or had finished her shift, she'd pick me up and drive us to Manuella Lake. Swimming, my body weightless in the blue depths, was one of the only forms of exercise I could do—and one of the only times I felt like a normal teenager. The sun, waves, and wind went a long way toward restoring my spirits.

Then and now, I'm grateful that Lynn went out of her way to accommodate my altered circumstances. Just as the weightlessness of the water diminished the burden of my body on my injured back, the weightlessness echoed in my heart. I felt happy and optimistic, my spirits brighter. When we share one another's burdens, we lessen the load. As the hands and feet of Jesus in this world, we can encourage our friends through actions that reflect his love and care.

— *Kristin*

— Today's Act of Friendship —

Think of a friend who is bearing a burden—whether emotional, physical, or circumstantial—and find a way to lighten their load.

The Love Found in Mentorship

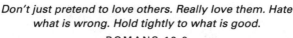

*Don't just pretend to love others. Really love them. Hate
what is wrong. Hold tightly to what is good.*

ROMANS 12:9

In the hypercompetitive world of parenting one-upmanship, my friend Mardi is a breath of fresh air. Her daughter is a confident, accomplished young woman a few years ahead of my Lizzie, and I find myself patterning my own parenting after Mardi's.

Mardi is a wealth of information and encouragement, letting me know about hidden land mines in the years ahead of me, telling me honestly about what worked or didn't, and giving me a glimpse into the good and the hard parts of her own parenting. I treasure my friendship with Mardi apart from our conversations around parenting, but because my values align with hers, and because our daughters share similar personalities, I especially appreciate her willingness to share what she has learned in that realm. And, in turn, I've been able to share honestly and vulnerably about my parenting journey as my children enter middle school, asking questions and seeking her advice as I strive to strike the right balance.

The gift of mentoring is invaluable. Taking the time and energy to share wisdom, so that the woman coming along a step behind you might avoid even one mistake you made, is the very definition of generosity—it is allowing others to learn from the prices you have already paid, without requiring a price of their own. It is loving others enough to spare them heartache and regret rather than secretly hope they get caught in the same traps you either got caught in or narrowly avoided.

It's easy to say we love others, but if our actions don't match our words, aren't we just pretending? Love requires action, and guiding someone else through a new experience, through a hard season, through the application of new knowledge helps them grasp what is good while avoiding choices that might harm them.

Mentoring can focus on anything: a career, parenthood, marriage, a hobby, a skill set. It can span any age: someone younger can mentor someone older. I've found that co-mentoring can be an especially sweet arrangement—with each person bringing their own strengths to the relationship and both walking away stronger for the shared knowledge.

– Julie

– Today's Act of Friendship –

Consider who you could mentor and who
might be willing to mentor you.

Relationship Restored

I pray that God, the source of hope, will fill you completely with joy and peace because you trust in him. Then you will overflow with confident hope through the power of the Holy Spirit.

ROMANS 15:13

I've joked that when Tim and I "grow up," we want to be like my brother-in-law Phil and his wife, Marlene. As retired engineers, they own a consulting business and tackle projects as they have the time and inclination. Their hard work is interspersed with lengthy trips abroad immersed in countries like India, Japan, and Turkey.

As someone who loves to travel, I'm inspired by their adventures, but I'm even more impressed by their heart for others. As consummate hosts, they have welcomed us—and our friends—into their home on numerous occasions. They take a genuine interest in our lives, love our children, encourage us in our parenting, and are just plain fun to be around.

To me, the sweetest part is that it's a relationship restored. Back in 2006 when my husband and I met, he and his brother rarely spoke. The two of them are twenty-three years apart in age and didn't grow up in the same household, never developing a strong connection. During my husband's childhood and young adulthood, Phil and Marlene were busy with their own children and careers, and their interactions with Tim were infrequent. It wasn't really a surprise when they decided not to attend our wedding, but my husband was still a little crushed. Resolving to make a real effort to get to know his brother, he began to forge a connection, beginning with our first trip out to California to visit them in 2008.

Over the past decade, the relationship has strengthened. Tim and Phil are brothers but also friends, both possessing the same goofy sense of humor. Their relationship is a reminder to me that we serve a God of hope—one who can heal and restore relationships. When we trust in his timing, that God-breathed hope can provide us with the courage to reconnect. Though time and distance may fray our friendships, unless the connection is harmful or unsafe, there is always the hope of restoration.

— *Kristin*

— Today's Act of Friendship —

Think of a friendship or relationship that needs restoration, then take one step toward mending the relationship.

Lean In

*You should clothe yourselves instead with the beauty
that comes from within, the unfading beauty of a gentle
and quiet spirit, which is so precious to God.*

1 PETER 3:4

Karen's small group gathers weekly with their pastor to discuss a wide range of faith topics. She loves this group—made up mostly of fellow retirees—and the thoughtful, carefully considered conversations that take place among people who have lived a lot of life and who have had time to let their thoughts marinate before they speak them aloud.

Of particular delight is Millie, an older woman with Parkinson's who, because of her disease, can speak no louder than a whisper. Millie is quiet but deeply contemplative, and when she chooses to speak, everyone in their group leans in close to hear what she might say.

I love that image of collectively leaning in, of drawing close to listen to whispered words of wisdom—words many would rush past on the way to hear someone whose exterior dazzles with youth, beauty, wealth, or power. How often do we choose glamour over wisdom, brash over gentle, boisterous over quiet? Our culture certainly gravitates toward the loudest among us and tends to drag us in that direction by default.

Scripture teaches us that true beauty is inward, that a gentle spirit holds more lasting beauty than the physical characteristics that disappear with age. Some of my dearest friends are quieter and gentler than me. They bring a depth and contemplation into my life that other friends tend to lack by nature of their louder personalities. I find myself seeking out their advice, wanting to hear from someone who views the world through a more introspective lens. There is something inviting and spiritually refreshing about gentleness, and I find myself both drawn to it and trying to emulate it more often in my own life. It is when we intentionally speak less, so that we can focus on listening, that we find wisdom.

– Julie

– Today's Act of Friendship –

Look for a quieter, introspective woman in your
circles and invite her out for coffee.

A Place to Feel Accepted

Worry weighs a person down; an encouraging word cheers a person up.
PROVERBS 12:25

I was overwhelmed. As a new mother of two children, what I thought would just be double the work suddenly felt more like quadruple, plus ten. Between hormonal changes, middle-of-the-night feedings for a fussy newborn, and chasing around a thirteen-month-old, I was beyond tired and feeling crushed by the burden of motherhood.

My sister-in-law April observed my distress and sent me an encouraging message about a moms' group that she was a part of. She wondered if I'd like to join the group that would be starting again that fall. She eased my fears as she shared about the other moms and the topics we'd talk about throughout the year. Mostly, she stated, it was a place for women to come together and feel like they weren't alone. A place where they could hear from moms who were going through similar struggles.

On the morning of the first meeting, I gathered my children as quickly as I could to drive the short distance to the church the moms' group met at. I parked and laboriously slung the baby carrier and diaper bag on one arm, while also attempting to hold the hand of my very small toddler with the other. April met me at the door with a huge smile on her face, ready to help me to the childcare rooms, settling my kids in and showing me to the meeting room.

Years later, I do not recall that first meeting around the table at all; I only remember April's smiling face and open arms. She exuded a calming warmth and extended friendship to me when I was most vulnerable, and I am forever thankful that she did.

Worry can weigh a person down, but an encouraging word from a friend can cheer a person up. We all go through seasons of worry where we need friends who can come alongside us and encourage us, and other times where our words can cheer someone else up. All it takes is a little intentionality to notice someone who is struggling and then offer them some encouragement.

— *Kendra*

— Today's Act of Friendship —

Think of a friend who is weighed down with worry,
and use your words to help cheer them up.

The Power of Words

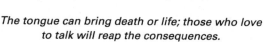

*The tongue can bring death or life; those who love
to talk will reap the consequences.*
PROVERBS 18:21

My friend Carisa owns a health and wellness business. She's enthusiastic and encouraging, and I've yet to hear her say an unkind or gossipy word about anyone. Along with speaking at corporate events, hosting online classes, and being a personal trainer, she is featured regularly on a local television station's morning news show. Her innate charisma makes her the kind of person you instinctively want to know, and her upbeat nature helps spur her success.

Yet because of the public nature of her television appearances, she is exposed regularly to both compliments and condemnation. People have messaged her to complain about the way she wears her hair, tell her the way she dresses is a joke, say she should never wear glasses in public, or ask if all her body parts are real. Some of the criticism is posted publicly, but the ugliest criticisms are often sent privately.

No one would say that the people trolling Carisa's posts would consider themselves to be her friends, but their words still wield power. Proverbs reminds us that words can be bearers of death or life. Whether our words are used as a weapon or a balm, we will reap the very real consequences of what we choose to say. Our responsibility to others—whether they are strangers or friends—is to choose our words wisely. Whenever we actively belittle a friend, quietly question her motives behind her back, or silently grumble about her in our minds, we reinforce a narrative about her character that may not be true.

As people who understand the power of friendship, let's resolve to be women who champion others. Let's go out of our way to encourage our friends with our words, recognizing them for who they are and propelling them to become the women God wants them to be.

— *Kristin*

— Today's Act of Friendship —

Consider the words you speak or think about
others, particularly friends. Adjust your narrative to
believe—and speak—the best about them.

The Power of Friendship

Ruth said, "Do not urge me to leave you or turn back from following you; for where you go, I will go, and where you lodge, I will lodge. Your people shall be my people, and your God, my God."
RUTH 1:16, NASB

"I only use disposable dinnerware because I am literally studying soooooooooo much that I don't have time to do my dishes."

I listened politely to my law school classmate as she smugly told me how very, very much she was studying each day, even as *Liar, liar, pants on fire* played in singsong meter in my mind.

That was the moment I decided I didn't need friends in law school. I made sweeping judgments about every woman in my first-year class, deeming them ultra-competitive and unsafe, and then preemptively rejected all of them. I was polite and kind, but with the exception of one woman with whom I was carefully friendly, I invited no one into the vulnerable space of genuine friendship.

I created a false narrative that I carried with me for more than a decade: attorneys cannot be good friends; they are unsafe in friendship by personality and training. Any attorney who didn't fit my narrative was explained as not being a "real" attorney—meaning there was something about his or her personality that made them different from the hundreds of thousands of legally trained individuals in our country that I had rejected.

I wish I could go back to that younger Julie and unpack for her the story of Ruth and Naomi—two women who loved one another fiercely, and who took turns spiritually carrying one another when the other was too weary to continue. The book of Ruth is far more than a love story. It is an instructional tale about the immense power of friendship that has both encouraged and convicted me as I've let go of the lies I've believed about women.

Younger me desperately needed girlfriends in law school, but my false narrative blinded me to the potential friendships all around me. My regret over those lost opportunities fuels not only how I teach my daughter about friendship but also reminds me not to reject other groups of women based on stereotypes.

— Julie

— Today's Act of Friendship —

Is there a group of women you have preemptively rejected, perhaps based on clothing choices, denominational affinity, or some other stereotype? Invite someone from that rejected category out for coffee and get to know her.

September

Friendship by Extension

He makes the whole body fit together perfectly. As each part
does its own special work, it helps the other parts grow, so that
the whole body is healthy and growing and full of love.

EPHESIANS 4:16

My husband grew up playing sports. He enjoyed baseball and played football all the way through college. He loved being part of a team.

Me, on the other hand? Well, I'm much less athletic. I did a measly year of basketball, and I gave up playing volleyball and golf after a few years of halfhearted attempts. Although I was a cheerleader in high school, most of my pursuits were academic and social in nature. Even now, years later, I begrudgingly work out on the elliptical several days a week—but only if I can simultaneously watch TV to take my mind off the fact that I'm exercising.

So when my husband joined CrossFit, I cheered him on but decided to remain on the sidelines. I love that he loves it; it's just not for me. But over the years, I've realized what draws him in isn't really the exercise at all—it's the people. He feels like he's part of a team again. He teases, encourages, and holds a deep affection for the friends he's made—and they return it in equal measure.

As a bystander, I have basked in the reflected glow of healthy community. Because by extension, they've been just as kind to me as they have to him. They've chatted with me when I show up at events, feeling out of place. They've read my books, written kind reviews, and recommended them to their friends. The camaraderie they display speaks to a healthy environment of mutual support.

Like Tim and his friends from CrossFit, we as Christians should model the same care and respect for others. Paul reminds us in Ephesians that we are different parts of one body, and that when we work together, the whole body transforms into one that is strong and vibrant, characterized by love. Each of us has unique qualities that, when joined with those of our friends, support the mutual well-being of us all.

— Kristin

— Today's Act of Friendship —

Encourage a friend by recognizing a characteristic or skill
they possess that you don't—one that complements your own
unique skill set, making the two of you a better team.

Whom Can I Befriend?

We love each other because he loved us first.

1 JOHN 4:19

We were invited to a team-building party at the beginning of a new year of dance for my daughter Jasmine. As we walked into the hotel pool area, my eyes scanned the room. Jasmine headed off to join some girls in the pool, and I saw my friends gathering chairs to one side. But I also noticed a new mom just sitting down on the opposite side of the pool. I decided to go and sit by her instead of joining my friends.

I greeted her and asked who her daughter was. Our conversation flowed from there to talk about where we were from and a bit about our families. The hour passed easily as we found things we had in common and realized there were people we both knew.

Finally, we all got up to leave and said goodbye. I collected my daughter, and we headed out to our car. On the way home, I mentioned to Jasmine how I had intentionally chosen to walk in looking for someone who might be new, even though I knew it would be easier to just go sit by my friends. I explained to Jasmine that we always want to try to be the inviters, the ones who look for those who need to be included. She nodded understanding as we pulled into our driveway.

Later on that evening, I received a message through social media from the mom I'd just met.

"Thank you for coming and sitting by me tonight," she stated. "It meant a lot that you would do that."

I quickly responded, letting her know what a pleasure it was to meet her.

It doesn't matter our age or how confident we are, it is always nice to be included when entering a new situation. As Christians, we should be some of the most welcoming and loving people around, reflecting the way Christ has first loved us. Out of that place of knowing God's love for us, we are able to pour out to others, inviting them in and showing them love and friendship. We don't have to wait for anyone else; we can be the ones to befriend first.

– Kendra

– Today's Act of Friendship –

Look for someone who is new, whether at work, church, or some other activity you are a part of, and start up a conversation.

Redefining Friendship

The godly give good advice to their friends; the wicked lead them astray.
PROVERBS 12:26

When my children started day care, I first encountered the casual use of the word "friend," and as my children grew, the trend continued. Early elementary teachers, staff, and other parents referred to classmates as "friends," and while my kids were too young to grasp the distinction between a friend and a classmate, the use of the two words interchangeably made me slightly uncomfortable.

As my children grow into young adulthood, Aaron and I are intentionally redefining the word "friend" for them. Their classmate relationships are built on proximity, and there is a large range of interests, perspectives, and personalities in their classrooms. While we teach that everyone is to be treated with respect and kindness, it is also important to accurately distinguish friend relationships from other types of relationships with the people in our life circles.

Our American culture has diluted the word "friend" by extending it to far too many relationships, and it creates confusion about what being a friend actually entails. We are in varying degrees of relationship with people in our lives based upon proximity, commonalities, and intersecting interests, and we sometimes forget that we can live peacefully and respectfully among others outside of a friendship relationship. I hold to the definition of *friend* (a person whom one knows, likes, and trusts according to the American Heritage Dictionary).

Scripture teaches us that we should invest in godly friends who give wise advice. Who is it we are listening to? Do they have our best interests in mind? Do we seek the advice of people who love us and point us back to Jesus? Rather than listen to poison being peddled by rabble-rousers—those who love to stir up drama—let's seek counsel from those in close friendships with us. We must carefully consider to whom we are turning for advice.

— Julie

— Today's Act of Friendship —

Make a list of those you allow to advise you and take that
list to God. Who might you need to remove or add? Ask
God to refine the kind of advice you give to others—always
pointing them back to God, not leading them astray.

Friendship That Rallies

They worshiped together at the Temple each day, met in homes for the
Lord's Supper, and shared their meals with great joy and generosity—all
the while praising God and enjoying the goodwill of all the people.

ACTS 2:46-47

The incoming text from my husband chirped during the rush of morning errands. "Eli's been in a car accident," it read. "Can you find out how he is doing?" My immediate call to his wife, Ashley, went unanswered, and I began to pray as I waited to hear more.

It wasn't long before the details of his condition emerged. After being hit by another car and breaking his femur, Eli now awaited surgery at the hospital. From the sidelines, texts volleyed among a group of friends, all working together to figure out how to help. One friend picked up car seats from Ashley and returned them home for the couple's children, who were being cared for by family members. Another friend arranged for their lawn to be mowed. Groceries were delivered, and a gift card for meals was dropped off. By the time I stopped over in the late afternoon and placed a homemade dinner in their refrigerator, mine was the fifth meal to arrive that day.

Witnessing the way so many rallied around our friends to help fill their needs reminded me of the actions of the early church. The believers devoted themselves not only to the teachings of Jesus but to spending time together and supporting one another. Sharing all that they had was an integral part of their faith; they even went so far as to sell personal possessions in order to give to those in need. Those early believers were unsparing in their generosity and joyful in their giving.

If I'm honest, that attitude of generosity doesn't always come naturally. Yet I've also come to realize that nothing helps us overcome our own reflexive self-interest like joining with others to serve those in need. It's when we step outside the comfort of our insulated homes and work together in unity to help those in need that we can experience the true breadth and depth of friendship.

— *Kristin*

— Today's Act of Friendship —

Give something you possess (or sell an item and
use the funds) to share with a friend in need.

Books and Wings

The heartfelt counsel of a friend is as sweet as perfume and incense.
PROVERBS 27:9

About a year ago, my husband started a book club. Aaron reads several books about business and leadership each year and thought a few of his male acquaintances in our business community might be interested in having conversations about these topics. Aaron picked out a book he had found invaluable and sent out email invites to join him at a local wing joint for the inaugural meeting of Books and Wings.

I have loved watching Books and Wings evolve. The group soon segued from reading purely business and leadership books into reading a book on the tragedy of the Donner Party wagon train in 1846 and watching a Ken Burns documentary on the Vietnam War. They continue to explore a wide-ranging selection of nonfiction topics.

Even more than witnessing my husband explore topics I'd never in a million years think to read about, I've loved watching him build a community of healthy male friendships outside of our normal circles. I have spoken to so many women whose husbands simply hang out with the husbands of their friends, content with relationships built solely on proximity. And while there is nothing wrong with a man befriending the husband of his wife's friend, we can also encourage the men in our lives to grow friendships around their own hobbies and interests.

Aaron engages in friendship differently than I do, and I've come to realize that most men are different from women in this way. Because of this, my "helpful" tips for his friendships often don't translate well, and I've learned not to interfere (even with the best of intentions) in how he and the men in his circles do friendship. But despite our different approaches, Aaron's need for solid male friends is no less than my need for solid female friends. God created us for community, and as Proverbs reminds us, sharing burdens and seeking counsel within the intimacy of healthy friendship has a tangible essence to it—like the sweet aroma of incense or perfume.

– Julie

– Today's Act of Friendship –

Encourage the men in your life to make time and space
for friendship with other men without offering "help" in
dictating what those friendships ought to look like.

Friendship Knows No Age

It is good when you obey the royal law as found in the
Scriptures: "Love your neighbor as yourself."

JAMES 2:8

My four-year-old, Ashlyn, likes to visit our neighbors. If I'm not watching carefully enough, she'll sneak out of the house, hop on her bike, and head out to find someone to talk to. We live on a quiet cul-de-sac and have kind neighbors, but it's a work in progress to teach her about boundaries. I've chased her down the street on her way to Joyce's, caught her as she hoofed her way up the driveway to Finley's, and snagged her just as she was about to ring Shelly and Denny's doorbell. I've repeatedly reminded her that she can't just visit whomever she likes without checking with me first, but she's mostly unrepentant.

I'll often hear about my children's exploits after they happen. Since my daughters spend the better part of every waking hour outside during the summer, that's not really a surprise, although the stories often are. My neighbor Jack told me recently that Ashlyn stopped over when he was working outside and asked if she could help him garden. Jim stopped me the other day to commend the calm way my oldest daughter relates to his dog. Debbie has picked up my children more than once when they've fallen off their bikes. And I've even found one of my children sunning themselves in Jayme's driveway, lying next to her slumbering cat Zoe.

Though there have been a few awkward moments and misunderstandings over the years, I love that my children see the value in having good relationships. We may have some different interests and perspectives, but I appreciate the wisdom my neighbors possess—be it in regard to parenting, gardening, or what's happening in the community. This is why I encourage my children to seek friendships with all neighbors of diverse ages and experiences. It's one of the greatest gifts I can give them in helping them learn how to love their neighbor as they do themselves.

— Kristin

— Today's Act of Friendship —

Invite a friend or neighbor who is older or younger than
you to go for a walk around the neighborhood.

Stick Together

A person standing alone can be attacked and defeated,
but two can stand back-to-back and conquer. Three are even
better, for a triple-braided cord is not easily broken.

ECCLESIASTES 4:12

My daughter Jasmine was so excited: she and a few of her friends had been asked to perform a dance for a local event. The girls spent the week leading up to the evening practicing, and the night of, we all showed up early so the girls would have extra time to prepare. As we were running through the dance a final few times, the minutes slipped away from us, and before we knew it, we were close to being late to the performance. We grabbed all of our things and rushed through the hallways toward the event, but as we got close to the auditorium doors, we heard the music start. My heart sank.

"What should we do?!" the girls all exclaimed, wide-eyed.

Everyone looked at each other, concerned and unsure. One mom suggested the girls just go out and start anyway, but still the girls hesitated.

Then Jasmine exclaimed, "I'm going." She ran out to the floor and began the routine.

The other moms quickly followed suit, giving their girls a quick hug before telling them to go out as well. "Do not leave your friend out there alone!" one mom stated.

We watched as all the girls fell into line and performed the dance beautifully. Once they were finished, the crowd cheered for them, and as they walked off the stage, many congratulated them for having the courage to go out, even after the music had begun.

Although I left that evening proud of my daughter's quick decision to begin the dance even if no one else did, I most resonated with the encouragement the other moms gave their girls not to let Jasmine perform alone. It's a good reminder that when we stick together and don't leave our friends to face life alone, we are all stronger for it.

— Kendra

— Today's Act of Friendship —

Think of a friend who needs a reminder that they aren't alone. Say
a prayer for them, and then let them know you are there for them.

Seeing the Best in Others

*I am certain that God, who began the good work
within you, will continue his work until it is finally
finished on the day when Christ Jesus returns.*

PHILIPPIANS 1:6

My friend Carol is an expert at championing others. As the director of a women's ministry that hosts events for thousands of people each year, she oversees a large advisory group and hundreds of volunteers. In the midst of all the work that entails, she consistently takes the time to recognize the contribution that each person makes.

"I can see you being really good at that role," she will tell someone when encouraging them to step into a new area. "You are so good at this," she will say to someone else. "Thank you for the work you are doing!"

Carol's leadership is effective because, instead of focusing on herself, she focuses on others. She finds the good—and praises it. Carol is one of those people who makes you want to do things for her, not out of obligation or guilt, but because she is so good at cultivating community that you simply want to be a part of it. She actively calls out the skills and talents of others and utilizes them to be the hands and feet of Jesus. I recall one situation in particular where a young woman had experienced some difficulties in her personal life and bowed out of the ministry for a while. When she returned, Carol went out of her way to make sure the woman knew she was loved and accepted despite the ugly circumstances she'd faced in the interim.

"I really want this to be a win for her," she confided.

One of the greatest gifts we can give a friend is to recognize a characteristic or skill they possess and encourage them to use it. God has called and equipped all of us to do his work and see it to completion, yet it can be hard to have the confidence necessary to try something new. As friends, let us recognize the innate talents others have to accomplish the tasks God has for them to do and encourage each friend to step out with holy confidence.

– *Kristin*

– *Today's Act of Friendship* –

Go out of your way to encourage a friend in their gifting, whether by sending an encouraging note or connecting them with an opportunity.

Choosing Your Battles

Love your enemies! Pray for those who persecute you! In that way,
you will be acting as true children of your Father in heaven.
MATTHEW 5:44-45

Heather's daughter, Natalie, has had a tumultuous eighth-grade year. One day Natalie came home with yet another story of facing off with some of the popular boys in her classroom, a story punctuated by familiar themes of power struggles and unfairness.

"What war are you fighting?" Heather asked quietly. "What battles could you strategically let slide so that you can win the war?"

Befuddled, Natalie paused for a long moment before saying, "My war is to survive eighth grade."

"Hmm." Heather shook her head as she wrapped Natalie in a hug. "I believe you are made for more than merely fighting the war to survive eighth grade. What bigger war might you be fighting?"

As Natalie paused, turning contemplative, her mom asked a follow-up question: "As a girl who loves Jesus, where is he in your war?" These two questions led to a crucial conversation about handling conflict.

These questions apply as much to us as they apply to an eighth-grade girl. When I find myself in conflict, I should be pausing to consider where Jesus is in this particular battle. Am I demanding my rights, or am I defending the rights of another? Am I causing harm to the cause of Christ, or am I living out what he taught? Sometimes we must forfeit a battle so that we might win the larger war of reflecting the love of Christ. This isn't always easy to determine, especially when our emotions are involved.

The question Heather ultimately posed to her daughter was this: "Does this battle honor God?" If not, perhaps the battle is not ours to fight. Our ultimate goal is to live like children of God in the battles we choose and to love our enemies even as we are in conflict with them.

– Julie

– Today's Act of Friendship –

Reexamine current and future conflicts through the lens
of this question: "Does this conflict honor God?"

Listening Well

*God did listen! He paid attention to my prayer. Praise God, who did
not ignore my prayer or withdraw his unfailing love from me.*

PSALM 66:19-20

It had been a long day, and I was tired. Everyone was out of the house except for
my teenage son. I'd just sat down to eat when he walked in and asked me a few
questions while also explaining about his upcoming lacrosse game that evening. My
response at first was brief. I was in the middle of reading an important email and
was caught off guard by his presence.

As he left the room, the thought flitted across my brain, *Don't miss this chance
to connect.* I quietly shut my email down and called a question to him in the next
room. He walked back in to answer, and we discussed school and how he was feeling about his game. Just as quickly as we'd begun, the conversation ended; my son's
friend had arrived, and he needed to leave. I wished him luck as he walked out the
door, and he turned to give me a grin and a nod.

It took only ten minutes to connect with my son, just enough time for him
to feel heard and, even more, to know that I value and love him. I hate to admit
how often I miss the opportunity to listen well to those around me. I love my to-
do list, and although getting things done is good, sometimes it can get in the way
of building relationships. I'm not perfect at setting things aside, but I am getting
better—it's a skill I am intentionally pursuing.

The psalmist tells us that God listens! He pays attention to our prayers, he
doesn't ignore us or withdraw his unfailing love from us. We don't have to wonder
if he's listening. As Christians, we can follow his example and listen to those around
us as they share their lives with us. It's one of the most endearing qualities in a
friendship, this ability to listen well.

— *Kendra*

— Today's Act of Friendship —

Lend a listening ear to a friend who needs you.

The Cheerleading Faux Pas

*Walk with the wise and become wise;
associate with fools and get in trouble.*

PROVERBS 13:20

It wasn't my idea. But when the sophomore cheerleader in charge of our small squad told my freshman friend and me that she wanted us all to pair two layers of tight white tank tops with our skirts instead of wearing our regular cheerleading uniform, I didn't say no.

Which is how I found myself, a few short minutes later, facing the stern reprimand of a woman from my church who was seated in the crowded gymnasium.

"These outfits are not professional," she said firmly, pulling us to the side of the bleachers and telling us in no uncertain terms to get back into our regular uniforms. Shamefaced and not a little embarrassed, we did as she asked and quickly returned to an otherwise uneventful evening. When I saw her at church that weekend and at future basketball games, she never brought up the faux pas again.

Proverbs reminds us that the people we choose to spend time with will rub off on us, influencing us in positive and negative ways. I was usually a Goody Two-shoes, but in this instance, I had ignored good sense. With the wisdom of hindsight, I can see how our outfits must have appeared to the woman from my church, and why it was inappropriate to alter our clothing without seeking the input of our advisor or another adult. Standing front and center in the gymnasium, or even along the edges, we were still ambassadors of our school and the student body, and we needed to dress as such.

That encounter is still a reminder to me, even now, to be cautious in my friendships. Following the path of "there's nothing wrong with it" can lead us further and further down the road to ruin if we aren't careful. As a mom to three daughters now, I'm grateful that the woman intervened and encouraged me to make a better choice. Let us intentionally foster friendships with those who lift us up and encourage us to be a better version of ourselves. Just as I was an ambassador for my school in my days spent cheerleading, we are called to be ambassadors for Jesus through our actions and reflect the love, grace, and mercy he demonstrated.

— Kristin

— Today's Act of Friendship —

Analyze your friendships to consider whether you have
a friend who is nudging you toward bad choices.

The Gift of Mothering

*A friend is always loyal, and a brother
is born to help in time of need.*

PROVERBS 17:17

"Are you taking your pain meds? You need to stay on top of the pain." My text zinged off before I fully appreciated that I had just mothered a woman who was close to my mother's age.

I quickly followed up with an apology, explaining that I care about her, that I had a feeling she was trying to tough out the pain of her broken wrist, and that I just wanted her to be comfortable so her body could focus on healing rather than pain.

"Oh, Julie. Thank you for mothering me. My mom has been gone for a long time, and I sometimes need to be mothered," she texted back. Her response was gracious, and it had me pondering the gift of mothering in the weeks since our conversation. While we should be careful about giving unsolicited advice to acquaintances, there is sometimes a need for gently mothering the women in our circles.

What is mothering? It is advice and gentle admonishment, often about self-care, wrapped up in a warm hug of affection and love. It is reminding another woman that she is important, that she has worth, and that what she has to offer the world is valuable. It is being another woman's confidante, her prayer support, her cheerleader. It is being willing to set aside the to-do list to meet for coffee and hash out a hard situation another woman is facing, pointing her always back toward God. It's always having her best interests at heart—in all the words we say and in all the actions we take. Mothering is gently pushing another woman into taking the jump into what God is calling her to do, it is challenging the lies she is believing, it is loving her despite her imperfections.

In a loyal friendship, we can mother another woman by being there spiritually and physically during a time of need. Regardless of whether we are earthly mothers in the traditional sense, we are called to spiritually mother one another.

– Julie

– Today's Act of Friendship –

Think of a friend in your circles who needs mothering,
whether a coworker, a neighbor, or an extended
family member. Reach out in motherly love.

Just Sit Down

They sat on the ground with him for seven days and nights.
No one said a word to Job, for they saw that his
suffering was too great for words.

JOB 2:13

One of my dear friends, Christa, told me that when she was a child, she was very attached to her mother. Being the youngest of four children, she spent her days as a young girl with her mom. As kindergarten approached, she was scared. She didn't want to leave her mom. Each day loomed over her as she dreaded those first few weeks of school.

Once school began, each day would start with Christa sitting in the classroom crying for her mom. On one of the very first days this happened, another little girl grabbed some Kleenex and sat down next to Christa. Every day after that, she would do the same, handing Christa a tissue and sitting with her until she'd finished crying. Christa said that as the first few weeks went on, she began to look forward to seeing her new friend at school. Her comfort increased and her loneliness decreased because of another little girl who noticed her sadness and decided to offer her comfort. Christa said that she is still good friends with that woman today.

As Christa told me her story, it reminded me of Job's friends in the Bible. They may have said things to him that they shouldn't have, but when they first came to Job, they wept with him and sat with him in his suffering for seven days. Sometimes we think that we need to have the perfect words to say to someone who is going through a hard time, and if we don't know what to say, we'll simply avoid the person or situation. In reality, just being willing to be present with someone is often enough. I love how Christa's friend could understand this truth, even as a child. It's simple but profound to the person who is hurting, when we are willing to sit down.

– Kendra

– Today's Act of Friendship –

Spend time with a friend who is going through a hard season of life.

Hands and Feet of Christ

Your kindness will reward you.
PROVERBS 11:17

As I hobbled across a parking lot early on a weekday morning, my prayer was more of a wave of strong emotion sent toward God rather than anything formal. And, on this day, I pulsed sadness at God.

My sciatic nerve had first twisted into excruciating pain during my pregnancies, and it has been an on-again, off-again presence in my life ever since. I'd had a painful flare-up three weeks previously, and here I was, limping slowly across the asphalt on the way back to my car, feeling immense sadness not only for my own pain but also for the pain of a friend facing an impossibly hard situation. Aaron and I had been helping in a variety of ways, none of which felt like enough, and we were heartbroken along with her.

"Ma'am, are you okay?"

I turned toward the voice. A man I'd never met had noticed me, and his stride was eating up the ground between us faster than I could hobble away in humiliation. Head cocked to the side, he introduced himself as a pastor, and his next words were my undoing: "May I pray for you?"

I could not contain my tears as he gently prayed for my healing. Thanking him with a watery smile, I maneuvered carefully into my car and paused for a moment as the pain subsided. I know that God is capable of healing anyone, anywhere, in any way he wants. However, I also know that healing in the way we ask isn't always his will—for a variety of reasons we don't always understand this side of heaven. I whispered a soft amen as a still, small voice spoke clearly to my heart: *Julie, don't you think that I can take care of you even as you are taking care of those I love?*

That parking-lot moment was the start of my healing. I immediately felt my hip start to unwind, and within a week I was back to full mobility. More importantly, those words God whispered to my heart have stayed with me. It's when we are the hands and feet of Christ that our own needs are met in unexpected ways. It's as we pour out kindness on others that God pours out kindness on us.

– Julie

– Today's Act of Friendship –

Be the hands and feet of Christ to a friend who has a need.

You Can Do It!

I can do everything through Christ, who gives me strength.
PHILIPPIANS 4:13

"I know this is hard, but I believe you can do this," I told my friend. She was contemplating whether she really had what it took to go back to college after being away for several years. Her thoughts were warring inside her, and insecurity and doubt had taken hold as she listened to her fears about not being able to complete school. But I knew my friend, and I knew what she was capable of accomplishing if God was asking her to finish school. I knew the passion in her heart to help others once she finished her degree.

I became her voice of reason, reminding her of all the truths about herself that she couldn't see at the moment. "You are capable of doing this," I told her. "God is going to use you. I believe that you are able; you have everything you need to do this well!"

She gave me a lopsided grin as I willed her to believe these things for herself.

But my words weren't just empty platitudes; I believed them to the core of my being. I could truly see all of the wonderful things about her, and I knew, even if she couldn't see it then, that she could do it. I had no doubt. Over the next several months of starting back to school, anytime she needed encouragement, she'd call me, and I'd cheer her on.

Sometimes we can be our own worst enemy, and it takes our friends to remind us of what is true about us, our purpose, and our place in the world. And just as often as I cheerlead others, I find I need them to speak into my life when I am overwhelmed or believing lies. Don't be afraid to reach out when you are struggling or to encourage others when they are as well, remembering that we can do everything that God is asking us to through Christ, who gives us strength.

— *Kendra*

— Today's Act of Friendship —

Offer encouragement to a friend who is struggling
to see what is true about themselves.

Healing Not Hurtful

Some people make cutting remarks,
but the words of the wise bring healing.
PROVERBS 12:18

It was little things, at first. A snide comment about how she would never let her son play the sport my friend's son was in because it was too dangerous. An offhand remark about how she didn't really struggle with parenting. At every opportunity, she cultivated the image of perfection—perfect mom, perfect kids, perfect family—while she aimed flaming arrows of doubt at my friend's life and parenting skills.

My friend ignored this woman's hurtful words, but eventually they took a toll. Finally, when the woman told my friend that she couldn't imagine having four kids—the number of children my friend had—because she felt like you'd never be able to devote quality time to them individually, my friend felt like she'd had the breath kicked from her lungs.

"In my mom-guilt moments, that comment resonates over and over in my head," my friend told me later. "And I begin to question our decisions." Over time, the toxic comments and comparisons beat down my friend's confidence, until she finally recognized that her "friend" wasn't really a friend at all.

"When I picked myself up out of my puddle of tears, I knew that these four boys were God's perfect plan, and I rest in that," she said. With new eyes, she reevaluated her interactions and took steps to avoid the toxic friend.

Although the woman's words hurt my friend, the opposite is often true as well. When we choose to speak words of life to our friends—affirming their parenting, congratulating them on milestones at work, recognizing the unique and lovely aspects of their character—our words can be a source of healing. Like a well-timed gift, kind words are a balm to the soul. Though a friend may accidentally speak a careless word here and there, larger issues are at hand when they repeatedly speak unkind words with no consideration for feelings. Sometimes, the best thing we can do for ourselves is to put boundaries in place and choose to instead spend time with friends who speak healing over our lives. And, in return, we can proactively choose to be friends who do the same.

— Kristin

— Today's Act of Friendship —

If a friend's words or actions consistently tear you down, reevaluate the relationship and consider implementing healthy boundaries.

Liquid Grace

To each one of us grace has been given as Christ apportioned it.
EPHESIANS 4:7, NIV

Carol has a keen eye for when someone is not okay. And that morning at the coffee shop, Carol quickly saw that our friend was struggling. As Carol leaned across the table and whispered, "Let's pray," the tears our friend had been holding back started to silently fall.

Listening to Carol pray, in my mind's eye I saw Jesus pouring out liquid grace over my friend's head with it streaming like rivulets down her hair and over her person until she was soaked in it. So that was what I prayed for—for liquid grace to cover all the tender spots that had been rubbed raw, to provide a barrier of God's love over the most painful places.

We all need grace. I've found myself praying for grace on a daily basis these last six months; grace over my friends when their internal voices are being cruel; grace over parent-child relationships in the midst of friction-filled seasons; grace over marriages as wives and husbands are so busy raising children that they are more roommates than spouses; grace over myself when I've fallen short.

Christ has set aside grace for each of us, but sometimes we need a friend to recognize our need for it, who will gently remind us that grace is always undeserved when we claim to be unworthy, who can see our situation from the slightly broader perspective of being outside looking in, who speaks God's truth over us when we are starting to believe lies. We need friends who are like Carol, discerning and wise, who are willing to stop in the middle of a conversation to turn to Jesus in prayer, tipping that proverbial bucket over our head, so that liquid grace might cover us from head to toe.

And when we walk in God's grace, we find the capacity for extending kindness, compassion, and forgiveness to those around us. It's in that extension of forgiveness, compassion, and an undeserved kind response that we find life. Liquid grace brings life—to ourselves and to those around us.

— Julie

— Today's Act of Friendship —

Pray God's liquid grace over your friends and over yourself.

SEPTEMBER 18

Standing Up for Others

*We know what real love is because Jesus
gave up his life for us. So we also ought to give up
our lives for our brothers and sisters.*

1 JOHN 3:16

Tears filled my daughter Jasmine's eyes as she casually said that some girls on the bus had been saying unkind things to her and that it had been going on for some time. She shrugged her shoulders as if to brush off the comments like they didn't matter, but we could all see that they did.

My sons were in the living room with us, listening as Jasmine explained how often it had been happening lately, almost daily. I immediately felt sadness mixed with anger as I saw how hurt she was by their careless words. Before I could say anything, my son Donnie spoke up. "Why don't I ride the bus with Jasmine tomorrow?" he said. "I'll stand up for Jasmine when those girls say something again." I smiled at his indignation and the protective way he spoke about Jasmine.

"Thank you for offering, buddy," I said. "But I don't think you'd be able to ride the bus with Jasmine since you don't attend her school." Instead, we talked about another way that Jasmine could handle the girls on the bus, starting with telling the bus driver about her concerns and making a plan for the future.

Afterward, we were able to have a conversation with our children about the love that we feel for one another, especially when one of us is going through a hard time, and how it mirrors Jesus' love. Because of his sacrifice, we are free to love others and give up our lives for one another too. Jesus is the perfect friend, and when I remember he laid his life down for me, I can lay down mine for others.

— *Kendra*

— *Today's Act of Friendship* —

Stand in the gap for a friend who is going through a hard time—whether with your time, words, or resources.

It's Okay to Cry

Now I am giving you a new commandment: Love each other.
Just as I have loved you, you should love each other.

JOHN 13:34

As someone who is perhaps overly empathetic, crying is my response to a lot of situations. News stories and sappy movies can make me cry, but so do many circumstances in my everyday life. Sadness, joy, anger, and frustration can all surface as tears. While I recognize that my tears are part of my sensitive nature, I'm often dismayed when they emerge—especially if it's at an inconvenient, work-related time. I've cried during a podcast recording; I've cried during dinner at a work conference. I've been on the verge of tears in some of the biggest moments of my working life, simply because I felt uncertain or overwhelmed.

All of those situations were immensely frustrating to me because, even though I appreciate the tender heart God has given me, I hate when my tears hinder the message I'm trying to convey. Luckily the ladies I work with are also dear friends. In every situation, without fail, Kendra and Julie are unfailingly kind. They never make me feel bad about a characteristic that can sometimes embarrass me. Instead, they respond with grace and understanding.

"It was fine!" one will say when I bemoan my tears.

"I thought it was great," the other will say, assuring me that the situation turned out okay.

I imagine that when Jesus commands us to love each other the way he loved us, this is what he meant. My friends love me for who I am. They recognize that my soft heart is an innate part of my nature, and they don't try to change me—they simply accept me, and they encourage me to do the same. And isn't that what Jesus does with us? He loves us, just as we are. He welcomes us, accepts us, and shows grace and mercy in the face of our many weaknesses. As friends, let us treat one another with the same measure of love that Jesus does.

— Kristin

— Today's Act of Friendship —

Thank a friend for affirming an aspect of yourself
that is sometimes hard for you to accept.

Newbies Need Friends

A servant of the Lord must not quarrel but must be kind to everyone, be able to teach, and be patient with difficult people.

2 TIMOTHY 2:24

A gentle knock on my office door had me smiling as Hassan hovered in my doorway, coffee cup in hand. He has spent a few minutes each day lingering just inside my door for months now, checking in on the new girl hired to teach a business law class in his department at a small liberal arts college.

Navigating my new role as adjunct faculty has been challenging. The phone system is a mystery. The copy machine requires a NASA-level education to operate. I don't know where the forms live in the byzantine internal computer system. And my first test had my students in a near panic because it was far too long and far too hard.

Hassan's routine check-ins are an answered prayer. I've peppered him with technical questions about how he runs his class, questions about small, mundane administrative tasks everyone else has absorbed as institutional knowledge, and slightly philosophical questions about how to be an instructor who teaches with mercy, encouragement, and high standards. In addition to shop talk, I've gleaned small pieces of information about him as we've chatted about children and families, about the communities we live in, about a new course he is developing. It's a tendril of friendship in a position that I'm learning can feel solitary much of the time.

It's easy to forget how hard it is to be the new person. Transitions—to a new school for your children, a new church, a new job, a new community—require patience as we figure out new systems, different procedures, and even unfamiliar subcultures. Having someone who takes the time to check in on a regular basis is such a blessing—it invites the asking of "silly" questions (those we feel a bit sheepish to ask), allows an easy transfer of information about all sorts of little details, and builds community and a sense of belonging around the newbie. Reaching out in regular and sustained welcome is the epitome of our role as God's servant—patient, kind, and willing to show the new girl the ropes.

– Julie

– Today's Act of Friendship –

Find a newbie at your job, in your neighborhood, or in your church, and check in with them, offering to answer questions and simply making them feel welcome.

Investing in Friendship

*Let's not get tired of doing what is good. At just the right time
we will reap a harvest of blessing if we don't give up.*

GALATIANS 6:9

I met my friend Edwin in college. Although I was an English major, I'd always loved history, and I ended up taking two of the classes he taught as electives. His sense of humor and engaging style made the class feel fun, and as time went on, we connected outside of class on things like music. When he moved on to a tenure track professorship in his native Canada, we kept in touch. He sent condolences when my sister died, congratulated me on my marriage, and wished me well when each of my daughters were born.

Each time a letter arrived, I immediately sat down and read through it. He sent newsy updates: postcards from his research travels to France, lengthy letters about the climate and adventures in the place he lived. Yet to my shame, I've only returned a fraction of his letters. He has been a much better friend to me than I have been to him.

Of course, I recognize that there are seasons in life that can interfere with our good intentions, especially when it comes to things like friendships. I'm in a season that includes small dirty footprints on the floor, Barbies in the bathtub, and Magic Tree House books tucked into unlikely nooks. Yet I also know that friendships are a precious gift, one I never want to take for granted. With that in mind, I finally sat down and wrote out a long letter to Edwin, thanking him for the generosity of his friendship over the years.

Sometimes, in friendship, we are the ones giving more than we receive. Sometimes, we're the ones receiving more than we give. The imbalance can feel frustrating, yet if we recognize that seasons in friendship can happen and believe in the overall value of the friendship, our persistence in doing good will eventually pay off. When we invest in friends without expectations, we leave room for God to work.

— *Kristin*

— Today's Act of Friendship —

Jot a quick note or write a long letter to a friend.

Generous Community

*The generous will prosper; those who refresh
others will themselves be refreshed.*

PROVERBS 11:25

Kendra, Kristin, and I attended a writer's conference that was billed as part networking opportunity with other authors and part teaching sessions on a wide variety of writing topics. We were longing for author friends—women who loved books and words as much as we did, who were a step or three further along in their writing journey and able to answer questions, give guidance, and offer encouragement.

Our secret fear, of course, was that we would be exposed as imposters, called out by "real" authors, snubbed because what we write wasn't enough when measured against some secret author test we didn't yet know about. What we found instead was a community of women and men who were lavish in sharing wisdom, ideas, and encouragement. In our case, it was about writing, but it could have been any skill set, hobby, or industry we were hungry to learn more about. We witnessed women with twenty years of experience chatting over key lime pie with newbies, listening carefully and offering suggestions when the new girl was stuck. Everywhere we turned, we saw women making sure the quiet girl was invited to dinner, for outings, for chats in the lobby. While we arrived hoping for a friend or two, we left the conference with an entire community of authors—numerous new friends who loved Jesus and words and who were generous in their support of one another.

The secret to building a strong, deeply rooted community is generosity: generosity in the sharing of wisdom; generosity in genuine, no-strings-attached support of another's project; generosity in inviting others to sit at your proverbial table. We serve a God who owns the cattle on a thousand hills, and there is more than enough for all of us. When we understand that our heavenly Father does not operate from an attitude of scarcity, we can be lavishly generous in our own circles and communities, knowing that God will provide even as we pour out. And when we are generous, we prosper.

— Julie

— Today's Act of Friendship —

Practice lavish generosity, asking God to show you what that looks like.

Seeing Your Potential

Encourage each other with these words.
1 THESSALONIANS 4:18

Several years ago, a woman relayed a story about a dream she'd had for many years. She wanted to be a speaker and writer who ministered to single mothers like herself, but in the wilderness of her current circumstances, it seemed like an impossible aspiration. She told no one, hardly daring to say it aloud, until one day she worked up the courage to tell a friend and mentor. Her trusted friend paused, then said, "I can see that potential in you."

That affirmation gave her the added boost of confidence she needed to pursue her dream—a ministry that eventually grew and led to her speaking onstage and traveling the country, sharing with others.

My friend Andrew has a similar ability to see the potential in others. When my husband and I tried to follow an easy, noncommittal route and volunteered as greeters at church, he challenged us to work in the kid classrooms instead. Later, he pulled us out of our comfort zone by asking us to step up as leaders of a small group—a challenge that he would make repeatedly over the next several years, prompting us to lead numerous women's, couples, and family-themed groups in our home and community.

What I appreciated most about Andrew was that his boldness wasn't due to arrogance; it was a holy expectation of God's provision and timing. He recognized a need in the church and saw that we could meet that need. Sometimes other people can see our potential for leadership, a new role, or something outside of our comfort zone much more clearly than we can. As friends, how can we encourage the potential in those we love and care about? The encouraging words we choose to use can be just the boost our friends need to get moving. Let's recognize the potential in our friends and encourage them in their pursuit of God-sized dreams.

— *Kristin*

— Today's Act of Friendship —

Reach out to a friend, encouraging her to step out in
an area where you can see she has potential.

The Legacy We Leave Behind

*Choose a good reputation over great riches; being held
in high esteem is better than silver or gold.*

PROVERBS 22:1

It's been many years since my sister Katrina died of breast cancer—the year of her death coincided with the year my husband and I got married. With each passing year, I wonder if she is being forgotten by others who knew her, though I sometimes unexpectedly receive a message from one of her high school friends, reminding me that they still remember her. It's a bit of a surprise since we moved to what I now consider my hometown when Katrina was entering her junior year of high school. With only two years left, it seemed like it would be a challenge to find good friends. But Katrina had a welcoming personality and always made friends quickly.

Katrina's time with her high school friends was brief but sincere. And the kindness I have received from them in the years since her death brings tears to my eyes. Not long ago, I received a message from one woman who told me her daughter decided that she wanted to follow Jesus and that it reminded her of my sister.

"I find myself praising Jesus for your sister and how she pointed so many to the Throne of Grace! What a legacy she left," she wrote.

I smiled as I read her words, reminded once again that God uses all of our lives, and even in death our legacy can live on.

It is true that a good reputation is better than wealth because it shows how our life had an impact on other people. Whether we realize it or not, we are all creating a legacy in the way that we interact with others, a legacy that can leave ripples of good long after we are gone. Katrina's life reminds me that it doesn't matter how long or short our time is with people, we can have a lasting impact on others by the way that we extend friendship and love to them.

– Kendra

– Today's Act of Friendship –

Remember someone whose life and legacy has had an impact on you, and let one of their loved ones know what they meant to you.

Trailblazing

*I am about to do something new. See, I have already
begun! Do you not see it? I will make a pathway through
the wilderness. I will create rivers in the dry wasteland.*

ISAIAH 43:19

"Oh, Lord," I whispered, "I hope I heard you right when I said yes to this." Nausea rolled over me as my prerecorded interview started to play at a business women's conference, my image flickering to life on a gigantic screen.

Eighteen months prior to the video's debut, I had traded a fifteen-year legal practice for an ambiguous journey involving writing, mothering, and trusting God with what might be next. My heart was bruised and tender as I continued to grapple with issues of identity, and now the story of that journey was being played for several hundred business women made up of former coworkers, clients, opposing counsel, and countless other women I'd done business alongside in one way or another.

It is one thing to share hard parts of your faith journey with someone over coffee; it is an entirely different thing to watch an enormous, on-screen version of yourself wipe away tears about making hard choices, going through identity crises, and trusting God as you choose his unknown thing over the path the entire world would say was the smart thing to do. What I did not entirely expect were the tender conversations I would have with so many women after I shared my story. Countless women approached me in the year following to tell me they found encouragement in the midst of their own desert wanderings and to thank me for having the courage to share honestly from the middle space, before there was a neat and tidy ending to the story.

God sometimes asks us to be trailblazers through the wilderness for other women, extending a hand and inviting them to walk alongside us. We build the courage we need to do what God is calling us to by hearing the stories of other women who are in the midst of doing the same.

– Julie

– Today's Act of Friendship –

Ask God what parts (and how much) of your story need to be shared
with a woman in your circles, and create an opportunity to share.

Sharing in the Joy

Rejoice with those who rejoice; mourn with those who mourn.
ROMANS 12:15, NIV

It was late, but I didn't care. The glow of the moon shone through the entry window as I tiptoed up to my sister Katrina's bedroom. Walking quietly past my niece and nephew's rooms, I slipped through her door and approached her side of the bed, attempting not to wake my soundly sleeping brother-in-law.

She half opened her eyes as I took her hand, signaling her to be quiet as I guided her into the bathroom. Then I shut the door and turned on the light. As she blinked against the sudden brightness, she saw my outstretched hand and newly placed ring as she squealed with delight.

"Oh my goodness, Kendra! It's gorgeous!" she exclaimed. "I am so happy for you! Tell me all about it." She sat on the edge of the tub as I recounted the details of the evening Kyle proposed to me.

Katrina was so excited for me, and over the next several months she became my wedding planner, carefully crafting all the details and helping me make every decision. At the time I thought nothing of it, but now looking back, I see what a huge sacrifice that was for her because she was also battling a cancer that had come back for the third time. All of her planning happened between doctors' appointments and treatments, but she never let on that she couldn't do both at the same time. She told me she wanted to help plan the happy occasion, and so she did. In turn, I stayed by her side on the hard days, helped with her kids, and listened when she shared her heart.

Joy and pain often run side by side in our lives. It seems even in the joyous times there are struggles and burdens to carry; we may rejoice with our friends at the same time as they mourn with us. All of our lives are to be shared, the good times and the hard times.

— Kendra

— Today's Act of Friendship —

Determine to rejoice with a friend who is celebrating
and to comfort a friend who is mourning.

Hope Bringers

The LORD is close to the brokenhearted;
he rescues those whose spirits are crushed.
PSALM 34:18

"Mom, Shiloh is living in the Gateway hotel."

My heart broke at Jonny's words. I knew that hotel from my law-clerking days when I worked for a local judge. Nothing good happens there, especially for kids. Shiloh and Jonny are roughly the same age, and while Jonny doesn't know her well, he knows part of her story.

I was unprepared to help my children navigate relationships with peers walking through impossibly hard circumstances. The death of a parent, divorce, the messy aftermath of divorce, foster care, homelessness, adoption, childhood cancer: the issues facing my children's peers are as hard and real as life gets, and I often find myself at a loss as I consider what the kids in the vicinity of my children are facing. But I've begun to realize that God has placed my children in circles that are different from mine, and they are sent into this broken world to be "hope bringers" in places and spaces I cannot walk. They have unique relationships with their peers that I will never have. And so I have to equip them with the tools to be hope bringers.

When Lizzie or Jonny tells me the hard story of a neighbor, teammate, or schoolmate, my momma heart aches as I ask the question: "Why might God have put the two of you in the same sphere? Why might you have found out about this information?"

Aaron and I have empowered our kids to be hope bringers, people who reveal the love of God twice as much through their actions as they do through their words. We equip them with the power of prayer—sending them out to be pray-ers over their schoolmates, classmates, and friends. God often deploys his people to the broken-hearted and the crushed as tangible love and help, and I'm learning that he deploys our children to do the same if we've raised them to be hope bringers.

— *Julie*

— Today's Act of Friendship —

Equip the children in your life to be hope bringers through kindness and prayer. Help them practice the art of verbalized prayer (even secretly) and remind them to look for ways to show kindness.

Tell the Truth

Never let loyalty and kindness leave you!
Tie them around your neck as a reminder.
Write them deep within your heart.

PROVERBS 3:3

A dear friend of mine was going through a really difficult time. Her family was being pulled apart at the seams, and she was looking for a way out. Although I completely understood where she was coming from, and my heart ached for her, I knew her emotions were guiding her actions. Before responding to her texts, I quickly said a prayer and called my mom.

My mother is a woman of faith who prays hard and keeps confidences. She is quick to offer compassion and slow to judge others and their actions. She knows all too well her own human frailties and often speaks of God's mercy toward her own propensity to error.

I briefly explained what was going on and then asked, "Mom, can you pray?"

"Of course," she responded, "but honey, you have got to tell her the truth."

I nodded through tears as my mom prayed for my dear friend and her situation, as well as for wisdom for me to speak truth wrapped completely in love. I felt peace as I hung up and called my friend.

Our conversation was honest but laced with grace and the shared understanding that no matter what, I loved my friend and her family dearly and only wanted the best for them.

We all walk through challenging situations sometimes, and we need those who love us to remind us of what is true, even when we ourselves don't feel it or see it. Proverbs tells us to keep loyalty and kindness close, allowing them to guide us in all we do. In friendship, this allows us to have honest and hard conversations with those we love, out of that place of true affection. We all need friends who will lovingly speak truth to us at times, and when we've built a foundation on kindness, we're able to navigate even the most difficult of conversations.

— Kendra

— Today's Act of Friendship —

If there's a difficult or challenging conversation you have been putting off, pray for that friend and then lovingly approach them with the truth.

Establishing Traditions

*How wonderful and pleasant it is when
brothers live together in harmony!*

PSALM 133:1

My husband and I love food. Tri-tip steaks, bacon-wrapped scallops, and beer can chicken grilled on our Big Green Egg are some of our favorite meals to make at home. We love trying new restaurants, whether they're farm-to-table, sushi, fancy, or casual. We enjoy watching shows like *Top Chef, Chopped,* and *MasterChef.* And whenever we travel, we've been known to plan our calendar around which restaurants we'd like to visit.

Luckily, our friends Ryan and Emily are foodies too. Several years ago, we decided to start visiting new restaurants in the Twin Cities together. We compiled a running list of restaurants, gleaned from magazine articles and recommendations from friends, and started working our way through them. The number of restaurants we visit varies from year to year, depending on the season of life we're in, but we make it happen at least a few times each year. Every dinner date is a chance to catch up and enjoy something new.

It's fun to establish traditions in friendships, and our standing new-restaurant dates are one of my favorite traditions. I'm much more likely to be adventurous when the people I surround myself with are willing to be adventurous too. By trying new things with our friends, I've created a list of favorite restaurants that Tim and I return to again and again for birthdays and anniversaries.

The writer of Psalms reminds us of the joy that comes when we live in unity with our fellow Christians. As friends, some of that unity comes from having a mutual interest or passion for a hobby, sport, or other activity. After all, it's just as important to foster community through fun and laughter as it is through the more serious parts of life and ministry. Seeking and finding common points of interest is foundational in the pursuit of lifelong friends.

— Kristin

— Today's Act of Friendship —

Brainstorm a new friendship tradition you could
establish with a friend, couple, or group.

How Can I Help?

Two people are better off than one,
for they can help each other succeed.

ECCLESIASTES 4:9

One of my adopted children has always struggled with some separation anxiety. It came to a climax one fall after months of tears over simple things like leaving for school in the morning and going to piano lessons. My husband and I finally decided it was time to seek some professional intervention, and we made the necessary appointments to help our daughter manage her anxiety.

At the same time, I confided in a good friend about the struggles we were having, and after relaying my fears and praying together, she asked, "How can I help?" She wanted to know practical ways she could support our family, and as she has a daughter who is the same age and a friend to my child, she came up with several suggestions for ways they could help our family through this time. She offered each idea with grace in mind, and her response to my child's struggle with anxiety was loving and compassionate. We made a plan that my daughter would test some of her new ways to manage her fears while at her friend's house, all with the understanding that her mom knew what was going on and would bring her home at any time if things got to be too much. This helped my daughter gain confidence, and over time her anxiety lessened, making me forever grateful for a friend who listened and supported our family through a hard season with kindness and compassion.

We're so much better and stronger together. One of the greatest things we can do for a friend going through a hard time is to ask, "How can I help?" and then listen for their answer. It also doesn't hurt to offer some specific ways you could help support them. There is no better comfort than knowing that you are not going through something alone, that your friend is right there with you, praying for you and walking with you through the difficulty.

— *Kendra*

— Today's Act of Friendship —

Spend some time listening to a friend who is going through
a hard time and then ask how you can help her.

October

The Friends Who Have Our Back

We are confident that he hears us whenever
we ask for anything that pleases him.

1 JOHN 5:14

Before my sister Katrina passed away from cancer, she gathered a group of close friends around her. As I think back on her life and the time we had together, especially toward the end, the memories that most often surface are of those friends.

These were the women who saw Katrina through her sickness, rallied when she was ill, celebrated when she was well, and grieved with us after her death. Over the few years they had together as dear friends, they celebrated the births of babies, kids' birthdays, wedding anniversaries, college graduations, business starts, and new careers. They are the ones who, in turn, have listened as I've cried, encouraged my dreams that felt too small to even whisper aloud, offered grace for my mistakes and my feeble attempts at apologies, and loved me well. They are the ones who still have my back. They are not fickle or petty. They love long and well and gracefully. These are the rich friendships of life. The ones you scarcely think you deserve.

And they all began from a little prayer my sister whispered so many years ago, simply asking God for some friends.

You may be lonely for good friends, even as you're surrounded by people, or already have a close group. Either way, it's important to remember that good friendships take time and commitment to grow strong. I believe that friendship with others pleases God. I've seen the power that friendship has in life, and I believe that God would desire for each of us to have deep, lasting friendships. Prayerfully invest in your friendships, and ask God to help them grow.

– Kendra

– Today's Act of Friendship –

Thank God for the friends who have your back, and choose
a way to support one of those friends in turn.

Starting from Scratch

All of you should be of one mind. Sympathize with each other. Love each other as brothers and sisters. Be tenderhearted, and keep a humble attitude.

1 PETER 3:8

I knew exactly how the next day's newspaper cover should appear. As the copy editor tasked with designing the front page during my shift, I planned it out right after our afternoon meeting ended. As soon as I heard which stories had been assigned to appear on the cover and which arts and sports stories would be teased along the top, I knew that the top right corner would feature a cutout image that perfectly complemented the overall page layout. Excited to see it come to life, I dove into perfecting the design.

A couple of hours later, I was told offhandedly that the news had changed, and with it, my perfectly planned cover. I would need to scrap my plan and start from scratch. As my frustration welled, I excused myself from the room, but not before the editors saw tears gleaming in my eyes.

"Didn't she know that this happens sometimes?" they asked Kate, my boss.

"Of course she knows," Kate told them. "But she put a lot of work into what she was doing. She's frustrated because she has to start over now."

I felt embarrassed over my instinctive reaction, but as Kate finished relaying her conversation to me, I straightened up. She was my direct boss, yes—but she was also my friend. At that moment, I felt grateful that she was willing to be an advocate for me. I wasn't upset that I had to fix something; I was upset because I felt as if I had wasted my time. I was grateful to her for recognizing the source of my frustration. I knew she had seen my hard work and was acknowledging it. She modeled for me what it meant to work together in harmony by sympathizing with how I was feeling.

All too often, whether it's at home or work, we perform tasks that go unseen and unsung. As friends, we must work to build each other up.

— Kristin

— Today's Act of Friendship —

Encourage a coworker or other friend by thanking them for the unseen work they do.

Made in God's Image

God created human beings in his own image. In the image of
God he created them; male and female he created them.
GENESIS 1:27

I sat quietly listening as all the women chatted together in the kitchen. We were meeting at my friend Sam's house to share a meal and recipes. We were women of all different ages and backgrounds, some new to the country, some visiting as teachers and here for a short season—all wanting to get to know one another better and learn about one another's lives. Each of us had brought a dish that was meaningful to us—a family recipe or traditional dish in our country. We all tried new foods made with ingredients and spices we'd never had before—foods that, once experienced, we vowed to taste again.

As I listened to the conversation of the women around me, I was struck by the familiar threads. We talked about work and education and balancing all of life. We spoke of dreams and hopes for the future, of food and cooking, of staying healthy and the few extra pounds some of us would like to lose. We spoke of concerns over children and families, parenting and schedules.

As I continued to quietly observe the women, I realized how much we are alike—how emotions such as happiness, joy, anxiety, and fear play through all of our lives—and I thought, *We aren't so different after all.* We all want jobs, safe places to live, food, and clothing. We want our children to be educated and secure in the places they grow up. We want to dream and pursue our goals in life.

Looking around the room, I realized that each of these women was made in the image of God. Their lives have value and meaning, just as mine does, because God is the creator of us all. And because of this, we can celebrate our differences and freely try new things, hear about others' experiences, and befriend those who, at least on the surface, appear very different from us.

— *Kendra*

— Today's Act of Friendship —

Take some time to get to know someone who appears to be different
from you—listen to their story and share a part of your own.

Grace for Grumpy Days

My grace is all you need. My power works best in weakness.

2 CORINTHIANS 12:9

I knew before we'd even arrived at the park that it was too much. We'd had a series of late nights, and we were all feeling slightly out of sorts, but I didn't want to cancel the playdate. I hadn't seen Beth in a long time, and I really wanted to catch up on her recent adventures. It was a lovely day to play at the park, and lovely days can be hard to come by in late autumn.

After trying to gently redirect grumpy children several times in a variety of ways, I gave up. Smiling ruefully at Beth, I apologized and said that we simply needed to leave and make plans to try it again on another day.

This is the thing: we are human. And our humanness has a tendency to show up in a spectacular way when we are tired, hungry, stressed, or stretched a bit too thin. That is where God's grace comes in—for me, for Beth, for our children. I sent a quick text that night apologizing again and explaining that my children had been stretched too thin—and that I had unfairly tried to pull off one more activity when I knew I should cancel. Beth was gracious in her response, and we both moved past a tough day with nothing further to be said.

I am not a perfect friend. In fact, I am a deeply imperfect friend—I forget important dates, I say the wrong thing, I get grumpy, I mess up in a multitude of ways. Because I'm a bit of a hot-mess friend, I've learned to reach quickly for grace—both for myself and others. It's in our weaknesses that Jesus shines, because he gets the credit and the glory, and grace is one of the greatest gifts he gives us and that we can give others.

– Julie

– Today's Act of Friendship –

We all have bad moments, bad days, bad weeks, and sometimes, bad months. Show grace to yourself and others in moments of weakness.

When You Need a Friend

Share each other's burdens, and in this way obey the law of Christ.
GALATIANS 6:2

I was sitting in the doctor's office one morning with my middle daughter after a sleepless night when Jen's call came in. Unable to take the call, I let it go to voice mail. Once we returned home, I thought of Jen as I pulled out my phone and listened to her message. Tears sprang to my eyes as I heard her concerned voice across the line. "Hello! Just checking in to see how you and Jasmine are doing," she said. She went on to offer encouragement for a concern that had recently presented itself in our family.

I choked back a cry, too worn out to call her back, but so grateful for this friend who always seemed to remember the little things. As the day went on and I felt stronger, I called her back, and the warmth of her words flooded me once again. I hung up encouraged and feeling better than I had before her call.

I told my sister later that week how I felt a bit embarrassed by how often Jen had been reaching out to me lately and how I felt like I'd not been there for her in the same way.

"That's okay," Kristin responded. "Sometimes we're the friend supporting others, and sometimes we're in a season where we're the one needing a friend. Jen understands this and wants to be there for you right now. So let her."

I nodded agreement, knowing her words to be true.

Sometimes it's hard to be the one needing a friend. If you're like me, I love to help others but feel a little uneasy when I am the one in need. It doesn't have to be this way. We are supposed to share each other's burdens. Don't be afraid to reach out for support from your friends when you need it.

– *Kendra*

– Today's Act of Friendship –

Contact a friend and honestly tell them about what is going
on in your life. Let them share the burden with you.

One of the Cool Gifts

Kind words are like honey—sweet to the soul and healthy for the body.
PROVERBS 16:24

Scrolling social media as I sipped my morning coffee, I noticed a friend's post and felt prompted to pray for her. As the morning continued, I went about my tasks, but she remained in the back of my mind. So, I dashed off a quick message to her. In it, I told her how much her encouraging nature and ability to connect with others had inspired me and how I was trying to become more intentional in the words I spoke to others because of her influence.

Not long after, she messaged me back to tell me that my impromptu note had arrived at just the right time and had brought her to tears. Two weeks earlier, on a day she was home by herself, she had spent some of her time alone questioning Jesus. She asked him why she hadn't received one of the "cool gifts," why she wasn't someone or something more exciting. While her family was out running errands, she sat on her couch for two hours, tearfully asking Jesus to make her something more than "nice."

Although she did eventually dust herself off and remind herself that God uses our gifts and talents in unique ways and that someone needs what she has to offer, it took her a while to recover.

"Thank you for making me feel like I got one of the cool gifts," she said. "This really means so much to me."

I love how God uses us for his purposes—at just the right time. The words I wrote to her were kind and honest, and though I didn't think they were earth-shattering, they offered hope on a hard day. They confirmed her uniqueness and the fact that she was impacting others (like me) with her life.

When we obey the prompts of God to speak encouraging words to a loved one, drop off coffee for a friend, or tell someone we are praying for them, God can use us to accomplish his aims. As friends, may we always be open to fulfilling the gentle nudges of the Holy Spirit. I couldn't have known how my words would resonate with my friend—but God did. He knew exactly what she needed to hear.

— Kristin

— Today's Act of Friendship —

Send a friend an encouraging note, letting them
know something you appreciate about them.

Far-Flung Friends

"You must love the LORD your God with all your heart, all your soul, all your strength, and all your mind." And, "Love your neighbor as yourself."
LUKE 10:27

It was the one last hurrah that did me in: a farewell potluck dinner on the backyard patio to wish Carmen safe travels before she returned home to China. We'd had two years, four road trips, and countless meals together. I had promised myself I wouldn't cry, but when it came time to say goodbye, I suddenly burst into tears.

There is no dumb question between Carmen and me, and we speak without fear of unintentionally offending. We've explored hard topics as well as the mundane and have laughed until our sides hurt, sat in comfortable silence, and quietly shared hard parts of our stories, our family's stories, our country's stories. I have glimpsed pieces of Chinese life and culture unreported by any news media and unavailable to most of my fellow citizens. As women of roughly the same age, we have a deep respect for each other that transcends the politics of countries and policies of leaders, and her greatest gift to me has been her friendship.

I've learned to separate people from their countries—especially when it comes to foreign policy. My Chinese friends are not China any more than I am the United States. We miss out on the opportunity of deep and abiding friendships when we paint millions of people with the foreign policy decisions of their country's government. When Jesus commanded us to love our neighbors, he defined "neighbor" by telling the parable of the Good Samaritan. Remember, it was the Samaritan—the despised enemy of the Jewish people—who was the hero, the man who stopped for the stranger lying on the side of the road, knowing full well that had roles been reversed, the favor likely would not have been returned.

Loving my neighbor is not constrained by national boundaries. I count myself immeasurably blessed to have done life alongside Carmen for two years and am already making plans to visit her in Changchun someday.

— Julie

— Today's Act of Friendship —

Invite someone from another country to your house for dinner.
Local universities often have foreign students hoping to experience
a dinner with an American family, so that is a great place to start.

Befriending Those in Prison

I was sick, and you cared for me. I was in prison, and you visited me.
MATTHEW 25:36

One of our friends spent a season of his life in prison. As I got to see firsthand the struggle he experienced, I began to think about and feel burdened for people who were incarcerated. I started to pray for people who were in prison and asked God to give me an opportunity to somehow minister to and connect with them if it was appropriate.

Several weeks later, I saw a post on one of my social media feeds about an organization that seeks to connect Christian women with women who are incarcerated, as a way to offer encouragement and friendship to them. They take very literally Scripture's command to remember those who are in prison and to build bridges of connection with them.

As I've started writing and receiving responses, I've found the women who write me back are not so different from me—we're all people with hopes and dreams, emotions and feelings. Mistakes may have been made, some they've paid a high price for—but all are trying to do better.

I joined the group initially to encourage other women, but I've found that I receive just as much—or more—encouragement from them. As they share their stories of pain, heartache, and what they are doing now to improve their circumstances, the thread of redemption is apparent. I've realized these women are not unknown enemies or even outcasts because they are in prison. They are children of God, just as I am.

Some commands in the Bible are more challenging than others, but that doesn't mean we get to choose which ones apply to us and which ones do not. We are called to do many things, including ministering to those in prison.

— *Kendra*

— Today's Act of Friendship —

Pray for a person or group that may need befriending, such
as prisoners, those in hospice, the homeless, or refugees.

Choosing Love

Make allowance for each other's faults,
and forgive anyone who offends you.
COLOSSIANS 3:13

I studied abroad during college in Oxford, England. I loved seeing the skyline's spires, hearing the resonant ring of church bells every hour, exploring the hushed vastness of the Bodleian Library, and losing myself in the maze of cobblestone streets. My peek into British life and culture was simultaneously daunting and exhilarating, as there are more than thirty colleges that compose Oxford University. I loved being part of it all, if only temporarily.

I lived in a building that housed students from all over the United States, and though I became friends with many students in the program, my closest friend was a Californian girl. She was smart and funny and fun. I loved our philosophical debates, our midnight trips to get chips (fries) and cheese from the food trucks dotting the city, and the boisterous dinner and karaoke we enjoyed together during a trip to Italy. When we returned home from England, we stayed in touch. She had family who lived in my part of the country, and when she visited them, I drove there and stayed the weekend.

But I had a secret—I was dating a mutual friend and hadn't told her. In fact, I didn't tell her for months. By the time I did, damage had been done. Our halcyon memories together in Oxford were tainted by the recognition that I hadn't been honest. Some secrets have the power to destroy, and my lie of omission had cut deep.

Thankfully, my friend chose love over unforgiveness. She didn't turn away, try to shame me, or hold it over my head. Yet the situation was a sharp reminder that, in friendship as in life, there are consequences for our actions. Though my friend and I still exchange annual Christmas cards, our friendship lacks its former depth. Even though I apologized, it took time to regain my friend's trust. Even now, I regret what happened, but I can appreciate the lesson it taught me. As friends, let us always choose the loving response—whether we are the one who needs to be honest or the one who needs to extend forgiveness.

– Kristin

– Today's Act of Friendship –

If a friendship has been damaged by dishonesty, choose love—
by apologizing or by choosing to forgive, as appropriate.

Virgil's Garden

It is more blessed to give than to receive.
ACTS 20:35

Virgil's flower garden was once tucked into the triangle intersection of the three walking trails winding through my neighborhood. Technically city property, it's a roundish mound that he filled with annuals each summer. In my children's early years, it became a favorite place for us to pause and spy the hundred tiny creatures peeking through the blooms, half burrowed beneath the leaves. One summer it was lizards. Another it was frogs. There was always something to notice for those of us who cared to look closer, and my children were enchanted with pointing out the colorful little creatures.

Virgil's garden is gone now, becoming neglected when he moved into a nearby assisted living facility after his wife died. His backyard, which bumps up against the walking trail, now belongs to someone who doesn't want to expend the extensive time and effort Virgil poured into that little pile of city-owned dirt. As I talked to a neighbor who lives closer to Virgil's garden than we do, I learned that Virgil had befriended her children, bringing them freezies and ice-cream sandwiches across their backyards. He found joy in bringing delight to others—friends and strangers alike—even as his own circumstances were impossibly hard. His generosity brought blessing to those around him, and in doing so, he found himself blessed.

I've been thinking a lot about Virgil this fall. He and I never met, but he built a friendly corner and a sense of community with his garden—and the remaining neighbors keenly feel the loss of it. His generosity with his time, money, and talent had ripple effects that reached a young mother and her children, giving them the gift of a fun distraction and happy memories. I wonder in what ways I could be more generous in building community in my own neighborhood, creating a space for others to belong, to feel welcome, to build happy memories.

– Julie

– Today's Act of Friendship –

Find ways to use your temporary currencies of time, money, and talent to bring community, friendship, and joy to those around you.

The Same, but Different

Our bodies have many parts, and God has put each part just
where he wants it. How strange a body would be if it had only
one part! Yes, there are many parts, but only one body.
1 CORINTHIANS 12:18-20

It's good to have friends who have strengths where we have weaknesses, who can step in to help us out and fill in for our shortcomings. Friends who don't shame or embarrass us but simply smile and do what we cannot. That is my friend Staci. She loves to work with her hands and can create and sew things that I just cannot. She isn't afraid to suggest a project and then carry the bulk of the load to implement it, while laughing good-naturedly at my ineptness with a sewing machine or needle and thread.

But instead of becoming insecure, I embrace her strengths, letting her know how much I appreciate her. She, in turn, is quick to remind me of the ways that I help her out too. We each bring to our friendship a mutual support for one another, and it is beautiful to behold.

It is unrealistic to think that we can do everything in life without any help. Understanding that God gave us friends to fill in our gaps is one of the best blessings we can receive in life. We need one another, and recognizing not only my strengths but also my weaknesses and allowing others to help me in areas where I lack skills makes my relationships that much richer and deeper.

We don't need to pretend to have it all, and we shouldn't. God created us each to be unique. We are all individual parts that make up one body, the body of Christ. And because of this, we are free to walk in our strengths, while also appreciating and utilizing the strengths of those around us. Don't be afraid to let your friends help you; that is the way that God designed his body to function.

— *Kendra*

— Today's Act of Friendship —

Thank a friend who has a skill or strength
in an area where you are weak.

Leading the Way

*Make me truly happy by agreeing wholeheartedly
with each other, loving one another, and working
together with one mind and purpose.*

PHILIPPIANS 2:2

Emily and I trained as copy editors on the same day. A New Jersey native, she was a couple of years older, more experienced in our new position, and had obtained a master's degree before moving to the area with her husband. I, on the other hand, was a recent college graduate who felt a little out of my depth.

Over the years, our friendship deepened. Emily's sense of humor and appreciation for shopping and good books matched my own, and we met for countless lunch and coffee dates. She attended my wedding and was excited when I found out I was pregnant with my oldest daughter.

After Elise's birth, I began to appreciate Emily's friendship in a new way. Her son was a little older than my daughter, so she had walked the same path not long before I had. She knew what it was like to juggle home and work life and to feel the pull between the two.

My choices felt complicated because, as a new mom, I struggled to find my footing with my child. I loved my daughter fiercely but didn't always feel like I measured up to an ephemeral mom-standard that was always shifting on me. In those precious early months of Elise's infancy, it was a relief to go to work and feel like I was good at something and that I knew what I was doing. My friend's encouragement, steady presence, obvious care, and wisdom on how to walk this uncertain road was the compass I didn't know I needed.

In Scripture we're told to love one another and work together, because doing so fosters a united vision and purpose for the church as a whole. That solidarity isn't just so that we can accomplish the things we're called to do; it's a gift from a God who sees and knows how much our souls need someone to come alongside us and say, "You're doing a great job. You're doing the right thing. You're not alone." Friendship is his way of sending us the people we need most, right when we need them.

— Kristin

— Today's Act of Friendship —

Encourage a friend who is walking through a season
or circumstance that you've experienced.

Letting Others Step In to Help

Keep on loving each other as brothers and sisters.
HEBREWS 13:1

My daughter Jasmine was several hours away at a friend's cabin and having what appeared to be a slight allergic reaction to a large amount of pollen in the area where they were staying. As I talked to Jasmine on the phone, I could tell that she was crying. Her friend's mother, Angela, was with her and was so sympathetic and caring, offering to give Jasmine some antihistamine and oils. We hung up the phone while she was still a little teary, and I felt so helpless to do anything to comfort her. All night long, I tossed and turned, praying that she was sleeping well and feeling better.

The next morning, as I was waiting for a text from Angela about how the night had gone, I called Julie and told her my concern. She listened and then immediately offered to pray for Jasmine. As she did, she reminded me that sometimes as mothers we have to allow others to step in and mother our children when we cannot. That is what good friends are for. As I sat thinking about her words, Angela texted me back: "Good morning! Jasmine feels great today. The girls fell asleep watching a movie last night and slept well all night! I got up a few times to check on them just in case. We are so relieved Jasmine is feeling well!" Relief washed over me as I saw her words, and then gratitude followed as I realized this other mama was willing to care for Jasmine when I could not.

We cannot be another person's everything—even our kids will find that they need to depend on others from time to time, and that is a good thing. We weren't created to be anyone's savior. We need to recognize that God gave us family through the friends around us and that we are to love and help each other as if we were brothers and sisters. We were meant to do life within a community of people who can support us (and our kids!) when we aren't able. Don't be ashamed of needing help from others; we weren't meant to go through life alone.

— *Kendra*

— Today's Act of Friendship —

Don't try to do everything on your own—ask a friend for help.

Casting Out Fear

Such love has no fear, because perfect love expels all fear.
1 JOHN 4:18

"Your community made the national news." My brother's text message was accompanied by a link to a lengthy *New York Times* article highlighting the angst embroiling my community over refugees, religious tension, and cultural clashes. Somehow, my central Minnesota town of approximately seventy thousand people had become the epicenter of a national debate on refugees, with both sides of the political spectrum chiming in about what a cesspool we are—for completely opposite reasons.

As I read the article and then skimmed the horrible comments about my community, my heart was heavy, and I thought, *No one will ever want to move here. No one will ever want to admit to being from here. Why did you root us so deeply in this hard place, Lord?*

The truth is that our community is allowing fear to dictate our responses, drive wedges, and highlight differences rather than embrace similarities—on both sides. Fear is the root cause of so much of what has made us internet infamous.

My response to those who fear is this: I wish you could meet the young Somali men who watch soccer with my husband on Saturday mornings. I wish you could meet my Iraqi friend who shares her cultural heritage through her love of cooking. I wish you could take a road trip with my Chinese friends as we talk frankly about trade wars and the devastation it visits upon ordinary people. I wish you could meet my friends from countries we fear; people I love. People Jesus loves.

Fear is not from God. And as followers of Jesus, we are called to walk in love, not fear. While I am not foolish, I am also not fearful, and I will not listen to the voices whose primary message is fear.

– Julie

– Today's Act of Friendship –

If you've allowed fear to keep you from relationships
with neighbors, coworkers, or community members,
resolve to reach out in spite of the fear.

Being the Advocate

*After David had finished talking with Saul, he met Jonathan,
the king's son. There was an immediate bond between them, for
Jonathan loved David. . . . And Jonathan made a solemn pact
with David, because he loved him as he loved himself.*

1 SAMUEL 18:1, 3

A friend's parents were in the early stages of bitter divorce proceedings, and my friend's stepmom had messaged her some ugly accusations about her father. When my friend relayed the situation to me via text, I could tell she felt shaken, and I immediately picked up the phone.

"That is not okay," I told her when the call connected. "I don't care that you're an adult; in this situation, you're still their child, and the way she's chosen to involve you is completely inappropriate. She needs to know that it's not okay." Pausing, I listened as a silence thick with tears and a few deep swallows descended on the line.

I'm generally not one to rush to anger, but in this case I felt a fierce desire to protect my friend. She didn't want to get mired in the middle of her parents' divorce but felt helpless to extricate herself from the sticky situation she found herself in. Sometimes, we must be advocates for our friends when they can't advocate for themselves.

This idea is demonstrated by the story of the friendship between David and Jonathan. As King Saul's son, Jonathan could have considered David—the man who would eventually succeed Saul—a rival. Instead, a deep friendship arose between the two men, so much so that when Saul wanted to kill David, Jonathan advocated for his friend's life by reminding Saul of the many things David had accomplished.

Jonathan's actions and the advocacy he demonstrated are a reminder that if we care for our friends as fiercely as we care for ourselves, we will be intensely for them. We will want the best for them, just as we want the best for ourselves. We will be willing to speak the truth in love, reflecting God's grace and mercy and love through our own demonstration of those qualities.

— Kristin

— Today's Act of Friendship —

If a friend is facing a confusing or challenging situation,
remind them that you are on their side. Offer to advocate
for them if they can't advocate for themselves.

Put Love into Practice

Love is patient and kind. Love is not jealous or boastful or proud or rude. It does not demand its own way. It is not irritable, and it keeps no record of being wronged.

1 CORINTHIANS 13:4-5

Kristin, Julie, and I have been friends now for many years. As we've started to speak and attend events around our state, we've often heard other women comment on our friendship—how our love and respect for one another is evident in the easy way we speak to one another, banter back and forth, and sometimes even finish one another's sentences. From outward appearances, it can look like it hasn't taken much effort for the bond to form between the three of us, but the truth is we've had our share of misunderstandings, annoyances, and mistakes. We've learned to apologize, and we've learned to forgive. We've held one another's secrets and prayed each other through hard seasons. This friendship brings us great joy, it's true, but it has been tested and tried and proven.

No one gains friends just by happenstance. You may meet someone and connect in an instant, but you've got to put in the work to make it a lasting friendship. It takes time, energy, and commitment. A recent survey showed that even with how connected everyone is today through social media and cell phones, loneliness is at an all-time high, in part because social media gives the appearance of connection without any real accountability. We can use it when it's convenient for us and leave it when it isn't. But this, in turn, only creates surface-level relationships without any real depth or lasting connection.

If we want true friendship, then we must be willing to practice loving others by showing patience and kindness, not being rude or jealous of their successes. We can't demand our own way all the time or be overly sensitive. We must be willing to forgive and let things go. Must we do it perfectly all the time? Absolutely not. But we must create habits of loving people well if we want to have good friends.

— Kendra

— Today's Act of Friendship —

Extend love to a friend by offering patience, kindness, and forgiveness in your tone and words, not by demanding your own way.

The Gift of an Introduction

How wonderful and pleasant it is when brothers live together in harmony!
PSALM 133:1

"How did the interview go?" My text zinged off despite the early hour. I was too eager to wait a moment longer. Rachael was interviewing for a dream job, and her second interview had been the afternoon before.

"It went great! The first thing Tom said to me was, 'Julie told us we'd be foolish not to hire you.'"

I paused for a moment, trying to remember my conversation with Tom. I think I said it a bit nicer than that, but I was glad he read between the lines!

Tom and I have worked together professionally on several projects. He works for a great company, and when I learned he was hiring for a position I knew Rachael would love, I sent her the hiring notice. Rachael and I, originally coworkers, have developed a friendship that has transcended job changes and her move to a different community. I knew her personality and working style would be a good fit for Tom's company. As Rachael submitted her résumé, I reached out to Tom directly with a glowing recommendation for Rachael, both professionally and personally, that he apparently took to heart.

I responded to Rachael's text, and my heart lifted as she explained more about the interview and how they had asked her about potential start dates.

One of my favorite things is being a connector. As I go about my day, I keep my eyes and ears open, listening and filing away information about skill sets, dreams, and needs. When I sense a good match between a need and a corresponding resource (it can be the right person for an open job, or two women whose ministry passions are complementary), I offer to make an introduction. Before I connect them, I give each person a preview of the very best the other has to offer. I set the foundation for a professional or personal relationship whenever possible, and then I let them and God figure out the rest.

Positive "gossip"—intentionally wagging our tongues with truthful, complimentary information about others when they are not in the room—is transformational. It builds a community of harmony and unity and pulls people together instead of sowing seeds of discord and tension. Let's choose to foster connection by spreading positive words about our friends.

— Julie

— Today's Act of Friendship —

Help make a connection by spreading positive information
about a friend to coworkers, neighbors, extended
family members, or fellow church members.

Assuming the Best

Fix your thoughts on what is true, and honorable, and right, and pure, and lovely, and admirable. Think about things that are excellent and worthy of praise.

PHILIPPIANS 4:8

"Why wasn't I invited?" the woman asked. "Did I do something wrong?"

Stunned, my friend paused to formulate her response. The woman had pulled her aside at church to ask about an event my friend was hosting at her house in the coming weeks. As families bustled through the hallway and conversation buzzed all around them, my friend felt caught off guard and bewildered about how to respond.

She quickly explained that no, of course the woman hadn't done anything wrong. They had invited a smaller group of friends because of space reasons; they simply couldn't fit more bodies into their home. But later, as my friend and I analyzed the interaction, she wondered, "Why would she have assumed that she had done something wrong? It had nothing to do with her at all. When I see other people together, I don't assume that it's a reflection on me but a reflection on them."

Yet how often do we, as friends, assume things about our friendships? How often do we take up an offense, read something into someone else's response, or obsess about a conversation we had? How many times do we see a group of friends together on social media and wonder why they didn't invite us—did we do something wrong? Is our friendship not as strong as we thought it was?

Just last week, my husband saw a photo of a group of our friends at an event, and his instinctive response was to feel hurt. Why hadn't they invited us? he wondered. Yet when I gently reminded him that they hadn't excluded us on purpose, he agreed.

As Christians, we're called to push through our gut-level, human responses. God asks us to dwell on things that are true, lovely, and worthy of praise. In friendship, that may mean that rather than feeling hurt or worried over a friend's actions, we trust their intentions. We recognize that our feelings aren't always the best litmus test for what's true. And we always choose to assume the best.

— Kristin

— Today's Act of Friendship —

The next time you're scrolling social media and see a group
of friends spending time without you, actively choose
to quell your hurt and instead assume the best.

Mentoring Friendship

Timely advice is lovely, like golden apples in a silver basket.
PROVERBS 25:11

As a young twentysomething, I had just graduated from college and started my career while living at home with my parents. It was a transitional period in my life in which I was moving toward adulthood while still clinging to bits of my childhood. One Sunday I was invited to participate in a Bible study some of the older women in our church were starting as a way to mentor younger women, both married and unmarried. I immediately accepted their invitation, excited to learn from these wise women.

Each week we would gather in one woman's home, share a meal that we would make together, complete a short Bible study, and then spend time praying for one another. Every time we gathered, I found myself drawn to these women and the stories they told about marriage, raising children, juggling careers, and keeping a home. I loved every week and learned so much. Their prayers over my life and my future would often leave me in tears, and the tender way in which they encouraged me as a young woman still affects me positively today. They intentionally poured their knowledge into each of us, and I still use many of the tips they gave us! They loved well and didn't shy away from harder topics, sharing honestly the struggles they've walked through and allowing a place for us to share our own concerns.

Many times throughout Scripture we see that older men and women are encouraged to mentor those who are younger. In my own life, such mentoring has given me great encouragement when I had little experience with the goodness of God and his faithfulness throughout all of life. We need those who are older to tell the younger generation of the mercy and grace of God—such good words are truly like apples of gold to those who receive them. Whom can you encourage today?

– Kendra

– Today's Act of Friendship –

Share with a friend a part of your story that can encourage
them in something they are going through.

Divine Appointments

*Live in harmony with each other. Don't be too proud to enjoy the
company of ordinary people. And don't think you know it all!*
ROMANS 12:16

"Are you a local or visiting from afar?" I asked the woman sitting next to me. We were on the same bench at the Mall of America, waiting on kids in line for a roller coaster that spun while also looping through a track suspended under the ceiling of glass. As easy as that, I found myself in a delightful conversation with a stranger about rural Tennessee, about the species of birds visiting her feeder, about the flowers she can grow (and those she cannot). We winced in unison as children went spinning by on the track, laughing ruefully about how motion sick we felt merely watching them.

That conversation took place because I intentionally left my phone in my purse, out of sight and slightly out of reach, determined to see who was around me while I waited rather than reach for the easy distraction of my screen. It's a social experiment I've been doing of late—standing in lines, waiting on benches or sidelines without distraction, looking for someone to invite into a small conversation with a simple question or a smile.

I believe God sends us divine appointments. I don't know whose life I'm intersecting for an eternal reason, and I don't want to miss a single one of them. Paul's gentle admonishment to the Romans is one we need to heed if we don't want to miss the people God sends our way. We should be careful in the strength of some of our opinions, we should be careful of the judgments we lay on people based upon initial impressions, and we should be—as followers of Jesus—seeking to live in harmony rather than stirring up controversy and chaos in the day-to-day. I want to be a woman who sees others, who isn't too proud or too scared to approach them, and who lives in the present.

– Julie

– Today's Act of Friendship –

Keep your eyes open and remain available for the
divine appointments God sends across your path.

It's Not You

You must be compassionate, just as your Father is compassionate.
LUKE 6:36

I was recently talking with a friend about a mutual acquaintance. My friend used to wonder if this other woman liked her, because sometimes the other woman would greet her and be friendly, and other times she would almost seem to ignore her altogether.

My friend wondered if she had said or done something to upset this woman, until one day she noticed several posts in the other woman's social media feed about managing anxiety and how challenging it is for her at times. My friend's understanding of this woman changed after she saw her posts, and now when the other woman doesn't respond, she doesn't take it personally and instead feels compassion for her. She told me that now she just thinks, *Maybe her anxiety is getting the best of her today*, and continues to show kindness and extend friendship to the woman regardless of how she is treated in return.

My dad used to always say to treat others kindly because you never know what they may be dealing with that you cannot see. These words came back to me as my friend shared her situation. I said she was wise to consider the other woman's situation before she rushed to make a judgment about her and treat her unfairly based on that judgment.

We can so easily take up an offense against someone for behavior that may or may not actually have anything to do with us. Oftentimes people have struggles in their own lives that we know nothing about. We can be compassionate, even when we do not understand the full backstory to someone else's life, because God is compassionate to us.

— Kendra

— Today's Act of Friendship —

The next time someone appears to slight you, consider what
may be affecting them behind the scenes and choose to
show them kindness and be friendly to them anyway.

Compassion at the Cookie Booth

Be happy with those who are happy, and weep with those who weep.
ROMANS 12:15

We were barely on time for my daughter's Girl Scout cookie booth. As we drove into the Walmart parking lot, I breathed a sigh of relief—until I looked a little closer at the group of adults and kids milling by the entrance, greeting passersby as they walked in and out of the building. Frowning, I realized that I didn't recognize any of them. I quickly pulled into a parking space, grabbed my phone, and found the event details.

"Oh no, we're at the wrong place!" I burst out, throwing my car into reverse and then forward again to exit back onto the road. As the engine roared, Elise and I flew back in our seats a bit. Muttering under my breath, I felt anxious at every red stoplight, frustrated by every small delay. When Elise asked me an innocent question, I responded sharply. By the time we arrived at the right location, I felt completely discombobulated and apologized profusely.

"Oh, are you late?" the cookie mom asked, peering at her watch. "I didn't even notice."

While the girls sold Caramel deLites and shortbread, the other moms and I chatted. One asked how my husband was doing. As I related the story of how he had ruptured his Achilles and was now recovering, I found myself in tears. My husband was fine, but in the wake of his injury, I felt like I was buried under a mountain of mothering responsibilities. Our lateness that morning was just one more symptom of the helplessness I'd been battling.

Yet as I rubbed at my eyes, the other moms responded with sympathy and understanding. They waved away my apologies, said they knew how I felt, and continued on to talk about our kids and lives. As the shift wore on, I felt myself relaxing, their understanding a balm to my aching heart. Sometimes we can be discomfited in the face of someone else's grief or hurt, but as friends, the unconditional love we provide is just as important in those moments of heartache as it is in moments of happiness.

— *Kristin*

— Today's Act of Friendship —

Extend words of sympathy and compassion the next time a
friend tells you about a difficulty they're experiencing.

You Deserve Friends

As iron sharpens iron, so a friend sharpens a friend.
PROVERBS 27:17

We'd planned an evening out, just us moms, with no kids or responsibilities. As we gathered in the corner of a coffee shop, cups of brew in hand for a few hours of uninterrupted time, it felt so good to just sit and catch up. Most of the women around the circle I'd met at a local moms' group, and many still had small children. As the conversation moved from the lighthearted to the more personal, one topic that came up often was how little time the women had with friends now that they had children. There was almost an undercurrent of guilt for leaving their kids for any amount of time, and putting their own friendships on the back burner during this season seemed like a common occurrence within our little gathering of women.

As the evening went on and conversation continued, it became very obvious to many of the moms around the circle just how desperate they were to connect with other women (and many hadn't even realized how badly they needed it). Each woman left feeling heard, encouraged, and loved. We closed with prayer and a promise to get together again soon, even choosing the next date so we knew it would really happen.

You don't have to have children to feel as though making time for friendships is sometimes frivolous, especially in light of all the daily responsibilities we have. Often our to-do lists are long, our sense of responsibility is strong, and spending time with friends just doesn't seem like we'd be accomplishing anything of value, and so we let that go. But when we do this, we can find ourselves in a place where we are accomplishing much but feeling very lonely. To-do lists are important, but they are not more important than relationships. It may take some imperfect balancing, but life is meant to be lived with others. We strengthen one another by listening and giving wise counsel, comfort, and support. You deserve friends and time with them—don't let your other responsibilities tell you otherwise.

– Kendra

– Today's Act of Friendship –

Contact a friend or group of friends and plan
a day and time to spend together.

Exceeding Expectations

*Let's not get tired of doing what is good. At just the right time
we will reap a harvest of blessing if we don't give up.*

GALATIANS 6:9

It was kind of a flop. Not in an "I can't show my face in public" kind of way, but rather in an "I had hoped for something more" way. A few weeks earlier, I had decided to invite the women of my church to a ladies' night in. Our church didn't have a women's ministry, and I had begun to feel stirrings that women were missing out because of it, myself included. My casual event was one small step toward what I hoped would be deeper connections. So, feeling hopeful, I posted the event in our church's social media group and enlisted the help of my friend Andrea.

Andrea came early to help cut up cheese and fruit, and we chatted as we waited for the doorbell to ring. As the hour arrived and women began to trickle through the door, I looked around and couldn't help but feel a little stab of disappointment in my gut. Rather than the houseful of women I had hoped for, I had a handful.

I took a deep breath, welcomed the women, and enjoyed the next few hours of food and conversation. There were a couple of women I didn't know well, and as the night progressed, I learned details of their lives I never would have known from passing conversation. As Andrea and I said goodbye to the other women and cleaned up, we talked incessantly. My contacts felt positively glued to my eyeballs, yet we still lingered, hesitant for the night to end.

Here is what I love about our God: when we are faithful to do what he asks us to do, he exceeds our expectations. From an outsider's perspective, the night looked like a flop. But as the evening progressed and the conversation deepened, I felt profoundly thankful that I hadn't missed the beauty of those connections because things didn't look the way I had expected. The deep conversations were well worth the effort I'd put in, as was the one-on-one time with Andrea at the end of the evening. If we don't give up on friendship, on trying, on doing what God asks us to do—he is faithful.

— Kristin

— Today's Act of Friendship —

Invite someone you don't know well to spend time with you.

Creating Community

Let us not neglect our meeting together, as some people do, but encourage one another, especially now that the day of his return is drawing near.

HEBREWS 10:25

For months Aaron and I found ourselves engaging in similar conversations with three different couples—wrestling with what it looks like to be followers of Jesus in an increasingly international community rooted in the heart of the Midwest. We had all known of one another for at least a year or two and had periodically spoken to one another about the tension within our community, our churches, and our own hearts as we discerned how God might be using us and our families in new ways.

As we spoke with each couple in different settings, we sensed kindred spirits on a journey with only slightly overlapping circles—each of us attending different churches, our children attending different schools, our jobs taking us into very different spheres of influence. Despite this, I enjoyed conversations with them when our lives did overlap. I learned from their experiences and spiritual wisdom as I also sought to hear from God on where he was sending my own family.

I sent the texts separately, inviting each couple to a periodic dinner book club, explaining the vision of wrestling together through issues we've been navigating as individual couples and giving them express permission to decline with no need for explanation. The responses were immediate and enthusiastic—yes, yes, and another yes!—letting me know that the Holy Spirit was at work as much in their lives in this area as he was in ours.

Community built around a similar calling is immensely powerful, and I've learned to create my own when I can't find what I need. People are often willing to join when invited, and I've become bold in being the inviter. Being in community with one another is critical to our spiritual journey. Our lives lived in community serve as iron sharpening iron, and gathering together brings encouragement and accountability and breathes fresh life into us.

— Julie

— Today's Act of Friendship —

Consider where you are longing for community, and ask God whom you might invite into a book study or semiregular coffee date around an area of struggle.

Hobbies and Friends

Wherever your treasure is, there the desires of your heart will also be.
MATTHEW 6:21

It began as a hobby. In the middle of the night, as I soothed the baby back to sleep while scrolling Instagram to keep my eyes from falling closed, I ran across people who were selling preloved clothing on their Instagram accounts. Intrigued, I followed a few boutiques to see how they did it. Then, I purchased a few items. Finally, I decided that I'd like to try it out myself.

Within a few months, I had joined a few online groups with other women who had the same business model, cross-promoting our items. There was one group that chatted almost every day, and as time went on, I began to see them as friends rather than simply fellow business owners. Two of them were even located in Minnesota, several hours' drive from where I lived.

As the months bled into years and our friendship deepened, one of my Minnesotan friends told us that she was going to move and couldn't take her inventory across the country. If I was willing to drive up to get it, Rose said, I was welcome to have it. Her offer was generous and completely unexpected, and I jumped at the chance to pick up the hundreds of items she had on hand and to meet my friend in person.

As the appointed day dawned bright and sunny, I hit the freeway and arrived around noon. Over the next several hours, we went out for lunch with another friend, returned to Rose's house and met her children, and finally settled down into cushy chairs to spend time talking about our lives. The time flew by.

As I left that evening, it struck me that the visit wasn't about clothes at all. My friend's generosity didn't just extend to the bags of clothing we had hefted into my trunk; it was also revealed in the caring, thoughtful conversations we had together. Both of us treasured one another—not because of the material items we used as a pretext for our visit but rather because of the friendship we strengthened that day.

— Kristin

— Today's Act of Friendship —

Give generously of your time or a resource to a friend.

I'm Not Your Friend—Yet

*Children born to a young man are like arrows in a warrior's
hands. How joyful is the man whose quiver is full of them!*

PSALM 127:4-5

"Honey, I love the future, thirty-year-old version of you so much that I'm willing to let the current version of you be furious at me."

My children have heard these words from me in the midst of battles over boundaries, homework, and other formational decisions. As their mother, I am not their friend—although I hope more than anything to someday be a best friend to each of them. I cheer for them, encourage them, and love them, but I've also been honest in telling them that I am tasked with setting boundaries, holding them accountable, and guiding them as they grow into the young man and woman God has called them to be.

It can be difficult not to blur the line between parenting and friendship. In fact, it's tempting to bend the boundaries, revoke consequences, and ignore rules when everything is smooth sailing because I usually know when my refusal to let something slide is going to open the proverbial can of worms. I don't like cans of worms. Honestly, I'd much prefer to pretend the can of worms is not there—skipping over it in blissful and willful ignorance, so that everything can remain calm on the surface.

My current role in my children's life is not based on friendship, and I sometimes need to remind myself of that as much as I need to remind them—because my current role as mom is far more important at this stage in their life. My job is to open the cans of worms, confront hard things in healthy ways, and raise them to be young adults who love God and love others. I want them to be arrows in the quiver of God's army—men and women who make a difference in the world and in the lives around them. They have many friends, but they have a limited number of mother figures—women who will go toe-to-toe with them over the hard things and stand firm.

— *Julie*

— Today's Act of Friendship —

Consider your role with young people in your life: Are you
a mothering figure or a friend? Determine not to blur the
line, and gently confront hard things when necessary.

Friendship Remains

*No one has ever seen God. But if we love each other, God lives
in us, and his love is brought to full expression in us.*

1 JOHN 4:12

It was our tenth Hope Hike. A year earlier, we had decided that this would be our
final endeavor. Afterward, we would give away the remaining funds in the foundation we had established in honor of my sister—Katie's Club—and that would be it.
At the time, it felt right, but the finality of it hit me hard as our week in Colorado
progressed.

We stayed with friends in a big mountain house full of laughter, shared meals,
and children running rampant. One evening, a friend asked how I felt about the
climb. I paused, plunging dishes into scalding soapy water in an effort to distract
myself from my turbulent feelings. I was unable to articulate how I felt. But late at
night and in the early light of dawn, I thought a lot about my sister, and it left me
searching for breath to pull into my lungs. In some ways it felt like my sister had
died all over again, and I was left bereft, wondering, *What now? What is her legacy,
if not all this? How do I find purpose in the circumstances of her death if I can no longer
see these tangible reminders of her life?*

Yet even as I felt the weight of my friend's question and the grief that lingered,
I encountered the reminders of my sister's life. I remembered that Jesus himself
was the Word made flesh who dwelled among us (see John 1:14), and I considered
how often God chooses to reveal his intangible attributes to us through the world
around us and in the people we encounter. After all, it's in friendship that we can
see the love of God, reflected in the faces of those who love him.

At the week's final event, I looked around at the friends who knew my sister or
came simply because they loved us—friends willing to sacrifice vacation time and
money. I was struck by the sense that the soul-deep friendships and community my
husband and I had found were her true legacy. As we packed up our luggage and
left the mountains, that certainty remained. And in purpose, in heart, in spirit—my
sister remains too.

— *Kristin*

— Today's Act of Friendship —

Think of a friend who has reflected the love of God
to you. Send a note to say thank you.

Befriending the Friends of My Friends

This is my commandment: Love each other in the same way I have loved you.

JOHN 15:12

Arriving home one evening after playing a rousing and hilarious game of cornhole with Kendra's dance-mom friends, I decided that I wanted them to be my friends too. They are funny, smart, and compassionate—exactly the kind of women I wanted to do life alongside. They were already friends with Kendra, so I was a surprise bonus friend simply by being in Kendra's life. And who doesn't love a MOGO (make one, get one free) kind of deal? I have yet to meet a woman who doesn't love a MOGO friend.

My favorite way to make new friends is by getting to know the people who are already in friendship with those I love. I trust my loved ones' judgment of people, and their friend circles are a great way to find new people with whom I have a lot in common. To be clear: I don't steal the friends of my friends, and I don't cause drama. I don't interfere in the relationships between my friend and my new friend in any way—unless it is wildly and wholeheartedly in support of that friendship.

My friends know they are always welcome to invite their friends to events at my house—and so they do. Aaron and I are in the business of building community, and that means intentionally bringing people from our various circles together over food, game nights, and anything else we can think of that will encourage new relationships between people from different circles in our life. We are called to love people in the same way Jesus loved us, and in order to love people we need to meet them.

People are desperately hungry for community, and as believers in Jesus, we create a space for community to happen—with us and with others—in our home, in our backyard, in our family. We keep our circles open, and we are always looking for new friends.

— Julie

— Today's Act of Friendship —

Cohost a party with a friend, and invite people from both of your friendship circles who may not have met before.

Always Remember

God blesses those who mourn, for they will be comforted.
MATTHEW 5:4

"I want you to know that I'm praying for you and your family today. Katrina was a light in a dark world. I still remember."

The message came through as I woke early on the anniversary morning of my sister's death. It's been several years since she passed, and yet each year I receive a message from this friend reminding me that she has not forgotten my sister or our loss. I wiped away tears as I sent back a quick reply, thanking her for remembering and for praying. It feels so good to be known and remembered. A little while later another message came through on social media from someone else who was remembering and praying for me. I smiled as I sent a thank-you in response.

Years earlier when I'd been training for a hospice program, I'd learned to always ask people their loved one's name and then refer to that person in conversation by name. This is important because it is a way to honor the loved one who is no longer alive, and it's a lesson I've not since forgotten. And after losing my sister, I understand why it is so important for people to still speak about the deceased, especially by name. It matters greatly to those of us who are missing them and still grieving the loss, even years later.

How many of us can relate to losing a loved one? Or know someone close to us who has recently lost someone who was dear to them? We can offer comfort to those around us in the way that we listen and in the way that we remember those who are gone. Don't underestimate the significance a few simple words of concern can have for someone who is grieving, even if it is many years later. I believe your friend will be grateful that you still remember their loved one.

— Kendra

— Today's Act of Friendship —

Reach out to a friend who is grieving and offer them comfort by sharing a memory you have of their loved one (and, please, call them by name).

Taking the Kids

Whenever we have the opportunity, we should do good to everyone—especially to those in the family of faith.

GALATIANS 6:10

Life is made up of seasons that ebb and flow, and I found myself in a season of insanity. Aaron was frequently traveling for work during a particularly busy time of parenting and work for me. It was short term and doable, but the phrase "ships passing in the night" was an apt description of our situation. Aaron and I didn't have much choice in the moment other than to get through it and talk about how to avoid that level of chaos the next time, because there is always a next time. That's just the way life works.

On the phone with Kendra about something initially unrelated, I explained that Aaron and I weren't seeing much of each other, and I lamented the fact that our choices—none of them individually bad—had erased the margin I tried to keep in our lives and had pushed me over the edge emotionally.

"Why don't I take the kids this Friday night for a sleepover?" Kendra asked. A quiet pause stretched for a long moment before I simply said an exhausted thank-you, accepting her unexpected gift without argument.

While my children love her children and sleepovers between our families are a semiregular occurrence, it's usually a divide and conquer deal; she takes the boys, and I take Jasmine and another friend to round out the trio of our girls who are practically sisters. Her offer to take both of my children overnight left me with an empty house on a Friday night with no place to be and a newly returned husband who had been traveling all week.

Kendra is a defender of my marriage. She, with a wink and a smirk, whisked my kids away to join her family for the night and told Aaron and me to go on a date and have fun. Her family coming alongside mine during a chaotic time is exactly what Paul is talking about in Galatians—seeing and responding to the needs of our faith sisters who are facing a season of weariness.

— *Julie*

— Today's Act of Friendship —

Be a defender of marriages and families by offering to watch someone's children for a few hours or overnight.

November

Leading by Example

You yourself must be an example to them
by doing good works of every kind. Let everything you do
reflect the integrity and seriousness of your teaching.
TITUS 2:7

I want my daughter to have good friends, and that means that I must set a good example and show her what friendship looks like among women. I cannot teach her something that I am not practicing as well. Over the years I've had a few groups of good friends, and I am quick to let Jasmine know the inner workings of our friendships. I'll explain to her about the time one of my good friends and I had a disagreement and how we resolved it while remaining friends or how I've cheered on another friend as she pursued her dreams. In terms she can understand, I share with her how misunderstandings are handled, tell her about times I've been vulnerable and asked for help, how I've come to the aid of others, and how we support and cheer for one another. Jasmine asks a lot of questions, and I answer them as honestly as I can. I want her to know that grown-up friendships aren't perfect, but they are worth it.

This isn't a conversation that is ever really complete; it is an ongoing process of her watching how I interact with other women. I want her to see friendships based on a solid foundation—things like believing the best of one another, giving the benefit of the doubt, practicing good communication, seeing one another's strengths, being loyal, holding one another's confidences, not backbiting or gossiping—just to name a few. I believe that as we do this, she will grow up in the confidence of having good friends, and in fact, she already is. I see her celebrate her friends' successes, listen as they cry, and offer encouragement when they are low. She is beginning to take on these traits herself, and it starts with watching me and my friends.

You do not have to be a parent to lead by example. Whether we realize it or not, we all have people around us who are watching the way we interact with others. You never know the positive impact your example could have on a younger woman. What kind of example do you want to set for those who may be watching you?

– Kendra

– Today's Act of Friendship –

Intentionally take the time to encourage a younger person by sharing
with them the successes and failures you've experienced in friendship.

Working Together

*Are your hearts tender and compassionate? Then make me truly
happy by agreeing wholeheartedly with each other, loving one
another, and working together with one mind and purpose.*

PHILIPPIANS 2:1-2

"Sorry I'm late!" I said, breezing into the room. The women (and a handful of babies) who were already present looked up and waved off my apology with a smile. With three young daughters, it's a challenge to make it to church on time—one daughter couldn't find her tights, another ran from me each time I tried to comb her hair, while the third informed me as she was buckling her seat belt that she hadn't eaten breakfast—so the other ladies are used to me arriving breathless and harried.

I started volunteering every other week in the church nursery a few years ago, and it's one of the highlights of my weekend. My kids are out of the baby and toddler stage, and I miss those years of pudgy cheeks and drooly smiles. An hour every other week is the perfect way to get those baby snuggles I miss while giving their parents a break.

But as much as I enjoy the babies, I also look forward to my time with my fellow workers Brittany, Molly, and Jerian. There's a special camaraderie among those who are volunteering their time for the benefit of others, a sense that working together with the same purpose is fostering community—not just among the four of us, but in the church as well.

Together, we've talked about parenting challenges, work, and daily life. Sometimes friendship can be brash and bold, but it can also be quiet and gently supportive, and that's how these friendships feel. I appreciate the godly wisdom and encouragement each woman offers, even as she goes about the business of rocking a fussy child or feeding endless Cheerios to another. As friends, working together with a united purpose can help provide a commonality on which deeper friendship can be built.

— *Kristin*

— *Today's Act of Friendship* —

Seek to foster a friendship with a coworker (or covolunteer).

A Taste of Home

Since God chose you to be the holy people he loves,
you must clothe yourselves with tenderhearted mercy,
kindness, humility, gentleness, and patience.

COLOSSIANS 3:12

When I was newly married, I joined my husband's Thanksgiving tradition of traveling to Iowa for an extended family gathering. Aunt Marigrace always hosted, and her home was filled with dozens of people and comfortable chaos. As we sat down to eat one year, I was pleasantly surprised to see that Aunt Marigrace had added my mom's wild rice salad (a favorite of my childhood holidays) to the ample spread.

It wasn't until years later, one fall Sunday as I was preparing the menu for a Friendsgiving we were hosting, that I finally, finally understood the depth of the intention behind that dish. Flipping through recipes, I suddenly realized that my mother-in-law, Connie, must have told Marigrace about my favorite holiday side. Marigrace had added it to the menu as an unspoken welcome to the new girl in the family, a taste of my childhood family grafted into my new family.

As my girlfriends become mothers-in-law, I've started pondering what it means to be the mother who welcomes newcomers into the family, who cedes her role as a central figure in her child's life to their new spouse, and does it well. Hollywood tropes of terrible in-laws often suggest that we will fail in this important relationship, that it is not possible to be friends with your in-laws. And, in some cases, it is not. People can be so broken and hurt by past traumas that they simply cannot do this relationship in healthy ways. But that is not what God intended.

If you are a new mother-in-law, you have the advantage of wisdom gleaned over decades, an opportunity to welcome the insecure newcomer with mercy and tenderness, compassion and patience, loving the younger woman in ways she might not entirely understand until she is a mother herself, well into her parenthood journey. And if you are a new daughter, you can find ways to honor the role of your husband's mother with love and humility, understanding there may be some grieving happening as her son shifts his loyalty and priority to your newly formed family.

— *Julie*

— Today's Act of Friendship —

Write a note of appreciation to a woman who has welcomed you as the newcomer, or write a note of welcome to a newcomer in your circles.

Build Bridges

*If you need wisdom, ask our generous God, and he will
give it to you. He will not rebuke you for asking.*

JAMES 1:5

At just twenty years old, my husband, Kyle, had moved out of his parents' house, dropped out of college, and was living with friends while working full time. He wasn't making the healthiest choices, and his parents knew it. His mother, Kathy, told me years later that she prayed constantly for him during that season and that she felt God's response was for her to just keep loving him and remaining positive in his life. She knew that berating him about his choices wasn't going to do any good, and she wanted to keep their relationship intact by not burning any bridges.

She talked with him about Jesus and kept praying for him, but ultimately, she entrusted his life to God. She told me it wasn't easy, but she knew it was the best way to handle the situation. Little by little, she and her husband began to see their son grow once again in his relationship with God. It didn't happen overnight, but they knew if they remained patient and trusted God, Kyle would come back around, even though they could not see it at the time.

Even now, the truth of Kathy's words lingers in my mind as I think about relationships that I am currently in with people who are not always making the best or healthiest choices. We all need wisdom from God to know how to navigate relationships with others, whether family members or friendships, and the Bible is clear that if we need wisdom, we can ask God and confidently know that he will give it to us. We don't want to unnecessarily break ties or burn bridges with others who are making poor choices in their lives but rather give them to God in prayer and act in wisdom and love toward them.

— *Kendra*

— *Today's Act of Friendship* —

Seek wisdom from God and then reach out to a friend
who is in the middle of a wandering season.

Ask the Question

Keep on asking, and you will receive what you ask for.
Keep on seeking, and you will find. Keep on knocking,
and the door will be opened to you.

MATTHEW 7:7

A family friend had just had a new baby, so I offered to bring them a meal—my standard, easy-to-double baked ziti recipe, along with salad, bread, and a dessert. I asked Tim to drop it off after work one day, and he mentioned it in passing to a friend.

"How did you convince them to let you bring them a meal?" the friend asked Tim incredulously. "I talked to them about having people from church bring meals after they had the baby, and they said no!"

Tim didn't know the reason, and when he asked me I could only shrug. "I don't know," I said, noncommittally. "I just asked them."

Sometimes, in life and in friendship, it's as simple as that—asking a question, sometimes more than once. Maybe our friends weren't comfortable with a multiday meal train that required coordinating schedules for drop-off, or maybe I simply caught them at the right moment.

Whatever the reason, in friendship, you and I can't accomplish the things we'd like to if we don't bother asking in the first place. If I'm honest, there have been many times when I didn't ask a question, even though I should have. I've refused to verbalize a question in class or at work at the risk of sounding silly or uninformed; I've avoided asking a friend about a questionable life choice they were pursuing because it felt uncomfortable; and I've refused to open myself up and ask an acquaintance to coffee or lunch because I feared rejection. Yet Jesus tells us to ask, seek, and knock. All of those actions require us to face a situation with bravery, knowing that rejection is a real possibility. Yet I believe it's when we're willing to face our fears that we find, oftentimes, the doors we feared were closed to us are already open. It's possible that a friend is already on the other side of that question, just waiting for you to have the courage to ask.

— *Kristin*

— Today's Act of Friendship —

Be brave and ask a question—whether it's asking an acquaintance out for coffee, a friend if she needs help, or a coworker if they could offer their opinion on a project.

A Brand-New Tradition

We love each other because he loved us first.
1 JOHN 4:19

The year my husband and I started dating, my soon-to-be mother-in-law suggested that since my family lived in the same town, we could host Thanksgiving together. Little did she know, that first year would start a tradition that has continued to this day: fifteen years later, our families still celebrate Thanksgiving all together. Her suggestion resulted in a wonderful new tradition that ensured both sides of our family would be together at least once a year. Each Thanksgiving we rotate homes and decide who's bringing what to eat—some new foods and other dishes we've brought every year without fail. Over the years we've created bonds and memories that we never would have if we hadn't decided to start a new tradition and create a new kind of family.

But it hasn't stopped there. Opening our homes up on Thanksgiving has also opened our hearts to others who may be alone on the holiday. Rarely a Thanksgiving celebration goes by that is not attended by at least one new person, usually several. Our families have learned to be flexible, and new faces are always welcome to join our rather rowdy (albeit very loving!) group. We love to open our doors to others, and it has created a wide circle that is always inviting new friends in to celebrate. Everyone knows they are always welcome to bring along a friend to our family gatherings.

Do you have a favorite way to celebrate holidays? Have you, like my family, opened your doors to others or started new traditions? If not, this may be the year to start something new. It often starts with just one person. Who around you needs a family to spend the holidays with this year? Who is lonely? Who is in need of a friend? We are free to love others because we first have been loved by God. When we fully grasp this truth, we can invite and include others more readily.

— *Kendra*

— Today's Act of Friendship —

Invite someone who may be lonely and in need of
a friend to your family's holiday gathering.

Meeting Needs

When God's people are in need, be ready to help them.
Always be eager to practice hospitality.

ROMANS 12:13

"I hate to ask, but could you pick me up tomorrow after surgery?" Mary's question came during our conversation about my canceled plans and how my schedule for the next day had unexpectedly cleared.

Mary is a single mom whose family lives far away. She was having outpatient surgery, and my heart squeezed at her words—knowing it was humbling for her to have to ask for help and immensely sad that she was navigating what it means to be a single parent through no choice of her own.

As I visited quietly with her in the recovery room while she waited to get discharged, my thoughts circled back to the unfairness of this—having me, a friend, sitting in the chair usually reserved for spouses and family, the intimacy of the nurse handing me the discharge papers as she gave me instructions for the prescription and aftercare. I silently prayed that I would be more sensitive, more discerning when it came to Mary. I asked God to show me ways that Aaron and I could support her family not only as she recovered but also going forward.

In the months since her surgery, we've looked for little ways to ease her burden. We've prayed for her and with her over the things beyond her control, offering a safe place to vent when frustrations are simply too much. When Mary expresses gratitude but also regret at needing help, I gently remind her that this is a season for her to receive, and I promise her that God will use her once again to be the helper, the giver, the one who comes alongside with loving generosity and hospitality.

We were never meant to do life alone, despite our American culture's celebration of fierce independence and the false narrative of pulling ourselves up by our bootstraps. God built us for community, and then showed us through Scripture what it looks like to have spiritual brothers and sisters who look out for those around them and who generously give and humbly receive as life ebbs and flows.

— *Julie*

— Today's Act of Friendship —

Consider which of your friends could use extra help in the form of
a listening ear or an extra set of hands, and then meet her needs.

The Encourager

Kind words are like honey—sweet to the soul and healthy for the body.
PROVERBS 16:24

Have you ever read *The 5 Love Languages* by Gary Chapman? In it, he lists five ways people give and receive love: quality time, gifts, acts of service, words of affirmation, and physical touch. My husband and I read it early on in our marriage, and it was enormously helpful for me to realize why my husband loves to spend all day watching movies together (his primary love language is quality time) and for him to understand why I was so upset when he did all of his Christmas shopping on December 24 (mine is receiving gifts).

Recognizing a person's primary love language can be helpful not just in romantic relationships but in other areas of life as well. Despite the fact that I spend my days as a writer, the love language I struggle with the most is words of affirmation. Using affirming words with my children comes naturally, but I often find myself tongue-tied with others.

Thankfully, I have a friend who has mastered the art of encouraging others through words. Carisa uses words of affirmation to foster connections. She starts by introducing people not by what they do but by the qualities she admires most about them. She then follows up by intentionally introducing women to one another— whenever she sees commonalities between two friends or acquaintances, she makes an effort to connect them. Every once in a while, a group chat that she's created will pop up, including me, her, and one other person. They typically read something like this:

Do you know each other? If you don't, you should. You are both amazing women who do everything for Jesus. Anyway, you two would really hit it off. You both have such HUGE hearts and are both so talented. I hope you meet up for coffee someday and love on each other.

The fact that Carisa is others-focused is the very reason she draws people in. Her consistent verbal encouragement makes others want to be around her. And because she's intentional in speaking words of kindness and love, as her friend, I want to do the same in return. As friends, let's choose to encourage others with our words, cultivating an atmosphere of love and mutual respect—even if affirmation is not our primary love language.

– *Kristin*

– *Today's Act of Friendship* –

Encourage someone by speaking words of affirmation
about a quality or characteristic you admire.

The Comparison Trap

*Pay careful attention to your own work, for then
you will get the satisfaction of a job well done, and you
won't need to compare yourself to anyone else.*
GALATIANS 6:4

Scanning the audience that bright wintry morning, I took in a sight that never fails to make my knees knock: tables filled with women dressed "jeans cute," with outfits perfectly on trend and expertly applied makeup. All I could think was, *How do these ladies have multiple toddlers and babies and still manage to look polished and beautiful?* Memories of my days with two kids under three sucker punched me, and I suddenly doubted my own mothering—because a decent percentage of the time during those toddler years, I didn't look polished and put together.

Lest you think that I am intimidated only around beautifully dressed women, I also found myself growing uncomfortable and insecure recently during a conversation about female leaders in my community—feelings that were completely unintended by my conversation partner.

My secret is out: I'm easily intimidated by other women, even when they don't intend to intimidate. The thing is, I probably unintentionally intimidate others on the days when I look polished and professional. My insecurities stem from taking the very best attributes of another woman and comparing her best public qualities to my worst secret qualities. It's a ridiculous comparison, one so stacked against me that I'll never win—a comparison Jesus never asked me to make in the first place!

Jesus has called me to serve in places specific to where I am in my own faith journey; he has something different for the woman next to me, and there is no need for me to be glancing around with envy or intimidation in my heart. In fact, when I start focusing on what Jesus has called the women around me to do instead of what he has for me, I stumble in what I'm supposed to be doing. Paul's words in Galatians remind us that we need to focus on our task, finding satisfaction in a job well done rather than being distracted and sidelined because we're focusing on what God has asked of the women around us.

— *Julie*

– Today's Act of Friendship –

Think of a way you secretly compare your worst to someone else's
public best, then bring those comparisons to God and leave them there.

NOVEMBER 10

No Small Prayers

God did listen! He paid attention to my prayer.
PSALM 66:19

My parents moved to a larger city when my dad started a new business. My mom, Annie, was excited for my dad but was also a little sad to be leaving the community they'd lived in for several years since they had a wonderful church and good friends that my mom was loath to leave.

An introvert by nature and now an empty nester, my mom wondered if she'd be able to make friends in their new city like she'd had in their previous town. So she decided to pray, even for just one good friend, while telling no one of her desire. The weeks went by, and as they settled into their new home she got a call from a woman named Gail, who'd heard that my mom was a quilter. Gail invited her to a quilt guild, and my mom happily accepted the invitation. Little did she know that Gail would soon become her very best friend.

"It wasn't hard to get to know Gail," my mom said. "We both knew we would be good friends right away."

The two started quilting together and quickly found other interests they both enjoyed, and it wasn't long before they were getting together with their husbands as well. My mom found friendship, support, and love with Gail, and she is grateful that God answered her simple prayer for a friend.

Do you have a friend you just clicked with right away? Maybe you had a shared interest or passion for a common cause. If you do, thank God for the friendship. If not, pray and ask God for a good friend, because we know that he will listen and pay attention to our prayers. It is not too small of a request to ask God for a good friend, and I believe it's a prayer he'd love to answer. Once you've prayed, keep your eyes open and heart sensitive to who God will bring across your path and be willing to take the initiative to make a new friend today.

— Kendra

— Today's Act of Friendship —

Tell a good friend how much you appreciate their friendship, and keep your eyes open for a new friend God may bring across your path.

Supportive Motherhood

May God, who gives this patience and encouragement,
help you live in complete harmony with each other,
as is fitting for followers of Christ Jesus.

ROMANS 15:5

When my daughter Noelle was a curly-haired toddler, I decided to find someone to watch her and Elise two mornings a week so I could accomplish work and tasks without interruption. After posting on our church's private online group, I got a response from a woman named Angie, who came over the following week to meet our family.

Angie's youngest daughters had just started school, so she was looking for flexible work during the day. Even better, she was willing to watch the girls at my house. So, for the past five years, she has done just that—spending ten or more hours a week at my house taking care of my (now three) daughters. On writing days, when I'm perched on the plush floral chair in my bedroom with a bird's-eye view of the backyard, I can see her at the playground—a calm force in a sea of chaos.

More than the help I now rely on, over the years, I have come to admire Angie's strength and ability to withstand adversity. As a single mom with daughters of her own, she's an amazing advocate for her children. Though we may have different approaches to certain things, she is a friend who supports me in my motherhood, just as I support her in hers. I always know she'll refer my daughters back to me if she's unsure how to respond to something. In my children's best moments, she cheers alongside me. In my children's worst moments, she offers the sympathy of shared understanding.

In an age of social media perfection and the internet's obsession with parent shaming, the ability to be authentic and vulnerable with our friends on a tender topic like parenting is invaluable. God, the source of patience and encouragement, has encouraged us to live in harmony with one another. Yet harmony is often achieved when we can find friends who are willing to be in the trenches alongside us. This idea doesn't just apply to parenting. Who is alongside you in the trenches of school or work? Who is experiencing the same medical, financial, or relationship struggles that you are? Who can you encourage?

— Kristin

— Today's Act of Friendship —

Thank a friend who is in the trenches with you for their encouragement.

Joyful Tomfoolery

A cheerful heart is good medicine.
PROVERBS 17:22

Zing. I snickered as the meme bounced off a satellite and landed in Kendra and Kristin's phones. It was a ridiculous picture captioned with something silly, and it was completely unrelated to whatever business thing we were currently discussing via text. The laughing emoji responses I received were soon followed by more memes in response, and we spent a few minutes laughing over nonsense before returning to the more serious discussion we had temporarily abandoned.

People often ask us what it is like to work as a trio—running a small business together as equal partners. There are a hundred reasons why we love working as a collective, but there are also moments of frustration. Our individual strengths are almost always complementary, but sometimes our different perspectives require compromise. We've discovered that humor goes a long way in strengthening our bond as friends even as we work alongside one another as professionals. Laughter acts as a buffer and gives us a mental break. Humor reminds us of one another's humanness and keeps us connected when we are physically apart, and often speaks to a deeper, harder truth beneath the surface laughter.

I've come to cherish that lighthearted connection so much that I've adopted it in other situations. My brothers periodically get something from me that falls into the "just for fun" category, as does my husband. If I see something silly and it makes me think of someone I love, I take a moment to send it their way with a funny little note, letting them know I'm thinking of them and love them.

As adults, it's so easy to fall into rhythms of responsibility in our relationships without setting aside time for silliness and fun. We disregard the importance laughter plays as it smooths over rough spots and hard moments. We forget that a joyful heart is good medicine—as good for our spirits as it is for our relationships.

— Julie

— Today's Act of Friendship —

Pick one relationship to start injecting a little extra silliness
into, and make it a regular habit going forward.

Listening without Agreeing

I want your will to be done, not mine.

LUKE 22:42

I've noticed that my daughters seem to get the most upset when they think I'm not listening. In response, they'll repeat their statement over and over again until I finally say, "I heard you!"

It's not so much that I'm not listening; it's that they've confused "listening" with "agreeing." My seven-year-old daughter Noelle explained it to me this way: "Mom, when you *listen* to the teacher, you do what she says. So you're not listening!" In other words, because I wasn't doing what she wanted me to do, she assumed I hadn't heard her—when really, I just didn't agree that she needed to stay up later than her usual bedtime because someone else's parents let them go to bed later in the evening. I heard her loud and clear, but because we had different perspectives, we disagreed on the best way to proceed.

Although this may sound like a childlike trait, I've seen this happen in friendship, too. Just the other day, I told my husband about a challenge I was having with friends of mine about coming to a consensus on a decision.

"Why don't you tell them that's how you feel about it?" he asked me.

"I did!" I said. "I just don't feel like they're listening!" If I'm honest with myself, however, I can recognize that my friends were listening—they just didn't agree with my conclusion.

We may also experience this frustration in our friendship with God. How often does this listening-without-agreeing happen in our prayers to Jesus? As our friend who sticks closer than a brother, he understands us intimately. But it can be easy to fall into the trap of thinking that if we pray and something doesn't go the way we'd like or we don't hear the answer we expect (or any answer at all, for that matter), he must not be listening. But it may simply mean that our heavenly Father views our circumstances in a very different light than we do. How powerful it is when we consider the big picture—unseen to us, but visible to God—and shift our mindset, recognizing that he can listen without agreeing! Doing so can go a long way to deepening or restoring our trust in him.

— *Kristin*

— Today's Act of Friendship —

When a friend or family member seems to be listening without agreeing, try to see the issue from their point of view.

The Sixth Love Language

*Live in harmony with each other. Don't be too proud to enjoy the
company of ordinary people. And don't think you know it all!*

ROMANS 12:16

I have a freezer full of homemade Chinese dumplings. Why? Because Carmen knows my children love the dumplings she and her mom make, and so they made and froze dozens of dumplings for my children before they returned home to China. I can't make authentic dumplings, and the versions in the store or at any of our restaurants in the US can't even begin to compare to the real thing—so this treasured gift of friendship is an extraordinary culinary delight in its own right that had my children jumping for joy.

Aaron and I have discovered that hosting a potluck and asking people to bring a favorite family dish provides a safe way to explore someone else's culture, and it is the perfect way to ask them to share parts of their stories as we grow in friendship. There is something powerful about sharing a favorite, culturally important food—it shrinks the differences between people as commonalities are discovered and highlighted. Discussing the ingredients of a particularly yummy dish soon turns into sharing stories about the version Great-Grandma made, about where the dish came from originally and then—suddenly—you are laughing and talking about something entirely different with someone who is no longer a stranger to you.

We've hosted football game "dip nights" in which our local central Minnesota families bring all the cheesy and creamy dips we're known for to the culinary surprise and delight of our visiting Chinese interns. We've hosted pancake feasts for the young Somali men Aaron plays soccer with so they can watch their favorite soccer teams on the basement TV on a full stomach. And we've laughed until our sides hurt as we've stood in my kitchen making lopsided dumplings alongside Carmen, in celebration of the Chinese Spring Festival.

Inviting others into your family's food traditions and expressing interest in trying theirs is one of the easiest ways to grow friendships as you bring people together in harmony and learn parts of their story. It's our favorite way to intentionally build community among people being introduced to one another for the first time.

— Julie

— Today's Act of Friendship —

Plan a food-themed dinner party that will bridge
gaps and get your guests talking.

We Can All Be Cheerleaders

Let everything you say be good and helpful, so that your words
will be an encouragement to those who hear them.

EPHESIANS 4:29

Not long ago a friend texted me to tell me about a dream she believes she should start pursuing. As I encouraged her to take a step, she replied, "How do I stop feeling anxious?" To which I responded, "You don't." I told her that fear is normal, especially when doing something new, and sometimes you just have to step out and do it afraid. We talked more about specific first steps she could take toward her dream, and then I told her to pray and take just one step that week.

I continued to check in on my friend, asking her how she was doing and what she was working on. I tried to encourage her and remind her of the truth of God's Word even when she couldn't quite believe it for herself. Over time her dream grew and began to come to fruition. I was thrilled for her and shared in the joy of knowing she was pursuing all that God had for her life. I loved being able to celebrate her success with her all along the way.

Perhaps that's where you find yourself today—maybe you've had a dream you've wanted to pursue but simply haven't yet, or maybe you don't know where to start, or maybe you've had no one tell you that you can do it. I believe that if God has given you a dream, he will be the one to bring it to pass, if you are obedient to take one step at a time. But we cannot do it alone! We need our friends and community to help us, encourage us, and remind us of God's truth when we forget or get discouraged. We need to be honest about our hopes and fears and allow others to speak truth to us. And we need to cheer on our friends as well when they are in need of encouragement.

– Kendra

– Today's Act of Friendship –

Encourage a friend who is pursuing a dream and ask how you can help.

Remaining Openhearted

All have sinned and fall short of the glory of God, and all are justified freely by his grace through the redemption that came by Christ Jesus.
ROMANS 3:23-24, NIV

After a lull in the conversation, Sarah began telling me a story of her days in seminary two decades ago. She was living in California, and she and her cohort went on a mission trip to Central America. As they served alongside young people from several Central American countries, they became especially good friends with José, a young man who was on fire for God and who acted as their translator. They had an amazing time, adopted José into their crew, and promised to stay in touch with their new friends as they reluctantly returned home to continue their studies.

It was about six months later that they learned that José had come to the United States and was living in the same community. Life was busy, they were busy, and she quietly told me that not one of them had reached out to José. She fell silent, looking into her mug, then said, "The last I heard, José left his faith."

We both wiped away tears that evening. Over José. Over that younger version of Sarah and her classmates. Over the other friends we've loved and lost.

I have yet to meet a woman who doesn't have a friendship regret. We have all fallen short of the glory of God, and that means we may hurt others and be hurt in return, often unintentionally, through our sinful preoccupation and negligence rather than maliciousness.

What are we going to do with the hurt caused through friendship? When we've been hurt, we may be tempted to harden our hearts, closing them off so that no one else can come close enough to hurt us again. When we've been the cause of hurt, we may internally beat ourselves up for decades, convinced we cannot do friendship well and that there is no place for a second chance. But what if we took the hurts—both received and inflicted—and laid them openhearted at the throne of God, giving him the opportunity to redeem them and us and to strengthen our future friendships through it all?

— *Julie*

— Today's Act of Friendship —

Examine the state of your heart. Spend the time necessary
with God processing your regrets and asking for forgiveness
even as you forgive those who have hurt you.

Putting Others First

*Don't be selfish; don't try to impress others. Be humble,
thinking of others as better than yourselves.*
PHILIPPIANS 2:3

"We really feel called to leave the church," our friends told us somberly. "We aren't sure what's next; we've just felt God tugging at us to do something else and have been praying about our next steps."

In the stillness of the evening, while our collective children slumbered in the hotel rooms adjoining ours on our joint family trip, the quiet statement fell like a box of rocks on the floor, discordant and unexpected.

"What?!" my husband exclaimed, nearly jumping out of his seat. "That's terrible! Who in the world could ever replace you guys?"

Seated next to him, I shot him a not-so-subtle death glare, hinting he should stop talking. Realizing his mistake, he backtracked a bit. "I mean, of course we support you guys no matter what. This is just unexpected."

In friendship as in life, it can be hard for us to consider someone else's needs first. Our natural impulse is to wonder what the ramifications of someone else's choice will be for us, not them. We may feel disappointed, worried, or hurt, wondering how things will change or what something will mean for our own life. Selfishly, we may even wish that our friends would make a different choice, one that wouldn't challenge us or change the status quo.

And yet, we are called to consider the needs of others—not just alongside them, but before our own. That tension is a challenge that, if I'm honest, I have yet to master. Thankfully, true friends will offer us grace when we realize that we've overstepped our boundaries and give us the benefit of the doubt when we find ourselves backtracking. In the case of our friends, they graciously accepted the apology we sheepishly offered for our knee-jerk reaction. Together, the four of us instead resolved to pray over the weighty decisions our friends faced.

— Kristin

— Today's Act of Friendship —

If there's a situation in which you've felt tension with a friend,
consider whether the tension is due to how the situation affects
you rather than how it will affect them. Pray about how you
might resolve those tensions, and then follow through.

There Is Always Hope

This High Priest of ours understands our weaknesses, for he faced all of the same testings we do, yet he did not sin. So let us come boldly to the throne of our gracious God. There we will receive his mercy, and we will find grace to help us when we need it most.

HEBREWS 4:15-16

We pulled into our driveway after a nice Thanksgiving dinner with family when our headlights shined a spotlight on him. Standing in the middle of our yard was my husband's good friend Jerry. Even from this distance, we could see that he was inebriated. My husband and I locked eyes as an understanding passed between us. I quickly shooed the children inside while my husband slowly walked up to his friend, greeting him softly and asking him what was going on.

Jerry has dealt with many demons in his life, and alcoholism is one of the worst. Tangled around his mind and heart, his addiction has left in its wake a history of poor choices, broken dreams, and damaged relationships. My husband came to know Jerry through a friend and forged an immediate bond with him. For all his struggles, Jerry is also very kind and genuine, funny and cheerful—when he's not drinking.

My husband decided to take Jerry to the hospital for detox as my kids stared at me from around the kitchen island. They know Jerry struggles with drinking too much, and they also know what a wonderful man he is.

"Why does he do it, Mom?" they asked.

I stumbled over my words as I tried to explain to them the complicated nature of addiction.

"Can we pray for him?"

"Of course," I replied. And we did. We ended our prayer by talking about hope. Hope in Christ. Hope for freedom from addiction. Hope for Jerry.

Maybe you, too, know someone who struggles with addiction (or maybe you are that person). It's comforting to know that Jesus understands our weaknesses and that we can come boldly to him where we will find mercy and grace when we need it most. No one is beyond the reach of God. We can believe that for ourselves and for our friends who struggle with addiction.

— Kendra

— Today's Act of Friendship —

Reach out to a friend who has been battling addiction, letting them know you are there for them and want to prayerfully help them.

Friendsgiving

Don't forget to show hospitality to strangers, for some who have done this have entertained angels without realizing it!

HEBREWS 13:2

We've started a new tradition around Thanksgiving that I swiped from one of my goddaughters—Friendsgiving. It's a more casual version of the big day, but with many of the same foods. I've come to consider it a dry run of sorts, a place to try a couple of new recipes while also cherishing the dishes that have become traditions in our respective extended families.

Aaron and I got the idea one Thanksgiving evening when we found ourselves swinging by a large indoor Somali soccer tournament to cheer on the young men on his pickup soccer team. As we visited with them before their next match, we discovered that most had never been invited to a Thanksgiving gathering and had never celebrated it, despite having lived in the United States for a significant portion of their lives. As we laughingly told them about the famous Katie's Salad (named after our niece and consisting only of whipped cream, apple chunks, and Snickers) as a favorite family food tradition, Aaron extended an invitation to join us next year for a Friendsgiving the weekend ahead of Thanksgiving, with a promise to include all the Fisk/Brotzler traditions and fixings.

Friendsgiving is a way for us to welcome those around us who don't have a place to go or whose own cultural traditions don't include turkey, gravy, and football. I've become increasingly attuned to inviting others to participate in holiday celebrations because those are some of the hardest, loneliest times of the year for any number of reasons.

Relationships are built over shared meals, and friendship is often birthed out of hospitality to near strangers. I don't know if I've ever entertained angels, but my life is filled with depth and richness from the friends I've made through simple acts of hospitality. God has sent people through my door who have touched my heart and the hearts of my family far more than the simple meal cost me in terms of time, money, and action.

— Julie

— Today's Act of Friendship —

Host a Friendsgiving this year, inviting the friends of friends of friends to join you.

A Catalyst toward New Friendships

Let the peace that comes from Christ rule in your hearts.
For as members of one body you are called to
live in peace. And always be thankful.

COLOSSIANS 3:15

They seemed like the perfect friends. They were about our own age, with kids near our kids' ages, attended the same church, and had many of the same interests and hobbies. Their home was even relatively close to ours.

"I want them to be our friends," my husband told me, and we agreed to intentionally reach out to them to foster a friendship.

But despite all the things we had in common—all the reasons they could have become our friends—it never happened. For one reason or another, they were always too busy, their schedule too full. Despite invitations on numerous occasions, they always regretfully declined. It didn't seem like a polite brush-off—we had nice conversations at church and at mutual events—but frankly, they already had enough friends. Though they were always kind, their circle was firmly closed to us.

Still, no one likes feeling rejected, and it would have been easy to take up an offense at their apparent disinterest in becoming our friends. We could have questioned their character or their life choices. We could have felt bitterness or envy, wondering why they thought their already-established friends were "better than us"—when, really, it had nothing to do with us at all.

It's a normal, human gut reaction to feel a twinge of hurt when we think we may have been snubbed. But as Christians, let's dust ourselves off and transform the situation into an opportunity to take stock of our current friendships. Let's use it as an opportunity to look around and be grateful for the friends we do have, while also reminding ourselves to keep our own circle open to those who may feel overlooked or ignored.

— Kristin

— Today's Act of Friendship —

Jot down a list of three people who are acquaintances or
casual friends that you think may feel overlooked. Choose one
and invite them to a meal or activity within the next week.

Already Proud of Me

What shall we say about such wonderful things as these?
If God is for us, who can ever be against us?
ROMANS 8:31

Several years ago I began speaking in front of women's groups. This was not something that came naturally to me, as I am an introvert. Before these speaking events I would pray and ask God for wisdom and help, almost begging him to help me not screw up or make a fool of myself. I'd end my prayer by saying, "I just want to make you proud."

Inevitably, I'd get up, give my talk, and immediately sit down and think about all that I did wrong and what I could have improved. I'd find myself apologizing to God, promising that next time, I'd do better. This went on for a year or two until I was asked to speak on the love of God.

As I was preparing, I began to see God's love toward me in a new way. A picture came to my mind of God sitting in the crowd I was about to speak in front of with a smile on his face, already proud of me before I'd ever said one word. In that moment, I felt his love like I hadn't before, and it struck me that I had nothing to prove, that God loved me fully, just as I was—if I messed up or not, if people liked what I said or not, if it came out perfectly or not—he was already proud of me simply for being obedient. This truth of God's love for me has transformed not only the way I speak but other areas of my life as well. I am braver now that I understand the truth and the depth of his love for me.

It is much easier to welcome others in and extend friendship when we fully know we've been included by God. Accepted and loved. Forgiven and free. We'll want for those around us what we ourselves know we have available to us in Christ. There is no fear in love because if God is for us, who could ever be against us? Accepting his love allows us to offer friendship to others as well. How have you experienced God's love and friendship toward you?

– Kendra

– Today's Act of Friendship –

Thank God for his friendship and love for you.

A Rope of Three Strands

*A person standing alone can be attacked and defeated, but
two can stand back-to-back and conquer. Three are even
better, for a triple-braided cord is not easily broken.*

ECCLESIASTES 4:12

"How are you? Are you doing okay?"

As I read Kate's text early one morning, I shook my head in wonder. She always seems to know when I'm having a hard day, and this morning was no exception. I appreciate that I can be gut-wrenchingly honest with Kate. When she asks how I'm doing, she is asking because she senses something isn't quite right. She has an incredible gift of discernment, and she is tuned in to those around her with a gentle sensitivity I've never encountered before.

Kate is a fierce defender of me in prayer, and I've received her prayers in just about every form of communication available—in text, in person, over the phone, in letters, and everything in between. And I do the same for her. I can't tell you how many times we've prayed over one another on the phone, each of us sitting in the parking lot at our respective offices, followed by a check-in text at the end of a tough day.

One of the things I love most about Kate is that she doesn't shame me in my weaknesses. She knows the places I tend to struggle, I know the places she tends to struggle, and we are the gap-standers for one another in those areas—we recognize when the other is starting to believe a lie instead of God's truth and gently remind each other of who we are, to whom we belong, and how God is using our skill sets.

I love the image of a triple-braided cord as a picture of my friendship with Kate. I treasure our friendship for a number of reasons, but especially the central role Jesus plays in it. He is the third strand of our cord that is not easily severed, and our relationship is among the biggest blessings in my life.

— Julie

— Today's Act of Friendship —

Invite Jesus to be the third strand of your friendships by
actively praying for and with your friends for a month—
you will see a difference in your life and theirs.

Nothing Can Separate Us

Can anything ever separate us from Christ's love? Does it mean he no longer loves us if we have trouble or calamity, or are persecuted, or hungry, or destitute, or in danger, or threatened with death? . . . No, despite all these things, overwhelming victory is ours through Christ, who loved us.

ROMANS 8:35, 37

In the darkness of the moonlit car, my emotions were roiling. Hurt, confusion, and frustration had me on a slow simmer that was quickly heating into a rolling boil.

It began earlier in the day when a dear friend admitted that she wasn't always honest with me. Wary of women who have betrayed and hurt her in the past, she continually struggles with building close relationships, the vulnerability and fear of rejection too high a hurdle.

I tried to ignore my welling tears, even as I wondered: *How many times do you have to say "I love you" before someone believes it?* It's hurtful to feel like I constantly have to prove myself, even after years of friendship.

But I've come to realize that while I may have an easier time trusting in human relationships, God has sometimes been an object of distrust for me. If life is good, my kids are behaving, and it's a good hair day, God clearly loves me. But on days when I hear grisly abuse stories or horrific sex trafficking statistics, I wonder: *If God is loving, how can he see a hurting world and seemingly do nothing?*

All too often, how we relate to others in friendship mirrors how we view God. If we see our relationship with God as a true friendship—one based on the love and mercy demonstrated by Jesus' death and resurrection—we understand why nothing can separate us from his love. Because we know we can trust God, we are willing to take the chance on trusting our friends. On the other hand, if we don't fully trust or know God, we may transfer our distrust to other relationships, always waiting for the other shoe to drop.

Yet I wonder if God has the same question for us that I did for my friend: "How many times do I have to say 'I love you' before you believe me? You're enough, just as you are." As women who deserve to be unreservedly authentic in our friendships, let us begin by considering if we are allowing our view of God to influence the level of trust we're willing to place in others.

— Kristin

— Today's Act of Friendship —

Jot down a brief description of your relationship with God, considering whether you trust him and his love. Pray about how your perspective influences your relationships with others.

Don't Let Fear Hold You Back

*After this I looked, and there before me was a great multitude
that no one could count, from every nation, tribe, people and
language, standing before the throne and before the Lamb.*

REVELATION 7:9, NIV

It was late and we were driving home from an event when my dear friend Sally told me about a conversation with an Uber driver that she could not forget. She grew up in the community that we currently live in and over the years has seen a change in the population. Because she was unfamiliar with the new groups of people coming into town, she was afraid.

While recently on a work trip to an unfamiliar city, she had to take a ride back to the airport alone, and the man driving the Uber was of the same nationality of the population that has moved to our community. Sally told me she was overwhelmed by his kindness and friendliness to her over the twenty-minute drive to the airport. He asked her about her family, told her about his, made jokes about the city they were in, and wondered with concern if she'd be able to get lunch before her flight. She was taken aback at his sincere and honest approach to her. And this had gotten her thinking since she returned home that maybe she could be more open in her community to people who are different than she is.

I sat and listened to her story as I nodded in acknowledgment of all that she was feeling and thinking. "I think that is where we all start," I stated, "just being willing to be open to others."

Days later, I was still thinking about the impact one man had on my friend in just a twenty-minute car ride. We never know what our simple acts of extending friendship to others may have on them, even breaking down stereotypes or barriers in their minds and hearts. We can all be intentional, as this Uber driver was, to be friendly and hospitable to the people we meet each day. All people are invited into God's family, and because this is true, we needn't fear people who look different from us.

— *Kendra*

— Today's Act of Friendship —

Be friendly with a person or people group you
have previously disliked or even feared.

Aspirational Community

Wise words are like deep waters;
wisdom flows from the wise like a bubbling brook.
PROVERBS 18:4

As I walked into the group exercise class at my local YMCA for the first time, I glanced around the room. Women were grabbing dumbbells twice as heavy as the ones I had selected, and they looked like what I was hoping to look like in the not-too-distant future.

As I told my friend after the class, I pick which classes I attend by looking at the women who are in them. I want to be in the classes with the women who are slightly ahead of me, who are where I want to be someday. Rather than finding them intimidating (which they could be if I let them), I find it motivating and encouraging to see what they've achieved.

I do the same thing in my spiritual life: I look for women of wisdom who are loving God and loving others well, and then I support their ministries so I can learn from them simply by being in their circle. Having others come along in quiet support is encouraging and life-giving, and what starts as me simply serving and learning from a distance often blossoms into friendship on some level.

Carol, a spiritual mother to me, came into my life in this fashion. I volunteered for years in her organization, learning from her from afar, before she and I got to know one another. She is a treasured friend and a rare find. Almost as importantly, I have also developed a number of mentoring acquaintances through this approach—women I have coffee with once or twice a year, picking their brains, listening to what they are doing (or not), asking questions, and learning from their wisdom and experience, even as our circles overlap only tangentially.

I am influenced by those I surround myself with. I very intentionally seek out women of spiritual depth, women whose lives look like the one I am journeying toward, so that I might learn from them. Wisdom bubbles up and flows around us when we sit in proximity to the wise.

— *Julie*

— *Today's Act of Friendship* —

Consider who is spiritually wise in your already-existing circles
that you can draw closer to or what aspirational community you
might join so that you can grow through their influence.

Teenagers Need Mentors Too

*Do not judge others, and you will not be judged. Do not
condemn others, or it will all come back against you.*

LUKE 6:37

I was a bit of a rebellious teenager. I loved my family and had faith in God but often sought the attention of my peers who were engaging in unhealthy activities like partying. When most people wouldn't bother with teenagers, Joyce, an older woman and mother at my church, was different. She always made sure to greet me warmly and let me know that she cared. She was kind and loving, even when I wasn't living the way I knew I should have been. Even now, I can see her smiling face, void of judgment, as I'd enter our little church. I could sense that she was always happy to see me as she greeted me warmly each week.

At the time, I appreciated Joyce's welcome but didn't think too much of it. Today, I think a lot about Joyce and the friendship she showed me as I look at the young people around me. I wonder if I am always drawing in teenagers or if it's easier to just leave them be. If I'm honest, teenagers can sometimes be intimidating. If they're moody or have an attitude, it can seem easier to just ignore them. But they need mentors just as much as anyone else does, and befriending them is important.

As my own children grow into the teen years, I see just how necessary it is for them to have mentors who can speak into their lives alongside my husband and me. As parents, we need a supportive network of people whom our kids will listen to. But if we are going to mentor teenagers, we must be willing to not judge or condemn them, even if they make poor choices. We can be honest and offer correction, while also showing kindness just like Joyce did for me.

— *Kendra*

— *Today's Act of Friendship* —

Thank someone who has been a mentor to you and then
look for a teenager whom you could come alongside to
befriend with encouragement or even as a mentor.

Showing Up

Dear children, let's not merely say that we love each other; let us show the truth by our actions.

1 JOHN 3:18

"Did you know Matthew started selling camel milk?" a friend asked recently.

"No," I said, astounded and amused. "Why in the world would he do that?"

Matthew and his wife, Elizabeth, are great friends of ours, and since he's witty and funny, my first thought was that he was playing a joke on our mutual friend. What else could possibly explain the seemingly offbeat decision to sell camel milk?

The next week when we encountered Matthew, he was quick to laugh over our bewilderment and offer an explanation. As part of his family's ministry of connecting with refugee and immigrant communities in the area, he decided to sell camel milk. In East African culture, it's considered a healthful delicacy and is a sought-after commodity. Matthew's work as a middleman between the supplier and the local ethnic grocery stores in the area means that he's connecting with the very people with whom he'd love to build relationships.

In friendship, it's important to meet people where they're at, just as Jesus meets us where we're at. Instead of just saying that we love and care for someone else, proving the truth of our words through our actions is the best way to demonstrate our love and care for our friends.

Of course, not everyone likes camel milk, but there are lots of other ways we can use our actions to show our friends that the things they care about matter to us as well. Showing up to watch a softball game they're playing in, cheering them on from the sidelines while they run a 5K, offering to read a book they're currently reading in order to discuss it over coffee at a later date, or meeting up for dinner at a restaurant that serves their favorite kind of food are all small ways to show our friends that they matter to us.

— *Kristin*

— Today's Act of Friendship —

Think of one tangible action you can take to demonstrate to a friend how much you care for them.

Be Willing to Get Close

*Always be humble and gentle. Be patient with each other, making
allowance for each other's faults because of your love.*

EPHESIANS 4:2

I first met Beth when I joined the leadership team of my local moms' group. A decade or so my senior, Beth is a few steps ahead of me in raising children and in life in general. I love seeing her example as a mom and appreciate her willingness to answer questions about kids and teens. The realness with which she approaches me and the other younger moms is encouraging and honest.

Beth is frank about her life experiences and shares openly with others who may be going through a difficult or challenging time. She is quick to encourage and offer to pray for you. She is confident in who she is and loves to call out the gifting of others, encouraging women to pursue what God has for them. Beth has shown me what it looks like to allow others to be near in friendship. She doesn't keep people at a distance but is kind toward those who need a friend, inviting women into her circle and loving them well.

If we want to have close friendships and be supportive of others around us, we must model our lives after Scripture. What makes a good friend? Someone who is humble, gentle, patient, and allows for others to be imperfect and have faults, while still deeply loving them. This sounds amazing, but most of us have probably had a different experience at some point in our lives. Often the world and our culture are quick to judge and approach others with harshness, while keeping others at a distance, but we, as Christians, are called to something much more sacrificial. We are called to love others. And to do this, we must let others get near to us. We must allow them to see our faults and mistakes, along with our successes. We must ask for help or prayer when we need it. And we can accomplish all of this by being willing to get close, by being comfortable in sharing even our messy parts, and by listening as others share theirs in return.

— Kendra

— Today's Act of Friendship —

Share a need or concern you have with a
friend and ask them to pray for you.

Ghosting or Grace

*Now go and learn the meaning of this Scripture: "I want you to show
mercy, not offer sacrifices." For I have come to call not those who
think they are righteous, but those who know they are sinners.*
MATTHEW 9:13

Emily and Jess served in the same church, and while they knew of each other, it was
only in passing. Jess was a rising star, asked to speak in their church and other churches
on a regular basis—until something happened, and she was dropped overnight.

Ghosting is breaking off a relationship suddenly and without explanation. I
didn't fully understand the concept until Emily cried while recounting the story of
Jess's experience in her church. She told me that because she was connected to Jess
on social media, she saw Jess's angry posts about being abandoned by people she
once thought were friends. My friend felt wretched and uncertain about what to
do, if anything. As I thought about Emily, Jess, and the women who had warmly
embraced Jess before suddenly distancing themselves from her, other instances of
what I now recognize as ghosting crept into my consciousness.

When people get messy, fail in a very public way, or admit to a crisis of faith,
there can be a mad scramble as Christians distance themselves from the sinner, as
though sin is an infectious disease they might catch. And while sometimes that
might be the appropriate response, it wasn't Jesus' response to sin. Jesus regularly
shared meals with those the religious elite of that day had ghosted—or worse yet—
had never bothered with in the first place.

Jess's experience came to mind when I found myself visiting with Candace, the
daughter of a pastor who—decades ago—had a very public fall from grace. Candace
spoke of the one (and only) fellow pastor in their denomination who had reached
out to her dad and her family during that hard time. He brought love, mercy,
friendship, and hope when everyone else had disappeared. He offered mercy and
redemption to her father. Today, Candace is a woman who is faithfully serving God
in a number of ways, and it was his influence that kept her heart turned toward
God when she might have turned away during that difficult time.

The difference between those two stories has stayed with me when I'm confronted
with the choice of responding to a friend's bad choice. We can make an impact on
the lives of hurting people—if we reach out to them with grace.

– Julie

– Today's Act of Friendship –

Reach for grace wrapped in loving accountability
instead of ghosting when friends have sinned.

That's Just the Way We Like It

Gentle words are a tree of life; a deceitful tongue crushes the spirit.
PROVERBS 15:4

My friend Carol is relentlessly optimistic. I mean that in the very best of ways, because when you have a job as demanding as Carol's, optimism in the face of adversity is necessary. Carol is the director of a women's ministry that puts on events throughout the year that host thousands of people. She has a large advisory group and hundreds of volunteers that need oversight, and with so many personalities and moving parts, it's inevitable that things will sometimes go awry.

Yet her standard phrase is, "That's just the way we like it." Funds not fully raised yet? That's just the way we like it. An item the team expected to hand out to hundreds at the conference stuck somewhere in the morass of customs? That's just the way we like it. Disgruntled vendor? That's just the way we like it.

Of course those situations aren't ideal, and no one likes having troubles arise. But Carol's phrase is a reminder that though we may face challenges, as Christians, we choose to take the optimistic view. Nothing is impossible with our Jesus—no hurdle, no obstacle, no impediment—nothing. He is in control.

As friends, how can we encourage each other with our words? Despite the scads of people and situations Carol is required to oversee, she has the unique ability to make each person feel seen and heard. She's an encourager. And she always says thank you, no matter how small of a role a person plays. The words she says are a reminder to me that I, too, need to choose optimism in the face of adversity. Our words have power, and we can use them for harm or for good. Carol has chosen to speak words that bring life. Her own optimism, expressed aloud, fuels the rest of her team to accept the obstacles and find ways to overcome them together. And—truthfully—that's just the way we like it.

— *Kristin*

— Today's Act of Friendship —

Find a way to verbally encourage a friend while
choosing to view a situation with optimism.

December

When We Join Together

Live in harmony with each other. Let there be no divisions in the church. Rather, be of one mind, united in thought and purpose.

1 CORINTHIANS 1:10

Each December, our family commits to doing an act of kindness each day. We began in 2012 when I had a rambunctious toddler and a chubby-cheeked baby at home. In the intervening years, we've added another daughter to our home, but our commitment to refocus on Jesus and his love by showing kindness through the Advent season remains unwavering.

Each November, I sketch out the following month. We've brought our girls' teachers their favorite coffee drinks, filled up the gas tank of a local serviceman on his way to the airport for a deployment, donated to food shelves and animal shelters, and bought toys for other children. My kids love making "candy bombs"— small candy-filled cellophane bags—to place on windshields at the hospital. And the day when we leave treats and a gift card in the mailbox for the mail carrier is always one of their favorites.

All of these activities are things my children love doing, but what I appreciate most is recruiting others to do these kind acts along with us. Each year when I ask for ideas on social media, my friends generously comment with their best ideas, giving me fresh insight and an appreciation for their creativity and generosity. Last year, one friend told me that she joined with us our first year and has continued to do so each year with her family. For eight years, she's partnered with us on our Advent adventure! As we traded ideas, she told me that her daughter likes to volunteer at an animal shelter, and her son likes to ask a cashier what his or her favorite candy is while waiting in the checkout line, and then he purchases the candy and gives it to them. Together, my friend and I brainstormed ideas for the next year.

In life, we are better when we join together with friends. Our good ideas are strengthened, multiplied, and even passed on to the next generation when we work with one another. When we are united in our desire to show the love of Jesus to others, we will spur one another on to more and more acts of love and grace and mercy, strengthening our friendships—and our faith.

— *Kristin*

— Today's Act of Friendship —

Brainstorm ideas—whether they're related to a work project, a ministry, or an upcoming event—with a friend.

Sharing Burdens

*Most important of all, continue to show deep love for
each other, for love covers a multitude of sins.*

1 PETER 4:8

For months my friend's child had been bullying others on and off the soccer field, and my friend hadn't had a clue. It wasn't until the coach called her up one morning and gently let her know the unkind things her daughter had been saying and doing that she became aware. Shame and disappointment flooded over her as she hung up, right after apologizing and vowing to talk with her daughter.

She then called me, crying. I tried to listen through the tears as she laid it all out. "I'm just so angry," she said. "And embarrassed and sad. I knew my daughter was having a hard time, but I didn't realize she was taking out her pain on other people."

I understood. Her daughter had struggled ever since my friend had left her unhealthy marriage, and the daughter's relationship with her father had disintegrated along with the family unit. Even so, my friend knew her daughter's actions were not okay, no matter what was happening in their own lives.

"What should I do?" she asked.

"Let's start by praying," I answered. And so we did. Afterward, we talked through some helpful things she could say to her daughter and how she could rectify the situation. "She is going to be all right," I told my friend. "You're going to be all right too."

She agreed as we hung up, ready to begin the work of helping her daughter stop bullying and start being a friend again.

There are many times in our lives where we can face something painful or even shameful, and whether it's something we've done ourselves or something a loved one has done, it can be embarrassing to reach out to others. But it's in these times when we can pray and seek counsel from good friends who love us and our kids. We don't have to carry the burden alone. Letting others in on our shame and pain is part of being a good friend and showing our deep love for one another.

— Kendra

— Today's Act of Friendship —

Tell a friend about a struggle you are having, and
let them carry the burden with you.

We All Win

All the world is mine and everything in it.
PSALM 50:12

Jim hired me straight out of law school to be his fifth judicial law clerk. He was a district court judge in a rural Minnesota county, and my husband and I were twentysomethings moving to a community in which we knew almost no one.

I attended his funeral, almost exactly seventeen years from the day he interviewed me. As I hugged law clerks number one, three, seven, and eight, I couldn't help but recognize Jim's enormous influence on my life—on so many of our lives—despite our tenures as his law clerks being only a year or two.

Jim cheered for each of us, calling out our best qualities before we knew enough to recognize them for ourselves. He let us sit in on every aspect of legal decision making—for example, his wrestling over lunch about a particularly hard decision in a case that would have no winners. He was training us to leave him, and it showed. He developed us, refined us, and then did his best to help launch us forward into a wide variety of jobs using his networks and his influence. I eventually went to work for Jim's former law firm, and Aaron went to work for Jim's former client. He leveraged his connections endlessly on our behalf—probably in some ways I'll never realize.

As I work with women coming up behind me, I now find myself emulating so much of what Jim did for me. My success and the success of the woman next to me are not mutually exclusive. I can be fully and enthusiastically in support of another woman, introducing her to all of the people in my circles without fear that she will move forward at my expense.

This is God's economy—and there is enough for her and for me. Her win is not my loss, and our success (both hers and mine) are not mutually exclusive. There is no scarcity in God's economy; after all, he owns the whole world.

– Julie

– Today's Act of Friendship –

Consider which women need access to your circles of influence at work, at school, in the neighborhood, and in your extended family, and be wildly on their side.

Friendship Knows No Age

*Let each generation tell its children of your mighty
acts; let them proclaim your power.*

PSALM 145:4

We race up the stairs, seeing who can reach the top floor first. My kids and I have traveled these steps countless times over the past few years, the worn tread of the carpet as familiar as our own home. Al stands just outside his door, waiting for us with a smile and wave. We rush down the hall, giving side hugs as we each walk past him to the small living room and find a seat.

Al is a former neighbor who remains a dear friend. He's old enough to be my children's grandpa, and he relishes the relationship he has with my kids, not having any grandchildren of his own. Even though we are on opposite ends of life's spectrum, we consider Al to be a close friend. We love our regular visits to his apartment, and he loves hearing all about the kids' activities.

I often wonder what our life would be like if we'd never met Al. For years he lived across the street from us with little interaction until one summer my husband and I decided we needed to be more intentional in getting to know our neighbors. That is when we first really got to know Al, and he is an absolute gift to our family. It makes me sad to think we missed starting a relationship with him sooner, and I don't want to make that mistake again.

Friendship knows no age. In fact, we should have friends in all stages of life. Older friends bring wisdom and understanding to life as well as a perspective young people often miss. They can remind those who are still inexperienced of the mighty acts of God. And in return, young people can bring an energy and excitement that may be missing for those who are later in life. There is a richness in relationships that span the decades, a bond in which commonalities can be found and differences celebrated.

— Kendra

— Today's Act of Friendship —

Reach out to someone who is in a different stage of life than you
are, and let them know what their friendship has meant to you.

The Hands and Feet of Jesus

*When we get together, I want to encourage you in your
faith, but I also want to be encouraged by yours.*

ROMANS 1:12

The doorbell began to peal as women arrived, trickled into the kitchen, and spilled over into the dining room. Laughter rang out, cutting through the hum of conversation and the clatter of plates being filled with snacks.

We were gathering together in my home for a special craft night, one where each of the women would create two boxes of handcrafted items: one for us, and one for a woman in Minnesota who had experienced abuse or been trafficked. The boxes were the vision of Rachel, the creator of Uplift a Box, who wanted to reach women who often feel alone, forgotten, or unheard—women who need to be reminded that they are loved by God.

Using the materials and instructions provided, each participant worked on creating a tasseled key chain and beautiful ombré coasters. Working steadily, we assembled the boxes with care, ending with each woman writing a note or a prayer on a slip of paper and tucking it into the box. Sneaking a peek at the notes, I saw heartfelt messages and Bible verses penned with love and accompanied by smiley faces and hearts, encouraging each woman who received a note to recognize how loved, valued, and beautiful she was. As the night ended and I closed the door behind the last friend, I felt profoundly grateful for the opportunity to unite with friends for such a worthy cause.

Friendship is fun, but it's often when we join together with one another that we find our friendship deepened and our faith strengthened. As we work toward a common goal—whether it's sitting next to each other at an event like our craft night, volunteering side by side within the community, or cooking a meal together at the local homeless shelter—our faith is simultaneously challenged and encouraged. As friends, let's spur one another on to be the hands and feet of Jesus in the world. Not only will we have the opportunity to encourage others but we'll find ourselves encouraged as well.

— Kristin

— Today's Act of Friendship —

Find an opportunity to help out in your community and
ask a friend to join you in volunteering together.

DECEMBER 6

Wholesome and Sweet

The LORD has told you what is good,
and this is what he requires of you: to do what is right, to
love mercy, and to walk humbly with your God.

MICAH 6:8

"Julie, I was trying to be catty. I forgot that you are my wholesome and sweet friend." Anita's laughing response to my polite attempt to redirect a casual but slightly derogatory remark made me pause for a moment.

Wholesome? Sweet? Those words have been used to describe me on more than one occasion, usually with a slight sneer because the speaker thinks I'm some sort of Pollyanna. I cultivate a habit of calling out the good in people and in situations (including when they are not in the room), and some people confuse my extension of grace with being naive—an extremely uncool trait in a world that loves snark.

Although Anita spoke with love instead of with a sneer, I inwardly rebelled over those sugary words that have oftentimes been used to insult me. Jesus knows me, and he could tell you all the times that my response was neither wholesome nor sweet. But I stilled my tongue as a thought washed over me: *Your friendship looks different enough from her other friendships that she has set you apart.*

And that is my prayer. I pray that I would reflect Jesus—despite my many imperfections—to the world around me. I long to be the kind of Jesus follower whose life makes others pause, wondering what it is that I have, what it is about my life that causes me to respond with loving grace instead of snark and mild derision. I want people to have met Jesus in me long before I speak the words of invitation. In order to do that, I need to know what Jesus asks of me. We are called to walk with God in humility, extending grace, standing against injustice, and doing what is right.

If that means I am labeled (and sometimes dismissed) as wholesome and sweet, so be it.

— Julie

— Today's Act of Friendship —

Take time to consider how friendship with you looks
different from friendships with people who do not yet
know God. If there's something about your behavior that
needs to shift, ask God to help you make that change.

Celebrating Our Friends' Successes

Don't just pretend to love others. Really love them. Hate
what is wrong. Hold tightly to what is good.
ROMANS 12:9

"Are you still planning to come?" my friend Mary asked over text. She'd invited me to the first get-together she was hosting for her new in-home business.

"Of course!" I responded. "I wouldn't miss it!" I was so excited for my friend and wanted to celebrate her new venture with her.

It's not the first time I've celebrated another's success. As a small-business owner myself, I know the effort it takes to put yourself out there and try something new. Many of my friends have home or side businesses, and when it fits my schedule and budget, I try to support them as much as I can. I've hosted several parties in my home and attended grand openings, graduation parties, and new-home gatherings. Anytime there is something to celebrate, I want to be one of the first to tell my friends how proud I am of them and how I am cheering them on in their lives.

Celebrating another's successes or even their attempts is one way that we show love to our friends. Whether it's starting a business, going back to school, starting a new job, or any other change that comes to our lives, it's important that as friends, we are the first to cheer for one another. There are enough negative opinions in the world, and even thoughts in our own heads, that we often need to balance them out by being the cheering section for those around us. We don't want to just pretend to love others, we want to really love them, and one way that we do that is by being the first to celebrate our friends' endeavors. The world around us is competitive enough; let's be friends who support and love one another well. Who is trying something new around you and could use a little encouragement? Be the first to cheer them on.

— *Kendra*

— Today's Act of Friendship —

Celebrate a recent success (or even attempt!) by a friend
and let them know how proud you are of them.

The High Road

See that no one pays back evil for evil, but always try
to do good to each other and to all people.

1 THESSALONIANS 5:15

"I felt like packing my bags and running away," Mary said.

Sara and I leaned in a bit closer over our small table at the coffee shop, wanting to lend support as Mary spoke of a time that clearly still stung, even though it was two decades ago. She spoke of deep betrayal—a knife in the back from a man who was a best friend and business partner. His actions ultimately boiled down to money, saving face, and pride. Her husband became the scapegoat in a business deal gone wrong, and their combined circle of friends, their small town, and their church picked sides, with almost all of them choosing the friend because his family wielded far more wealth and social influence. Her family lost everything, and she and her husband found themselves starting over at age forty.

While Mary spoke of humiliation and devastation, she also spoke of her husband choosing the high road, over and over. He refused to go on the offensive in an effort to clear his name, refused to seek vengeance for intentional actions that had destroyed his family financially. They did not repay evil with evil, and they did their former friend no harm in return.

Now, two decades later, she and her husband have prospered in a different way. My friend wields enormous spiritual influence across our nation and across the globe; her advice and counsel are sought by men and women in highly placed pastoral positions. She is wise and discerning; her advice is measured always against Scripture, and being in her presence brings the peace of Christ even in the midst of chaos.

After a few beats of silence as we processed her story, Mary observed that Jesus, too, was betrayed—perhaps, in part, because he knew most of us would face the heartache of betrayal and that we would need to know that our Savior experienced the same devastation we feel. He asks us to trust him when he tells us to take the high road and not to seek our own vengeance. He redeems. He restores. He elevates us when we take the high road.

— Julie

— Today's Act of Friendship —

When a friend wrongs you, take the high road and
trust God to provide for and guide you.

Gifted by God

All of you together are Christ's body, and each of you is a part of it.

1 CORINTHIANS 12:27

I have a friend who is a really talented writer. She's a natural storyteller, has a great sense of humor, and her attention to detail and ability to connect with the reader's emotions make her one of my favorite authors to read. Yet, despite my encouragement, she's never sought publication—even though she's confided that it's a dream of hers. While it may be true that she's simply too busy, hasn't had the time to pursue it based on other commitments, or just simply isn't ready, I wonder if she struggles with imposter syndrome.

It's a common affliction for people in general and writers in particular. We feel like our writing isn't good enough or think that someone else is more talented or could do it better. If someone we care about dismisses it as "just" a hobby or belittles it, our self-confidence gets bruised and it confirms our deepest fears. You may not be a writer, but perhaps you struggle with imposter syndrome in other ways—feeling uncertain in your parenting when you see your child's screaming-in-public tantrum next to another child's seeming perfection, wondering why someone else got a promotion when you thought you worked harder and longer for it, questioning the choices you've made when it comes to your finances or relationships. It doesn't help that when we look at social media, we see mostly celebration, not struggle.

As friends, let us affirm the gifts and talents that we see in others. Even more, let us go out of our way to encourage our friends to put those skills to use. I recently sent my friend a message, asking how her writing was going and encouraging her to pursue it in a professional capacity. I can't take the next step—only she can do that—but I can be willing to hold her hand along the way. Each of us is equipped with gifts, qualities, and skills that God gave us on purpose as members of the body of Christ. He knows who we are and, what's more, he never asks us to be anyone other than who we are.

— *Kristin*

— Today's Act of Friendship —

Message or call a friend to tell them three qualities,
gifts, or skills that you admire in them.

Standing Firm

Yes, speak up for the poor and helpless, and see that they get justice.
PROVERBS 31:9

My daughter marched through our front door with a particular fierceness. Cassie, a friend and classmate, had spilled tears when one of the popular boys smacked into her and then apologized insincerely. As other kids began rallying around him, Cassie began to face ridicule instead of compassion, and what should have been a minor interaction began to spiral into something bigger.

Cue my daughter and her unwillingness to let injustice slide. She verbally jumped into the fray and got shoved, and the boy doing the shoving ended up in the office. My daughter's indignant stride as she walked into the house had me suddenly navigating the line between wanting my daughter to be safe while also recognizing the fire God has placed in her heart against injustice.

While a part of me longs for my daughter to always play it safe, the Jesus follower in me wants my daughter to be a woman who stands firmly alongside those who cannot defend themselves, whether it is a friend or a stranger. We are the hands and feet of Christ, and sometimes that requires us to speak up or act on behalf of someone else—even when it puts our own best interests at risk. In this case, it was getting shoved, but what happens when we are asked to speak up on behalf of a friend or coworker being treated unjustly by our employer or to take the side of someone being marginalized unfairly by those wielding influence or power? Standing against injustice comes with potential risk—physical, emotional, and financial—and there may be a price to pay for our stance.

How do we know when we are being asked to take a stand versus when we are running ahead of God and taking matters into our own hands? It requires discernment and prayer, having read what Scripture shows us about how Christ commands us to live. It requires us to be in an intimate relationship with our Father, so that instead of allowing fear or anger to color our response, we listen to the still, small voice of the Holy Spirit.

— *Julie*

— *Today's Act of Friendship* —

Consider how God is asking you to respond to unjust situations your friends and others around you are facing, and take a stand if necessary.

Believe the Best

*Now, dear brothers and sisters, one final thing. Fix your thoughts
on what is true, and honorable, and right, and pure, and lovely, and
admirable. Think about things that are excellent and worthy of praise.*

PHILIPPIANS 4:8

I wasn't invited, and I was feeling hurt. I had inadvertently found out about a gathering of friends that my husband and I hadn't been included in, and I was more upset than I cared to admit.

"Why weren't we invited?" I asked my husband, who simply shrugged and tried to tell me it was okay if we weren't always included in everything this group of friends did.

I knew that it was true, and I told myself it was fine, but I still felt like a middle school girl who'd been uninvited to a party, and I hated the old insecurities it brought up. I honestly stewed for a while, and then realized I hated the way I was feeling and the things I was thinking about my friends. Determined not to let the feelings consume me, I decided to combat them with what I knew to be true about our friends. I reminded myself of all the ways I've been included and comforted and loved by them over the years. I told myself that I knew they cared for me and would never do something to intentionally hurt me. I prayed and asked God to bless these friends, and slowly, I began to feel better. I chose to believe the best about my friends, and when I did, those old insecurities went away.

We all have a choice to make each day regarding what we will believe about other people. We can choose to fix our minds on things that are pure and lovely and honorable, or we can choose the opposite. It can be easy to allow our minds to go to a negative place when we feel rejected, but reminding ourselves of the ways we have been included can offset those insecurities when they arise. We all need friends who will believe the best about each other.

— Kendra

— Today's Act of Friendship —

When you struggle with insecurity in friendships, choose
to focus on the ways others have loved you well.

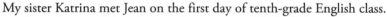

DECEMBER 12

Friendship That Lingers

Let your good deeds shine out for all to see, so that everyone will praise your heavenly Father.

MATTHEW 5:16

My sister Katrina met Jean on the first day of tenth-grade English class.

"I was curious," Jean later said. "I sensed a profound kindness under her calm, quiet demeanor. I wanted to be her friend."

Their deepening friendship was tested the following spring when Jean's dad announced he was leaving their family.

"I was angry but never outward," Jean said. "I turned it in, I withdrew, I hated. I made plans to leave high school early and start college. It was my version of running away."

That summer, she and Katrina spent a lot of time together.

"She was always there to listen and be what I needed most," Jean said. "Katrina introduced me to her family, who made me feel loved and safe. One day while at her house I quipped about how fun it would be to drive her dad's new truck, a sporty red pickup. Katrina came back and announced, 'You can!' I couldn't believe it. Why would he trust a sixteen-year-old he just met? But he did. He trusted. I never took that for granted."

The friends kept in touch over the years, but when Katrina died at twenty-eight, it would have been easy for Jean to sever the family connection. Instead, she has stopped at my parents' house and welcomed out-of-the-blue phone calls from them.

There's an intimacy that builds in soul-deep friendships, and sometimes those connections spill over to those around us. In the case of Jean, it's meant a lot to my family that she has continued to make an effort to stay connected, even years after Katrina's passing.

"I don't think her family knows just how much they carried me through one of the darkest times in my life with simple acts of kindness that I see now were always rooted in Christlike love," Jean said recently. "I see now that is what I was drawn to in Katrina—Christ's light within her."

Sometimes friendship doesn't need to be proclaimed loudly—rather, it's a quiet presence made known by our actions, by the care we show others when words aren't enough. And it's a witness and testimony of our love and our faith, even over a period of many years.

— *Kristin*

— Today's Act of Friendship —

Reconnect with an old friend you haven't talked to in a while.

Girlfriends' Christmas

Dear friends, let us continue to love one another, for love comes from God. Anyone who loves is a child of God and knows God.

1 JOHN 4:7

"Who's picking names this year?!"

I saw the text on my phone in the middle of making dinner. Some of my closest friends and I were planning our annual girlfriends' Christmas, never mind that it was only late October. We all like to get an early start on finding the perfect gift for the person whose name we draw (although we always end up getting a small gift for everyone regardless, a tradition my late sister Katrina started almost twenty years ago).

I smiled as I saw the back-and-forth about whose husband would choose the names so it would be a surprise, and the reminder to "please make sure you don't tell anyone who you have after he sends you the text with your name." We're supposed to keep a secret whose name we receive each year, although we rarely make it to our dinner without finding out who the others have.

Each December it's the same: we go to the same restaurant, eat as many cheesy biscuits as possible (calories don't count on this night), catch up on families and what everyone is up to, open presents from one another that we've planned all year, take a picture in front of the lobster tank, and then head off to the mall to find the wackiest pajamas we can to try on and take pictures of. We end the night completely full, with sides and cheeks hurting from all the laughter.

Do you have friends that you've known for years? Thank God for them. And if you do not, pray and ask God to bring you to people who could be good friends. I do not see the girlfriends I get together with each Christmas all the time throughout the year, but I know that they are consistently there for me and would step in anytime I need a hand. Reliability, loyalty, and genuine love for one another will help friendships last throughout the years, even if you are not with one another frequently. Take the time to intentionally start a tradition of getting together with friends, even if it's just once a year.

— *Kendra*

— Today's Act of Friendship —

Plan a get-together with old or new friends.

DECEMBER 14

Just Call Me Sister

See how very much our Father loves us, for he calls
us his children, and that is what we are!
1 JOHN 3:1

Arms laden with gift baskets, I carefully made my way up the carpeted aisle. As worship music boomed from the speakers and a countdown scrolled on the projectors, I placed the items on the stage and found a chair that would allow me to jump out of my seat at a moment's notice.

From the stage, my sister Kendra—one of the Single Moms' Retreat emcees—gave me a nod as she continued to make last-minute production changes. Within minutes, she was smiling onstage, exchanging witty repartee with her co-emcee and announcing all the details attendees would need to know. As she moved on to giveaways, I hurried up the aisle, ready to hear who had won so that I could hand them their prize.

But then she paused.

"This is Kristin, and she hates to be the center of attention," she said as my face turned ten shades of red. "Everyone smile and say hi!"

As the crowd laughingly complied, she added, "It's okay. She's my sister."

As the giveaways continued and the event rolled on, I found myself with a new nickname: Sister. I heard it while standing in the line that snaked out the door, waiting for lunch. I heard it as I walked across the pathways that crisscrossed the camp or helped out at one of the conference booths in the back of the worship center. Wherever I turned, women called me Sister, usually with a smile.

There is an instant connection and camaraderie that is achieved when someone feels like they're on the inside of a private joke. In a sea of women, many of whom came alone and at the last minute, I was suddenly a familiar face. And as the weekend rolled on, I began to view the nickname in a whole new way. As children of God, we are a family. At its best, friendship is a sisterhood. Though the women I encountered may have had different backgrounds, hobbies, or parenting styles, each of us could connect as God's children, wholly and deeply loved—not just as friends, but as sisters in the family of God.

— Kristin

— Today's Act of Friendship —

Consider friends who have become spiritual sisters to you.
Reach out to one of them to thank her for her friendship.

Casting a New Vision

Let the message about Christ, in all its richness, fill your lives.
Teach and counsel each other with all the wisdom he gives.

COLOSSIANS 3:16

"Oh, this space is perfect!" I exclaimed as I toured her new apartment, taking in the beautifully decorated space for the first time. My friend and her husband have downsized, and after decades of hosting hundreds of people in their large home, I could tell this move was a little hard. She spoke warmly of the move and of their home, but there was a hint of wistfulness in her voice.

As we moved through her new rooms, I spoke not of the smaller square footage but dreamed aloud of the endless possibilities for continued hospitality without the work of maintaining a house that had become a bit too much. I pointed out the beautiful view of the wooded acreage just beyond their small balcony and listened as she told me about the common room that could be reserved for bigger gatherings. I turned to her in excitement and said it again, "This is absolutely perfect for you guys!"

She paused for a long minute before wrapping me in a fierce hug and whispering in my ear how much she loved me. Releasing me, she confessed that she had been struggling and that the enemy of our souls had been whispering lies to her about this move, about this apartment, about how she could not host in such a small space.

She simply needed a friend to view the situation with fresh eyes, a woman who pointed out all the promise of the future despite it looking a bit different from what she had previously known. She needed someone to speak truth and life over her and over her new situation louder than the enemy's whispered lies. And that's what we are called to do as women who follow Christ. We are called to draw near to Jesus, to know who and what he is—and then liberally pour out that wisdom on the women around us. We are to be hope bringers, vision casters, and truth tellers, pointing women always back to Jesus.

— Julie

— Today's Act of Friendship —

Reach out to a friend in your circles who needs a
fresh perspective, encouragement, and hope.

Taking a Risk

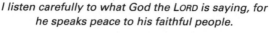

I listen carefully to what God the LORD is saying, for
he speaks peace to his faithful people.

PSALM 85:8

My sister-in-law April told me about a woman at her church whom she first knew only through their work together in the preschool room. That was until one Sunday when Monica asked April if she'd like to have dinner together. Even though Monica was a single widow without children and April was a married mom of three, April happily agreed and felt honored to be asked. They spent the evening getting to know one another, and since that first night they have formed a friendship that supersedes any differences they may have. April told me, "We give one another perspective on where we each are in life and remind one another of the gifts of the season that we are each in." Having a friend in a different stage of life has offered April a different viewpoint, one she often needs in her own life but has a hard time seeing for herself. Monica reminds April of the good in singleness, and April always leaves her visits grateful for Monica's perspective.

April told me how brave Monica was to reach out to her when they really did not know one another except in passing. Monica told her that she did so because she felt like God was nudging her to, and she wanted to be obedient. But what if she hadn't listened or obeyed? They both could have easily missed out on the blessing that their friendship has been to both of them.

Being sensitive to God's nudging in friendship is so important because we never know who God may bring across our path that could potentially be a good friend. We are told to listen carefully to what the Lord is saying, and that applies to many things in life, including relationships with others. We never know who around us may be in need of a friend or how great of a blessing they may be to us if we'll only be obedient to step out and meet someone new.

— Kendra

— Today's Act of Friendship —

Invite someone to coffee or dinner when you feel a nudge
from God to do so, and see if you do not gain a new friend.

Working Together

Whatever you do or say, do it as a representative of the Lord
Jesus, giving thanks through him to God the Father.
COLOSSIANS 3:17

Writing—though I love it—is often a solitary occupation. As an introvert, I don't usually mind it. It's not uncommon for me to slip into the corner of a coffee shop or hide out in the big floral chair in my bedroom when I'm in the middle of something, only emerging when my stomach rumbles or my neck muscles spasm. Although working with Kendra and Julie is a collaborative effort that lends itself well to brainstorming and encouragement, the three of us still find ourselves writing in isolation.

My husband, Tim, on the other hand, sees clients all day long at his job but rarely sees his coworkers. Few of them even live within the same state. Yet despite the distance, he has strong work relationships. Some of his coworkers were groomsmen and ushers in our wedding. Two of his closest friends, whom he has spent countless hours talking to on the phone about work and family, live several states away.

Every corporation or work community has its ups and downs, but Tim's approach has inspired me to become more intentional in my work life. So I've found myself calling up my coauthors more frequently to talk about what I'm working on and where I feel stuck. The three of us have a running text thread filled with work updates and silly memes about how our kids drive us crazy. I've become part of a local group of writers who meet every other month. All of these practices help me feel less alone and more connected, and the friendships I've made through these avenues have encouraged me on the days when work feels tough.

Your work life may require you, like me, to spend hours alone on a computer. On the other hand, it may call for you to spend your entire day with other people, be they children or adults. Yet everything we say and do is as a representative of Christ. As ambassadors for him, we are called to show love, grace, and mercy in all of our relationships—including work relationships. As women who understand the value of befriending others, our work relationships can be life-affirming, too.

— *Kristin*

— Today's Act of Friendship —

Find a way to connect with someone at work who has a similar
interest or passion, be it work-related or more personal in nature.

A Brotherly Perspective

The heartfelt counsel of a friend is as sweet as perfume and incense.

PROVERBS 27:9

As I walked through the door of the local gathering place in my hometown, I swallowed my nervousness, unsure of what my twenty-year reunion would be like. Immediately I was met by warm smiles and familiar faces. As I started talking with a group of classmates I hadn't seen in almost twenty years, someone sidled up next to me—my dear friend Blake. We hugged and began talking about our lives now.

Our small group of reunion goers spent the rest of the evening reminiscing and telling old stories that I'd long since forgotten while also showing photos of family and sharing about career choices, places we'd lived, and dreams for the future.

Several days later I was still warmly remembering how much I appreciated Blake's friendship throughout high school. He was supportive and kind, often offering me a listening ear and being a sounding board for all my teenage angst. Even as a teen, he was always considerate of others and what was going on in their lives, not just his own. His male perspective was helpful to me as I began to navigate healthy relationships, and I learned a lot from him during that time. He was a good friend to me during a season when I really needed one, and today, I am grateful for his friendship over those high school years.

Too often we can befriend only those who are just like us, but I am grateful for my young experiences of friendship with both sexes. Learning early on in life to interact with a young man in a purely platonic way, a man who was more like the brother I never had, taught me a great deal about navigating relationships with men—skills that I still draw on today. It set me up for healthy relationships at work, in college, and even with my husband. We all need and can benefit from a variety of friends with varying perspectives and experiences to help us navigate life and relationships because the counsel they give us will be like sweet perfume.

— Kendra

— Today's Act of Friendship —

Thank a friend who brings a different perspective to your
life, and let them know why you appreciate them.

Unwavering Faith

Let us run with endurance the race God has set before us.
HEBREWS 12:1

Death was *not* the way the Katrina's story was supposed to end. One of my dearest friends and the sister of Kendra and Kristin, she had a firmly rooted faith like no one I've met in person. She conquered cancer repeatedly during a five-year saga before it suddenly came roaring back to overtake her at twenty-eight, and she left behind two babies and a husband.

In the midst of my grief I almost missed seeing how her unwavering faith, her trust in the goodness of God through the hardest things, was somehow magnified by her death, encouraging and strengthening the faith of thousands who had been following her journey via email in a pre-Facebook world. She finished her Hebrews 12 faith race stronger than anyone I'd ever seen, and people were noticing and reexamining their own faith in ways I'd never imagined.

My grief-stricken prayer as I decided to go all in on my own faith race was that I might be allowed to carry a piece of her story of unwavering hope forward with me to women who never had the opportunity to meet her. That exhausted, broken prayer started a new journey. I found myself sharing the story of Katrina the following week and then continually week upon week, month upon month, unending for more than fifteen years.

Katrina is the silent fourth partner in the story of Kristin, Kendra, and me. She introduced the three of us originally, and she is as much a part of our ministry, The Ruth Experience, as any of us. We carry her story with us everywhere we go, and everything we do is a part of her legacy. It was through her that we learned firsthand that God is our strength, even in the hardest of hard circumstances, and we strive to run our individual Hebrews 12 races the way she showed us. Our prayer is that we would finish our races with the same tenacity and strength that Katrina had and that others would always find the hope of Jesus in our lives, no matter the circumstances.

— Julie

— Today's Act of Friendship —

Evaluate your faith race, determining to run with
unwavering faith, even when things are hard.

Wedding Guests

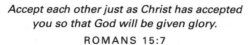

*Accept each other just as Christ has accepted
you so that God will be given glory.*

ROMANS 15:7

The summer before I entered fourth grade, my family moved from Grand Rapids, Minnesota, a forest-filled area with the shimmering waters of the Mississippi River winding through town, to the grassier farmlands of central Minnesota.

When we moved, we left behind my aunt, uncle, and cousins, as well as various friends. One year, we made one of our many trips northward to attend the wedding of the son of a family friend. Still a teenager living at home, I tagged along, curious to see if I would run into any old friends.

That day, while cooling my heels in a Lutheran church on the edge of town, I spied the teenage versions of kids from our old church whom I'd last seen at age nine. Despite my shyness, they quickly made me feel at ease and even offered to take me along with them around town. Having gained my parents' permission, we spent the next several hours driving around my old hometown, visiting places that had grown murky in my memory. With a keen eye, I saw the new library built in part through the largesse of the paper mill, the businesses downtown that had failed or thrived in my absence, and the old church building I once attended that felt smaller than it used to. By the time they returned me to the wedding and my parents, I was grateful for their kindness and the opportunity they'd afforded me to see my old town through their eyes.

Friendship isn't just about established friends—the ones we have now, the ones we feel the strongest pull toward—it's also about our willingness to keep our circle open. There is a generosity in including others and accepting them the same way that Jesus has accepted us—viewing others not as strangers, but rather as long-lost friends to rediscover. Though the old friends' offer to include me in their plans may have started as a polite overture, their willingness to include me gave me a chance to feel at home, even in a town I no longer claimed as my own.

— *Kristin*

— *Today's Act of Friendship* —

Go out of your way to include a new acquaintance or old friend.

Protecting Your Loved Ones

Her husband can trust her, and she will greatly enrich his life.
She brings him good, not harm, all the days of her life.
PROVERBS 31:11-12

Holly Ball is the fanciest annual gala in my community. A fundraiser for our hospital's hospice and cancer centers, it is an opportunity to dress in tuxes and glittering gowns as everyone mingles and dances in our event-center-turned-bejeweled-wonderland for an evening.

As Aaron and I waited in line for an appetizer among the glitz, we chatted with Carissa and Mark—a couple around our same age and stage in life. We caught up on kids and work and what was new since we had last seen one another. It didn't take long to notice that Carissa's comments were laced with an undercurrent of derision as she jokingly revealed minor but unflattering truths about Mark. His responses were defensive and slightly derisive in return—which left Aaron and me feeling awkward and casting about for neutral topics to diffuse the tension as we silently plotted our escape.

Because I am a woman writing to women, I'm going to address the female half of that relationship while fully acknowledging that he was not an innocent victim. It was clear that her negative slant in conversation about her spouse was not a one-time occurrence, and she is far from alone in this conversational trap. I regularly run across female commentary in break rooms, church lobbies, moms' groups, and on social media in which exposing a husband's (or a friend's) less than flattering characteristics acts as fodder for casual conversation.

As women who love Jesus, we are to bring good to our husbands, our loved ones, and our friends with the words we speak—not harm. Guard the words you speak about your husband and your marriage in casual conversations, and don't expose his idiosyncrasies to acquaintances. The same goes for friends. Don't expose your girlfriend's weaknesses to others the moment she walks out of a room. Let's be women who call out the best in our loved ones, who share stories painting them in a favorable light, who build them up—especially when they are not present.

– Julie

– Today's Act of Friendship –

Practice calling out the very best qualities in your spouse
and in your other friends to those around you, both when
that person is present and when he or she is not.

Faithful Presence in a Hard Place

*Never let loyalty and kindness leave you! Tie them around your
neck as a reminder. Write them deep within your heart.*

PROVERBS 3:3

I first met Karen and Paul when our family started attending weekly services at a local shelter in our community, only two blocks from our house. Karen and Paul were two of several leaders in the kids' program at the time. Each week I would go to the kids' area since my youngest was afraid to go alone, and after several weeks Karen warmly offered to allow me to be one of the weekly helpers, to which I happily agreed. Every week I watched as Karen and her assistant, Paul, faithfully served alongside several other helpers.

As the months went on, a few of the workers' attendance dwindled and then ended completely. Eventually, I asked Karen and Paul what had happened. Karen shrugged her shoulders and they explained how the helpers were using drugs again. They then affirmed their commitment to the people and families who come through the shelter's doors.

Karen and Paul's love of the kids is obvious, and they have a passion for serving that is inspiring and incredibly hopeful to me. Their example reminds me that each person, no matter what they struggle with in life, has value and is made in the image of God. The Scripture verse they recite with the kids each week is simply that God loves us. Karen and Paul are living examples of never letting loyalty and kindness leave them. They wear it like a reminder for all to see, and you know it's written deep in their hearts.

When we remain faithful, even in a challenging place, we will exude the same kind of hope that Karen and Paul do. We may not all be called to work in a shelter, but I believe that there are hurting people around each of us whom God would want us to befriend.

— *Kendra*

— Today's Act of Friendship —

Befriend someone who is going through a hard time, faithfully
pursuing them with texts, phone calls, or showing up even
when they don't or can't return the friendship in kind.

More Than Piano Lessons

There is no greater love than to lay down one's life for one's friends.
JOHN 15:13

"Please pick up the kids ten minutes late."

The text from my children's piano teacher made me smile. Karen is the music teacher at our elementary school and has been our piano teacher for years. My children have spent countless hours sitting on her piano bench and in her classroom.

As they sit alongside her, they confide about troubles with classmates, hopes for their summer breaks, theories about the latest Marvel movie, and all the things almost-tweens think about. She listens and responds with the kind of advice she is perfectly positioned to give as a teacher, a mother of grown children, and a mentor who shares their school world. She echoes all the same words their father and I speak over them—but from a different perspective that sometimes resonates louder than our parental voices. And this year, I've periodically received a text telling me to come a bit later than when the lesson would normally end, because they've decided to chat over a small bowl of ice cream.

My son confesses these little ice cream breaks to me with a sly grin at the end of the lesson as Karen and I make eye contact with our own sly grins over the children's heads. Having another adult who loves my children and will speak words of accountability, truth, and life over them is a gift beyond measure. I am forever grateful for Karen's investment of time, energy, and love in the lives of my children—and of all the children who sit on her piano bench or stand on her choir risers at school. She is fiercely on the side of all of her kids, and mine are far from the only ones who have been loved well in her orbit. She perfectly balances friendship and mentoring with her students, and the sacrificial love she pours into her students impacts the families in her orbit far more than she'll realize this side of heaven.

– Julie

– Today's Act of Friendship –

Befriend someone younger at your church, your workplace, or in your neighborhood, coming alongside them in loving guidance.

Serving Together

We are members of his body.
EPHESIANS 5:30

"He's autistic," his aunt said, somewhat distracted as she snagged another wayward child strolling along by the arm. Standing in front of the battered card table where we were wrapping gifts, she nodded at the child in my arms, who was concentrating on my round silver necklace, repeatedly dropping it and picking it up again. "That's why he's a runner."

And boy, could he run. When he first arrived at the table, I caught a gleeful smirk as he eluded my grasp, happy to play this game. But now, he was tired of running and didn't mind being rocked by me. As the presents for his family members were wrapped one by one, he fell asleep, head nodding, cookie crumbs clinging to his mouth.

Even as my arms fell asleep and my fingers went a little numb, I held onto the sweetness of the moment. Kids' Hope Shop—an event where at-risk kids from the community can come and "shop" for their families for free—is always a highlight of my Christmas season.

Looking around, I saw my friend Samantha arriving in the doorway with another group of kids, cheeks flushed and feet stomping snow on the ground. I was just down the row from my friend Molly, another friend, Cheri, was across the room, and other friends from church were scattered throughout the event, all working toward the goal of making local children's Christmases just a little brighter.

When we work together as friends united by a common goal, the sum is always greater than the parts. Jesus and his disciples, whom he considered friends, provided the best example of how we should work together. They were united in their goal of sharing the grace and mercy made available through Jesus.

As friends, some of our holiest work happens when we band together to serve others. That evening, even as I wrapped countless children's gifts, I blessed the pause of holding someone else's child until he fell asleep. After all, I had friends who were willing to step into my place behind the table to continue wrapping, working steadily onward to complete our goal.

— *Kristin*

— Today's Act of Friendship —

Choose a goal (or an event) to work toward together with friends.

No Striving Necessary

*No power in the sky above or in the earth below—indeed,
nothing in all creation will ever be able to separate us from the
love of God that is revealed in Christ Jesus our Lord.*

ROMANS 8:39

"Why does this season fall disproportionately on women?" Kendra's question ended on a sigh. Christmas seems to carry a universally heavier than normal burden on our girlfriends—women who quietly speak of feeling overwhelmed as they strive to make this season appear both magical and effortless despite the chaos often swirling just below the surface. I recognized the truth in her question as I reflected on the many conversations I've had with girlfriends this past month.

Overwhelmed and exhausted are the themes I hear as the women I love navigate hard relationships, mourn the loss of loved ones, and strive to get all the details perfect for Christmas morning. It is an emotional and physical load that is often unavoidable, even as we look for ways to balance it better every year.

That is not what Jesus has for you, for me, for all of us today. Our American culture has made Christmas far more complicated than it was ever meant to be, and we get inadvertently caught up in the vortex of cultural and familial expectations.

In the midst of all the magic-making, let's pause for a lingering moment to bask in the truth of today: God loves you, loves all of us so much that he sent his only beloved Son to redeem us. Jesus is a priceless gift with no strings attached, a Savior who offers a path back to God despite sin and our unworthiness. There is no striving, no to-do list, no preconditions, just a humble acceptance of his freely offered salvation.

You are beloved. There is nothing you can do (or fail to do), no place you can go that will separate you from the love of Christ. In a season that can feel chaotic and hard, Jesus' unconditional, inextinguishable, unending love is a balm for our weary souls.

— Julie

— Today's Act of Friendship —

Spend a few quiet moments with your Savior this Christmas.

DECEMBER 26

Quiet Friendship

*If you are wise and understand God's ways,
prove it by living an honorable life, doing good works
with the humility that comes from wisdom.*

JAMES 3:13

One day in December, I cooked up a pan of baked ziti, a Tupperware bowl of ham and wild rice soup, and fudgy brownies and paired them with bread and salad from the store. I then packed it all up in a sturdy box and drove over snowy back roads to give the homemade meals to an amazing mama friend who has children with medical challenges. They had just survived a week at the hospital with one of her children and were spending a well-deserved day at home in their pajamas.

As I surveyed my box of plastic and aluminum containers, I couldn't help but think of how unglamorous my box looked. No one would take a picture and post it to Pinterest or Instagram; no one would stop scrolling social media to admire my efforts. It reminded me of how often friendship, at its deepest level, is unglamorous. It's often shown in quiet moments, in unseen encounters. It happens amid the mundane moments of our lives. Friendship is not always picture-worthy—and yet, it's profoundly memorable.

When I dropped the items off, my friend didn't see the ugly containers. Instead, she saw two meals she didn't have to cook. She smelled the mouthwatering fudginess emanating from the brownies. She noticed the hug and smile I offered. She felt the care and concern directed her way.

Sometimes friendship requires quiet, discreet acts of kindness. Our good works committed in a spirit of love and service aren't meant for public fanfare; they are a reflection of the care and loving-kindness Jesus has shown us. If that's you today—if you are doing things that feel overlooked or minor to you—I recognize the care and love that you're offering to others. And, more importantly, I know that God sees you and honors the spirit in which your acts of friendship are accomplished.

— *Kristin*

— Today's Act of Friendship —

Commit to doing an "unglamorous" act of friendship,
be it making a meal or something else.

Unlikely Friends

*Pure and genuine religion in the sight of God the Father
means caring for orphans and widows in their distress
and refusing to let the world corrupt you.*

JAMES 1:27

They come from all corners of Minnesota—a ragtag group of mechanics who meet together once a year with the common goal of fixing single moms' cars—all for free. They've been coming to the single moms' retreat for this purpose for almost ten years now.

Their reasons for being there are as varied as they are. Some were raised by a single mom, others have close friends or family members who are single moms, and some just want to help out in any way that they can. But no matter their reasons, their goal is the same: to bless as many single moms as possible. To do this, they show up early on a Friday afternoon and begin working as soon as the moms arrive. Taking only short breaks to eat, they work through the night, not wanting any woman's car to be overlooked or missed. They work right up until the women are ready to leave on Saturday afternoon. Many of them faithfully come back year after year to let single moms know that they care. They're quick to shrug off any thanks we try to bestow on them, claiming they're simply glad they can help. Their presence reminds the women that they are loved, valued, and not forgotten.

Each year I am in awe of the men who come to show support to women they never even meet. Their commitment is admirable and worth noticing. They are literally the hands and feet of Jesus. When asked, they will tell you that they wholeheartedly believe they are taking care of widows and orphans, and they are confident their small acts of kindness please the Lord. I wholeheartedly agree. When we remember those that Scripture calls out as vulnerable, we honor God, and I believe he is pleased by our acts of kindness and friendship. Even though they've not met in person, these women and mechanics would call themselves friends, united in their community of support and respect for one another.

– *Kendra*

– Today's Act of Friendship –

Look for a way to befriend a widow, a single mom, or
an orphan, offering them some practical help.

365 Notes

Worry weighs a person down; an encouraging word cheers a person up.
PROVERBS 12:25

Her card was the prettiest piece of mail I'd received in as long as I could remember—the hand-decorated, colorful envelope immediately stood out against the neighboring junk mail and bills. As I pulled it out of the pile for a closer look, I smiled. I'd met Lisa at a conference and immediately liked the funny, spunky woman with a streak of dark purple in her hair. She told me as she collected my address that she was on a mission to send 365 notes to 365 people this year, and that day it was evidently my turn.

Opening the card, I was surprised to see it covered—top to bottom—in her neat cursive. Her words were lovely and encouraging, but it was the effort expended that held my attention. She clearly spent thought and time on me—a woman she had met only once—and I can't explain what a blessing it was to receive her encouraging words and beautiful note, knowing that she was praying for me that week.

I know that 365 notes seems like a lot, but Lisa didn't start with a note every day; she started far smaller. But she so enjoyed the creative outlet for both her words and art that she slowly expanded over a number of years until this year's grand experiment. I can't help but be inspired both by her process and her finding the intersection of personal artistic outlet and blessing toward others.

As I thought of her being blessed while blessing someone else, I was reminded that God is so, so good. We don't have to copy Lisa (although I know she wouldn't mind a bit): God will use *our* talents and hobbies to bring joy to those around us, if we let him. We'll be his hands and feet, bringing desperately needed encouragement to others if we ask him to use us in our giftings.

— Julie

— Today's Act of Friendship —

Make a list of your hobbies and talents. Offer that list to God,
asking how you might be a blessing and encouragement
to others through the activities on that list.

A Remembered Prayer

*The earnest prayer of a righteous person has great
power and produces wonderful results.*

JAMES 5:16

I spotted Grace across the room, a friendly face in a sea of people who were mostly strangers. She smiled in acknowledgment, then turned to listen to the speaker who had just arrived at the front of the room.

At the event's next break, I found myself standing next to Grace in line, and she introduced me to a childhood friend of hers that she'd known since third grade. As we chatted about the event, she suddenly asked me a question: "Remember that church yoga group we did years ago?"

"Yes!" I exclaimed. "I was hugely pregnant with Ashlyn and thought I would fall over at any moment. My balance was nonexistent."

Grace told me that she had just been telling her friend about the group and one evening in particular that stood out to her. On that night, our church's small group leader had challenged us to pair up to pray for one another. Pulling our mats close together, Grace and I shared honestly about the challenges we were facing in our lives, then bowed our heads to pray, ignoring the roomful of other people quietly whispering in order to focus on each other and the presence of God.

Almost five years later, she still recalled with perfect clarity that single prayer I had prayed for her. And as we touched on some of the topics that arose that night—how my husband and I had made it our practice to pray together every day, as well as how and why that habit began—I realized how much that prayer had touched her.

As friends, it's important to reflect our care for others in our words and actions, but it's even more important to consistently make time in our prayer life. Prayer has the power to encourage us, to alter our perspectives, to influence our decisions, and ultimately to change our lives. In typical God-ordained timing, we may never know how profoundly our heartfelt words, prayed in earnest for a friend, will stay with them long after we part ways.

— *Kristin*

— Today's Act of Friendship —

Write a short list of friends you'd like to pray for
regularly. Then, call one in order to pray with her.

Shared Leadership

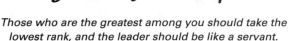

*Those who are the greatest among you should take the
lowest rank, and the leader should be like a servant.*

LUKE 22:25

I was in my early twenties and had just recently started attending a new church when the youth pastor approached me about working with the youth group. I was both thrilled and honored to be asked. Since my day job involved working with the elderly, I was happy to be volunteering with younger people.

Over the next few years, I was able to walk alongside Carl and his wife, Jenny, as they led the youth at our church. Each month, they would have meetings with the youth leaders and discuss upcoming events and topics for our Wednesday night gatherings. Carl was always quick to ask questions and listen to the opinions of others around the circle and often allowed us to step into the roles of teaching or leading. Carl was quick to share the leadership, encouraging others to pursue the gifts God had given to them.

Carl was a wonderful mentor to me and walked confidently in his calling. It was actually under his direction that I found my voice as a speaker and shared several messages with the youth that I felt God had given me during my time on that team. Because of their leadership style, Carl and Jenny became more than leaders in my life; they became dear friends and still are to this day.

As Christians, the best leaders should be the best at serving others. This comes in direct opposition to what the world would call leaders to do or be—keeping power only for themselves and taking every opportunity to make themselves known. But true leaders are ones who share their influence and platform and power with others around them, while also fostering friendships among those they work and do ministry with.

– *Kendra*

– *Today's Act of Friendship* –

Show friendship to someone you lead by giving them
one-on-one time to provide guidance in their role.

My Favorite List

Teach us to realize the brevity of life,
so that we may grow in wisdom.

PSALM 90:12

I'm a list-maker. In fact, so great is my desire to cross something off a list that—if I'm enumerating items—I'll include something I've already finished just for the pleasure of drawing a line through it. I have copious lists for work, for events that are approaching, for groceries to purchase, and for daily to-do items. I've got a summer bucket list that shapes how our family plans our summer months, full of day trips to museums and parks and experiences we want to accomplish while our daughters are young and not sailing in a million different directions. I even keep a year-round, ongoing list of ideas for Christmas gifts.

But I also have other, more private lists that only my husband and I ever consult. A list of friends, family, and acquaintances that we are praying for. There's also the wordy, but aptly named, "People We Want to See" list. It's a running list of people we are intentionally choosing to target—in the best sense of the word—for deeper friendship.

While I feel like all of my lists serve a purpose, our list of friends we want to spend time with is my favorite. Because no matter how important it is to write down places we'd like to visit or when I need to see the dentist again, the truth is that we intentionally choose to prioritize people over things. Each month, we sit down, find dates that are open, and make time for the people we care about.

I don't keep lists because I'm amazingly organized; I keep them because I'm not. The older I get, the more I realize how quickly life can pass us by. I don't want to get to the end of my life and wish I'd taken the time for more lunch or coffee dates, more deep conversations late at night, and more dinners where hearts are shared and confidences spoken. And so, I'll keep making my lists. I'll find spaces in my calendar. And I'll intentionally invite others into my life.

— *Kristin*

— Today's Act of Friendship —

Make a list of friends or acquaintances you'd like to spend time with
over the next month, and then follow through with invitations.

About the Authors

After a fifteen-year career as a lawyer, **Julie Fisk** decided to follow her childhood dream of becoming an author. She shifted her storytelling from courtrooms and boardrooms to dinner tables and backyard barbecues, where she uncovers truth about faith, kindness, and friendship. Together with her cofounders of The Ruth Experience, Julie connects with thousands of women online through real, raw stories of living out faith. When she's not writing or speaking, you can find Julie with her husband and their two kids filling their home and backyard with friends.

Do it afraid. **Kendra Roehl** has sought to live out that advice as a social worker, foster parent, mother of five, and public speaker. She has a master's degree in social work and has naturally become a defender of those in need, serving others in hospice, low-income housing, and veterans' affairs programs. Kendra and her husband are well-known advocates for foster care, taking in more than twenty children in six years and adopting three of them. As a cofounder of The Ruth Experience, she continues to care for others as a frequent speaker and an author of five books.

A career in journalism set **Kristin Demery** up to one day publish her own stories of living this wild, precious life. She is now an author of five books and part of a trio of writers collectively known as The Ruth Experience. Kristin formerly served as a newspaper and magazine editor, and her work has been featured in a variety of publications, including *USA Today*. She still works behind the scenes as an editor for others while writing her own series on kindness, friendship, and living with intention. An adventurer at heart, she loves checking items off the family bucket list with her husband and three daughters.

Truth for Women:

Meet with Jesus Every Day The One Year Way

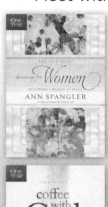

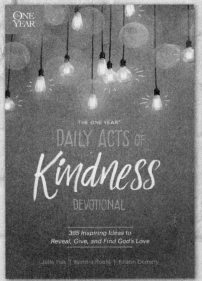
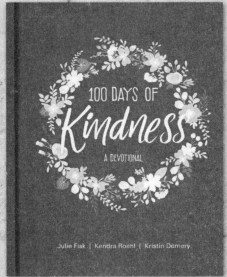

If you were inspired by this devotional,
check out the free

refresh
DAILY BIBLE
DEVOTIONAL APP